SCIENCE
AnyTime™

Harcourt Brace & Company

Orlando   Atlanta   Austin   Boston   San Francisco   Chicago   Dallas   New York
Toronto   London

Science AnyTime is a trademark of Harcourt Brace & Company.
Acknowledgments appear on page R30.

Printed in the United States of America
ISBN 0-15-304888-3
          7 8 9 10   048   97

Authors

Napoleon A. Bryant, Jr.
Professor Emeritus of Education
Xavier University
Cincinnati, Ohio

Marjorie Slavick Frank
Specialist in Literacy and Language Development
Adjunct Faculty, Hunter, Brooklyn, and
Manhattan Colleges
Brooklyn, New York

Gerald Krockover
Professor of Science Education
School of Mathematics and Science Center
Purdue University
West Lafayette, Indiana

Mozell Lang
Science Specialist
Michigan Department of Education
Lansing, Michigan

Carol J. Valenta
Director of Education
California Museum of Science and Industry
Los Angeles, California

Barry A. Van Deman
Director
International Museum of Surgical Science
Chicago, Illinois

Advisors

Betsy Balzano
Professor
State University of New York
Brockport, New York

Anne R. Biggins
Speech-Language Pathologist
Fairfax County Public Schools
Fairfax, Virginia

Walter Brautigan
State University of New York
Brockport, New York

Gerard F. Consuegra
Director of Curriculum Coordination and
Implementation
Montgomery County Public Schools
Rockville, Maryland

Robert H. Fronk
Head, Science Education Department
Florida Institute of Technology
Melbourne, Florida

Carolyn Gambrel
Learning Disabilities Teacher
Fairfax County Public Schools
Fairfax, Virginia

Joyce E. Haines
Instructor of Humanities
Haskell Indian Nations University
Lawrence, Kansas

Chris Hasegawa
Associate Professor of Teacher Education
California State University
Sacramento, California

Asa Hilliard III
Fuller E. Calloway Professor of Urban Education
Georgia State University
Atlanta, Georgia

V. Daniel Ochs
Professor of Science Education
University of Louisville
Louisville, Kentucky

Donna M. Ogle
Chair, Reading & Language Arts Department
National-Louis University
Evanston, Illinois

Young Pai
Interim Dean, School of Education
University of Missouri
Kansas City, Missouri

Susan Cashman Paterniti
School Board Member
Port Charlotte, Florida

Barbara S. Pettegrew
Associate Professor
Otterbein College
Westerville, Ohio

Stearns W. Rogers
Professor of Chemistry
McNeese State University
Lake Charles, Louisiana

CONTENTS

iv

Unit B

Caution: Endangered Species Ahead

Diversity and Adaptations

Unit C

Stage and Screen

Using Light and Sound

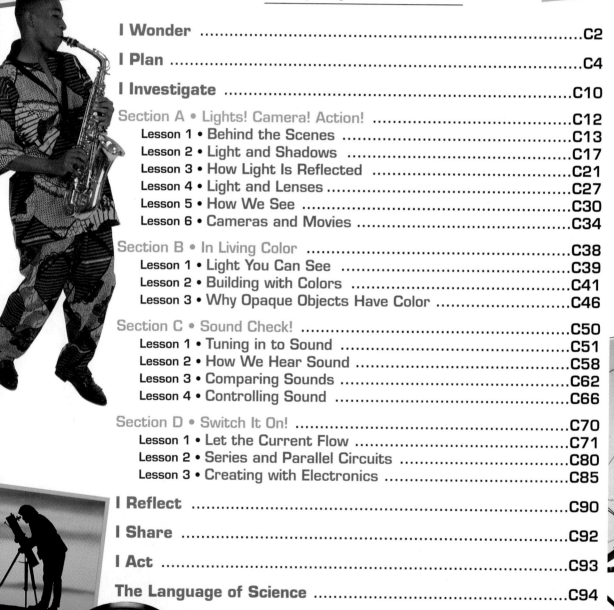

Unit D

SeaBase Nautilus

Exploring the Oceans

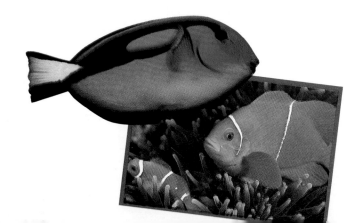

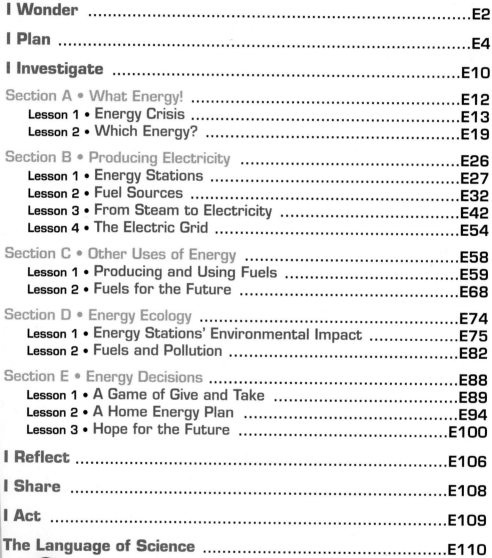

Unit E

Blackout!

Energy Uses, Sources, and Alternatives

Unit F

The Secrets Within Seeds

Plant Growth and Heredity

SCIENCE ANYTIME

Calvin seems to be rather disturbed in this cartoon strip. What is his problem? What does he intend to do about it? Then Hobbes, the voice of reason, enters in. Where will Calvin go? How will he solve his dilemma? These are questions you may have also. What other questions do you have as you study science and try to apply it to your daily life? The following pages show an exciting process you will use this year as you study science.

Wonder...

Many science discoveries begin
when someone says, "I wonder ..."
What do *you* wonder about?

I WONDER

Plan.

Scientists wonder and then plan how they will find answers to their questions. You too can be a scientist by planning ways to answer questions you wonder about. You may do some things with your class. Other things you may do in a small group or by yourself. However you work, your plan will guide you.

Investigate

Finding answers to your **I Wonder** questions will lead you to do investigations. Investigations can be activities, research, reading, talking to experts, using a computer, or watching videos.

Your investigations may answer some of your questions, but they may also lead to new questions.

Reflect.

Investigations are not complete until you reflect on what you did and what you learned. When you reflect, you think about something quietly and calmly. Reflecting helps you make sense of the science you are learning.

You will have many opportunities to share your science discoveries with others. By sharing, you will continue to learn about your topic and about communicating to others what you have discovered. As you listen to others share, you will also continue to learn.

I SHARE

Share...

Act.

People who make discoveries often try to use what they have discovered. You may take action this year by drawing up a home energy-saving plan, volunteering to help a group working to save threatened or endangered species, videotaping a presentation, or planting a flower garden at home or at school.

As you **wonder, plan, investigate, reflect, share,** and **act,** you will be a scientist at work. What an exciting year of science discoveries lies ahead!

RING OF FIRE

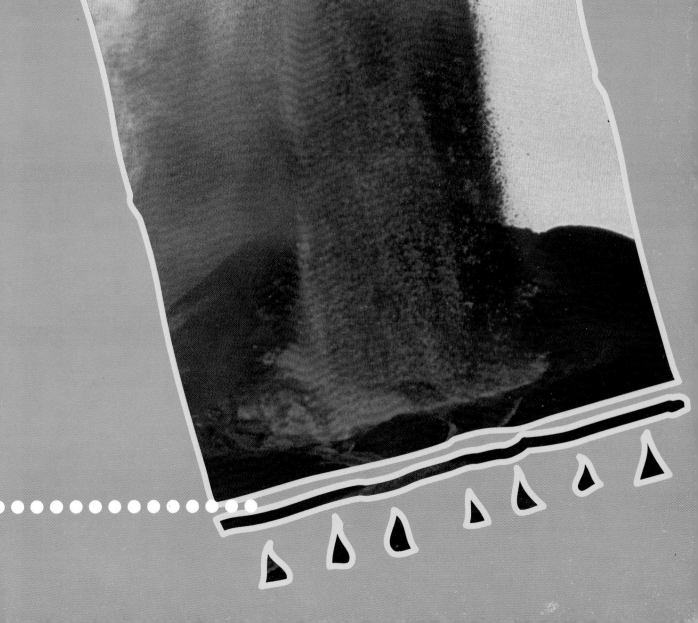

Unit A

Ring of Fire

Earthquakes and Volcanoes

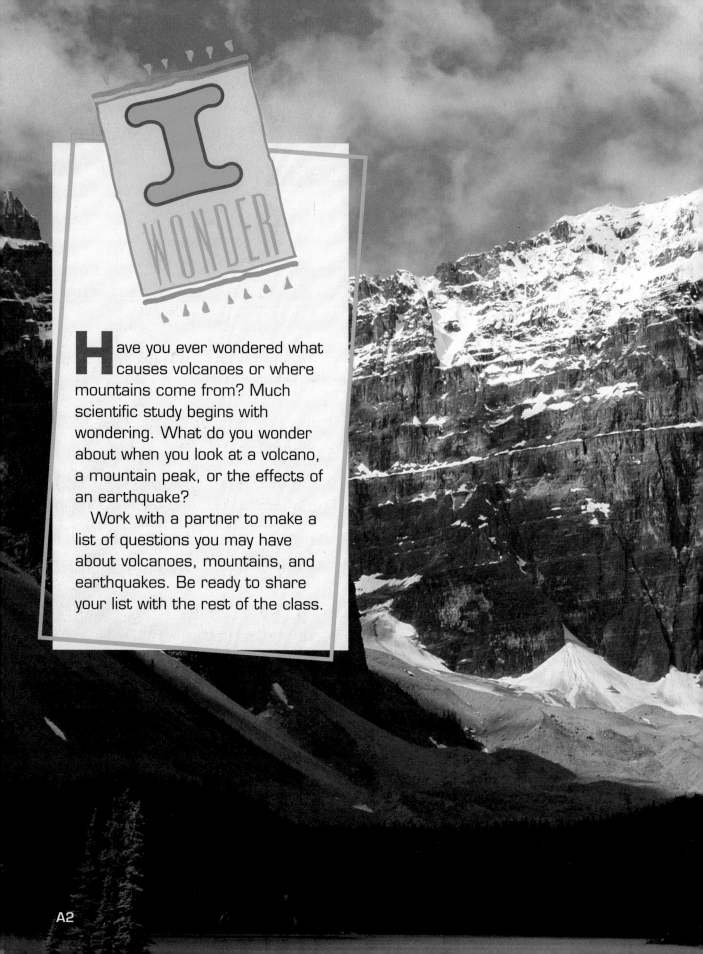

I WONDER

Have you ever wondered what causes volcanoes or where mountains come from? Much scientific study begins with wondering. What do you wonder about when you look at a volcano, a mountain peak, or the effects of an earthquake?

Work with a partner to make a list of questions you may have about volcanoes, mountains, and earthquakes. Be ready to share your list with the rest of the class.

Banff National Park, Alberta, Canada
Volcano in Indonesia

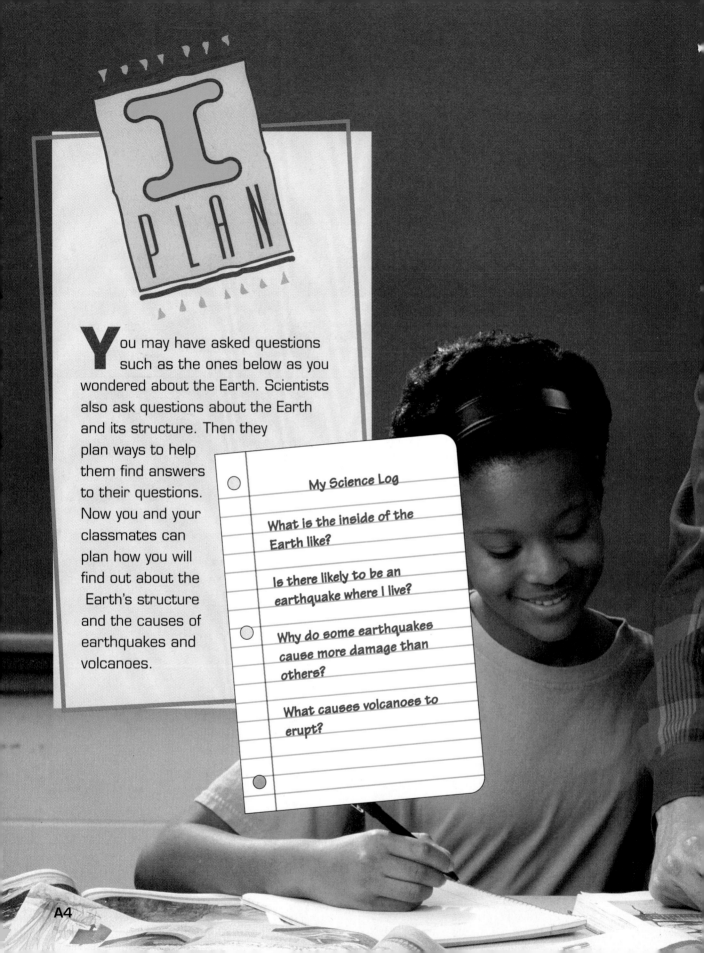

I PLAN

You may have asked questions such as the ones below as you wondered about the Earth. Scientists also ask questions about the Earth and its structure. Then they plan ways to help them find answers to their questions. Now you and your classmates can plan how you will find out about the Earth's structure and the causes of earthquakes and volcanoes.

My Science Log

What is the inside of the Earth like?

Is there likely to be an earthquake where I live?

Why do some earthquakes cause more damage than others?

What causes volcanoes to erupt?

With Your Class

Plan how your class will use the activities and readings from the **I Investigate** part of this unit. Decide what other resources you might use.

On Your Own

There are many ways to learn about the Earth and its structure. Following are some things you can do to explore earthquakes and volcanoes by yourself or with some classmates. Some explorations may take longer to do than others. Look over the suggestions and choose . . .

- **Projects to Do**
- **People to Contact**
- **Books to Read**

PROJECTS TO DO

VOLCANO BAKE

Hungry? Ask for help from an adult, and bake yourself a volcano to snack on. You will need a container of crescent-roll dough and some jelly. Open the container, and unroll the crescent dough. Cut or pull the crescents apart. Put a spoonful of jelly into the middle of each crescent. Fold the crescent in half, and pinch the sides closed. Use a plastic knife to poke a hole into the dough. Place the crescents on a baking sheet, and bake as the package directs. The jelly will "erupt" through the hole, just as lava erupts through the cone of a volcano.

SCIENCE FAIR PROJECT

Review the **I Wonder** questions you and your partner asked. One way to find answers to these questions is through a science fair project. Choose one of your questions. Plan a project that will help you answer the question. Discuss your plans with your teacher. With his or her approval, begin work by collecting materials and resources. Then carry out your plan.

ANIMATED PLATES

Make a series of diagrams that show either an oceanic plate collapsing in a trench or the action of sea-floor spreading. Each drawing in the sequence should depict a scene that is slightly different from the one before it. Staple your pages together, and flip through them. You will see an animated show of Earth's plates moving.

PEOPLE TO CONTACT

IN PERSON

The Earth trembles and buildings sway. What is it like to experience an earthquake? Talk with your friends, relatives, and neighbors to find out if they have ever experienced an earthquake. Ask what it felt like and what the person thought when the earthquake hit. You might make an informal survey to find out how many people you know have experienced earthquakes.

Take notes during your interview, and organize them so that you can share your information in an interesting and understandable way.

BY TELEPHONE

To learn how geologists study the Earth's structure, contact a geologist at a university in your area. Find out about the instruments geologists use to study the Earth's structure. Ask if you may tape-record the conversation and, if so, share the tape with your class.

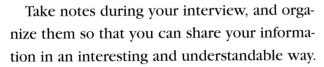

- American Geological Institute
- National Geographic Society
- U.S. Geological Survey
- State geological surveys
- National Park Service

You can contact many different agencies to learn more about the Earth and its structure. Here is a list of some you might call for more information.

BY COMPUTER

Use a computer with a modem to connect to on-line services or bulletin boards. Search for information about mountains, earthquakes, and volcanoes.

Perhaps your school's computers are connected to Internet, an international network of computers. Internet links computer users in more than 40 countries. Contact students in several parts of the world. Ask them if there are mountains in their area and, if so, what type of mountains they are.

BOOKS TO READ

Earthquake at Dawn

by Kristiana Gregory (Harcourt Brace, 1992). Read about Daisy, a 15-year-old, and Edith Irvine, a photographer, as they set out on a trip to Australia. Their journey is interrupted by an earthquake when they arrive in San Francisco. Desperate to save their own lives and to help those around them, they still manage to film the destruction of the city and the misery of the earthquake victims.

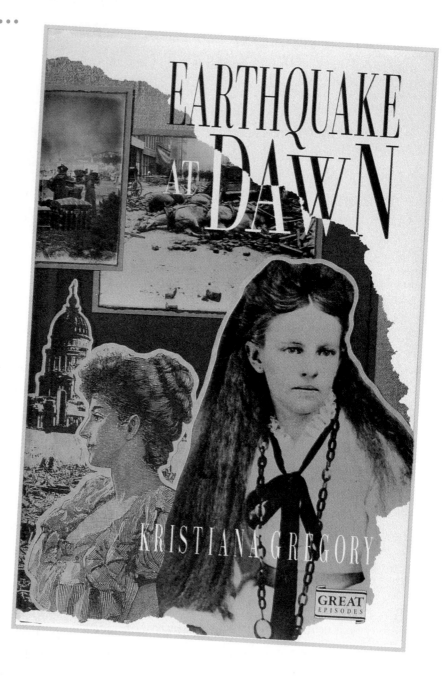

Surtsey: The Newest Place on Earth

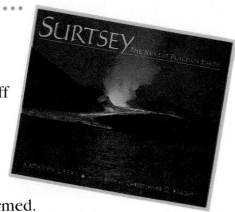

by Kathryn Lasky (Hyperion, 1992), Outstanding Science Trade Book. As fishers off the coast of Iceland stared, the sea boiled. Huge black feathers seemed to rise from its surface, topped by a steam cloud. Then the cinder cone of a volcano burst through the surface. A new island that would be named Surtsey had been formed. Read this book to discover the newest land on Earth.

More Books to Read

Could You Ever Dig a Hole to China?

by David Darling (Dillon Press, 1990). What would you find if you dug to the other side of the Earth? Ancient people and fiction writers have told tales of fiery underworlds and lost cities. Read about what scientists have learned through instruments and investigation. The real story is as interesting as the legends of the past.

Volcanoes and Earthquakes

by Mary Elting (Simon & Schuster, 1990). Throughout history there have been many recorded earthquakes and volcanoes. In this book, you will be a witness to several of them, sometimes from a distance and sometimes up close. There are also facts about earthquakes and volcanoes and explanations of their causes.

Powerful Waves

by D. M. Souza (Carolrhoda, 1992). Ocean waves are interesting to watch and fun to play in. A tsunami (su NAH mee) is one wave that is so powerful, it can uproot trees and tear apart buildings. It is caused by earthquakes or other forceful movements of the Earth. This book contains many pictures as well as charts and drawings that describe tsunamis.

How to Make a Chemical Volcano and Other Mysterious Experiments

by Alan Kramer (Franklin Watts, 1989). You might not be able to move great chunks of the Earth's surface, but you can make your own volcano. By constructing a model of a mountain and combining certain chemicals, you can make an "exploding" volcano.

Investigate

To find answers to their questions, scientists read, think, talk to others, and do experiments. Their investigations often lead to new questions.

In this unit, you will have many chances to think and work like a scientist. How will you find answers to questions you asked?

▶ **INFERRING** Inferring is using what you have observed to explain what has happened. An observation is something you see or experience. An inference is an explanation of an observation, and it may be right or wrong.

▶ **RECOGNIZING TIME/SPACE RELATIONSHIPS** Time relationships tell you the order of events. Space relationships tell you about locations of objects. Understanding these relationships can help you make accurate models.

▶ **INTERPRETING DATA** Data is information given to you or information that you gather during activities. When you interpret data, you decide what it means.

Are you ready to begin?

SECTIONS

SECTION A
Inside the Earth

Suppose you're playing a video adventure game. You come to a locked room without windows. You want to know what's inside the room, but the only way you can see into it is through a keyhole. You can't get a very good look. If you had a key, you could open the door and see the entire room.

Now, think about the Earth. The inside of the Earth is like that locked room. Scientists can't actually see what's going on in there. Yet they *have* been able to infer what's inside the Earth. How were they able to do this? What "key" did they use to unlock the Earth's secrets? And what's the inside of the Earth like? The readings and activities that follow can help you answer these and other questions about our planet. As you work through the investigations, keep careful notes in your Science Log for reference.

1 CRUST TO CORE

As you dressed today, you may have put on a T-shirt, a flannel shirt, and then a sweater. Over all of that, you might have worn a jacket. This way of dressing is sometimes called "the layered look." The Earth has a layered look, too. In the activities and readings in this lesson, you will find out about the Earth's layers and how these layers may have formed.

ACTIVITY

Gathering Together

Have you ever wondered how the Earth and the other planets formed? In the following activity, you can model the way many scientists hypothesize the Earth formed more than 4.5 billion years ago.

MATERIALS
- shallow pan
- water
- 2 plastic spoons
- paper dots
- Science Log data sheet

DO THIS

1. Half-fill the pan with water.

2. Scoop up a spoonful of paper dots.

3. As one partner rapidly stirs the water in the pan, the other sprinkles the paper dots over the water as evenly as possible.

4. Stop stirring, and watch the floating dots as the water motion stops.

THINK AND WRITE

1. What happened to the paper dots? Why do you think this happened?

2. Some scientists hypothesize that the Earth formed in a similar manner. If so, what might the paper dots represent?

From a Cloud of Dust

Many scientists have accepted the hypothesis that the Earth and the rest of the solar system formed from a huge cloud of gas and dust. As you look at the illustrations and read the captions, you will find out how this probably happened.

▲ Billions of years ago, a gigantic cloud of dust and gas swirled slowly in the vastness of space. Over time, the cloud shrank and began spinning faster and faster.

▲ Parts of the cloud formed individual whirlpools spinning around its center. At the same time, gravity pulled most of the gas and dust into the center of the shrinking cloud. Eventually, a star, the sun, formed.

▲ The whirlpools revolving around the sun also pulled gases and dust into their centers in much the same way. More and more gas and dust collected, and the centers grew larger.

▼ The centers slowly cooled and formed planets. Some of the planets, such as Jupiter, retained thick atmospheres, and some, such as Earth, developed rocky surfaces.

THINK ABOUT IT

Scientists hypothesize that the Earth and the other planets of the solar system are about the same age. How does this model support that hypothesis?

Eggs-actly Right

You can easily see Earth's rocky surface, but what is our planet like inside? The answer would be easy if we could just cut the Earth in half. However, there is a way to model Earth's interior. You might try it at lunch.

You will need: hard-boiled egg, plastic knife

Using the handle of the knife, crack the shell slightly by tapping around the center of the egg. Then, without removing the shell, cut the egg in half. In your Science Log, write a description of each layer you see. Also sketch the layers and label them *1, 2,* and *3.*

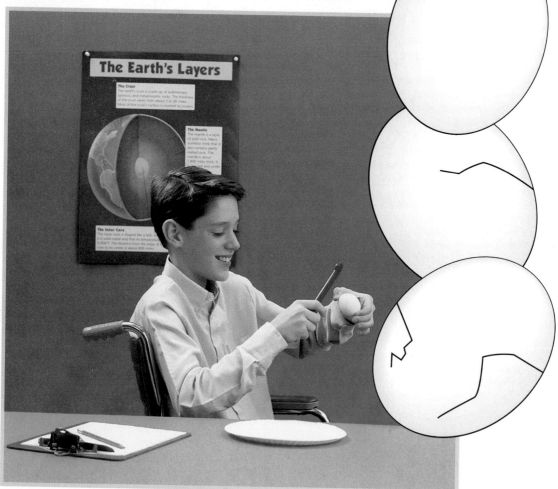

The egg represents the Earth. Like the egg, the Earth is composed of three major layers. What part of the Earth does the egg's shell represent?

A C T I V I T Y

Like a Rock

You know that, like an egg, the Earth has layers. You also know that the Earth probably formed from a swirling cloud of dust and gas. But how did the dust and gas form into layers? The following activity can help you answer this question.

DO THIS

1. Put 10 mL of potting soil and 10 mL of sand into the jar.

2. Measure 10 mL of water and 10 mL of vegetable oil, and pour them into the jar.

3. Add 10 mL of uncooked oatmeal to the jar.

4. Put the lid on the jar, and shake the contents vigorously.

5. Set the jar aside, and allow all the materials to settle.

THINK AND WRITE

1. In what order did the materials layer themselves in the jar?

2. Where in the jar are the heavier materials?

3. INFERRING Inferring is using what you have observed to explain what happens. Would you expect to find the heaviest layer of Earth on its surface or near its center? Explain how you made this inference.

Journey to the Center of the Earth

Gerardo Bacena is a research geologist—a scientist who studies the Earth—at a university in California. In addition to conducting research and teaching at the university, Dr. Bacena spends some of his time speaking to science classes about the Earth and its structure. Today, he is speaking to Ms. Claxon's sixth-grade class.

After being introduced, Dr. Bacena walks over to a globe he brought with him. Without saying a word, he picks it up, gently taps it on a desk, and breaks it open like an egg.

"Take a good look," he says. "Like a hard-boiled egg, the Earth has three major layers. This thin layer at the surface is called the **crust.** Earth's crust is composed of various kinds of rock. Think about the crust on a loaf of bread. It's thicker in some places than in others. The Earth's crust is the same—it's thicker under the continents than it is under the oceans.

"Earth's middle layer is called the **mantle,** and it's about 2,900 kilometers (1,800 miles) thick. The mantle is made up of heavy rock and is divided into two parts—the upper mantle and the lower mantle. Beneath the mantle is the **core,** which is also divided into two parts. The outer core is liquid and the inner core is solid.

"Of course, no one has ever seen the interior of the Earth, so you might wonder how we know about its structure. Scientists use instruments, such as a seismograph (sys muh graf), to study the Earth's interior.

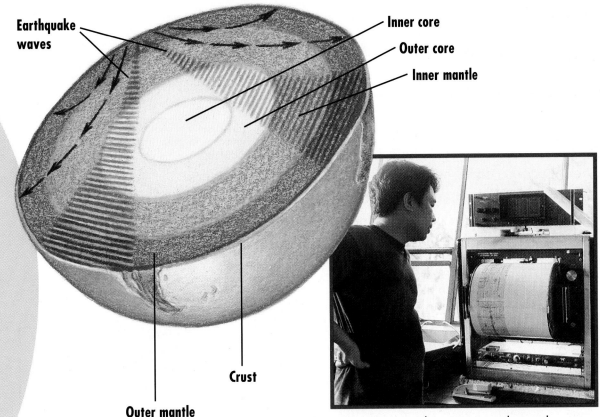

Earthquake waves

Inner core

Outer core

Inner mantle

Crust

Outer mantle

▲ A seismograph measures and records ground movements caused by earthquakes. The energy of an earthquake moves through the Earth in waves, like the waves formed by dropping a pebble into a puddle. Some waves can pass through both liquids and solids, but they move at different speeds through different materials. Other waves cannot pass through liquids. Studying these waves enables scientists to make inferences about the Earth's interior.

"In the middle of continents, the crust may be 70 kilometers (43.5 miles) thick. At the edges of continents, it's about 25 kilometers (15.5 miles) thick. However, under the oceans, the crust is only about 7 kilometers (4.4 miles) thick. Oceanic crust and continental crust differ in another way, too. The rock of oceanic crust is much heavier than the rock of continental crust."

Dr. Bacena explains that the rock of the upper mantle is pretty much like the rock of the crust. In the lower mantle, the rock is soft and pliable. You might compare it with modeling clay that can be stretched and pulled. The liquid outer core is composed of heavy metals, such as iron and nickel. The solid inner core is composed of heavy metals also. 🔖

QUICK CHECK

LESSON 1 REVIEW

❶ How do scientists know that part of the Earth's core is solid and part is liquid?

❷ In what way is the Earth like a hard-boiled egg?

2 Go with the Flow

Have you ever watched or run in a 5-kilometer (3.1-mile) race? At the start, the runners are all bunched together. Then, because some of the runners are faster than others, they begin to spread out. Most scientists theorize that the continents were once bunched together and then spread out, like runners in a race. In this lesson, you will examine evidence that led to this theory.

ACTIVITY

A Perfect Fit

If the continents had once been bunched together, you might expect them to fit together in some way, like the pieces of a jigsaw puzzle. In the following activity, you can check this out for yourself.

MATERIALS
- outline map of the world
- scissors
- blue construction paper
- glue
- Science Log data sheet

DO THIS

❶ Cut out the continents and large islands.

❷ Try to arrange the pieces so that they form one large landmass. Fit them together as well as you can.

❸ Glue the pieces onto the construction paper.

❹ Compare your landmass with those created by your classmates.

THINK AND WRITE

1. What did you discover when you put all the landmasses together?

2. Propose an explanation for how the continents might have moved to their present positions.

Adrift

In the activity, did you join Africa and South America? Many people think these continents fit together like the pieces of a jigsaw puzzle. Alfred Wegener was one of the first scientists to think so. Read to find out more about his ideas.

Wegener was a college student when he first noticed that the coastlines of Africa and South America look as if they could be fitted together. Several years later, he read about fossil animals in South America and in Africa that seemed to be very much alike.

These facts made Wegener really curious. What could explain the way the continents seemed to fit together? How could animals on continents separated by an ocean be alike?

Wegener concluded that South America and Africa must have been connected at one time. In fact, he hypothesized that millions of years ago, all of the continents were part of one single large landmass. He began looking for evidence to support his ideas.

In 1912 Wegener presented his ideas at an international meeting of geologists. He suggested that all the continents were once part of a giant continent he named Pangea. *Pangea* comes from Greek words meaning "all Earth."

▼ Pangea

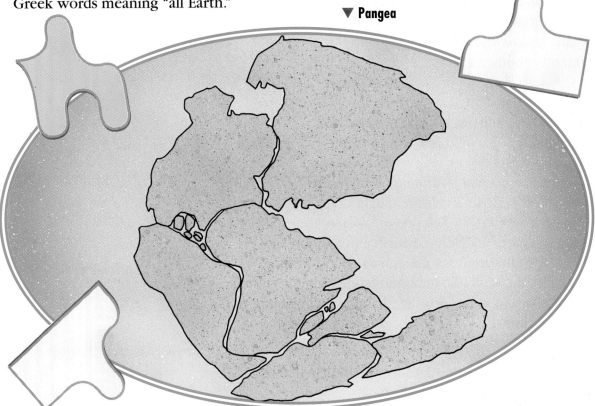

In 1915 Wegener published a book that presented his hypothesis about Pangea and offered evidence to support it. He noted that fossils of the same plants and animals were found on many different continents. For example, fossils of an ancient reptile were found in Antarctica, Africa, and India. Fossils of an ancient plant were found in South America, Africa, India, Australia, and Antarctica. He also pointed out that rocks on the western coast of Africa and the eastern coast of South America seemed to match.

▲ Alfred Wegener

Wegener thought the evidence supported his idea that the continents were once part of Pangea. He proposed that Pangea broke up for some reason and that the pieces drifted away from one another, forming the present continents. According to Wegener, *continental drift* could explain how fossils of the same organisms are found in places far away from one another.

Although Wegener concluded that the continents had drifted away from one another, he could not explain how these large landmasses could move. As a result, most geologists dismissed his ideas. They said that Pangea was nothing more than the product of Wegener's vivid imagination.

Wegener died in 1930 while on a scientific expedition to gather additional evidence to support his ideas. He didn't live long enough to see his ideas accepted by the scientific community. He didn't know that one day he would be considered a pioneer in geology.

▲ Fossil evidence

THINK ABOUT IT

Why do you think scientists in the 1920s did not accept Wegener's ideas?

ACTIVITY

Drifting Along

Wegener could not explain how continents could drift across the surface of the Earth. In the following activity, you will discover something that might help explain continental drift.

DO THIS

❶ Half-fill the dishpan with water.

❷ Cut away the top half of each foam cup.

❸ Float all the cup bottoms together in the dishpan and loosely loop the string around them.

❹ Guide the foam cups to the center of the dishpan.

❺ Use your hand to create waves by swishing the water underneath the cups back and forth.

❻ Remove the string from around the cups. Watch what happens to the cups as you swish the water.

THINK AND WRITE

1. What happened to the foam cups? Why do you think this happened?

2. **RECOGNIZING TIME/SPACE RELATIONSHIPS** Space relationships tell you about locations of objects. How might this help you explain the drifting of the continents to their present positions?

ACTIVITY

Spreading Apart

If continents somehow floated on a liquid, as the foam cups did in the last activity, it might help explain their drifting apart. But what could have started them moving? In this activity, you can model a process that could cause continents to move.

DO THIS

1 Cut a slit about 6 cm long and 4 cm wide in the bottom of the shoe box. Cut an opening in one side of the box large enough for you to reach inside.

2 Cut 2 strips of construction paper, each about 5 cm wide and 10 cm long.

3 Push the strips through the slit in the box so that about one-third of each strip is showing.

4 Place a small lump of clay on the exposed end of each strip of paper. The lumps of clay should just touch each other at the slit in the box.

5 Reach into the box through the opening you made. Grasp the free ends of the paper strips, and slowly push them up through the slit in the box.

THINK AND WRITE

1. What happened to the lumps of clay? Why?

2. If the clay represents rocks of the crust and the paper strips represent the upper mantle, how might this explain why continents move?

MATERIALS
- scissors
- ruler
- shoe box
- construction paper
- clay
- Science Log data sheet

Oozing Earth

In the last activity, you saw how pieces of the Earth can move, as if pushed by something below the surface. What provides the push for this movement? In this activity, you can find out.

DO THIS

❶ Gently tap the egg so that it cracks without breaking.

❷ Place the egg in a small pan, and cover it with water.

❸ **CAUTION: Be careful when using the hot plate.** Put the pan on the hot plate, and bring the water to a boil. Allow the water to boil for five minutes.

❹ Your teacher will remove the pan from the heat source, pour out the hot water, and cool the egg by running cold water over it.

❺ Look at the cooled egg. What do you observe?

MATERIALS
- raw egg
- small pan
- water
- hot plate
- Science Log data sheet

THINK AND WRITE

1. What happened around the crack in the egg?

2. Why do you think this happened?

3. Would the same thing have happened if the egg hadn't been cracked? Explain.

4. Suppose the Earth had cracks in it that reached down to the inner mantle. What might happen at the cracks?

Maybe He Was Right

You may recall that in the 1920s, few scientists accepted Wegener's ideas about continental drift. By the 1960s, however, more and more scientists thought he was right. Recently, Dr. Bacena wrote a magazine article that explained why scientists changed their opinions about Wegener and continental drift. Read the article to find out why scientists changed their minds.

We *FINALLY* Got Your Drift

by Gerardo Bacena

 In the 1950s and 1960s, new technology helped geologists explore the seafloor. For the first time, they were able to map the ocean floor and to study rocks taken from deep inside the crust. Their deep-sea explorations led to some exciting discoveries about the Earth.

Geologists learned that mountain ranges circle the Earth beneath the oceans. One of these underwater mountain ranges is the mid-Atlantic Ridge.

Surprised scientists found out that the ridge doesn't have a thick layer of sediments as most of the ocean floor does. They also found that the rocks closest to the ridge are much younger than those farther away. One other thing they learned is that the water near the ridge is much warmer than in other parts of the ocean.

Based on these discoveries, geologists formed a new hypothesis. The mid-Atlantic Ridge must have a crack in it, like a cracked egg. Have you ever boiled a cracked egg? If you have, you know the egg comes through the shell where the crack is.

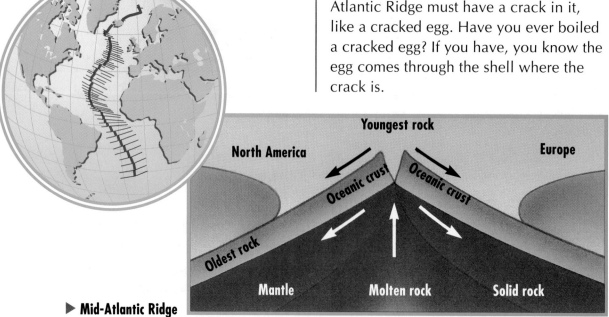

▶ **Mid-Atlantic Ridge**

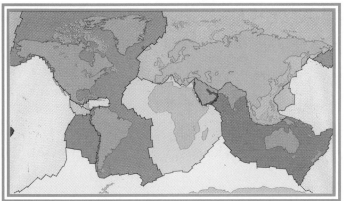

▲ Earth's major plates

Think about a jigsaw puzzle. It's made up of pieces that can be put together to form a whole picture. The Earth's outer shell is much like that. It has pieces, or plates, that come together to form the Earth's surface. And, like the pieces of a jigsaw puzzle, the Earth's plates are different shapes and sizes. The map shows Earth's major plates.

Even though the Earth's plates include the oceans as well as the continents, the theory of plate tectonics supports Wegener's idea of continental drift. Perhaps Pangea did exist—and not just in Wegener's imagination.

Scientists determined that the inner mantle's soft rock oozes up to the surface through the crack in the mid-Atlantic Ridge. Once at the surface, it cools and hardens. This new rock pushes older rock aside. Many geologists conclude that the floor of the Atlantic Ocean is spreading.

What does this mean? It means that North and South America are moving away from Europe and Africa. They are moving just as Alfred Wegener hypothesized.

Geologists learned that other parts of Earth's surface also have cracks. They used this information, combined with the ideas of continental drift and sea-floor spreading, to come up with a new theory. They called it the *theory of plate tectonics*. According to this theory, the Earth's outer shell, including the crust and outer mantle, is made up of rigid plates, and these plates are moving. The cracks are the places where plates meet.

LESSON 2 REVIEW

❶ What evidence did Wegener use to support his ideas about continental drift?

❷ Why would you expect to find a deeper layer of sediment away from the mid-Atlantic Ridge? Explain.

DOUBLE CHECK

SECTION A REVIEW

1. How did seismographs help scientists identify the materials that make up the Earth's layers?

2. Why did scientists change their opinions about Wegener's ideas of continental drift?

SECTION B
Boundaries

▲ Plate boundary

Do you play soccer, basketball, or tennis? If you do, you know that the playing area has boundaries. When the ball crosses a boundary, it is out of play. In a game such as basketball, a lot of action often takes place near the boundaries.

The Earth's plates have boundaries, too. And, just as in an action-packed game, a lot goes on near a boundary. What *does* happen at a plate boundary? Does the same kind of action occur at all plate boundaries? In this section, you'll discover the answers to these questions and others. Keep careful notes in your Science Log as you work through the investigations.

1 ON THE MOVE

Have you ever seen a bumper-car ride at an amusement park or a carnival? Some of the cars move away from each other, some scrape past each other, and some crash head on. Like bumper cars, the Earth's plates move. In the activities and readings that follow, you will discover what happens when the Earth's plates move.

Shake and Bake

In California, most people are familiar with *earthquakes,* or violent movements that shake the Earth's crust. But most people in Florida have probably never experienced these frightening movements. Why are earthquakes common in California but not in Florida?

In the last section, you read about the evidence that led to the theory of plate tectonics. You may recall that the Earth's surface is divided into many plates and that the plates are constantly moving. Some plates come together, some move apart, and others slide past each other. These movements are similar to the movements of bumper cars.

If you've ever driven bumper cars, you know what happens when two cars scrape past each other or crash head on. Now, think of the tremendous power of gigantic plates scraping past each other or crashing together. You would expect something pretty dramatic to happen, wouldn't you?

Ring of Fire

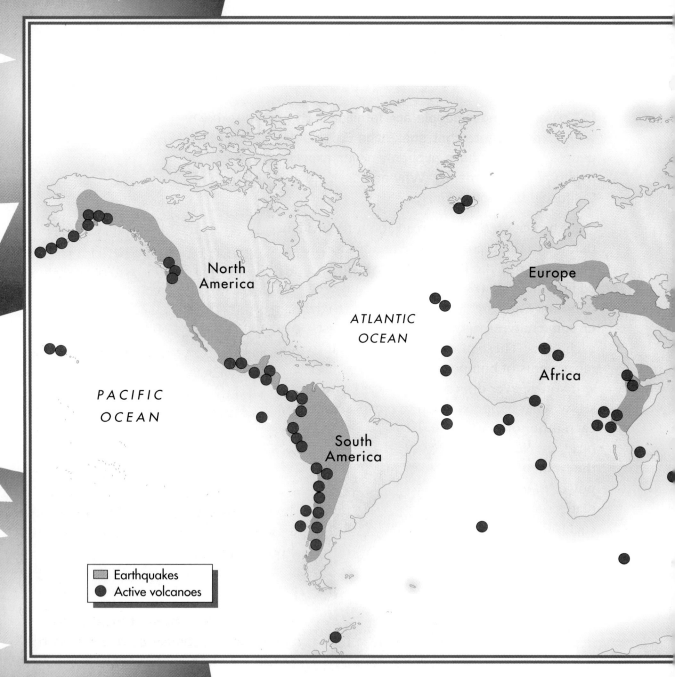

Legend:
- Earthquakes
- Active volcanoes

PACIFIC OCEAN

ATLANTIC OCEAN

North America

South America

Europe

Africa

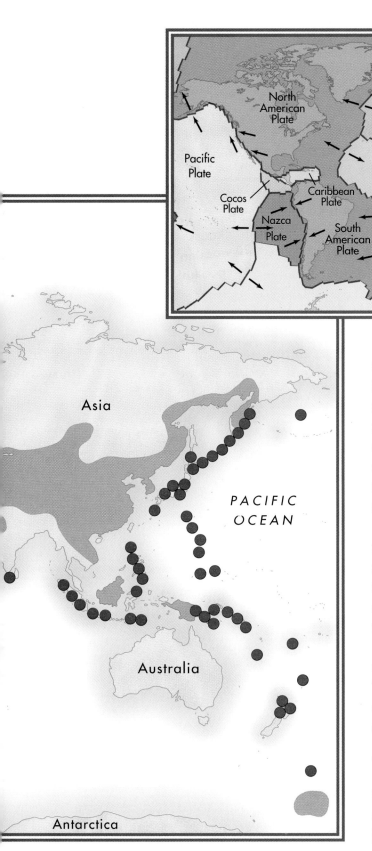

Compare the maps on these pages. One map shows the boundaries of the Earth's plates and the directions in which the plates move. The other map shows the locations of areas that have major earthquakes and volcanoes. **Volcanoes** are openings in the Earth's crust through which ashes, molten rock, and gases escape.

As you compare the maps, pay close attention to the area around the Pacific Ocean. So many earthquakes and volcanoes occur here that the area has become known as the *Ring of Fire*. As you can see, California is within that ring, but Florida isn't.

Earthquakes and volcanoes are two activities that take place near plate boundaries. You'll discover more about them in the next section. Trenches and mountains also form at plate boundaries.

THINK ABOUT IT

How does the location of most earthquakes and volcanoes compare with the location of plate boundaries?

A31

ACTIVITY

Coming Apart at the Seams

The Ring of Fire isn't the only place where plate movements produce dramatic results. The Atlantic Ocean is getting wider as the Eurasian and North American plates pull apart. In this activity, you can make a model of the effects of this movement.

MATERIALS
- 2 books of equal thickness
- 20 wooden blocks
- Science Log data sheet

DO THIS

1. Set the books on a table so that their spines are about 2 cm apart.

2. Place 4 blocks in a row between the spines of the books so that each block rests on both books.

3. Place 2 rows of 4 blocks each on both sides of the row along the book spines.

4. Slowly pull the books apart. As you do, observe what happens to the blocks.

THINK AND WRITE

1. What happened to the blocks along the book spines? What happened to the other blocks?

2. If the blocks represent the Earth's crust and the books represent the Eurasian and North American plates, what happens to the crust when plates move away from each other?

Moving Up

When plates pull apart, what happens to the molten rock beneath them? You can find out in the following activity.

DO THIS

1 Place the pieces of poster board next to each other on the gelatin in the middle of the baking pan.

2 Place the blocks of wood on each side of the crack on top of the poster board.

3 Press down on the blocks of wood, and slowly slide them away from the crack in the poster board. Observe what happens to the gelatin between the pieces of poster board.

THINK AND WRITE

1. What happened to the gelatin as you pushed down and moved the blocks of wood away from the crack?

2. If the blocks of wood represent the plates and the gelatin represents molten rock, what happens to the rock as the plates pull apart?

3. **RECOGNIZING TIME/SPACE RELATIONSHIPS** Time relationships tell you the order of events. In order for molten rock to emerge from the Earth, the plates must move away from each other at the same time the molten rock emerges. In this activity, how did you have to move the blocks of wood (which represent the plates) for the gelatin (or molten rock) to erupt?

On the Ridge

Iceland is a small island country in the northern Atlantic Ocean. Geologists like Gerardo Bacena go there to study the land and its features. Why is this small country of so much interest to geologists? Read to find out.

Look at the map of the Atlantic Ocean floor, and trace the mid-Atlantic ridge. Because of Iceland's location along the mid-Atlantic ridge, geologists can study valleys and mountains that were produced in the same way as those of the mid-ocean ridges.

When plates pull apart, Earth's crust cracks open. These cracks are known as *rifts*. Along some rifts, the crust drops and forms a sunken valley, as the blocks did in the Coming Apart at the Seams activity.

When the crust is thin or weakened, molten rock pushes up to the surface through cracks in the crust. The mid-Atlantic ridge formed this way, as did some of the landscape of Iceland. This process is similar to what happened in the Moving Up activity.

The last time Dr. Bacena was in Iceland, he visited the Skaptar fissure. The fissure, or crack, is part of a 24-kilometer (15-mile) rift that opened up in 1783.

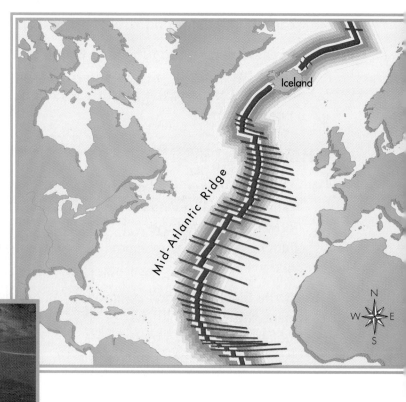

Iceland

Mid-Atlantic Ridge

THINK ABOUT IT

What effect can plates that are pulling apart have on the land?

◀ Skaptar rift

ACTIVITY

Crashing Plates

Since the Earth is not getting any larger, if some plates are moving apart, others must be crashing into each other. What happens to the landscape when plates collide? In the following activity, you will discover one possible result.

DO THIS

❶ Place the spines of the books together.

❷ With your fingers, push the books toward each other.

❸ Observe what happens along the spines of the books.

THINK AND WRITE

1. What happened to the spines of the books?

2. How might this be similar to what happens when two plates collide?

3. **INFERRING** Scientists infer when they explain observations. Based on your observation, make an inference about the type of landform that might be produced by plates colliding.

Over and Under

In the last activity, you observed a model of colliding plates. What actually happens when plates collide depends on the kinds of plates involved. The following diagrams show several different kinds of plate collisions.

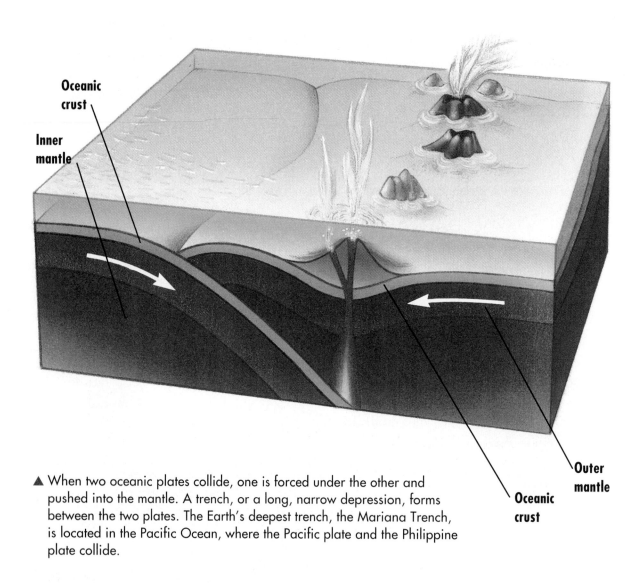

▲ When two oceanic plates collide, one is forced under the other and pushed into the mantle. A trench, or a long, narrow depression, forms between the two plates. The Earth's deepest trench, the Mariana Trench, is located in the Pacific Ocean, where the Pacific plate and the Philippine plate collide.

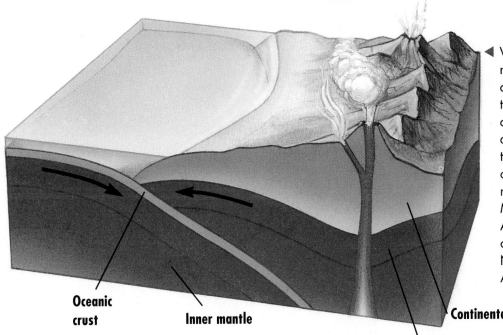

◀ When oceanic and continental plates collide, the continental plate rides over the oceanic plate. The oceanic plate is forced down. A trench forms in the ocean, and a mountain chain forms on the continent. The Andes Mountains of South America formed because of the collision of the Nazca plate and the South American plate.

Oceanic crust

Inner mantle

Continental crust

Outer mantle

▼ When two continental plates collide, the edges of the plates are pushed up to form large mountain ranges. The Earth's highest mountains, the Himalayas, formed because of the collision of the Eurasian plate and the Indo-Australian plate.

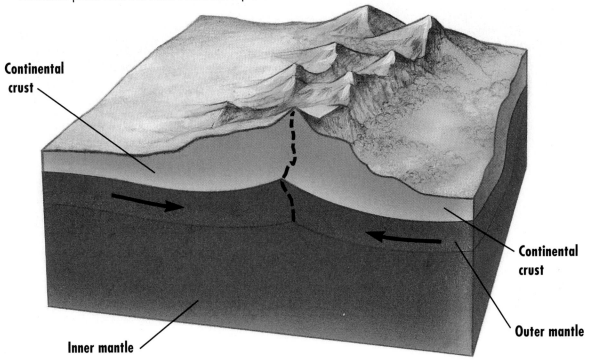

Continental crust

Continental crust

Outer mantle

Inner mantle

THINK ABOUT IT

Why does the effect of the collision of two plates depend on the kinds of plates involved?

Building Up and Tearing Down

All around the Ring of Fire, tectonic plates are pushing against each other or pulling apart. In some places, the Earth's crust is being destroyed as it is pushed down into the mantle. In other places, new crust is being made as molten rock flows up to the Earth's surface. The diagram shows where crust is being destroyed and where it is being formed.

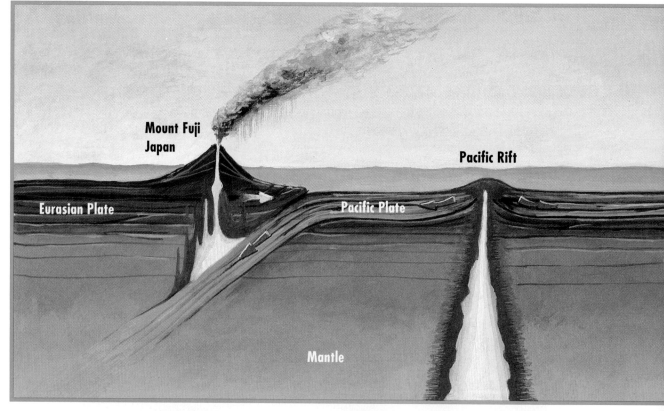

Mount Fuji
Japan

Pacific Rift

Eurasian Plate

Pacific Plate

Mantle

▲ The western edge of the Pacific plate is destroyed as it collides with and is forced under the Eurasian plate.

▲ At the Pacific rift, new crust is forming from molten rock pouring out of a crack in the ocean floor. The rift is located at the place where the Pacific plate meets the Cocos and the Nazca plates.

▼ The North American plate grinds past the eastern edge of the Pacific plate, forcing the Pacific plate into the mantle.

▼ The North American plate forms at the mid-Atlantic ridge. This plate pushes westward as it grows.

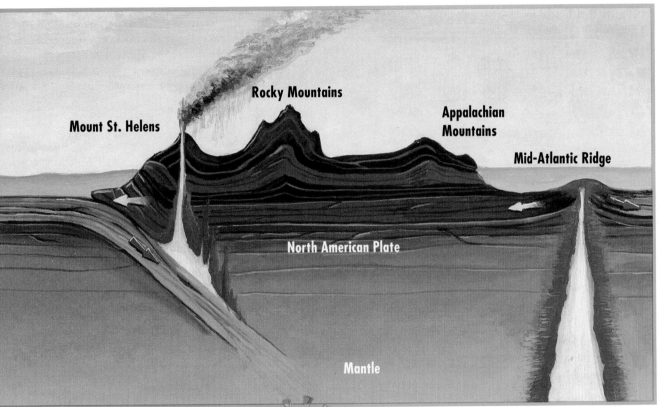

Mount St. Helens

Rocky Mountains

Appalachian Mountains

Mid-Atlantic Ridge

North American Plate

Mantle

▲ Because of the destruction of crust, the width of the Pacific Ocean floor decreases along its eastern, northern, and western boundaries.

LESSON 1 REVIEW

❶ How are the results of plates separating and plates colliding alike? How are they different?

❷ The Himalayas get several centimeters higher each year. Why do you think these mountains continue to get taller?

2 BUILDING MOUNTAINS

Have you ever seen or made origami figures? Origami is the ancient Japanese art of folding paper. Like paper, the Earth's crust can be folded. Folding paper makes beautiful designs. Folding the Earth's crust makes interesting landscapes. But how can the Earth's crust, which is mostly rock, be folded? You can find out in the activities and readings that follow.

ACTIVITY

Fold Neatly

What happens when pieces of the Earth's crust are pushed together? In this activity, you can model the action and observe what happens.

MATERIALS
- 3 hand towels
- table
- Science Log data sheet

DO THIS

❶ Work with a partner. Fold the towels in thirds lengthwise, and stack them on the table.

❷ With you on one end and your partner on the other end, gently push the ends of the towels toward each other. Observe what happens to the towels.

THINK AND WRITE

1. What happened to the towels?

2. How do you think what happened to the towels might be related to the folding of the Earth's crust?

May the Force Be with You

After leaving Iceland, Dr. Bacena traveled to Wales in Great Britain. While exploring the coast of Wales, he found many examples of the folding of the Earth's crust. Read to find out what causes the crust to fold.

▲ Folded rocks in Wales

In the last activity, the towels folded because you and your partner applied a force to each end of the stack. Forces are applied to the Earth's crust by such things as moving plates. **Folding** occurs when forces within the Earth push together, or *compress,* part of the crust. This compression of the crust causes rocks to bend.

The folded towels formed hills and valleys as they were compressed. The same thing happens to the Earth's crust when it's compressed. Areas where the crust bends upward are called *anticlines.* Many mountains and hills are anticlines. Areas where the crust bends downward are called *synclines.* Many valleys are synclines. Look at the diagram. Then identify an anticline and a syncline in the photograph above.

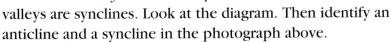

▲ The Alps

Many mountain chains have been formed by the folding of the Earth's crust. Think how strong the force must be to produce mountains like the Alps in Europe.

Forces within the Earth can be so strong that the rocks of the crust break, or *fracture,* rather than fold. If these forces cause the fractured rocks to move, a fault forms. A **fault** is a break in the crust along which rocks move past each other. The rocks may move up or down in relation to one another, or they may move sideways. The rocks on either side of a fault are called *walls.*

Dr. Bacena's home in California is near a famous fault—the San Andreas fault. The San Andreas fault is located along the boundary between the North American plate and the Pacific plate. At the boundary, the Pacific plate is drifting toward the northwest. The North American plate is also moving toward the northwest, but more slowly. Along the boundary, the plates grind against each other. In the next activity, you can model the movement of the San Andreas fault.

THINK ABOUT IT

How is the way the Alps were formed similar to the way the Himalayas were formed? How is it different?

ACTIVITY

It's Not My Fault!

Forces within the Earth cause the rock walls of faults to slide past each other. In the following activity, you can model the movement of the walls of the famous San Andreas Fault.

MATERIALS
- 2 blocks of wood
- fine-grained sandpaper
- tape
- Science Log data sheet

DO THIS

CAUTION

1. Tape a piece of sandpaper to one of the blocks of wood.

2. Put the blocks of wood together so that the sandpaper is between the blocks.

3. **CAUTION: Be careful when pushing and pulling the wood. It may slip and hit you or someone else.** Pull one piece of wood toward you, and push the other piece away from you. Observe what happens as you do this.

THINK AND WRITE

1. Did the wood blocks glide easily past each other? Explain.

2. How might this be similar to rocks moving past each other along a fault?

Finding Faults

Not all faults are like the San Andreas fault. In fact, there are three different kinds of faults. The differences between faults involve the ways the rock walls move past each other and the kind of force that produces the faults. Dr. Bacena is describing faults to Ms. Claxon's class.

 "The San Andreas Fault is a *lateral fault.* In a lateral fault, the walls of broken rock move sideways past each other. The force that causes a lateral fault is called *shear.*

"Ms. Claxon said you made a model of a lateral fault with blocks of wood and sandpaper. You probably observed that your blocks resisted moving at first, and then they suddenly moved with a jerk. In a real lateral fault, the jerky movement produces an earthquake.

"In another kind of fault, the crust is stretched. You know that if you stretch a rubber band far enough, it eventually snaps. The same thing happens to the Earth's crust. Forces within the Earth stretch the crust in some places. If this stretching, or *tension,* is great enough, rocks break. As tension continues along the fault, one wall will drop down. This kind of fault is called a *normal fault.*

▼ San Andreas Fault

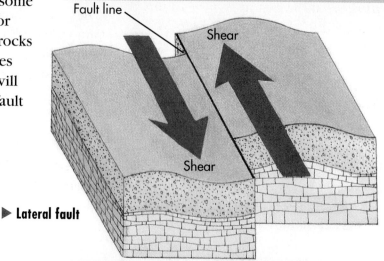

Fault line

Shear

Shear

▶ Lateral fault

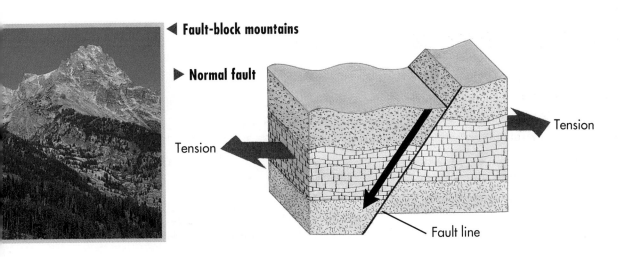

◄ **Fault-block mountains**

► **Normal fault**

Tension

Tension

Fault line

▼ **Reverse fault**

Fault line

Compression

Compression

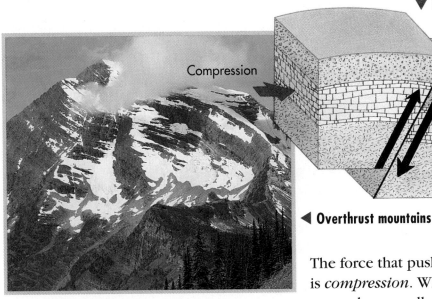

◄ **Overthrust mountains**

"If an area has many normal faults, ranges of mountains form as walls along the faults drop. Mountains formed by normal faults are called *fault-block mountains*. The Teton range in Wyoming is an example of fault-block mountains.

"As normal faults build mountains, they also produce valleys. Death Valley, the lowest place in North America at 86 meters (282 feet) below sea level, is a block of crust that dropped between normal faults to the east and west.

"While some faults separate because of tension, other faults are pushed together.

The force that pushes faults together is *compression*. When a fault is compressed, one wall moves up in relation to the other. This type of fault is called a *reverse fault*.

"At some reverse faults, compression causes one wall to ride up and over the other wall. The result is a range of mountains called *overthrust mountains*. Many mountains in Montana's Glacier National Park are overthrust mountains."

THINK ABOUT IT

How are the three types of faults similar? How are they different?

ACTIVITY

Another Fault

In the last activity, you made a model of a lateral fault. Remember, at lateral faults, rocks slide past each other. As Dr. Bacena just described, rocks move differently at different types of faults. In this activity, you will model and identify different types of faults.

MATERIALS
- shoe box
- scissors
- Science Log data sheet

DO THIS

❶ Cut the shoe box in half at an angle.

❷ Place the angled sides of the box together, and hold the joined box flat on the palms of your hands.

❸ Relax one hand, and allow one side of the box to drop down.

THINK AND WRITE

1. What kind of fault did this activity model?

2. What kind of force produces this fault?

3. What kind of mountain is represented by the side of the box that did not drop?

One More Fault

DO THIS

MATERIALS
- modeling clay
- plastic knife
- 2 wood blocks
- Science Log data sheet

1 Mold the clay into a block about 2 cm deep, 6 cm wide, and 10 cm long.

2 Use the knife to cut the clay block in half at an angle.

3 Place the cut block on a table, and with a partner, use the wood blocks to press the halves of the clay block together. Observe what happens to the clay-block halves as you press them together.

THINK AND WRITE

1. What kind of force did you use in this activity?

2. What happened as a result of the force?

3. What kind of fault did you model in this part of the activity?

4. What kind of mountain does the upper half of the clay block represent?

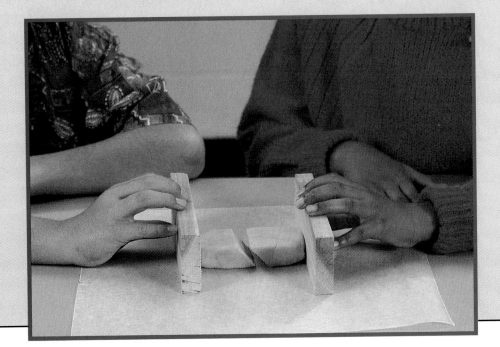

Sing, Sing, Sing

You have discovered how plate movements and folding and faulting have built mountains and produced valleys. The Jicarilla Apaches of the American Southwest have a legend that describes a much different method of mountain building.

HOW THE PEOPLE SANG THE MOUNTAINS UP

from *How the People Sang the Mountains Up: How and Why Stories*
by **Maria Leach**

Silence. Dark. There was nothing there. Only the Hactcins, the Holy Ones, were there from the beginning. They owned the stuff of creation. There was no light—just darkness and the Hactcins creating things in the dark.

It was dark down there where the people lived because there was no sun. So Black Hactcin called for White Hactcin to come, because White Hactcin owned the sun stuff.

"The people need light," said Black Hactcin.

White Hactcin looked in his bag and took out a little sun.

"This will make daylight," he said.

Then Black Hactcin looked in his bag and took out a little moon.

"This can shine in the night," he said.

The sun and the moon were very small and dim.

"You had better start singing," said Black Hactcin.

So they sang together to make the moon and the sun grow larger; and as they sang, the sun and moon began to grow; their light became strong and bright; and the sun and moon moved in their courses, just as they do today.

But it was still dim where the people were. The sun and moon were too far away, too high. What the people needed was a mountain.

The Hactcins made four little mounds of Earth for the people. In each one they hid the seeds and fruits which were to grow, and on top of each little mound they laid the leaves and needles of the trees which were to grow on the mountain.

The little mounds stood in a row, east to west. Then the Hactcins filled a black clay bowl with water (because nothing can grow without water) and they watered the little mounds.

All the animals and birds and people were there and helped to make the mounds grow. They all sang and the mountain began to rise. They were all using their power.

They sang and sang, and the mountain grew and the fruits and trees began to grow on the mountain. They sang four times and the mountain grew, twelve times and the mountain grew twelve

times. As it grew the four little mounds merged together and grew into one big mountain. This spread into a long beautiful range.

Then the people began traveling up the mountains. The birds flew up first, then came the animals and the people. They climbed and climbed and finally came forth into a sunny world.

When the people were all up on the mountains in the sun, the Hactcins put a white pot upside down on top of the highest peak, so all would remember it forever.

QUICK CHECK

LESSON 2 REVIEW

❶ How are mountains formed by normal faults and reverse faults?

❷ Most of the Earth's mountains are folded mountains. Would you expect to find many fault blocks in folded mountains? Explain.

DOUBLE CHECK

SECTION B REVIEW

1. Describe the effects of plates colliding and separating.

2. How are the forces of tension and shear similar? How do they differ?

Earthquakes and Volcanoes

▲ Earthquake damage

Suppose you're standing on a corner, waiting for the light to change, when a huge truck comes rumbling down the street. You feel the vibrations under your feet as the truck passes. The movement of the truck causes these vibrations, which are strong enough to shake the ground around and under you.

Now, think of the vibrations made by the North American plate scraping past the Pacific plate. You may remember that earthquakes and volcanoes occur along plate boundaries. But why are some more damaging than others? And why does a volcano that has not erupted in years suddenly erupt again? As you investigate earthquakes and volcanoes in this section, you will find answers to these and other questions. As you do, record them in your Science Log.

1 EARTHQUAKES

Long ago, people did not know about the forces within the Earth that move plates and cause earthquakes. Because of this, myths, or stories, were created to explain how earthquakes occur. Today our knowledge of earthquakes is based on scientific data, not myths. Read the myth of the namazu, and compare it with the scientific explanations that follow.

The One That Got Away

In the folklore of Japan, a story is told of a giant catfish, the namazu (nuh MAH soo). Namazu causes earthquakes by thrashing its tail.

According to this myth, the namazu lives in the mud, just beneath the surface of the Earth. A brave samurai warrior, Kashima, has to constantly hold a large, heavy stone on top of the fish to keep it from moving. As long as the warrior keeps the namazu under the stone, the Earth is quiet. But if Kashima relaxes and allows the fish to wriggle, an earthquake occurs.

THINK ABOUT IT

Why do people make up myths about things they can't understand?

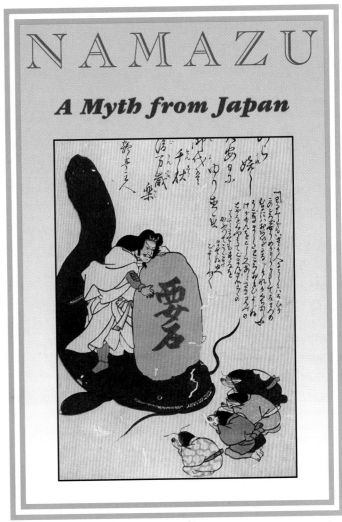

NAMAZU

A Myth from Japan

ACTIVITY

It Shakes Like Jelly

In October 1989, an area about 100 kilometers (62 miles) south of San Francisco experienced a fairly strong earthquake. Although the earthquake caused some damage locally, there was also a lot of damage in and around San Francisco. Why was the damage so widespread? This activity will help you understand what happens during an earthquake.

DO THIS

1 Place the plastic wrap over the gelatin in the baking pan. The plastic wrap must touch the gelatin.

2 Arrange the toys and other objects at various places on the plastic wrap.

3 Gently shake the pan in a back-and-forth motion. Observe what happens to the objects after you stop shaking the pan.

MATERIALS
- baking pan of gelatin
- plastic wrap
- toy houses, cars, trees, and other objects
- Science Log data sheet

THINK AND WRITE

1. How did the objects move? What kind of movement occurred after you stopped shaking the pan?

2. Why are buildings and other structures damaged during earthquakes?

Catch a Wave!

When you think of earthquakes, you probably think of the Earth shaking like gelatin, as you modeled in the last activity. Although this is sometimes the case, earthquake motion is usually much more regular. In the following activity, you can model two kinds of earthquake motion.

DO THIS

1 Tie one end of the elastic cord to a doorknob or another stationary object.

2 Hold the other end of the cord, and move back until the cord is partially stretched when your hand is at your side.

3 Slowly swing your arm forward and backward while observing the motion of the cord.

4 Now, shake the cord up and down or from side to side. Observe any differences in the motion of the cord.

MATERIALS
- 3-m elastic cord
- stationary object
- Science Log data sheet

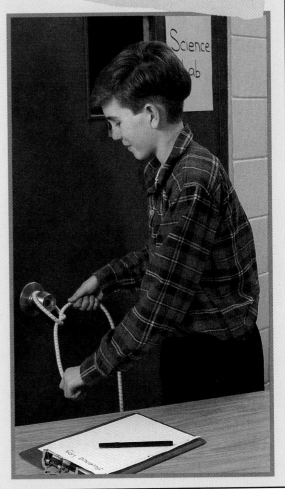

THINK AND WRITE

1. Describe the motion of the cord in steps 3 and 4.

2. Suppose that you represent the center of an earthquake. As you move the cord, in which direction does the motion travel?

A53

Mind Your P's and S's

In the last activity, the energy of your moving arm was converted to waves, which traveled the length of the bungee cord. The energy released during an earthquake travels through the ground, also as waves. Continue reading to learn more about earthquake waves.

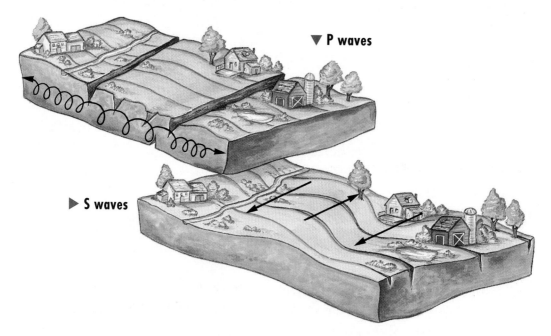

▼ P waves

▶ S waves

As with energy waves in a bungee cord, there are two kinds of earthquake waves. The first kind are primary waves, or *P waves.* The waves produced in step 3 of the last activity were similar to P waves. P waves travel fast, and they vibrate in the same direction that the waves travel. P waves compress the Earth's crust in front of them and stretch it out behind them, like the motion of a Slinky® being pulled across a table.

The second kind of earthquake waves are secondary waves, or *S waves.* S waves travel more slowly and vibrate at right angles to the direction they travel. S waves move the Earth's crust from side to side or up and down, like the waves you made by shaking the cord up and down or from side to side.

Although P waves and S waves both contain a lot of energy, they do not cause most of the damage seen after an earthquake. This is because P waves and S waves usually travel deep underground. In the next activity, you can see how earthquakes *do* cause damage.

THINK ABOUT IT

Describe the differences between P waves and S waves.

ACTIVITY

An Earthshaking Experience

When P waves and S waves act together, they produce a third kind of wave. In this activity, you can see how this process works and the results it produces.

DO THIS

1 Cover the gelatin in the pan with plastic wrap. The wrap must touch the surface of the gelatin.

2 Make several crouton "buildings" on top of the wrap.

3 Hold one end of the pan firmly, and gently tap the other end of the pan with your hand. Observe the motion, and note any damage to the buildings.

4 Repair any damaged buildings. Then gently move the pan up and down or side to side. Again, observe the motion, and note any damage to the buildings.

5 Once again, repair any damaged buildings. Now, move the pan up and down or side to side, and tap one end of it at the same time. Observe the movement, and note the damage. Compare the damage with that observed in steps 3 and 4.

MATERIALS
- baking pan of gelatin
- plastic wrap
- large croutons
- Science Log data sheet

THINK AND WRITE

1. Which step produced motion like that of P waves, and which produced motion like that of S waves?

2. How did the damage from step 3 compare with that in step 4? Why was there so much more damage in step 5?

Rollin', Rollin'

As you observed in the last activity, the combination of up-and-down or side-to-side motion (S waves) and Slinky®-like motion (P waves) produces a rolling kind of motion—something like that of ocean waves. This rolling motion is what causes so much damage.

The interaction of P waves and S waves produces *surface waves.* As the name implies, surface waves occur on the surface of the Earth, rather than deep underground. Surface waves cause the Earth to shake and roll, like a boat in rough water. You can imagine the effect this has if you think about the damage to the crouton buildings in the activity. If the gelatin were the Earth's surface, think what the rolling motion you created would do to real buildings, roads, bridges, trees, and people.

Severe earthquakes in heavily populated areas can cause massive amounts of damage and the loss of many lives. These photos show the results of some of the worst earthquakes along the boundary between the North American and Pacific plates.

▼ Surface waves

▶ The strongest earthquake ever recorded occurred near Anchorage, Alaska, in April 1964. The damage was massive, but the loss of life was low because most workers were at home for a holiday. Loss of life was also low in the January 17, 1994, Los Angeles earthquake, which occurred at 4:30 A.M.

◀ In 1985 a severe earthquake rocked Mexico City. The damage was extensive, and many lives were lost as poorly constructed buildings collapsed.

▲ In 1906, the city of San Francisco was almost destroyed by a severe earthquake and the resulting fire. Because of strict building codes, another strong earthquake in 1989 did much less damage, even though the ground shook very much like the gelatin in the last activity.

THINK ABOUT IT

Many heavily populated areas are located near the western boundary of the North American plate. How does this affect the way people live in these cities?

A57

ACTIVITY

How Does It Measure Up?

The 1964 Alaska earthquake was one of the strongest earthquakes ever recorded. How do scientists know that? How is an earthquake recorded and measured? In the following activity, you will see how scientists record and compare earthquakes.

DO THIS

1 Work with a partner. Roll the paper into a cylinder, and secure the ends with tape.

2 Place the turntable on top of the speaker. Turn the volume all the way down and the bass all the way up. Put a record on the turntable, and place the paper cylinder on top of the record.

3 Attach the marker to the string, and suspend the string over the turntable, letting the marker gently touch the paper cylinder. Have your partner set the turntable at its slowest speed and run it without music for a few seconds as the marker draws a line on the paper.

4 Now, play the record. Slowly increase the volume as the marker continues to draw on the paper.

THINK AND WRITE

1. How did the drawing change as the volume got louder?

2. **INTERPRETING DATA** As a scientist does, you have to interpret the drawings in order for them to have meaning. Why do you need a base line before interpreting data accurately?

Seismograph A seismograph is an instrument that records earthquakes. A *seismogram* is a drawing made by a seismograph. In the activity, you made a model of a seismograph. The drawing made by the marking pen was a model of a seismogram.

◀ Seismograph

▶ Earthquake damage

Who's the Strongest of Them All?

In the last activity, you made a model of a seismograph. Continue reading to see how a real seismograph records earthquakes and how seismograms are used to measure the strength of earthquakes.

A real seismograph is made of a rotating drum wrapped with paper, a pen, and a weight to hold the pen steady. It also has "roots." That is, unlike the one you made, a real seismograph is anchored to the solid rock of the Earth's crust. When the crust moves, so does the drum, and the pen records vibrations as zig-zag lines, just as your seismograph recorded vibrations from the music. As the music got louder, the lines the marker made got longer. Likewise, a powerful earthquake makes longer lines on a seismogram than a minor earthquake does.

Seismograms can be compared to determine the relative strength, or *magnitude,* of any earthquake. The magnitude of an earthquake is measured by the **Richter scale,** named after Charles F. Richter, the American geologist who developed this system of measuring earthquakes in 1935.

On the Richter scale, the higher the magnitude, the stronger the earthquake.

Originally, each number on the scale represented an earthquake 10 times stronger than one of the next lower magnitude.

However, scientists have determined that each number actually represents an earthquake 32 times stronger than the next lower one. The 1964 Alaska earthquake, for example, was 32 times stronger than the 1985 Mexico City earthquake, which had a magnitude of 8.1; 1,024 times stronger than the 1989 San Francisco earthquake, which had a magnitude of 7.1; and 16,384 times stronger than the January 1994 Los Angeles earthquake, which had a magnitude of 6.6. The table lists the strongest Pacific Rim earthquakes of this century.

THINK ABOUT IT

In order for scientists to accurately compare seismograms, why do the seismographs need to be about the same distance from the earthquake they are measuring?

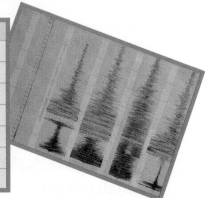

MAJOR PACIFIC RIM EARTHQUAKES		
Year	Location	Magnitude
1906	San Francisco	8.3 (estimated)
1906	Chile	8.6 (estimated)
1933	Japan	8.4 (estimated)
1964	Alaska	9.2 (revised)
1976	China	7.8
1985	Mexico City	8.1

Taking Precautions

The forces unleashed during an earthquake are powerful, but humans can take some precautions to protect themselves. Continue reading to learn how we can protect ourselves from the worst effects of earthquakes.

▼ In Iran, the site of many severe earthquakes, traditional mud homes are being replaced by reinforced brick structures. Concrete is replacing brick and mud structures in parts of Russia. People in Japan and the western United States have learned that wood-frame houses built on solid concrete can resist earthquakes.

▶ San Francisco, which had to rebuild after the 1906 earthquake, has wide streets to slow the spread of fires that often follow earthquakes. This also allows buildings to sway without hitting one another. The 255-meter (836-foot) Transamerica Building, pictured here, is built with concrete-covered steel columns. It should withstand a force twice that required by the city's strict earthquake-proof building codes.

THINK ABOUT IT

What can people do to protect themselves from earthquakes?

Karen McNally:
Seismologist

Every 30 seconds there is an earthquake somewhere in the world, or there are about 1 million earthquakes each year. Although most are small, a really strong earthquake occurs every 2 or 3 years. Seismologists—geologists who specialize in earthquakes—help increase our knowledge of the forces that change the Earth. The following describes a fairly typical day for one seismologist, Dr. Karen McNally.

7:00 AM

Dr. Karen McNally arrives early at her office. She studies data supplied by the National Earthquake Information Service in Golden, Colorado. In the data received today, she notices a sudden drop in the number of minor earthquakes around the Cocos plate in Central America. This might mean that a major earthquake is about to happen there.

8:00 AM

McNally works on the lecture she will give to her university class this afternoon. She is going to talk about hidden earthquakes within the Earth's crust.

8:30 AM

McNally returns a call from an architect in Los Angeles who wants to discuss the design for a new building near the San Andreas fault. Then she calls an oil company engineer in Alaska about using seismograms to find natural gas deposits.

9:00 AM

McNally gives the lecture to her freshman geophysics class. Geophysics is a science that deals with the Earth's physical forces, including weather, tides, earthquakes, and volcanoes.

1:00 PM

McNally talks to a scientist with the U.S. Geological Survey about predicting earthquakes. They discuss the data from the Cocos plate and conclude that an earthquake in that area is likely within the next few days.

1:45 PM

McNally meets with a group of geologists to plan ways to get grants for continued earthquake research.

4:00 PM

▲ Checking the seismographs

A call comes in from the Mexican government. Seismographs in that country have recorded additional changes in activity near the boundary between the Cocos and Pacific plates. McNally decides to join a team of scientists heading to Central America. They will set up more seismographs to gather data on the earthquake that will probably occur there.

6:00 PM

McNally meets with one of her graduate assistants to discuss a project he is doing on the 1985 Mexico City earthquake. She also prepares him to take over her university classes while she is gone.

9:30 PM

McNally makes final plans for her trip to Central America. Early in the morning she will be on a plane for Mexico City, where she will join the earthquake team. Then the team will travel to Guatemala and El Salvador to set up their equipment. There is always the chance that the expected earthquake will be a minor one or that there won't be an earthquake at all. But the scientists could gain valuable knowledge about our Earth, so the trip is an important one.

LESSON 1 REVIEW

❶ Why does so much earthquake activity occur near the boundaries between plates?

❷ How does studying earthquakes help scientists understand the forces that shape the Earth?

2 VOLCANOES

The word *earthquake* is fairly easy to understand. It describes perfectly what happens when the Earth's crust moves. But what does the word *volcano* mean? And what are volcanoes? Why do volcanoes exist in many of the same places where earthquakes occur? The following activities and readings can help you discover the causes and effects of volcanoes.

The Death of a City

Living near a volcano is dangerous. Read to find out about the people of Pompeii and their encounter with Mount Vesuvius.

During the first century A.D., the city of Pompeii, in what is now Italy, was filled with people living a carefree, pleasant life. Pompeii was a beautiful city. You could look in one direction and view a lovely seacoast. In another direction, the view was of majestic, towering Mount Vesuvius.

The people of Pompeii knew that Mount Vesuvius was a volcano, but they

didn't worry about it. After all, the mountain hadn't erupted for hundreds of years. Oh, there had been some minor earthquakes many years earlier. The mountain had rumbled a little, but since nothing

▼ Eruption of Mount Vesuvius

further had happened, the people of Pompeii repaired their damaged homes and went on with their lives. Suddenly, in August of 79, Pompeii changed forever. Mount Vesuvius erupted, burying the city and its people. Pompeii was buried under a hot, suffocating layer of ash. On that day, life in Pompeii stopped.

The same ash that entombed the people of Pompeii preserved the city and its inhabitants for 17 centuries. When Pompeii was finally excavated, 1,700-year-old bread was found undecayed in bakery ovens. Colorful wall paintings had been preserved intact. Slogans written on walls—graffiti—remained. And the remains of many of Pompeii's citizens were found preserved in the ash.

Mount Vesuvius has erupted several times since 79. And even though it hasn't again buried an entire town, after each eruption, people who lived near the volcano returned to their homes in the shadow of its slopes.

▼ **Ancient kitchen in Pompeii**

▼ **In the shadow of Vesuvius**

▲ **A victim of the eruption**

THINK ABOUT IT

What can people learn about volcanoes from the story of Pompeii and its people?

Myths of Fire

Why would people live near a volcano? Maybe it's because they didn't understand what could happen. Remember the myth of the namazu, the catfish that causes earthquakes by wriggling its tail? There are also myths about volcanoes, including one that explains how they were named. Read these two myths. Then make up your own myth to explain a natural event.

VULCAN

A Myth from Ancient Rome

Italy and the lands that made up ancient Rome are the sites of many volcanoes. It's not surprising that the word volcano *comes from* Vulcan, *the name of the Roman god of fire. Known as the blacksmith of the gods, Vulcan labored under the Earth. Over his eternal fire, he forged arrows for Apollo, the god of the sun, and Diana, the goddess of the moon. Vulcan also fashioned the armored breastplate of the Roman hero Hercules.*

PELE

A Myth from Hawai'i

The Hawaiian Islands also have many volcanoes, and the Hawaiians have a myth to explain them as well. Pele is a Hawaiian goddess who takes different human forms. Sometimes she is an old woman, and sometimes she is a young athlete. When Pele loses a contest with other athletes, her rage is terrible. She calls up boiling lava from the underworld, and she scorches the surface of the Earth until her rivals are defeated.

You can see how these mythical events resemble the natural event they attempt to explain. Both Vulcan and Pele are identified with fire and heat from inside the Earth. Volcanoes are scary enough to people who understand them. No wonder myths were created to explain events that must have terrified ancient peoples. In the next activity, you can discover the true nature of volcanoes.

THINK ABOUT IT

In what ways are the myths about volcanoes similar?

A C T I V I T Y

A Hot Topic!

Suppose you're observing a volcano from a safe distance. It's night-time. The volcano is erupting in a spectacular display of ash, bombs, and lava. Ash is a fine powder, like dust or talc. And bombs are hunks of solid rock. But what is lava—this material that flows like cold molasses and glows like molten steel?

DO THIS

1 Add several drops of food coloring to 10 mL of water.

2 In the mixing bowl, mix together equal parts of glue, colored water, and borax. Put the mixture in the plastic bag for an hour or so. Make sure the bag is tightly sealed.

3 After an hour, take the material out of the bag, and pour it into one end of the pan. Prop up that end of the pan with several books. The incline should be steep, but not steep enough for the material to slide to the other end of the pan.

4 Observe the material every hour or so, and describe the way it moves.

5 Let the material remain overnight in the pan. Then observe it again the following day.

MATERIALS
- red food coloring
- water
- mixing bowl
- white liquid glue
- borax
- zip-type plastic bag
- baking pan
- several books
- Science Log data sheet

THINK AND WRITE

How is this material similar to lava? How is it different?

Hawai'i, a Real Hot Spot

You may recall that the Pacific plate is lined with volcanoes. This is where the name *Ring of Fire* came from. However, not all volcanoes occur near plate boundaries. Some volcanic islands, like Hawaii, are in the middle of plates. Continue reading to discover how these islands form.

Inside the Earth, rock is partly melted by the tremendous heat and pressure there. When a volcano erupts, molten rock moves slowly toward the surface. Upon reaching the surface, the molten rock, now called *lava,* flows down the side of the volcano. As the lava cools, it stops flowing and eventually forms solid rock.

Some volcanoes form in the middle of plates, above areas in the crust called *hot spots.* Molten rock melts through a thin spot in the crust and forms a volcanic island. The Hawaiian Islands were formed in this way.

Look at the map of Hawaii. Notice that the islands lie in a northwest-to-southeast line, from left to right. Geologists hypothesize that Hawaii, the largest island and, currently, the last one in the chain, is over a hot spot. As the Pacific plate moves very slowly to the northwest, the volcanic activity stops in one area and starts up in another. Today, Hawaii is the only island in the chain with active volcanoes—Mauna Loa and Kilauea.

THINK ABOUT IT

Why would scientists be interested in studying Kilauea and Mauna Loa?

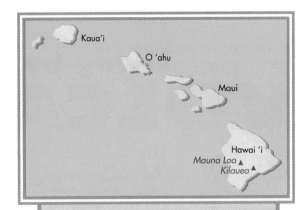

▼ Kilauea erupts regularly, and its lava flows out of the crater in a firey explosion.

▼ Hardened lava from Mauna Loa

A Mountain Explodes!

Although some volcanoes erupt peacefully, like Kilauea, many explode violently, like Mount Vesuvius. When Mount St. Helens erupted in 1980, many people were close enough to experience the effects of the biggest eruption in the history of the United States. The following article describes the effects of the eruption on one family that lived nearby.

Living by a
VOLCANO

by **Kay Saetre** from *Cricket*

 My dreams were suddenly broken by my mother's groan. The alarm clock said morning, but it was dark in my room. I wondered why the yellow glow of sunshine wasn't filtering through my window curtains.

"I'm glad all the animals are still locked up in the barn for the night!" I heard my dad say.

I jumped out of bed and ran into the hall. Mom and Dad were standing by the window.

"Mom, what is it?"

They turned and looked at me, worried. My mother answered slowly. "Mount St. Helens erupted again early this morning. We're getting the ash now." She sighed. "It's mixing with the rain."

I tried to look out the window, but it was covered with a thick gray film that looked like concrete. All the living-room windows were coated with the same stuff. That's why it's so dark, I thought.

I hurried after my parents into the kitchen, where my dad turned on the radio. A voice, high-pitched with excitement, blared that ash was falling in the area and that everyone should stay inside until the ash was tested. The announcer went on to say that the ash might contain a certain type of acid that, when mixed with water, could form a poisonous gas. I looked up at my dad. He smiled at me and said cheerfully, "We're still breathing, right?"

"Right," I echoed, relieved.

The radio announcer went on talking, but I wasn't paying attention. I was thinking of last Sunday. Mom, Dad, and I had been gardening when Mount St. Helens first erupted. Dark clouds of ash had been blown over towns to the east of us, but we hadn't received a thimbleful. Then, I had wanted the wind to blow some ash toward us. Now, I wasn't sure I liked it.

The radio announcer droned on. He reminded his listeners that the water supply for the area was an open reservoir, which could become contaminated, and that we should all fill bottles and jars with water.

We filled containers until the radio reported that the water supply for our area was not to be used any longer. Health officials had to test the water first, to see if it was safe to drink. Mom showed me the ash particles drifting slowly to the bottom of the last containers we had filled. We emptied these into the sink. Then Dad returned to the kitchen with the good news that we would have enough water for our livestock.

It was lighter outside now, and through the kitchen window, which was protected by our overhanging roof, everything appeared in gray monotones. I glanced at the clock. The animals should have been fed half an hour ago.

The radio announcer still hadn't mentioned if we could go outside yet. I was getting worried about our animals, when Mom started to dig into a drawer and came up with the soil-testing kit she had bought to use on the garden.

I wasn't allowed near the door as Dad quickly leaned out and scraped some heavy gray stuff off our front steps. Mom took the ash from him and measured it into the test tubes. When she added chemicals, the colors in the tubes started to change. Mom smiled.

Mom and Dad then hurried to put on the old clothing. I asked if I might go, too.

"Not until we hear the results of the government tests. I know you want to see the ash, but you could hardly call our soil test kit perfect," replied Dad.

"O.K." I sighed.

Looking out the window through streaks

of gray, I watched my bundled parents trudge to the barn. I stood there until I saw them returning, then ran to open the door. They hurried in, their clothes covered with the gray ash.

After they had removed their old clothes, Dad opened the door, to let me see outside. I could hardly recognize our yard, everything was so changed. The air smelled strange—pungent and faintly like rotten eggs. "Sulfur," Dad agreed when he saw my nose wrinkle.

After breakfast, the day stretched long before me. I tried reading, but my eyes kept straying back to the windows. I tried listening to the radio, but all they talked about was the ash. I felt so trapped! I would have given up a month's allowance just to be able to step outside for even a couple of minutes.

It was late in the afternoon when Mom called me into the kitchen.

"I'm bored!" I wailed. "I can't stand it in here. When will I be able to go outside?"

"There should be a report on the test results in about five minutes, if you can wait that long," Mom said patiently. We pulled up chairs and sat down. Dad came in from the living room and stood behind us. I was so eager to know if I could go outside, I could hardly sit still to listen. First came some boring news about fertilizer tests being incomplete, and then the magic words. It was safe to go outdoors!

I flew to the bag of old clothes, but I wasn't quick enough. Mom and Dad were putting on theirs before I could even find mine. As fast as I could, I slipped them over the clothes I had on. Laughing, Dad, Mom, and I joggled for first place out the door.

Mom went to see her plants and started to wash them off with the water hose. Dad tried to talk her into letting him use the hose to rinse the ash off the car. She told him living things had to breathe and plants should be rinsed off before a car. I ran to the shed for all the jars and containers I could find to fill with ash. As I looked around I felt as though I were on a different planet, all gray and still. There wasn't even a bird in the sky. The ash covered everything until it melted into one gray color. It stuck heavily even on the trunks of trees and when I touched leaves covered with ash, it felt like talcum powder, all fine and slippery.

When I had filled all the containers, I saw that Dad finally had the water hose

and was rinsing off the car. He told me not to touch it, because the ash acted just like a scrubbing cleanser and could remove the paint. Then he showed me how rubbing the fine ash on the chrome bumper could remove the rust. This was fun—my fingers seemed to make the rust dissolve. I helped Dad until he was finished with the car, and then we took a walk through the woods.

"As long as the ash particles are wet, it's O.K. to be out here without a face mask," Dad assured me.

"Will I have to stay inside or wear a face mask when the ash dries?" I asked hesitatingly. My dad stopped and looked solemn.

"I'm afraid so," he said. "But soon the only ash around here will be what you've collected."

"Where will it all go?" I asked incredulously.

"Into the ground," he explained. "With our rainy climate, it will be absorbed in a few months, if not sooner."

"But the volcano could explode again! What if more ash falls?"

He laughed. "I suppose we'll find some way to use it. Mom says it's a good fertilizer, and you saw how nicely it takes rust off metal."

I suddenly realized that the mountain had sent us a challenge along with the ash. "Maybe it would make a nice glue—it sure sticks to everything," I said eagerly.

Dad agreed, and we both laughed. As we walked back toward our house, a single bird's song broke the still air.

LESSON 2 REVIEW

Why do you think earthquakes and volcanoes are often found in the same parts of the world?

DOUBLE CHECK

SECTION C REVIEW

1. Describe how the Earth's crust is constantly changing.

2. From where do earthquakes and volcanoes get their energy?

3. Do you think scientists will one day be able to predict earthquakes and volcanoes more precisely? Explain.

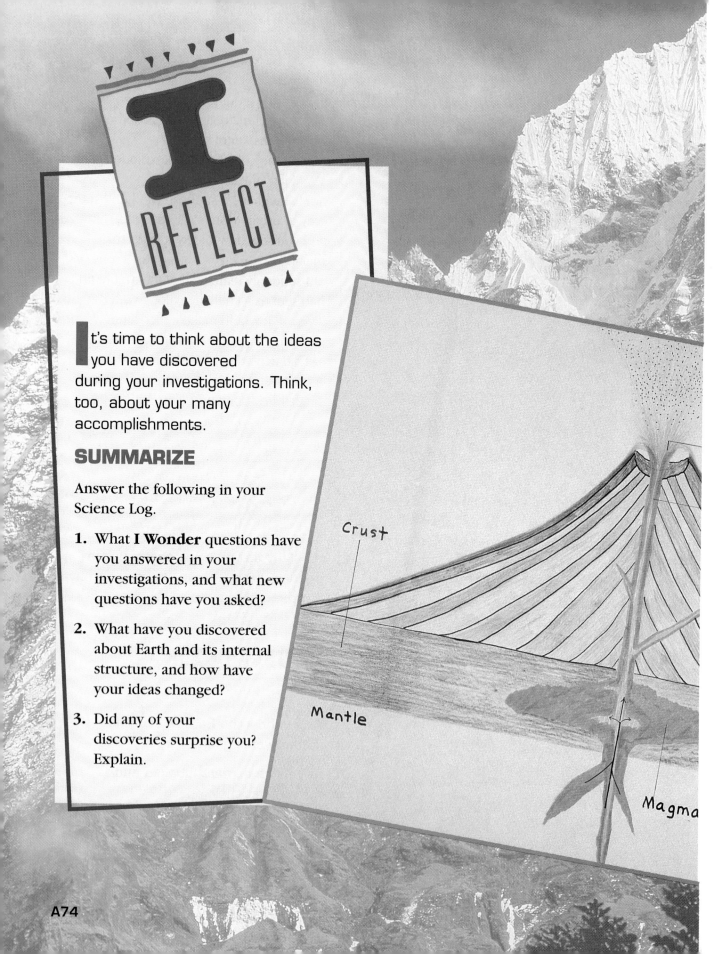

I REFLECT

It's time to think about the ideas you have discovered during your investigations. Think, too, about your many accomplishments.

SUMMARIZE

Answer the following in your Science Log.

1. What **I Wonder** questions have you answered in your investigations, and what new questions have you asked?

2. What have you discovered about Earth and its internal structure, and how have your ideas changed?

3. Did any of your discoveries surprise you? Explain.

Crust

Mantle

Magma

Ash

Crater

Conduit

Lava

CONNECT IDEAS

1. Why are earthquakes more likely to occur at the boundaries of plates rather than in the middle of plates?

2. How are compression and tension alike? How are they different?

3. Could there be a relationship between the mid-Atlantic ridge and the Andes Mountains? Explain.

4. Are all faults the same? Explain.

5. The island of Surtsey came into existence during the 1960s. Surtsey is near Iceland, along the mid-Atlantic ridge. How do you think it was formed?

SCIENCE PORTFOLIO

1 Complete your Science Experiences Record.

2 Choose several samples of your best work from each section to include in your Science Portfolio.

3 On A Guide to My Science Portfolio, tell why you chose each sample.

Scientists share their discoveries and ideas and learn from one another. How can you share what you've learned?

Decide

▶ what you want to say.

▶ what the best way is to get your message across.

Share

▶ what you did and why.

▶ what worked and what didn't work.

▶ what conclusions you have drawn.

▶ what else you'd like to find out.

Find Out

▶ what classmates liked about what you shared—and why.

▶ what questions your classmates have.

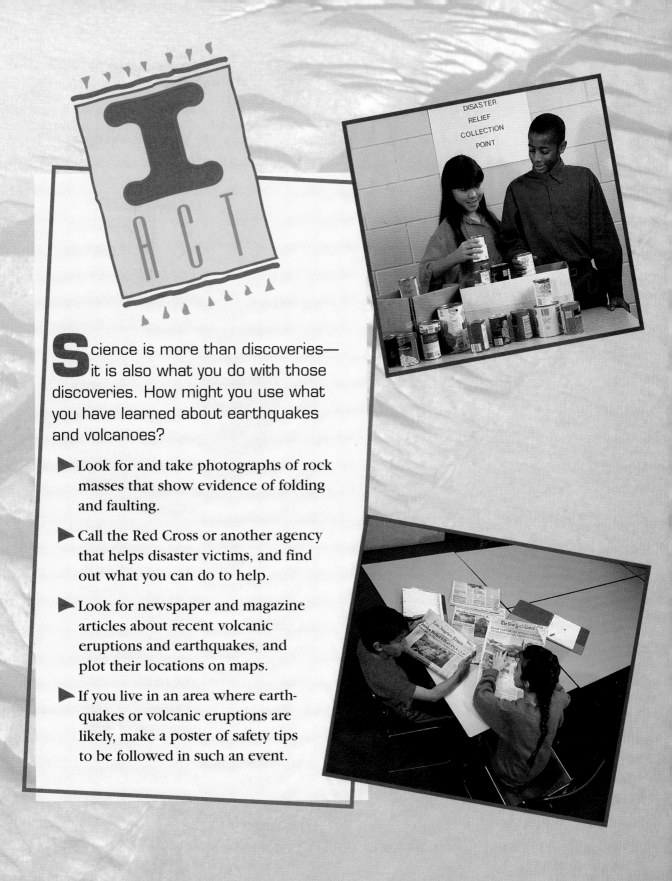

I ACT

Science is more than discoveries—it is also what you do with those discoveries. How might you use what you have learned about earthquakes and volcanoes?

► Look for and take photographs of rock masses that show evidence of folding and faulting.

► Call the Red Cross or another agency that helps disaster victims, and find out what you can do to help.

► Look for newspaper and magazine articles about recent volcanic eruptions and earthquakes, and plot their locations on maps.

► If you live in an area where earthquakes or volcanic eruptions are likely, make a poster of safety tips to be followed in such an event.

THE LANGUAGE OF SCIENCE

The language of science helps people communicate clearly when they talk about earthquakes and volcanoes. Here are some vocabulary words you can use when you talk about earthquakes and volcanoes with your friends, family, and others.

compression—the force that pushes rocks together at plate boundaries and reverse faults. (**A41**)

continental drift—theory stating that present-day continents drifted to their present locations. (**A22**)

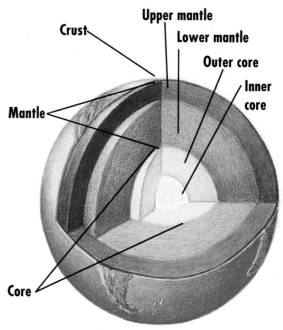

Crust · Upper mantle · Lower mantle · Outer core · Inner core · Mantle · Core

▲ Layers of the Earth

core—the innermost layer of the Earth. The core is divided into two parts. The *outer core* consists of liquid metals, and the *inner core* consists of solid metals. (**A18**)

crust—the thin layer of rock at the Earth's surface. Oceanic crust is thinner and heavier than continental crust. (**A18**)

fault—a break in the crust along which rocks move. There are three types of faults. At a *lateral fault,* the walls move sideways past each other. The San Andreas fault is a lateral fault. At a *normal fault,* the walls move apart. Death Valley formed because of a normal fault. At a *reverse fault,* the walls move toward each other. Some mountains in Glacier National Park formed because of a reverse fault. (**A42**)

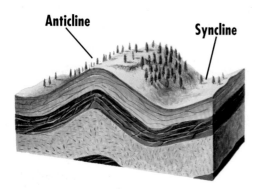

Anticline · Syncline

anticlines—areas where the crust bends upward. (**A41**)

folding—the bending of rock due to compression. **(A41)**

▲ **Folded rock**

fracture—a break in the crust. **(A42)**

lava—molten rock that flows across the surface of the Earth. **(A69)**

magnitude—relative strength of an earthquake. **(A60)**

mantle—the middle layer of the Earth's interior. The mantle has two parts. The *upper mantle* is made up of rock much like the rock of the crust. The *lower mantle* is made up of soft, pliable rock. **(A18)**

Pangea—giant continent that included all of Earth's present-day land masses. **(A21)**

Plate tectonics—theory that Earth's surface is divided into plates that move. **(A27)**

▲ **Pangea**

Richter scale—a scale that rates the strength, or magnitude, of an earthquake. One of the strongest earthquakes ever recorded occurred in Alaska in 1964. **(A60)**

Ring of Fire—the area around the Pacific Ocean where many earthquakes and volcanoes occur. **(A30)**

seismograph—an instrument that records vibrations caused by movements within the crust. A seismogram is the recording made by a seismograph. **(A59)**

▲ **Seismograph**

shear—the force that causes rocks to move sideways past each other at plate boundaries and lateral faults. **(A44)**

synclines—areas where the crust bends down. **(A41)**

tension—the force that pulls rocks apart at plate boundaries and normal faults. **(A44)**

walls—the rocks on either side of a fault. **(A42)**

waves—the form in which energy travels in an earthquake. *P waves* vibrate in the same direction that the wave travels. *S waves* vibrate at right angles to the direction of travel. **(A54)**

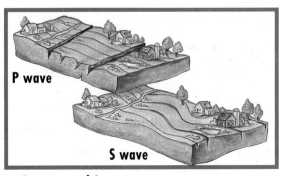

P wave

S wave

▲ **P waves and S waves**

CAUTION: ENDANGERED SPECIES AHEAD

Caution: Endangered Species Ahead

Diversity and Adaptations

I WONDER

The world is full of many unusual and fascinating plants and animals, as well as the common ones you see every day. Have you ever seen an animal like the one shown here? What questions come to mind when you see an animal or a plant you have never seen before?

Work with a partner to make a list of questions you may have about different kinds of living things. Be ready to share your list with the rest of the class.

Destruction of the rain forest

Jaguar

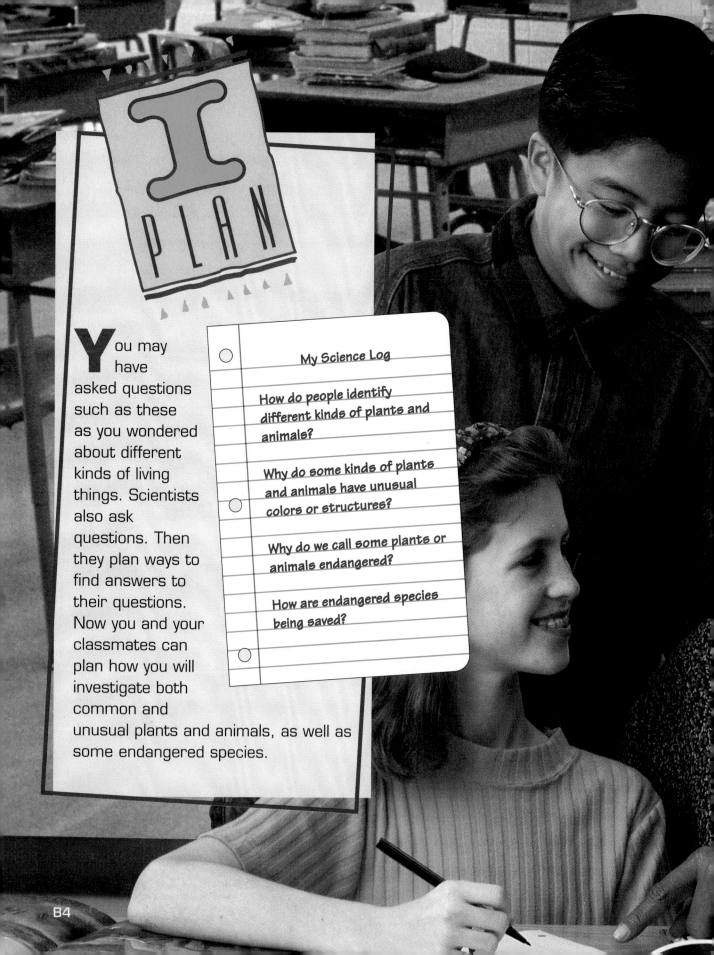

I PLAN

You may have asked questions such as these as you wondered about different kinds of living things. Scientists also ask questions. Then they plan ways to find answers to their questions. Now you and your classmates can plan how you will investigate both common and unusual plants and animals, as well as some endangered species.

My Science Log

How do people identify different kinds of plants and animals?

Why do some kinds of plants and animals have unusual colors or structures?

Why do we call some plants or animals endangered?

How are endangered species being saved?

With Your Class

Plan how your class will use the activities and readings from the **I Investigate** part of this unit. Decide what other resources you might use.

On Your Own

There are many ways to learn about endangered plants and animals. Following are some things you can do to explore endangered species by yourself or with some classmates. Some explorations may take longer to do than others. Look over the suggestions and choose . . .

- **Places to Visit**
- **People to Contact**
- **Books to Read**

PLACES TO VISIT

BOTANICAL GARDENS

Local botanical gardens and parks with nature trails
may provide information on rare and endangered
plants. There you may find live plants marked with
signs that identify them. You may also find books and
pamphlets about such plants. Take a guided tour
through a botanical garden. Ask the guide to point out
any endangered plants.

ANIMAL SHOWPLACES

A zoo, an aquarium, or an oceanarium may have endangered animals in its collection. Many of these places
care for sick, injured, or orphaned animals. Some breed
endangered animals and return them to the wild. Try to
arrange for a behind-the-scenes tour. Find out how the
animals are cared for.

REFUGES

Many states have set aside one or more areas,
such as a marsh, seashore, or prairie, as a
wildlife refuge. Find out whether there are any
wildlife refuges near you and what plants and
animals are protected there. Try to obtain information or go on guided tours.

Visit one of these places, and write down what you learn about
endangered plants and animals. Draw pictures, take photographs,
or collect pamphlets to help you. Compare your notes with those
of your classmates, and make a class list of endangered species.

PEOPLE TO CONTACT

IN PERSON

To learn about endangered species, talk to people who are interested in or work with plants and animals. Find out if there are any endangered plants or animals in your area.

Some people watch for and keep a count of endangered species of plants and animals. Talk to someone who does this. Find out what plants or animals in your area need to be protected.

- American Association of Zoological Parks
- National Audubon Society
- National Wildlife Federation
- Rainforest Action Network
- World Resources Institute
- World Wildlife Fund

BY TELEPHONE

In some places, people have worked to save wetlands, deserts, or other areas that have endangered species. Sometimes these people belong to national organizations.

There are many organizations you can call to find people who are concerned with endangered species. Listed to the left are some groups you might try.

BY COMPUTER

Use a computer with a modem to connect to on-line services or bulletin boards. You can look for news about endangered species from around the world. You can also talk with people near and far to find out what plants and animals need to be protected where they live.

Perhaps the computers at your school are connected to Internet, an international network of computers. Internet links computer users in more than 40 countries worldwide. Contact students in several parts of the world. Ask them about unusual plants and animals in their areas, and what is being done to protect them.

BOOKS TO READ

The Missing 'Gator of Gumbo Limbo: An Ecological Mystery

by Jean Craighead George (HarperCollins, 1992). This is a story about Lisa and other people who live in Gumbo Limbo Hammock in the Florida Everglades. Among the animals and plants in Gumbo Limbo is Dajun, a huge alligator. Lisa and her friends search for Dajun when they learn that he is missing. Read to discover whether they find him.

On the Brink of Extinction: The California Condor

by Caroline Arnold (Harcourt Brace, 1993). As the American West was settled, the California condor began to disappear. By the late 1980s, only 26 of these huge vultures remained, and all were in captivity. Scientists have been working to save the condor population and to return them to nature. You, too, can feel their excitement as condors born in captivity are released to soar freely once again.

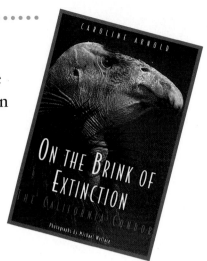

More Books to Read

Living Treasure: Saving Earth's Threatened Biodiversity

by Laurence Pringle (William Morrow, 1991), Outstanding Science Trade Book. *Biodiversity* describes the variety of living things on Earth. When we destroy environments, we interfere with life on Earth. Not all life forms are as appealing as pandas and dolphins, but each is important. This book will tell you how we can work together to save all living things.

Save the Tiger

by Jill Bailey (Steck-Vaughn, 1990). A tiger, searching for food, has been stalking the villagers' animals. The frightened villagers want to stop the stalking. Why has the tiger started to prey on their animals rather than on wildlife? What can be done to protect the villagers and the tiger?

The Voyage of the Beagle

by Kate Hyndley (Bookwright Press, 1989). In this book, set sail with the scientist Charles Darwin for a journey around the world. The year is 1831, and you will be gone for more than five years. Through his investigation of the many plants and animals found during the voyage, Darwin has come up with a new idea about animal change, called *evolution.* People will be talking about it for years to come.

Journey Through a Tropical Jungle

by Adrian Forsyth (Simon & Schuster, 1988), Outstanding Science Trade Book. Journey to a tropical rain forest in this book. Meet lizards as large as dogs, and stinging ants whose powerful jaws are used to close open wounds. This land is important to the Earth's water cycle and affects weather everywhere. We must learn about this forest to save it from destruction.

INVESTIGATE

To find answers to their questions, scientists read, think, talk to others, and do experiments. Their investigations often lead to new questions.

In this unit, you will have many chances to think and work like a scientist. How will you find answers to questions you asked?

▶ **CLASSIFYING/ORDERING** When you classify objects, you put them into groups according to how they are alike. Ordering is putting things in an order. For example, you might order things from first to last, smallest to largest, or lightest to heaviest.

▶ **INFERRING** Inferring is using what you have observed to explain what has happened. An observation is something you see or experience. An inference is an explanation of an observation, and it may be right or wrong.

▶ **COMMUNICATING** When you communicate, you give information. In science, you communicate by showing results from an activity in an organized way—for example, in a chart. Then you and other people can interpret the results.

Are you ready to begin?

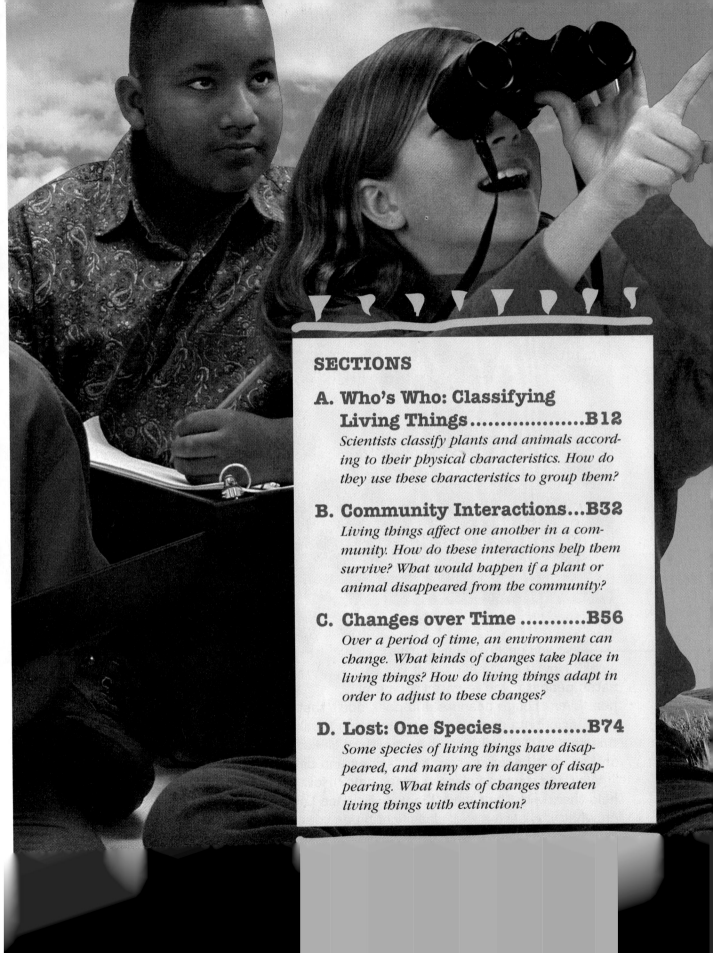

SECTIONS

Who's Who:
Classifying Living Things

▲ Peanuts

Have you eaten any peas this week? How about peanuts? If you've eaten peanuts, you've eaten a type of pea. Even though peanuts and peas don't taste alike, scientists group them in the same family. In this section, you will see how scientists classify plants and animals based on their similarities and differences.

Why do scientists classify organisms? How does classifying help them with their work? In your Science Log, keep careful notes on what you learn about classification as you work through the investigations that follow.

A PLACE FOR EVERYTHING

Scientists often study a single kind of living thing, such as whooping cranes or dogtooth violets. They also learn a great deal about plants and animals by studying how they are related and by classifying them in groups. In the activities that follow, you will see some of the different ways people have classified living things.

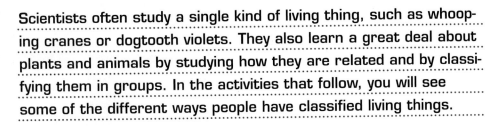

Will It Fly?

You will need: Science Log

Work with a group. Choose one member to take notes. First, make a list of living things that can fly. The list has been started for you. Write down as many as you can think of in 15 minutes.

Next, look over your list. Can the living things be organized in some way? Classify them by arranging them in groups whose members are alike in any way. Label each group.

Compare your classifications with those of your classmates. Did you come up with the same groups or different ones?

With your class, decide which groupings work best. Then, make a combined list of living things in groups.

Can any of the classifications on the combined list be divided into smaller groups? Choose one and try it.

Things that can fly

*robin
mosquito
bat
cardinal
goldfinch
butterfly
bee
sparrow
sea gull
eagle
ladybug
wasp*

*mosquito
butterfly
bee*

Family Pictures

Is a giant panda more like a raccoon or more like a bear? Is a banana tree really a tree? Is a tomato a fruit or a vegetable? The answers to questions like these depend on how you classify, or group, each of these things. As you read the following, think about the many different ways plants and animals can be classified.

▲ The banana plant is not a tree because it has no true trunk or branches.

If you're making a salad, you think of a tomato as a vegetable. A **botanist,** a scientist who studies plants, classifies a tomato as a fruit.

When you're standing in the shade of a banana plant, you think of it as a tree. To a botanist, however, it's a big flowering herb, not a tree, because it has no real trunk or branches.

Classifying is something most people do every day, even for simple things like making a salad or sorting the laundry.

In science, though, it's an especially important tool. It helps scientists see how living organisms are related to one another.

When a new organism is discovered, scientists classify it by deciding which group it belongs to. Classifying also helps scientists describe what makes that living thing different from all the other living things in the group.

All living things can be classified into one of five large groups called **kingdoms.** The two most familiar kingdoms are *plants* and *animals*.

Scientists divide each kingdom of living things into smaller groups, based on ways the members are similar to or different from one another. To do this, they may look at the structure of a plant or compare the body parts of an animal. For example, scientists place horses, zebras, donkeys, tapirs, and rhinoceroses in one large group of animals. They place sheep, goats, deer, pigs, and cattle in another group. Why?

▲ Deer hoof

▲ Deer

▲ Horse hoof

▲ Horse

What do these animals have in common?

Some of these animals have an odd number of toes, and some have an even number. Animals with a divided hoof, such as sheep, cattle, deer, and pigs, have an even number of toes—two. Animals with an undivided hoof have an odd number of toes—one. A rhinoceros has three toes. It is related to other odd-toed animals.

Each group of living things can be further divided into smaller and smaller subgroups. The smallest subgroup is a *species,* a group of living things that are alike in important ways, such as chemical makeup and structure, or body plan. Members of the same species can mate and produce offspring that can also mate and produce offspring.

Even though members of a species may be different in appearance—in size, color, or even shape—they are alike in all their important characteristics. For example, there are many breeds of domestic (pet) cats, yet all cats are members of the same species. When a species is classified, it is given its own two-part name, usually in Latin. The scientific name for all domestic cats is *Felis catus,* no matter what size, color, or breed they are.

You'd think that scientists wouldn't

▼ **Bear**

▼ **Raccoon**

▼ **Is the giant panda related to the raccoon or to the bear? Scientists have worked on that question for years.**

▲ **Giant panda**

have any trouble classifying any living thing they see—but that's not true. Sometimes an organism appears to belong in more than one group or not to belong in any group at all. For years scientists have tried to figure out whether the giant panda is more like a raccoon or more like a bear!

THINK ABOUT IT

Would you classify whales in a group with sharks or with cows? Write down your ideas. Then look up these animals in reference books. Write a paragraph explaining how you would group, or classify, them.

ACTIVITY

The Key to a Tree

To help identify living things, scientists often use a guide called a *key*. A key is a branching diagram that shows smaller and smaller groups into which things can be classified, down to the exact species. In this activity, you will use a key to identify a tree.

MATERIALS
- pictures of trees
- tree key
- Science Log data sheet

DO THIS

1 Work in groups. Each group will use one of the trees and the tree key on page B17. Ask your teacher which tree your group will use.

2 Read the first pair of sentences in the key. Decide which sentence describes your tree.

3 Read the instruction at the end of that sentence. Find the pair of sentences with that number.

4 Read the new pair of sentences and decide which one describes your tree. Repeat steps 3 and 4 until you find the name of your tree.

THINK AND WRITE

1. Make a key that would identify the kinds of supplies you use in your classroom. Write down some ideas about how you would do this and some of the groups you would use.

2. **CLASSIFYING/ORDERING** When you classify objects, you put them in groups according to how they are alike. Did you classify the supplies in your classroom the same way as everyone else did? How were the keys similar? different?

TREE KEY

1. Leaves are broad. ....Go to 2.

   Leaves are needles. ....Go to 3.

2. Leaves are oval. ....Go to 4.

   Leaves have parts that
   stick out. ....Go to 5.

3. Needles are grouped in
   twos or threes. ....Go to 6.

   Needles are not in groups. ..Go to 7.

4. Fruits are round and
   brown, with several on
   a stem. ....American linden

   Fruits are green, with a
   notch opposite the
   stem. ....American elm

5. Fruits are round and have
   a spiky covering. ....sweet gum

   Fruits are green and
   have two wings. ....sugar maple

6. Needles are grouped
   in fives. ....bristlecone pine

   Needles are grouped
   in threes. ....loblolly pine

7. The scales on the cones
   are closed. ....balsam fir

   The scales on the cones
   are open. ....Douglas fir

Who Thought of It?

For thousands of years, people have been trying to classify living things—to organize them in groups whose members are related in some way. As you read, notice how the ideas of many people have contributed to the ways of classifying that scientists use today.

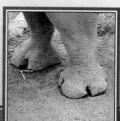

◄ **Cow hoof**

▼ **Horse hoof**

▼ **Rhinoceros hoof**

Aristotle

More than 2,300 years ago, Aristotle, a Greek philosopher, invented a system for classifying animals. He divided them into "blooded" animals with a backbone and "bloodless" animals without a backbone. He also tried classifying plants by their size and the way they grew, using groups such as bushes, herbs, and trees. His ideas were used for almost 2,000 years.

John Ray

During the 1600s, John Ray, an English scientist, worked on a way of classifying animals in large groups and then dividing the groups into smaller ones. For example, he divided all mammals into two groups: animals with hoofs and animals with toes. He then divided each of those groups into smaller groups. Hoofed animals were divided into animals with single hoofs, those with two-toed hoofs, and those with three-toed hoofs.

Ray believed that by dividing each group again and again, scientists could identify each different species of animal. Although his ways of grouping animals were changed by later scientists, his ideas about identifying species have become part of the way scientists classify living things.

Carolus Linnaeus

In the 1700s, Carolus Linnaeus, a Swedish scientist, worked out a way of classifying all living things by organizing and naming all the groups to which they belonged, from largest to smallest. In his system, each group had a name, and any organism could be classified by naming the groups. The last two group names became the name of a single species of living thing—like *Canis familiaris*. Many of Linnaeus's ideas about grouping are still used by scientists. His system of giving each species a two-part name, for example, is still used.

▲ What is the common name you call a *Canis familiaris*?

Gregor Mendel

In the 1860s, Gregor Mendel, an Austrian monk, began to experiment with breeding plants that had some easily identified characteristics, such as flower color. He observed that some of these traits really were passed from parent plants to offspring when the plants were pollinated and seeds were produced.

Thomas Hunt Morgan

In 1910 an American biologist, Thomas Hunt Morgan, was able to explain what Mendel had observed. He and other scientists studied how traits are passed along in fruit flies. They were able to show not only that small structures inside the cells of living things carried the traits from parents to offspring but that the traits were carried in a certain order, like a list.

◀ **Mendel experimented with garden peas.**

Scientists at work

Today's Scientists

Today, scientists study single molecules in the cells of living things to find out exactly how they are related. The cells of all living things contain molecules of a substance called *DNA*. Each species has its own pattern of DNA, like a finger-print. Species that are closely related have similar DNA. Studying these mole-cules has already helped scientists solve many classification problems. For one thing, they now know that giant pandas really are related to bears!

LESSON 1 REVIEW

How does classifying help people study plants and animals?

2 A NEW LOOK AT LIVING THINGS

As scientists explore new areas, they sometimes find information that leads them to change their way of classifying things. In this lesson, you will find out how scientists have gone about classifying living things, how their ideas have changed, and how their ideas are still changing today.

ACTIVITY

Seeing Seeds

Scientists make many of their classifications by observing how living things are alike. In this activity, you will classify things based on your own observations.

DO THIS

1 Work in groups. Look at one of each type of the dry seeds with a hand lens. See if any of them are alike in any way.

2 Now look at the seeds that were soaked in water. Split one of each type, and look for more ways they are alike.

MATERIALS
- 8 types of dry seeds
- hand lens
- wet seeds (same varieties as the dry seeds)
- plastic knife
- paper
- glue
- Science Log data sheet

3 Using your observations of both the soaked and the dry seeds, divide the dry seeds into two groups whose members are alike in some way.

4 On your paper, write the way you've classified each of the groups and glue the seeds in their groups.

5 Take eight more dry seeds. Use them to divide each group into smaller groups. Arrange the smaller groups, glue them down on the same paper, and label the way you've classified them.

6 Repeat step 5 until each seed has its own group. Share your classifications.

THINK AND WRITE

1. Which part of the classification was the easiest to do? How could parts of it be improved? Write down your ideas.

2. **CLASSIFYING/ORDERING** In this activity, you experimented with some ways of classifying and ordering things. How did you decide which things belonged in the same group? What did you look for when dividing a group into smaller groups?

Are You My Species?

With so many kinds of organisms in the world and with new kinds being discovered every day, scientists are learning a great deal about living things and about classifying, too. By reading the following, you will find out about some new ways of looking at and grouping living organisms.

▲ Animal

▲ Plant

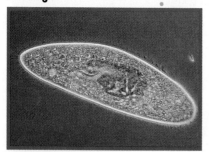

▲ Fungus

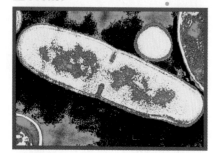

▲ Protist

▲ Moneran

How many kinds of living things are there on Earth? Scientists can't answer that question—but they can tell you that new kinds of organisms are constantly being discovered. So far, they have found more than 2 million kinds of living organisms. Every year they find more than 7,000 new kinds of insects—that's about 19 every day!

Without a way of classifying living things, scientists would never be able to record their findings or to tell whether a "new" organism had already been discovered.

Scientists still use some of the classifications that Linnaeus developed more than 250 years ago. But others have been changed as scientists have gained new information.

One big change has to do with large groups called *kingdoms*. At one time, there were thought to be only two kingdoms: plants and animals. Today, most scientists say there are five. The other three are *fungi* (mushrooms and related organisms), *protists* (protozoa and similar organisms), and *monerans* (bacteria and similar forms of life).

Why were these classifications changed? In studying certain organisms at the cellular level, scientists discovered that fungi, protists, and monerans were neither plants nor animals, although some of them resembled both. There were also differences in the DNA of some of these organisms.

Other changes have occurred as scientists studied related species. For example, harbor seals and sea lions resemble each other in appearance much more than they resemble walruses, which have larger, thicker bodies, square faces, and tusks. Walruses appear to be distant relatives of seals and sea lions.

However, scientists have discovered that sea lions are very closely related to walruses. Their skeletons follow the same basic plan. The vertebrae in their upper backbones are heavy and strong to support their chest muscles in walking. Their hind flippers fold under their bodies and support them on land.

Harbor seals and fur seals have a different body plan. Their backbones are very flexible, and the lower vertebrae are especially strong. Their hind flippers do not turn under to support them, and they move on land by using their front flippers and highly flexible bodies. By comparing the two body plans and by studying fossils of seal-like animals, scientists have learned that seals are a newer family of animals. They got their start millions of years later than sea lions and walruses did.

Is a zebra more like a donkey or a horse? Is an apricot more like a peach or a plum? Scientists can test cells from skin, hair, fruits, stems, and other tissues to find out. Because the cells of all living things contain molecules of DNA, they carry a record of all of the traits that get passed along from parents to offspring. Each species of living things has its own kind of DNA—its own "map" for making new organisms just like itself.

Scientists can use chemical tests to study and compare these "maps." They may find that two very different-looking organisms have similar DNA and are actually very closely related. And sometimes they may find that "look-alike" organisms have very different DNA and are not closely related at all. Modern classification depends more on chemical tests and microscopic structures than it does on outward appearances.

▼ Pacific walrus

◄ Sea lion

▲ Harbor seals

THINK ABOUT IT

Do you think that our system of classification will change again in the future, or will scientists continue to use the same system? Explain. What might cause the way we classify things to change?

One of a Kind?

Australia is a continent in the southern Pacific Ocean. It has many plants and animals that are not found on other continents. Read about one of these animals.

THE Puzzling Platypus

by **Kathy Walsh**
from ***Ranger Rick***

It's dusk. The surface of a pond in South Australia is as smooth as a mirror. Suddenly, a ripple appears. Then another. A dark bill breaks the surface, followed by two beady eyes and a furry body. The creature paddles around a bit. Then, *splash!* As quickly as it came, it disappears below the water's surface.

Hey—what *was* that? With a bill like a duck's and fur like a mammal's—it must have been a *platypus* (PLAT-uh-pus)! But it's not just any platypus. This one is special. It's one of a group of platypuses that live in a place called the Warrawong Sanctuary.

The platypuses were brought there by a man named John Wamsley.

Platypuses had been wiped out in the state of South Australia. So Dr. Wamsley made a special place where he thought platypuses would like to live. He had lots of ponds dug for the platypuses to swim in. And he put brush and dead branches around the banks of the ponds. That way, when the platypuses dug their burrows in the banks, the entrances would be hidden from enemies. Then he moved a few platypuses to the sanctuary from another part of Australia. So far, the platypuses are doing well in their new home!

▲ The ponds of Australia are home to one *weird* creature!

Are They for Real?

Even though they had become extinct in South Australia, platypuses have been doing just fine in other parts of the country. And that's good news, because they're such neat creatures. For one thing, they're so *weird!* They have a bill like a bird's. They lay soft, rubbery eggs like a reptile. And they have a furry body and feed their young milk like a mammal. So—just what *is* a platypus, anyway?

That's the same question scientists asked almost 200 years ago when someone first brought them a dead platypus. They thought the creature was a fake! It looked like someone had sewn a duck's bill onto an otter's body. The scientists pulled and poked at the bill, but they couldn't find any stitches. They were amazed.

Today, scientists know the platypus is a mammal. But they don't find it any less amazing!

Tough Customers

Even though it's so funny looking, a platypus can be tough. An adult male has a sharp *spur* (hollow claw) on the inside of each hind leg. When he

▲ Even though platypuses look cuddly, watch out! Males have sharp, poisonous spurs on their hind legs.

attacks, he pumps poison through the spur.

Platypuses use their spurs mainly against other males during the breeding season. These spurs can be bad news for people too. A person who gets stabbed will be in terrible pain, sometimes for days.

▲ The platypus's bill may look funny, but it's not a joke! It helps the platypus find food.

But there's not much danger of a person being spurred by a platypus. Many Australians have never even seen one of these shy creatures in the wild. That's because during the day, the animals are mostly resting in their burrows. They usually don't come out to find food until night. Then they'll swim around the pond, diving for insect larvae, worms, and shrimp on the bottom.

But wait—when a platypus swims, it keeps its eyes, its ears, and even its nostrils tightly shut! So how does it find its food? For years scientists puzzled over this question. But now they've figured out the answer. The secret is in the platypus's rubbery bill.

▲ When a platypus swims, it keeps its eyes, ears, and nostrils tightly shut.

Filling the Bill

The platypus's bill is covered with thousands of *pores* (tiny openings). Nerves inside these pores can "feel" vibrations as well as small amounts of electricity.

Where do the vibrations and electricity come from? When any animal moves, it gives off very weak electric signals. And when an animal moves in the water, it causes vibrations. The platypus picks up these vibrations and signals. Then it follows them to find its prey.

When a platypus hunts, it sweeps its bill from side to side as it swims along the bottom of a pond. It uses the bill to shovel aside stones and mud as it searches for food. And when a shrimp flicks its tail, the platypus can zero right in on the signals and snatch it up—even though its eyes and nostrils are closed.

A platypus stays under the water about two minutes at a time, grabbing food and storing it in pouches in its cheeks. Then it rises to the surface to breathe and eat.

Platypuses don't have teeth. So they grind up their food between hard, bumpy pads inside their bills.

Coated with Air

A platypus spends up to 12 hours a night in water that's often near freezing. But its thick, waterproof coat keeps it nice and warm.

The coat has two layers. There's an inner layer of kinky fur that traps warm air next to the platypus's skin. And there's an outer layer of long "guard" hairs. The coat traps so much air that when the platypus dives, lots of air bubbles rise to the surface. Long ago, people who saw all those bubbles thought the platypus breathed through its back!

Of course, platypuses don't breathe through their backs. They breathe through their lungs, the same as any other mammal. But they do swim differently.

Beavers, otters, and other small swimming mammals use their hind legs and tail to swim. But platypuses use their webbed front feet. The webs spread out beyond their claws. So when the platypuses come out of the water, the webs fold under. That way they can use their claws to dig.

A Burrow for the Babies

Platypuses are great little diggers. They make two types of burrows. One is a small resting burrow, where they stay during the day. And the other is a nesting burrow, which the females dig to raise their young in.

And speaking of platypus young, remember the platypuses Dr. Wamsley moved to his sanctuary? Well, guess what—they're so happy in their new home that they've had at least two young. This is the first time platypuses have been born in a zoo or sanctuary in almost 50 years!

Since platypuses have their young inside burrows, scientists still don't know everything about how platypuses breed. But they do know that the nesting burrow can be amazing—up to 100 feet (30 m) long. That's a lot of digging for one platypus!

The female often piles up loose soil in different places along the tunnel. That may help keep snakes and other enemies out.

At the very end of the nesting burrow is a little "room." The female lines this room with wet leaves and grass. Then she usually lays one or two rubbery, grape-sized

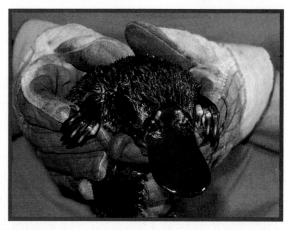

▲ A platypus is born with a tiny bill, webbed feet, and no hair. But after it grows hair, it looks kind of like a furry duckling!

eggs. She curls her tail around the little eggs to keep them warm.

After about 10 days, the eggs hatch. The newborn platypuses look just like miniature, hairless adults! They are each about the size of a kidney bean. And they have tiny bills and little webbed feet. After they hatch, they crawl through their mother's warm fur until they reach her belly. Then they drink her rich milk.

For the next three to four months, the baby platypuses live in the burrow drinking their mother's milk. During that time the little bean-sized babies grow fast—to more than half their mother's size!

Finally the day comes when young platypuses are ready to leave their burrow. They waddle down the long nesting tunnel to the burrow entrance. Then, one by one, they slide down the muddy bank and into the pond. With webbed feet working and bills searching for food, off they swim into their new lives. 📖

▲ Mother platypus stays in the burrow with her young for about three to four months. During that time, they live on her rich milk.

THINK ABOUT IT

Why were platypuses so difficult to classify?

ACTIVITY

More Plant and Animal Puzzles

Sometimes two species of living things that look alike really are closely related—they're like cousins. Appearances can be deceiving, though! Two living things can look very much alike and not be closely related at all. Try your hand at figuring out the classification puzzles in this activity.

MATERIALS
• Science Log data sheet

DO THIS

1 Look at each set of three pictures on pages B30–B31.

2 In each set, the organism pictured in the middle is closely related to either the one pictured on the right of it or the one pictured on the left of it.

3 Read the clue under each set of pictures to help you decide which two organisms belong together.

4 Write down the name of the organism that you think is more closely related to the one in the middle. Explain why you think the one you chose is more closely related than the other one.

5 Do this for each set of pictures.

▲ Violet

▲ Pansy

▲ Morning glory

Clue: Compare the petals.

▲ Platypus

▲ Beaver

▲ Squirrel

Clue: Look at the mouths of these animals.

▲ Camel

▲ Horse

▲ Rhinoceros

Clue: Look at the toes of these animals.

▲ Tulip

▲ Lily

▲ Iris

Clue: Look at the parts from which roots grow.

▲ Pear

▲ Apple

▲ Orange

Clue: Look at the fruit and seeds.

THINK AND WRITE

How did the clues help you decide which two of the three organisms were closely related?

QUICK CHECK

LESSON 2 REVIEW

What are some things scientists might look for when they try to classify an unfamiliar plant or animal?

DOUBLE CHECK

SECTION A REVIEW

1. Do you think dogs and wolves are in the same family of animals? Give reasons to support your answer.

2. Plants and some monerans can make their own food. If you found an organism that could not make its own food, could it be a plant? Could it be a moneran? Explain your answers.

SECTION B
Community Interactions

▲ Monkey

A plant takes root on a high branch of a tropical rain forest tree. A tree frog lays its eggs in the water-filled cup of the plant's leaves. A snake catches the frog and eats it. Each of these living things plays an important part in the life of the tropical rain forest biome.

How do living things in a biome interact? What kinds of things do they provide for one another? What could happen if a plant or an animal is removed from or added to the biome? Answering these questions will help you understand how the interactions of living things help keep the entire biome alive. Make careful notes in your Science Log as you work on the investigations in this section.

1 ▸ INSIDE A TROPICAL RAIN FOREST

From top to bottom, a tropical rain forest is alive with many layers of organisms, large and small. Each layer of the forest has its own communities of living things. You can discover many things about how these living things interact with one another if you explore the forest life layer by layer.

Into the Jungle

If you took a journey through a tropical rain forest, you would see many different plants and animals. Read to find out what Vanessa sees as she visits a tropical rain forest with her father.

A JUNGLE JOURNEY

from *Ranger Rick's NatureScope®*
Rain Forests: Tropical Treasures

Vanessa clutched the side of the boat as it chugged away from shore. *I'm finally going to see the jungle!* she thought. It seemed so long since her father had said he was going to Central America to study tropical rain forest insects and had told her she could come.

As the boat chugged along, Vanessa looked at the plants growing along the riverbank. A solid wall of leaves, trunks, vines, and branches grew on both sides of the river. She had heard that plants grew so thickly in jungles that people had to cut their way through them with big knives. Now she could see why!

The next morning Vanessa's father left very early to collect insects. But he had arranged to have Juanita, another researcher, take Vanessa on a walk in the jungle.

After breakfast, Juanita and Vanessa set out to explore. Once inside the forest, Vanessa stopped and looked around.

She noticed several things right away—how green the forest was and how dark and still. As she stood there, her eyes adjusted to the dim light. Here and there she could see shafts of sunlight shining to the forest floor, like small spotlights. The rest of the forest was bathed in a kind of greenish-gray light. All around her she could see the dark shapes of tree trunks. The trees were very tall and straight and their lowest branches were high above her head. Higher still, Vanessa could see flecks of light between the leaves of the trees. It seemed as if the leaves formed a roof over the forest.

"Hey, Vanessa! Come here!"

Vanessa stopped looking at the trees and other plants and ran over to where Juanita was standing. She was pointing at some dead leaves on the forest floor.

"Pretty neat, huh?" she asked.

"What?" Vanessa looked at her as if she were crazy. *What does she think is so special about dead leaves?* she wondered.

Then Juanita slid her foot closer and closer to one particular "dead leaf." Suddenly it flew off the ground, fluttered in the air for a minute, and landed on some other dead leaves several yards away.

"Wow!" cried Vanessa as she went after it, hoping for another look. "That's the best camouflage I've ever seen. What was it?"

"A moth," answered Juanita.

While Vanessa looked for the leaf-shaped moth, she noticed something else on the forest floor. "Hey, Juanita. Look at these ants. What are they doing?"

Juanita came over and looked at the parade of ants. Many of them were carrying little pieces of leaves.

▲ **Leaf-cutter ants**

"They're leaf-cutter ants and they're taking the plant pieces to their underground nest. If we follow their trail backwards, we should find the plants they're working on."

It didn't take long for Vanessa and Juanita to find the small tree the ants were working on. Its stems, branches, and leaves were crawling with ants. Vanessa bent over to watch the tiny creatures cut out pieces of leaves and lift them over their heads.

"What do they do with the leaf pieces when they get them back to their nests?" she asked.

"They clean them off and then let fungus grow on them," answered Juanita. And then, because Vanessa looked kind of confused, she added, "The ants eat the fungus."

Vanessa had never heard of ants that grew their own food. She stood by the tree and continued to watch them.

"Hey, Vanessa—want to see a living aquarium?" asked Juanita.

"A living *what?*"

Vanessa went over to where Juanita was standing.

"See that plant up there with all the long, pointed leaves?" Juanita asked, pointing to a plant on the tree. "Look inside it."

Vanessa stood on tiptoes and peered into the plant. All the leaves joined together at the base and formed a kind of cup. The cup was about half full of water. And swimming around in the water were some little creatures Vanessa guessed were insects. There was also a snail crawling around.

"Wow! It *is* like an aquarium."

"This plant is called a bromeliad," said Juanita. "And there are many different kinds. Lizards, snakes, monkeys, and other

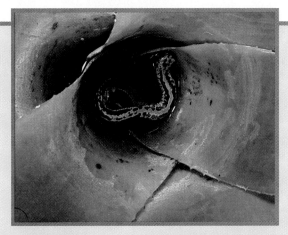

▲ Bromeliad

animals sometimes drink out of them. And frogs even lay their eggs in them!"

Just then a brilliant blue butterfly fluttered slowly by Vanessa and Juanita and landed in a nearby patch of sunlight. After a few seconds the butterfly took off, drifting out of sight.

"That butterfly was so beautiful," Vanessa said. "I never knew anything could be so blue! And . . . hey, what's that clump of stuff up there? I think it just moved."

Juanita looked up in the trees where Vanessa was pointing. "That's a sloth," she said. "They spend almost their whole lives hanging upside down in the trees, eating leaves."

"It looks like a green blob to me."

"Yeah. Sloths have tiny, green algae growing in their fur, which makes the sloths harder to see in all the green leaves. C'mon. There's a hollow tree up here I want you to see."

▲ Three-toed sloth

Vanessa took the flashlight and poked her head into the hole. Shining the flashlight upwards, she saw several brown, furry bodies. At first she didn't know what they were. Then a little head turned and looked at her, and she could see they were bats. *Neat-o!* she thought. She slowly turned the flashlight down, lighting up the inner walls of the tree. She saw crickets, giant roaches, and beetles.

They had explored only a tiny part of the jungle and had seen so much. She could hardly wait to explore more of it tomorrow.

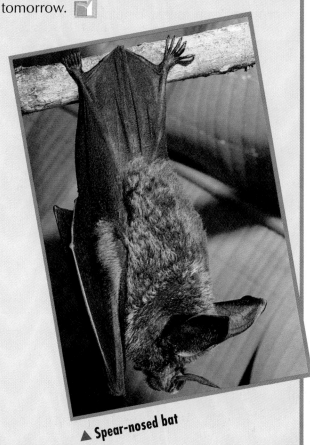

▲ Spear-nosed bat

THINK ABOUT IT

Why would plants grow more thickly along a jungle riverbank than under the tall trees of a tropical rain forest?

Make a Tropical Rain Forest

What does a tropical rain forest biome look like? What kinds of living things are found in each layer? You can use the following group activities to create a tropical rain forest display.

RESEARCH KEY FEATURES

Look for pictures of tropical rain forests in books and magazines about nature. Do not cut out the pictures. Find out about plant life, animal life, rivers, and other key features of these forests. Make a list of plants, animals, and other features that you'll try to include in your display.

BUILD A BIOME

Collect materials you can use to make a tropical rain forest. For example, you might decide on green yard bags for the background, heavy twine wrapped with crepe paper streamers for vines, long cardboard tubes for tree trunks, and construction paper or crepe paper for leaves.

Work in one corner of the room. Cover the walls with the green bags, and use the other materials to create your rain forest.

ADD PLANTS AND ANIMALS

Use materials such as construction paper, cardboard, crayons, and markers to make plants and animals for your tropical rain forest. For the upper layer hang plants and animals from the ceiling or from the vines and trees you've made. Attach other plants and animals to the tree trunks, or put them on the floor.

ADD SPECIAL TOUCHES

Here are some extra things you can do to make your tropical rain forest more exciting:

- If you have a sheet of blue plastic, such as a tarpaulin, use it to make a pond or waterfall.

- Bring in tropical houseplants, and add them to your rain forest.

- Hide a cassette player in the forest setting. Play a cassette tape of bird calls, animal sounds, or waterfall sounds.

OFFER GUIDED TOURS

Take groups of travelers from other classes on trips through your tropical rain forest. Point out and talk about the kinds of plants and animals that live in each layer, from top to bottom.

A Letter from the Treetops

Although the plants and animals of tropical rain forests differ some from place to place, they live, grow, and interact in similar ways. Here is what one student observed on a trip with his mother to rain forest communities in South America.

Strangler Fig

Anteater

Dear Dad,

I'm having a wonderful vacation with mom exploring the tropical rain forest. So far I've seen so many different plants and animals. I'm sending you some pictures of some of the neatest things I've seen.

This kind of tree isn't hard to climb — it has a hole in the middle. It's a strangler fig that grew around another tree. The other tree has died and rotted away, leaving a kind of round ladder of strangler fig trunk.

It's kind of hard to get used to seeing anteaters, but this one is really good-looking. It's a tamandua. Its brown, gold, and white stripes make it hard to spot when it's in a tree. Most anteaters eat ants (of course) or termites, but people say this kind loves to eat honey and bees.

Here's a puzzler for you, Dad. What's this jelly in a puddle on a leaf? Give up? It's frog eggs! There is so much rain here that the water collects in the leaves, and tree frogs lay their eggs there.

Now that I've seen a coati, I know what you mean. They do look like long-nosed raccoons! Mom tells me they eat just about anything — ants, grubs, and even scorpions! Sometimes, coati moms baby-sit for each other's kids, just like you and mom used to do with me and Aunt Marisol's kids.

As you can see, Dad, I'm having a terrific time. Tomorrow we're going on a boat tour. I can hardly wait! See you soon!

Love,
Jaime

Frog's eggs in bromeliad

Coati

LESSON 1 REVIEW

❶ What kinds of plant and animal communities might be found only in the treetops or only on the ground of the rain forest? What kinds might be found in more than one layer?

❷ How is a tropical rain forest different from other forest biomes?

B39

2 PLANT AND ANIMAL INTERACTIONS

Tropical rain forest communities can be found in the tree-tops, on the ground, and anywhere in between. Some of the members of the communities may never meet, but all of them interact. In this lesson, you'll investigate some of the ways living things interact in a tropical rain forest biome.

ACTIVITY

Woodworks

Climate helps determine what kinds of living things are found in a biome and how they interact. This activity will help you compare a tropical rain forest climate with the climate in your area.

MATERIALS
- local weather information
- graphs on page B41
- graph paper
- colored crayons
- Science Log data sheet

DO THIS

1 Research the average monthly temperatures for one year for your area. Record your findings.

2 Find out what the average rainfall is each month for one year where you live. Write down your findings.

3 Look at the two bar graphs on page B41. Copy onto your graph paper the bars that show the data about the average monthly temperatures in a tropical rain forest. Then, using a different color, include the data about your area by adding a bar to the right of each rain forest bar.

4 Repeat this procedure for the average monthly rainfall.

RAIN FOREST AVERAGE TEMPERATURE

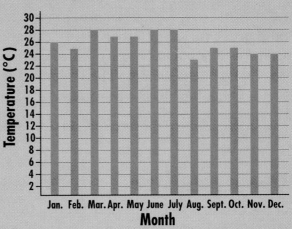

RAIN FOREST AVERAGE RAINFALL

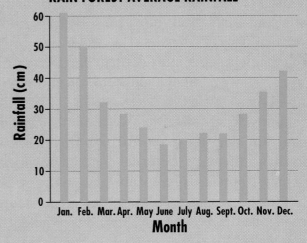

▲ Tropical rain forest

THINK AND WRITE

1. How does the amount of rain in a rain forest compare with the amount of rain where you live? How does the temperature compare?

2. **INFERRING** Inferring is using what you have observed to explain what has happened. In this activity, you compared a rain forest climate with aspects of the climate in your area. Could there be a rain forest in a place that has a cooler climate than the climate of a tropical rain forest? If so, how would the two types of rain forests be different?

Home Sweet Rain Forest

In a tropical rain forest climate, many species of large trees and a great variety of other plants thrive on the warmth and moisture. The plants, in turn, support many animal communities. Some of these communities have worked out unusual living arrangements and ways of interacting. Look for several of these as you read.

Room to Grow

For many plants and animals, living in a tropical rain forest is like being in a close-knit community or neighborhood. Everything plants need to grow fast and tall—warmth, moisture, and sunlight—is close at hand.

Tropical rain forest plants all try to get their share of sunlight. Some plants move into "high-rise" housing in the branches of tall trees. Their roots grow into the tree branches, but most of them don't feed on the trees. They get enough moisture, air, and sunlight to make their own food.

▲ Vine growing up a tree

Some plants climb their way into the sunshine, using the trees for support. That's why many trees look as if they have been decorated with vines. Some plants start as air plants high in the trees, but they don't stay that way! They grow hanging roots that drop to the ground and take hold. Some plants are on a "waiting list" for living space. For example, a tree stays small until a larger, older tree dies. When it does, the small tree gets more sunlight and shoots up rapidly to fill in the space.

◀ Epiphytes on a tree

Floors and Ceilings

Tropical rain forest animals are choosy about the places they live. Different animals live in different layers of the forest. Some may never meet each other, but others move up and down through several layers.

Some birds, such as toucans (TOO kanz), live in the highest trees. They have feet that grip almost like hands and have strong beaks for breaking open fruits and seeds.

Animals such as tapirs (TAY puhrz) and deer live entirely on the forest floor. Animals such as coatis (koh AHT eez) and anteaters move back and forth between the branches and the ground.

▲ Keel-billed toucan

What's for Dinner?

Some animals survive because they aren't fussy at all about their food. Coatis eat almost any small creature that moves, as well as turtle eggs, lizard eggs, and fruit. Some animals survive because they have a taste for one kind of meal that other animals don't eat. Some anteaters, for example, eat only ants, while other anteaters specialize in termites.

▲ South American tapir

Let's Make a Trade

Plants provide animals with food and even water. Animals in the treetops drink water caught in tree leaves and in the plants that take root on the tree branches. The animals' food can be almost anything—fruits, leaves, bark, or nuts and other seeds. Of course, some of the animals eat insects and other animals that live in the trees.

The fruits of rain forest plants may be brightly colored and sweet. These fruits attract birds, bats, and other animals, which eat the fruits and spit up the seeds or deposit them in their wastes. New plants often grow from these seeds.

▲ Giant anteater

THINK ABOUT IT

Suppose one species of tropical rain forest tree is cut for its fine wood. How might this affect other plants in the rain forest? How might it affect animals there?

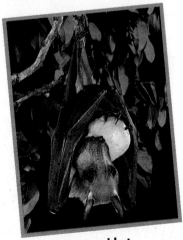
▲ Hammer-head bat

Twiners, Twisters, and Scratchers

How do tropical rain forest vines climb their way through layers of plant life into the sunlight? Take a close look at some of the ways these plants have adapted to tropical rain forest life.

▲ Tendrils winding around a plant

Climbing plants don't have fingers, but some kinds have tendrils—long growths that reach out from the stem and twine around another plant for support. The tendrils "tie" the vine to the plant, and the vine continues to grow until it reaches the top of the plant supporting it.

Is it a rope? No, it's a liana (lee AHN uh). A liana sends out a shoot from its tip and twists around any tree the shoot can reach. If the shoot holds fast, the liana wraps itself around the tree. New shoots grow whenever the liana reaches the end of its supporting plant.

▲ Lianas

Some palm trees climb and have spines. Instead of heavy trunks, rattan palms have thin stems that grow thorny "straps." The spines help anchor the palms to their supports and keep grazing animals away. However, people harvest rattan palms and use their stems to make furniture.

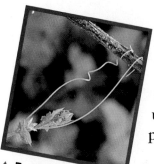

▲ Thorny straps

A monstera vine "walks" on its roots. As one end of the vine puts down roots and grows in a new direction, the other end dies away. When the vine finds a tree, it fastens new roots to the trunk and begins growing upward. Eventually, the roots on the ground die, and the monstera plant lives entirely in the tree.

▲ Monstera plant

THINK ABOUT IT

What characteristics do climbing plants have? What effect could the plants have on the trees they climb?

Life in a Tree

What kinds of organisms make their homes in or on a tree?
In this activity, you will study a tree near you to
find out what lives there.

DO THIS

1 Work in groups. Choose a tree to study
in detail.

2 With your group, study your tree
carefully for 10 to 15 minutes on
3 different days.

3 List all the organisms
you find on the bark,
branches, or leaves,
including other plants
or fungi. Use the hand
lens to help you
see them.

4 Measure and record
the size of each organ-
ism you find. Draw or
make notes about any
that are especially
interesting.

5 Share your information
with your classmates.

MATERIALS
- a tree near your school
- hand lens
- ruler
- colored pencils
- Science Log data sheet

THINK AND WRITE

Describe how the things you found are similar to and
different from what other groups observed. Write a short
summary of what all the groups found.

Plant and Animal Partners

Plants and animals in a biome can work together in different ways. Here are some plants and animals from different tropical rain forests. Try your hand at matching plant and animal partners.

◀ Some types of bats prefer nectar from a particular kind of flower. They fly a "beat" each night, looking for blossoms that have opened.

▶ Some orchids have large, showy flowers, but this type of orchid doesn't. Its flower looks like a bee!

◀ Flies are attracted by the smell of garbage, decaying fruit, and rotting meat.

◀ Passionflower vines have blossoms up to 15 centimeters (6 inches) across. They bloom a few at a time rather than all at once, and some kinds produce a sweet fruit.

▶ Bees collect nectar and pollen from many kinds of flowers. They can see colors, and this helps them recognize certain kinds of flowers. They also have a sense of smell.

▲ Rafflesias (ra FLEE zhee uhz) have huge flowers but no leaves or stems. The flowers are fleshy and smell like rotting meat.

LESSON 2 REVIEW

❶ What do tropical rain forest plants provide for animals? What do these animals provide for the plants?

❷ Are the types of things provided similar to or different from those provided in other biomes you've studied? Explain.

3 ▸ PEOPLE AND THE TROPICAL RAIN FOREST

Just as the plants and animals in a tropical rain forest community interact with one another, people interact with them. Tropical rain forests have added many things to people's lives, and the forests have been changed by people. In this lesson, you will explore some of the ways people interact with tropical rain forests.

Tropical Rain Forest People

All around the world, people live in tropical rain forests. They use the forests in different ways. As you read, look for some of the ways tropical rain forests are used and for some of the changes people make in the forests when they use them.

In a rain forest in Zaire, in the middle of Africa, a group of men and boys fans out. They are hunting whatever animals they find—sometimes large game, but most often small antelope and monkeys, rodents, and birds. While these males

▲ Harvesting peppers

B48

hunt, groups of women look for fruits, nuts, and seeds.

These people hunt and gather their food. They do not plow and plant the forest land, and they usually don't use up all the plants or animals in an area. Sometimes, though, a type of animal is overhunted and becomes scarce.

In Central America, Mayan farmers have lived for hundreds of years in the rain forests. At one time, the Mayan people even established a large kingdom there. The kingdom died out centuries ago, but farming in Central America's rain forest hasn't changed much.

Most farmers still "slash and burn" the land—they cut down trees and then set fires to clear the land. They farm it for a few years and then clear new land.

Slash-and-burn farming destroys trees and wildlife. It takes years for the forest to regrow. When the groups of farmers were small, not much land was used at any given time. The forest had a chance to regrow before the land was needed again.

Now, in some areas, more and more families are moving to the forest from the crowded cities. Most of these new arrivals use slash-and-burn farming. So more and more of the forest land is being destroyed every year. With so much farming, the land

◀ **Carrying bananas**

▲ **Slash-and-burn farming**

Gathering latex

wears out and has no chance to recover. If this continues, the rain forests in Central America will soon be gone.

Other ways of using tropical rain forests harm the forests very little. In fact, some people who live in tropical rain forests find unusual ways of making a living. In addition to fishing and farming, some people make a living by collecting tree sap to make rubber, by gathering and selling nuts, or by collecting oils, resins, and gums. Gathering these products doesn't destroy the forests, and it gives the people more ways to earn a living there.

THINK ABOUT IT

Suppose that you are the governor of a tropical rain forest area. A lumber company wants permission to cut and sell trees. Write down some reasons both for giving and for not giving permission to the lumber company.

Tropical Rain Forest Treasure Hunt

Tropical rain forests produce many things people use, and some of these products are very valuable. In this activity, you will hunt down the rain forest sources of some familiar things.

You will need: product cards, library books, cardboard, old magazines, and small objects from home

Work in pairs. Choose a product card from your teacher.

Decide what kind of product the card shows—for example, furniture—and what the product might be made of.

Use library books and magazines to find out what the product is made of and where it comes from. Write down some information about it. Find pictures of the plants or animals it comes from.

Make a display about your product. Use magazine pictures, newspaper ads, or small objects to show the product. Attach them to cardboard or poster board. If you know how your product was made or discovered, include that information on your display.

Also, include a picture of the plant or animal your product comes from. Find out whether that plant or animal is plentiful or rare. Share your information with the class.

They Save Tropical Rain Forests

Many people are concerned by what is happening to Earth's tropical rain forests. As more and more tropical rain forest disappears, scientists are studying the effects people are having on it and what can be done to stop its destruction. As you read the following article, you'll see how some scientists have dedicated their careers to preserving the plants and animals of the tropical rain forest.

RAP Team to the Rescue

by Deborah Churchman from Ranger Rick

As you read this, a forest is falling. Every minute an acre of rainforest like this one in South America is cut down or burned.

Then people move in and turn the land into farms and ranches.

Not all rainforests can be saved. So which ones are the most important to save? Good question.

Scientists know that all rainforests are valuable. But they think that some rainforests may be super-valuable. They've named these places *hot spots*.

The scientists believe these places may hold more species of plants and animals than other rainforests. The hot spots may also have more species that live *nowhere* else.

◀ Burning of rain forests

▲ Rain forests are turned into farms.

And they're in danger of being lost soon.

But scientists don't have a lot of information about these places. What if scientists could prove that the hot spots are super-valuable? Then that proof could be used to talk the local people into protecting the hot spots. So how do they get proof?

Meet the RAP team! RAP means Rapid Assessment Program. These scientists learn everything they can about a hot spot. And they do it in a great big hurry.

First, the team goes to one of the hot spots and joins the local scientists working there. Part of the team swoops over the area by plane to see what the whole place looks like. Then the team picks out parts to study. They walk, ride, or fly to these areas.

The RAP team members have just a few weeks to figure out everything they can about this place. They especially try to find rare plants and animals.

When the RAP team members are finished, they may have proof that shows why this forest is so valuable. They give the proof to the local scientists and other concerned people. Those people use it to show their government that the forest should be protected.

Ted Parker:
Birds

Ted Parker is the team leader. Ted can recognize the songs and calls of more than *3,000* different kinds of birds. That's more than any other bird scientist!

By aiming a microphone, he can pick up the faraway song of a bird such as the *blue-crowned motmot*.

He can also tell which other birds are calling at the same time and how many there are. Sometimes he can even tell whether the birds he hears are eating, fighting, or calling for mates.

Robin Foster:
Ecology

Robin Foster doesn't look for one type of animal. His job is to figure out how and why one part of a forest is different from another.

He starts by studying *satellite photos* (photos taken from space) of the hot spot. He also flies over the area to get a "bird's eye view." When he's on the ground, he checks the soil, water, and important plants.

Then he talks with the team about what they're finding. Finally, he puts all of the information together. That lets him see what makes this forest special.

Louise Emmons:
Mammals

Louise Emmons looks for creatures that are really hard to find. She searches for *mammals* (warm-blooded, hairy animals that feed mother's milk to their young).

During the day, she sets traps to capture animals for study.

She also looks for mammal tracks and droppings. These tell her which mammals are living in the area.

Many animals roam around only at night. To find them, Louise puts on a headlamp and sets out into the darkness—all alone.

Step . . . pause . . . listen and look. Louise tiptoes into the forest. She listens for cries and follows the slightest rustle. And sometimes her headlamp shines on animal eyes. By moving slowly and staying alert, Louise

finds mammals such as this *olingo*, which is rarely seen in the wild.

When Louise finds a mammal, she knows that its plant or animal foods must be there too. For example, *spider monkeys* usually eat the seeds of *virolas*. If she finds a lot of spider monkeys, she knows there are probably virola plants nearby. So learning what kinds of mammals are in a forest tells her something about what the forest must be like.

Al Gentry:

Plants

Al Gentry comes back to the team's campsite about the time Louise is leaving for the night. Carrying a huge sack of plant clippings on his back, he looks like a skinny, sweaty Santa Claus.

He preserves the plants by pressing them into folded newspapers.

Rare finds, such as this pink flower, can really make his day. Al was the first scientist to find this kind of flower in Ecuador, a country in South America.

In a rainforest, trees often look alike from the ground. The only way to tell them apart is to look at their flowers and leaves—50 to 100 feet (15 to 30 m) straight up.

No problem. Al straps on a safety belt, attaches climbing irons to his feet, and scrambles right up the tree. Then he reaches for a flowering or leafy branch. He uses a pair of tree-trimming clippers on a long pole.

When he's finished collecting, Al can tell what kinds of plants are there, which ones are new or rare, and how many kinds there may be in the whole forest. Ted can say the same about birds. Louise can say the same about mammals. And Robin has figured out what makes this forest different from other rainforests. They give the information to people who are working to save this rainforest.

Then they're ready to move on—and find out what plants and animals need to be saved in the *next* hot spot!

QUICK CHECK

LESSON 3 REVIEW

❶ How do tropical rain forests sometimes recover after people have used them?

❷ What are some things people do that can make it impossible for a tropical rain forest to recover?

DOUBLE CHECK

SECTION B REVIEW

What are some ways that living things in a tropical rain forest interact with one another? Which ways are helpful to the entire biome? Which ones are harmful?

Changes over Time

Dogs, horses, trees, grasses, song-birds—the living things we see every day don't seem to change much. Yet scientists have found evidence that these and other animals and plants were very different millions of years ago. Over time, living things evolve—they slowly change and sometimes take on whole new ways of life.

What kinds of changes take place in living things? What can scientists tell us about the reasons for these changes? In your Science Log, keep careful notes on what you discover about changes as you work through the investigations in this section.

1 KEYS TO SURVIVAL

Sometimes living things are confronted with changing conditions of life—a warmer or colder climate, a new predator, or a change in the food supply. These organisms must adapt to the changing conditions, or they will die out. In the activities and readings that follow, you will discover some of these changes.

The Great Voyage

It's easy to see how the Earth changes when an earthquake hits or a volcano erupts. It's much harder to see how living things change over time. As you read the story from *The Voyage of the Beagle*, note the evidence used to identify changes in organisms.

from *The Voyage of the Beagle* by **Kate Hyndley**

LITERATURE In 1831 an invitation was sent to Charles Darwin. He was a young student at Cambridge at the time, twenty-two years old and rather bored with his life so far. He was invited to join HMS *Beagle* on a surveying trip around the world as the ship's naturalist. Although Darwin did not seem particularly smart at school or at the university, he had always been interested in nature.

The offer came from Captain Fitzroy who was to lead the expedition. It was important that Fitzroy and Darwin should like each other as they

would have to share a cabin for the next five years. On September 5, 1831, Darwin traveled to London to meet Captain Fitzroy for the first time.

Fitzroy invited Darwin to go with him to see the *Beagle* at Plymouth where she was being refitted. She was a small ship, only 90 ft (27 m) long and weighing 242 tons.

Now that he had seen the ship, Darwin was very excited about the voyage. He set off immediately to say goodby to his family and to pack his clothes and equipment. He took with him a microscope, a compass, a book on taxidermy, binoculars, a magnifying glass and jars of spirits for preserving specimens.

 ◄ **HMS** *Beagle*

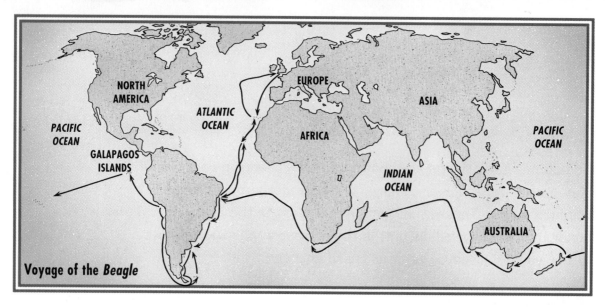

Voyage of the Beagle

At last, on December 27, 1831, the *Beagle* set sail from Plymouth. Darwin liked life on board ship but was very sea-sick. As they sailed closer to the South American coast, the sea grew calmer and Darwin was able to go out on deck and see the strange birds and sea creatures around the ship.

As soon as the *Beagle* arrived at Salvador in Brazil, Darwin went ashore to explore. He was amazed at the beauty of the tropical forests. The air was warm and steamy and there were brilliantly colored birds and flowers all around.

Walking along the shore one day, Darwin discovered a very strange fish called a diodon. When it was in danger it would fill itself up with water and air until it was round like a balloon. It could pro-tect itself by biting, or by squirting water at its enemies.

For several months Darwin was happy exploring the forests and observing and collecting all the new animals and plants he found there. In July the *Beagle* was ready to sail south again.

For the next two years the *Beagle* traveled up and down the east coast of South America, surveying the coastline and making maps. Darwin spent some of the time on the ship but also went on many inland excursions.

Darwin made one of his most exciting discoveries at a place called Punta Alta. While digging in the gravel and shingle, the explorers began to uncover large fos-silized bones. Not only did the bones belong to animals that had died out a long time ago but they were of an enormous size. Darwin soon real-ized that at one time these ani-mals must have existed in large numbers.

When Darwin brought the huge fossilized bones on board the *Beagle* he was teased for making the decks untidy. The crew was amazed at the "rub-bish" he brought on board.

The *Beagle* now sailed south again to the tip of South America, which was known as Tierra del Fuego (the Land of Fire). The landscape was impres-sive but not very welcoming with its huge mountains and deep, dark forests. The cli-mate was very cold and wet.

Darwin was pleased to leave Tierra del

Fuego, and in July 1834, the *Beagle* sailed up the west coast of South America to Valparaiso, the main seaport of Chile.

In March 1835, Darwin set off from Valparaiso to travel across the vast Cordillera range of the

Andes

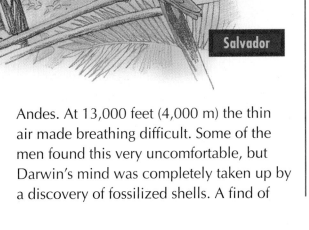

Salvador

Andes. At 13,000 feet (4,000 m) the thin air made breathing difficult. Some of the men found this very uncomfortable, but Darwin's mind was completely taken up by a discovery of fossilized shells. A find of

Galápagos Islands

fossil shells so high up meant that at one time even these high mountains had been under the ocean.

When he returned to Valparaiso, the *Beagle* was ready to sail to Lima in Peru. In September 1835 the *Beagle* left Lima to sail west across the Pacific Ocean. Their first port of call was a group of islands 600 miles (1,000 km) west of Peru called the Galápagos Islands. The word *galápagos* means giant tortoise in Spanish, and these huge animals thrived on the islands.

The islands were inhabited by strange and interesting creatures. Most of the creatures Darwin saw lived only in the Galápagos Islands. Darwin was very excited by this discovery.

THINK ABOUT IT

What evidence did Darwin find of extinct animals?

ACTIVITY

The Latest Beak

Darwin hypothesized that organisms change because of changing conditions. In some cases, this means parts of their bodies change. The following activity will give you a chance to try some different bird "beaks," to see which ones are best for eating certain kinds of foods.

DO THIS

1 Work in small groups. Each person in the group should have a paper plate. Choose one person to be the timekeeper.

2 Select three different kinds of food, and take them to your work area. Each kind of food represents a kind of bird food. Spread one kind of "bird food" over your work area.

3 Each person in the group should choose a tool to use to pick up the food. The tool you choose becomes your "beak." You may use only your beak to pick up food and move it to your plate. You will have 1 minute to gather as much of the food as possible. After 1 minute, record the number of pieces of food you were able to pick up.

MATERIALS
- **3 kinds of uncooked pasta**
- **raisins**
- **nuts**
- **gummy worms**
- **jelly beans**
- **small paper plates**
- **teaspoons**
- **tablespoons**
- **tweezers**
- **clothespins**
- **drinking straws**
- **chopsticks**
- **stopwatch**
- **Science Log data sheet**

4 Select a different tool, and try it again. Repeat step 3 until you find the beak that works best.

5 Repeat the procedure with another kind of food. Determine which "beak" works best on each kind of "bird food."

THINK AND WRITE

1. What would be the best beak for soft foods? liquid foods? moving foods? Write down some ideas for different kinds of beaks, and share them with your classmates.

2. **COMMUNICATING** When you communicate, you share information. You were asked to communicate the results of this activity to your classmates. How did you organize your information? What ideas did you think were important to explain?

Natural Selection

On the Galápagos Islands, hundreds of miles from the mainland of South America, Darwin discovered that the beaks of certain birds—finches—were different from island to island. In the last activity, you found that certain beaks worked best on certain kinds of food. Continue reading to discover how such differences can be an advantage to survival.

EXAMPLES OF FINCHES

Tool-using finch

Warbler finch

Small tree finch

Large ground finch

Vegetarian tree finch

Darwin observed that the finches on different islands ate different kinds of food. On each island, the finches with the best beaks for the available food got the most food and raised the most young. Eventually, all the finches on each island had the "best beaks."

Darwin had two related ideas to explain this. The first is called *natural selection.* Even in a single species, Darwin explained, each individual is slightly different from all the others. Some of these differences give the individual an advantage. Individuals with the successful differences survive, while individuals without these differences don't. In a sense, nature determines, or selects, the individuals that will survive.

The second idea is called *adaptation.* Darwin explained that, over time, changes in body structure or behavior enable an organism to survive in a certain environment. Organisms become adapted to their surroundings. The finches on the Galápagos Islands had adapted—over time, their beaks had changed. But Darwin couldn't explain how. It wasn't until later that the process of passing characteristics from one generation to another was understood. You will discover more about this process in a later unit.

It's not often that scientists can see natural selection and adaptation at work. But scientists in nineteenth-century England watched peppered moths change color in just a few generations.

Peppered moths live in areas where light-colored lichens cover the tree trunks. Most peppered moths are light-colored also, so they blend into this background, making it hard for predators to see them. Nature has selected light-colored moths as better adapted to survive. A few moths in every generation are dark-colored. Since they are easier to see against the light background, more dark-colored moths are eaten by birds, their natural predators.

During the nineteenth century, some of the areas where peppered moths lived were near cities with growing industries. When smoke and soot turned the tree trunks dark, light-colored moths were easy to see, and birds ate them. The moths that survived were dark-colored ones. Scientists observed that in peppered moth populations, the number of darker moths was increasing and the number of lighter moths was decreasing.

In some areas, pollution has been brought under control. The lichens have slowly been turning the tree trunks light again. So once more, the birds eat the dark-colored moths. In the moth population, the number of lighter moths is again increasing and the number of darker moths is decreasing.

THINK ABOUT IT

Why is adapting to environmental conditions important for survival?

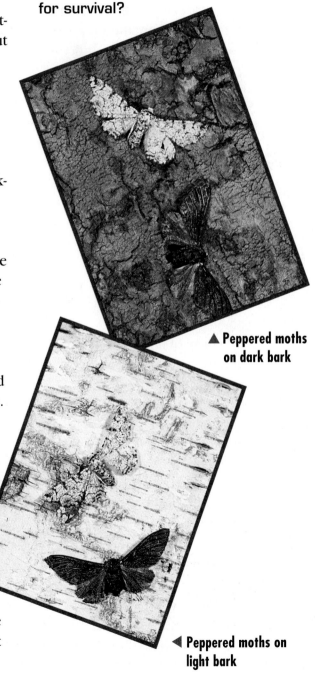

▲ Peppered moths on dark bark

◄ Peppered moths on light bark

Hop on Pop

Powerful hind legs and a long tail give kangaroos an unusual way of moving. How did they develop the ability to move in this way? Scientists would say that hopping kangaroos were better adapted to their environment and so were selected for survival. An Australian legend explains this adaptation in a more fanciful way.

WHY THE KANGAROO HOPS ON TWO LEGS

an Australian Aborigine Legend

This was the long-ago time, the Dreamtime. Kangaroo did not hop then. He walked on four paws, as Dog does, and he had four pointed teeth, just like Dog.

Once in the deep of night, Kangaroo heard singing. He had never heard such sounds before. He was curious, so he went to see who made the sounds.

The singing came from a circle of campfires between the hills. Outside the circle, women sat, singing and playing clapsticks and beating on skins. Inside the circles of fires, men danced. Bright designs were painted on their bodies, and tufts of Bird's feathers were stuck to the designs.

Drawn by the music, Kangaroo crept closer and closer. It was the most wonderful sound he had ever heard. More than anything, he wanted to dance. Finally, he could stand it no longer.

Standing on his hind legs, as the men did, he leaped into the circle and followed them—hop, hop, hop.

He did his best, holding his front legs up, just as the dancers held their arms. But he looked so funny that the women stopped singing and began to laugh.

When the men saw Kangaroo trying to dance, some of them were angry and wanted to kill him. But the oldest man of the tribe said, "No, let him dance."

So once again, the women began to sing and the men began to dance. But Kangaroo looked so funny that the men began to laugh, too. "I have an idea," the oldest man said.

The men followed him into the brush. When they returned, they all had tails made of grass hanging from their belts. Again they began to dance. But this time they danced the way Kangaroo did, with their hands in front of their chests, their grass tails flying, and their feet thumping the ground—hop, hop, hop!

At dawn the dance was over. The oldest man stood up in the ring of dying fires. "Kangaroo," he said, "you came to our dance without being invited. You danced without being asked. But you brought us a new dance that makes us laugh. We will make you one of us. But from now on, you and all your people will hop on your hind legs and hold your front legs in the air."

The dancers took Kangaroo into the brush, and they went through the ceremony that made him part of their tribe. It was the same ceremony that boys of the tribe went through to become men. As part of the ceremony, they knocked out Kangaroo's pointed teeth with a boomerang. And Kangaroo became their brother.

Ever since, no kangaroos have had pointed teeth. Ever since, kangaroos have hopped on two legs. And ever since, men wear long grass tails and dance like their kangaroo brothers. Ever since the long-ago time, the Dreamtime.

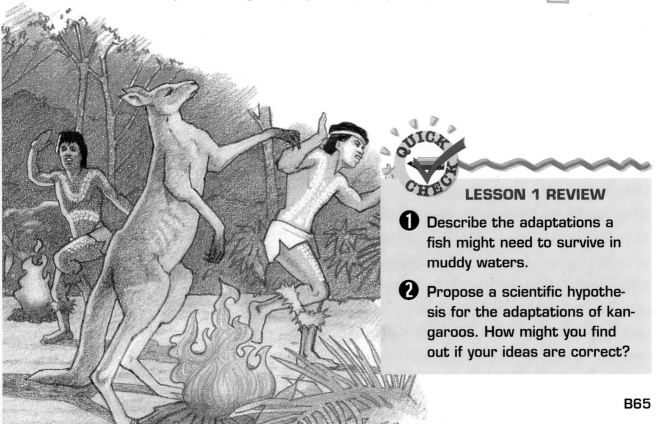

QUICK CHECK

LESSON 1 REVIEW

❶ Describe the adaptations a fish might need to survive in muddy waters.

❷ Propose a scientific hypothesis for the adaptations of kangaroos. How might you find out if your ideas are correct?

2 THE FOSSIL STORY

Scientists can study organisms to see how they have adapted to a certain way of life. Scientists can also study fossils to learn how organisms that existed long ago have changed. Putting together data about modern species and ancient species provides scientists with a clearer understanding of how organisms have adapted and changed or why they have become extinct. In this lesson, you will discover some of these things for yourself.

Feathered Tails and Shovel Teeth

Many of the plants and animals we know today have lived on Earth for millions of years. But the organisms that are so familiar to us are really just the "latest model" of earlier organisms. As you read, notice how the animals described have changed and adapted to changing environments.

In an ancient forest of tall trees, something glides from a high branch to a lower one. Then it flaps across a clearing and lands on another branch. Its long, bony tail, covered with feathers, hangs far below the branch it lands on, while sunlight glints off the claws at the ends of its wings.

The animal looks like a bird. In some ways, it is very much like modern birds, while in other ways, it is very different from birds today. It is called an *archaeopteryx* (ahr kee AHP tuhr iks). It may be the ancestor of modern birds.

The archaeopteryx lived at least 150 million years ago. Its fossil remains, found in layers of rock formed at that time, are both birdlike and lizardlike. In fact, the bone structure of an archaeopteryx looks very much like that of a dinosaur.

Fortunately, some very complete fossils from that time exist. They contain not only archaeopteryx bones but also the imprints of its feathers. From these remains, scientists can produce a fairly accurate representation of this ancestral bird.

The archaeopteryx was small, about the size of a pigeon. Its jaws were lined with pointed teeth. Its legs were long and probably used for running, and its tail was long and lizardlike. It also had a birdlike wishbone and bird feet, and its feathers were arranged like those of birds today.

The archaeopteryx probably flew clumsily and glided as much as it flew. If it landed on the ground, it probably climbed back into the trees, using its wing claws as hooks.

Over millions of years, birds developed a more useful body plan. A heavier breastbone could support larger flight muscles, allowing birds to fly more efficiently. The tail bones shortened to a stub and the legs shifted forward, giving birds better balance on the ground. Birds also lost their teeth and developed beaks. All of these adaptations have been found in fossils after archaeopteryx and can be seen in birds today.

▲ **Archaeopteryx fossil**

The basic body plan of birds has changed, or *evolved,* over millions of years. But changes can also be seen in animals that appeared much later.

Elephants, for example, are the only surviving members of a much larger family. The first species, which appeared about 50 million years ago, weren't much like elephants at all. They were about the size of a pig, and their noses were only a little longer than their lower jaws.

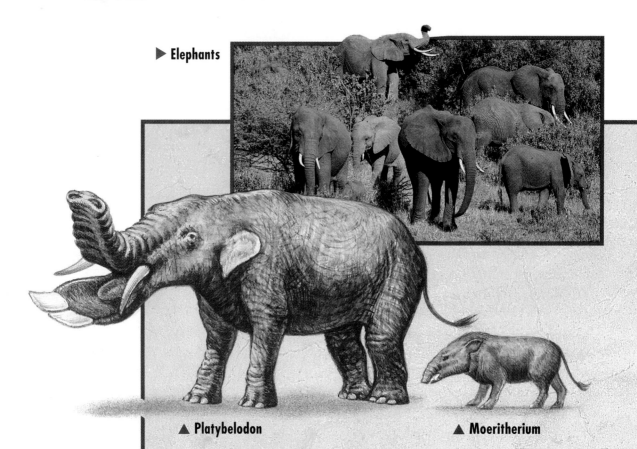

▶ **Elephants**

▲ **Platybelodon**　　　　　　　　　　　　　　　▲ **Moeritherium**

Over millions of years, their offspring became larger and their body plans evolved. The legs of later species were stronger and heavier to support their huge bodies, and their necks were shorter.

Many different kinds of noses and teeth evolved. Some early elephants had tusks and trunks, but they were different from those of modern elephants. The trunks were usually shorter. Some species were "shovel-tusked" elephants—two front teeth in their lower jaws were flattened into heavy, shovel-shaped tusks. And several shovel-tuskers had short tusks in their upper jaws, as well.

One of these early elephants, the platybelodon (plaht ee BEHL uh dahn), did not have a trunk like that of elephants today. Instead, it had a long, flat upper lip. Like a trunk, the lip could be lifted and curled.

Many of these early elephants died out because they were too adapted! Their body plans were very efficient for browsing or rooting in a forestlike environment. But as the climate changed and the forests were replaced by grasslands, they weren't able to adapt to grassland feeding. They died out, or became *extinct,* and were replaced by other species that were adapted to grazing.

Later elephants developed a body structure more like that of elephants today. As their necks became shorter and heavier, mak-

▲ **Woolly mammoth**

ing it impossible for them to bend down to graze, their trunks lengthened, enabling them to reach the ground. Later species also lost the tusks in their lower jaws. The tusks in the upper jaw became longer and often curved inward or upward.

As the climate changed and the Ice Age began, shaggy-coated mastodons and mammoths evolved. They took over in northern regions, while the ancestors of modern elephants moved farther south.

Mastodons, mammoths, and humans lived in the same areas for many years. In fact, mastodons and mammoths became extinct only about 10,000 years ago. Fossils of these animals, together with the remains of human campsites, suggest that they may have been hunted to extinction. Early peoples depended on them for food, hides, and bones, which were used for tools.

Based on a study of the gradual change, or *evolution,* of elephant ancestors, scientists would probably say that modern elephants are well adapted to their environment. They can feed on many kinds of plants, and they have few natural enemies. They are in danger from humans, who still hunt them. And they are also in danger where their habitat is changed by human beings, with whom they have lived for thousands of years.

THINK ABOUT IT

What are some ways in which changes in body structure help animals survive?

A Fossil Puzzle

Interpreting fossils is like solving puzzles. Fossils can show the structure of extinct plants and animals. They can also show other things, such as how a plant reproduced, what an animal ate, or what the climate was like. In the following activity, you can make and solve a fossil puzzle.

MATERIALS

- plant and animal materials
- shallow pan
- clay
- Science Log data sheet

DO THIS

1 Work in groups. With your group, decide what you want to show in your fossil puzzle. It might be what an animal ate, how it hunted, or how a plant spread its seeds. You may want to look through reference books for ideas.

2 Use chicken bones, dried plants, pine cones, seeds, or any other natural material to make your fossil. You may also make footprints or imprints of leaves, animal skins, or feathers.

3 Assemble your fossil puzzle in a shallow pan or box. Cover the bottom of the pan with a layer of clay. Then arrange your materials or make your imprints on top of the clay.

4 Write a description of what your fossil puzzle is supposed to show. Your teacher will collect descriptions from all the groups and put them in a folder.

5 With your group, take turns viewing all the fossil puzzles. Try to figure out what each one shows. Then check the folder to see if you were right.

THINK AND WRITE

Why did different groups come up with different explanations for some of the fossil puzzles? Do you think this happens when scientists try to interpret real fossils? Explain.

Digging Up Stories

Fossil bones give scientists important information about extinct animals. But animal fossils include things besides bones. What other kinds of animal fossils do scientists find, and what can these discoveries tell them? Continue reading to find out.

▲ Duck-billed dinosaurs

Some scientists have become egg hunters. In Montana one team found the eggs of duck-billed dinosaurs, nests of newly hatched young, and bones of half-grown young and adults. Around the nesting area were piles of plant material, wastes, and chewed food.

From these findings, scientists learned that duck-billed dinosaurs lived in large groups, built nests, and took care of their young until they were fairly well grown. The chewed food may be what the adults fed their newly hatched young.

Other scientists study rock and sediment where fossils are found. In the area where fossils of the duck-billed dinosaurs were found, there was once a great sea. As the sea dried, it became grazing land for large groups of duck-billed dinosaurs.

However, some things can never be learned from fossils. For example, no one will ever know what sound a young duck-billed dinosaur made or whether its skin was brightly colored or dull gray. As scientists find new ways to study fossils, they form more complete pictures of life in a world that was very different from ours.

THINK ABOUT IT

How can fossils provide information about the lifestyle of extinct organisms?

◀ Discovering fossil clues

He Found What?

Sometimes scientists find things that explain how and why living things evolved. It takes more than luck to make such a find. One scientist knew where to look and what to look for.

▲ John Horner at a dig

A boy growing up on a ranch might want to become a rancher. John Horner didn't. When he was eight, Horner found his first dinosaur fossil. From then on, he knew what he wanted to do—study dinosaurs.

Specifically, he wanted to study duck-billed dinosaurs. After college, Horner went to work at a museum in Montana, where he helped build a fine collection of dinosaur fossils. Horner knew that Montana was once covered by an inland sea, but he hypothesized that duck-billed dinosaurs nested on high ground, away from the water. He was also convinced that, like some birds, they nested in large colonies.

Horner was so certain of his hypothesis that he told friends he would be finding fossil eggs and young dinosaurs. He started his search in an area that would have been high ground but still close to the sea.

He found the first nest of young dinosaurs ever discovered! The next year he found more nests, as well as eggs and bones. The area he found is now known as Egg Mountain. Scientists are still digging there, finding thousands of duck-billed dinosaur bones.

THINK ABOUT IT

What did John Horner know that helped him find duck-billed dinosaurs? How did he use that knowledge?

▲ Duck-bill nest and eggs (museum display)

Why Did They Die?

Organisms become extinct for many reasons. As you read, think about what would happen if some species became extinct today.

Dinosaurs were very successful animals. They first appeared more than 200 million years ago and ruled the Earth for about 150 million years. Even though they survived for such a long time, about 65 million years ago, they all disappeared. There are several hypotheses about why dinosaurs died out. The one with the most evidence is that a giant meteor hit the Earth, causing a sudden change in climate. Most plants probably died, leaving little or no food for large animals such as dinosaurs.

In many cases, extinction is a natural part of evolution. Newer, better-adapted species replace older, less successful ones. Over millions of years, the loss of one species makes room for another.

Today, however, some species are being lost at a rapid rate—faster than new ones evolve. Human activities such as farming, building, hunting, and logging are speeding up the loss. The Earth has many fewer species today than it did even 200 years ago. You will discover more about species that are threatened with extinction in the next section.

LESSON 2 REVIEW

How can the extinction of one species be good for the evolution of another?

 DOUBLE CHECK

SECTION C REVIEW

1. Describe the kinds of changes in the environment to which a plant or an animal might need to adapt.

2. How does adaptation lead to the evolution of new species?

Lost:
One Species

Over millions of years, thousands of species have evolved into the modern species of today. Others have become extinct. Sometimes a species is in danger of becoming extinct for just one reason. It may lose its habitat or its source of food, or be overhunted. Often, a species becomes extinct when a combination of several changes take place.

When is a species in danger of dying out? What kinds of problems threaten living things and cause some of them to disappear? In your Science Log, keep notes on answers to these questions as you work on some of the investigations in this section.

1 DANGER: VANISHING SPECIES

Sometimes the population of a species becomes too small to replace itself. When this happens, the species is in danger of dying out and becoming extinct. In this lesson, you will investigate species that are in danger of becoming extinct and learn what can be done to save them.

Find a Story

When several problems threaten an environment at once, they can be hard to solve. In this activity, you will explore some of the problems a species may face.

You will need: reference sources

Work with a group to investigate and report on one of the following species or another one that you know is in danger of becoming extinct.

- **California condor**
- **desert tortoise**
- **orangutan**
- **rosewood trees**
- **Indian elephant**
- **green pitcher plant**

Use library books, magazines, and newspaper articles to find out as much as you can about the species you choose. Make a list of the problems the species faces and what causes them.

Put together a "TV special bulletin" about your species. Have different members of your group be the anchor-person; the on-location reporter; and people being interviewed, such as a conservation expert, a real estate developer, and a person who collects plants. Practice your interview, and present it to the class.

Put together a "front-page" report on your species. Include some quotes from the people you interviewed for your TV special. You may include pictures, maps, or graphs to present your information. Make a display of front pages from each group that has made a report.

Make a class list of the species all the groups found and the kinds of problems those species face in surviving.

Species Watch

Some species in danger of becoming extinct may be kinds of living things you have never seen before. Others may look very much like plants and animals you know. As you read, notice which problems these species share.

Kiwis

Kiwis are small flightless birds that live in the forests of New Zealand. They nest on the ground.

In the forest, kiwis can run as fast as a person can, but wild dogs, introduced by settlers, can catch them. Now there are very few kiwis on the two main islands of New Zealand.

Flying foxes

Flying foxes aren't really foxes at all—they're fruit bats with foxlike faces and large eyes. They eat fruit and sip nectar from flowers, and they help pollinate many plants.

Fruit growers in tropical Asia kill flying foxes to protect their crops. The habitat of flying foxes is shrinking as people clear forests. And because flying foxes are very tasty, they are hunted for food.

Key deer

The key deer, a tiny white-tailed deer, lives in the chain of keys, or islands, south of the tip of Florida.

A key deer refuge has been created to protect the deer. However, many people now live on the keys. Every year many deer are killed by cars. As houses are built, the plants the deer feed on are disappearing and their water is becoming polluted.

Indian pythons

Indian pythons are large, nonvenomous snakes. They eat small animals that they kill by constricting, or squeezing, with their bodies.

In Asia pythons are collected and sold as pets, and they are hunted for their skin, which makes fine leather. In some places, cattle graze and destroy the brush where pythons live.

THINK ABOUT IT

What problems do all or most of these endangered species share?

Going, Going, Gone!

Some living things are decreasing in number but are not yet in danger of dying out. Others will survive only if people make a great effort to save them. As you read, find out whether a plant or an animal is threatened or endangered, and determine when it is likely to become extinct.

On a list of plants and animals that are decreasing in number, some kinds are listed as threatened and others are listed as endangered. How do people decide which way to list them?

An organism appears on one of these lists if it is in danger of becoming extinct—dying out altogether. If it is likely to die out in 20 years or less without protection, it is put on the *endangered* list. If it is not endangered but is likely to become endangered within 20 years, it is put on the *threatened* list.

One of the biggest threats to a species is the destruction of its *habitat,* the part of the biome in which it lives. Most living things are adapted to live in a certain habitat. If the habitat is changed by grazing, by building, or even by too much camping or driving, species that can't adapt, such as marsh grasses or cactuses, may be lost.

A species may also be endangered or threatened because of its cash value. "Cactus rustling" by collectors who dig up cactuses and sell them to gardeners has endangered several species of cactuses. Some species of parrots are nearly extinct because collectors capture them to sell as pets.

Illegal hunting, or poaching, endangers some species. Rhinoceroses are hunted just for their horns, which some people think have medicinal uses. As a result, three of the five rhinoceros species are nearly extinct and the others are threatened.

Snow leopards, hunted for their beautiful fur, are dying out in the wild. They are being saved

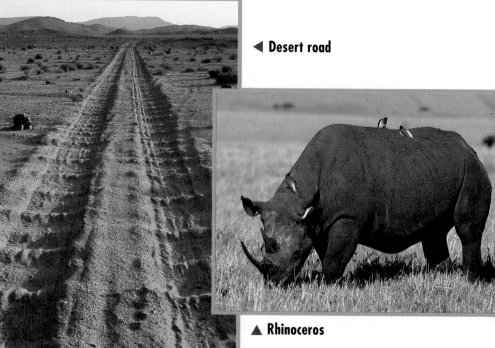

◀ Desert road

▲ Rhinoceros

only by being bred and raised in zoos.

Many countries and many states in the United States have laws that protect some plants and animals that are in danger of extinction. If the laws are enforced, endangered species can sometimes be saved. For example, American alligators, once almost extinct, have been saved by strictly enforced hunting laws. Their population has increased so much that limited hunting is allowed.

Sometimes, however, there are so few plants or animals left that it's hard to save them. Whooping cranes are alive today

▲ Art work showing endangered species

only because scientists went to great efforts to make sure they didn't die out. Some eggs have been placed in incubators, and the chicks raised by hand. Other eggs have been placed in the nests of sandhill cranes, which hatch and "adopt" the chicks.

It is too soon to tell whether the whooping cranes are a success story. Today there are a few small flocks, and scientists have found a few habitats where the cranes can be returned to the wild. If enough of these cranes can survive and raise chicks, they may reappear in the sky and disappear from the lists of endangered species.

▲ Whooping crane

THINK ABOUT IT

How is it possible to prevent a species from becoming threatened or endangered?

▲ Alligators

ACTIVITY

Threatened, Endangered, or Extinct?

Over time, a threatened or endangered species can be saved and a thriving species can become threatened, endangered, or even extinct. In this activity, you will investigate the changes in the status of some species.

DO THIS

1 Find lists of endangered species in reference books, or use your lists from other activities.

2 Choose several endangered plants or animals from the lists. Look for information about how their numbers have changed and what they are now.

3 Make a bar graph for each species you choose. Use one bar to show what the population was in an earlier year. Use a second bar to show what it is now.

4 Make a prediction about what will happen to the species in the coming years. Explain your findings, and share your prediction with the class.

THINK AND WRITE

1. What could happen that would change your prediction? Write down some ideas, and share them with your classmates.

2. **INFERRING** Inferring is using what you have observed to explain what has happened. In this activity, you used information to infer what is happening to an endangered species. How did your information help you? Did what you inferred help you make a prediction? If so, how?

Which Things Count?

Are some kinds of living things more important to save than others? This activity will give you a chance to share your ideas. Work with a group to perform the following activity.

You will need: Science Log

SOME ENDANGERED SPECIES

- black-footed ferret
- Santa Cruz cypress trees
- lady's slipper
- mission blue butterfly
- California leaf-nosed bat
- peregrine falcon
- salt marsh harvest mouse
- pygmy rattlesnake
- snakeroot
- jaguar

Your group runs the town government. A manufacturer wants to clear a large area of land to build a new factory. Some people in your town support the factory, because more jobs are needed. Others are concerned that clearing the land will destroy the habitat of a species.

At your town council meeting, there are council members, the head of a wildlife conservation group, the president of the manufacturing company, and several residents of your town.

Each member of your group should choose a role to play. From the list, select a species that could be endangered by the land clearing. Then discuss whether the factory should be built. Write down your ideas and any decision you make.

Choose another species and discuss the situation again. Were your ideas the same or different? Did you make the same decision? Share your group's results with the class.

QUICK CHECK

LESSON 1 REVIEW

❶ What can cause a species to become endangered?

❷ What can make an endangered species difficult to save?

2 SAVING ENDANGERED SPECIES

An endangered species might be saved if people protect it from being hunted, harvested, or hurt in other ways. But the species must also have a habitat that provides the things it needs to survive. This lesson will help you explore some ways of helping endangered species survive.

ACTIVITY

Contents:
Endangered Species

Take a look around you. Are there things people buy or use that can endanger a species? Are there other things that can be used instead that will help an endangered species survive? This activity will help you find out.

MATERIALS
- newspaper and magazine ads
- large sheet of paper
- markers
- Science Log data sheet

DO THIS

1 Work in groups. With your group, choose a category from the list.

CATEGORIES
- clothes
- household
- food
- pets
- furniture
- plants

2 Look for newspaper and magazine ads in the category you selected. Make a list of products that might be made from an endangered species. Include the name of the endangered species next to the product.

▼ **African elephant**

Ivory figurine ▶

3 With your group, look for information about the things on your list. Note whether harvesting or collecting a species, such as a tree, could endanger another species.

4 Make a table to display your findings. Use three columns: one for the things you would recommend using because they will not endanger a species, one for the things you would not recommend, and one for things that could be used instead.

5 Display your table and discuss it with the class.

Not Recommended	Recommended	Substitute
teak desk	maple desk	

THINK AND WRITE

1. What reasons did different groups have for their decisions? What reasons would make you think about adding, removing, or changing things in your table? Write down some ideas and discuss them with your group.

2. **COMMUNICATING** When you communicate with other people you share information. Write down some things that are important for you to communicate to other people about saving endangered species.

Looking for Answers

People need to use air, water, living things, and the resources of Earth itself in order to survive. Sometimes they can find ways to use what they need without doing permanent damage to the Earth and to living things. As you read, look for the uses that do the least damage to the environment.

A clearing of stumps and brush lies where a rain forest once stood. A river backs up behind a new dam, flooding a valley. Part of an area that once supported many species of plants and animals has been destroyed.

These events are no longer unusual. They happen more and more often. They will probably continue to happen for many reasons.

Perhaps the most important reason is that the human population of Earth is growing. In the last 150 years, the number of people has quadrupled. About 40 years from now, it will probably double again. People will need even more land for space to live and to grow food.

What happens when an area of rain forest is lost? Almost always, some species are lost. A few square kilometers of rain forest may support 200 or more species of trees and hundreds of species of smaller plants and animals. The more rain forest that disappears, the smaller the number of species becomes. Eventually, only a few species may survive.

Careful planning and careful use of the rain forest can lessen or limit some of the damage to it. One way to do this is to replace harmful uses with less harmful ones. Some rain forest products can be harvested with very little damage to plant and animal life. For example, vanilla beans, coconuts, latex, and other plant products can be collected regu-

◀ Burning rain forest

larly without harming the plants.

Fishing and some hunting can produce a steady supply of food if not too many of a species are taken. The remaining animals will breed and produce a new food supply. Even some timber can be harvested if enough trees are left to seed the area and the forest is allowed to regrow.

▲ Jaguar

But some uses of the rain forest change it permanently. For example, an area flooded by a dam is lost to rain forest species. So are areas cleared for towns, factories, or large ranches. A mine changes an area because living things are destroyed and soil is removed. And mining, manufacturing, farming, and even new towns can release chemicals or wastes into the air, the water, and the soil.

If changes to an environment can't be avoided, they must be handled in the best way. Planning how a rain forest will be used—how much logging will take place, where farming will be allowed, or how factories will control wastes—can help limit the damage to the environment.

Another way is to set aside parts of the rain forest to keep them unchanged by making them off-limits for living and working. Where this can be done, it may be the best way to save plant and animal species from possible extinction.

THINK ABOUT IT

How would creating new towns or farms decrease the number of species in an environment?

▼ Logging the forest

▼ Flooded rain forest

Can This Species Be Saved?

Sometimes an endangered plant or animal can be saved if it is simply protected from hunting or collecting. Sometimes it takes many changes and the cooperation of many people to keep a species from becoming extinct. As you read about this species, note what kinds of special help are needed to protect it.

It looks like a tiny lion with the face of a monkey, and that's how it got its name. It's a golden lion tamarin.

Lion tamarins live in the rain forests of Brazil. There are several types of tamarins but very few of each kind. Only a few golden lion tamarins are left in the world.

▲ Golden lion tamarins

At one time, Brazil had no laws protecting tamarins. In the 1960s, hundreds were captured and sold to zoos or to people who wanted them for pets. When laws were passed in the 1970s, animal traders still captured and sold tamarins illegally.

At the same time, the habitat of the golden lion tamarins was being destroyed. Tamarins live only in forests that are less than 300 meters (1,000 feet) above sea level. They can't survive at greater heights. When their forests were cleared for farms, they had nowhere to go.

There are two wild colonies of these small monkeys left. One is on land that has ocean-front housing nearby. The monkeys' land is being developed for housing, too. The other colony is luckier. It lives in a

NORTH AMERICA

Range of the Golden Lion Tamarin

ATLANTIC OCEAN

Brazil

SOUTH AMERICA

PACIFIC OCEAN

N
W E
S

reserve that was established for it in 1974. Only a small portion of the reserve has the right kind of forest for tamarins, and the area is not very well patrolled. Poachers still sneak in and capture tamarins.

Several zoos in the United States and Europe now have breeding programs. Enough golden lion tamarins have been raised so that they will very likely survive, but only in the protection of a zoo or animal park.

Can these tamarins be helped to survive in the wild? Right now, no one is sure, but people are trying. At the Primate Center in Rio de Janeiro, there are scientists who specialize in the study of monkeys and apes. These scientists are working with people at the National Zoo in Washington, D.C., and with the World Wildlife Fund to find a way to save the tamarins.

The scientists' first step is to study tamarins and the exact part of the rain forest biome in which they live. They need to know what tamarins need from their environment and what kinds of groups they form in the wild.

After that, their next goal will be to restore the forest and make it the kind of habitat the tamarins need. Their final goal will be to introduce tamarins into the restored forest.

▲ Learning about tamarins

If all of these things can be done and if the animals can be protected, golden lion tamarins may be able to take their place in the rain forest again.

THINK ABOUT IT

What things make it difficult for golden lion tamarins to survive?

Who Made It Happen?

Some endangered species have survived only because someone made a special effort to save them. Here is the story of one of those people.

What can an 11-year-old do to save an endangered species? Glenn Allen didn't know until he tried.

The Florida Keys, a string of low, coral reef islands at the southern tip of Florida, are the only home of the tiny key deer. These animals, a little more than 60 centimeters (2 feet) high, were endangered for two reasons. New homes were being built in the Keys, destroying the brush and open forest the deer needed to live. And venison, or deer meat, was highly prized, even from such small animals.

In 1949, Glenn started his project to help key deer. He read everything he could find about key deer. Then he began writing letters to anyone he could think of who would help—newspaper editors, state representatives, and local officials. He even wrote to Presidents Truman and Eisenhower to ask that a refuge be set aside for the deer.

During this time, Florida finally passed a law that made hunting key deer illegal, but Glenn knew that wasn't enough. Key deer were still being hunted illegally, and new housing developments were taking away their living space.

Glenn kept on writing letters, and so did people all across the country. Finally, in 1957 Congress established the National Key Deer Refuge on a group of 15 keys. The deer still need protection, but without Glenn's help, they would not have survived.

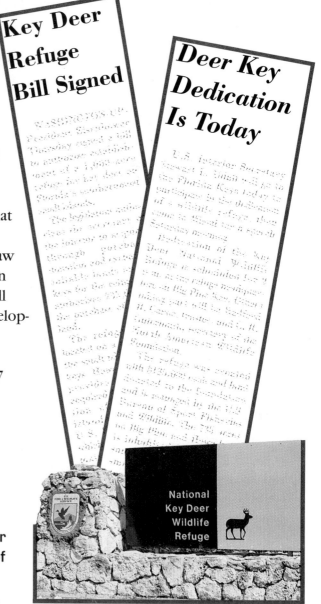

THINK ABOUT IT

Could Glenn Allen have gotten the key deer protected by working just with the state of Florida or just with Congress? Write a paragraph telling why you think as you do.

Honor a Species

Governments often issue stamps that honor a species of plant or animal. Here is your chance to design a stamp that honors an endangered species.

You will need: library books or magazines, postage stamps or pictures of stamps, ruler, heavy paper or poster board, colored pencils

Look through books or magazines for pictures of endangered plants or animals.

Look at some real postage stamps to see how they are designed and what is printed on them.

Decide on a design for your stamp.

Use the ruler to draw a 2.5-cm square on your paper or poster board. Draw your design inside this square.

Use the colored pencils to color your design. If you like, cut scallops around the edge to make it look like a real stamp.

Display your stamp designs in your classroom.

LESSON 2 REVIEW

1 What does an endangered species need in order to survive?

2 Why is it important to have enough members of an endangered species in one place?

DOUBLE CHECK

SECTION D REVIEW

1. In your own words, define the words *threatened*, *endangered*, and *extinct*.

2. What are some ways that people can help endangered species survive?

I REFLECT

It's time to think about the ideas you have discovered during your investigations. Think, too, about your many accomplishments.

SUMMARIZE

Answer the following in your Science Log.

1. What **I Wonder** questions have you answered in your investigations, and what new questions have you asked?

2. What have you discovered about endangered species, and how have your ideas changed?

3. Did any of your discoveries surprise you? Explain.

The Orangutans are an endangered species. Laws protect them in their ranges, but people are their major enemy. People are destroying their habitats.

CONNECT IDEAS

1. Name some ways living things can be grouped, or classified.

2. If one plant or animal in a biome becomes extinct, how can this affect the biome?

3. Choose one plant or animal, and describe how it has adapted to its biome.

4. How do endangered species affect you, your family, and other people you know?

5. How do people use the land? How can some of these uses be harmful?

6. What needs to be done to save endangered species?

SCIENCE PORTFOLIO

1 Complete your Science Experiences Record.

2 Choose several samples of your best work from each section to include in your Science Portfolio.

3 On A Guide to My Science Portfolio, tell why you chose each sample.

I SHARE

Scientists share their discoveries and ideas and learn from one another. How can you share what you've learned?

Decide

▶ what you want to say.

▶ what the best way is to get your message across.

Share

▶ what you did and why.

▶ what worked and what didn't work.

▶ what conclusions you have drawn.

▶ what else you'd like to find out.

Find Out

▶ what classmates liked about what you shared—and why.

▶ what questions your classmates have.

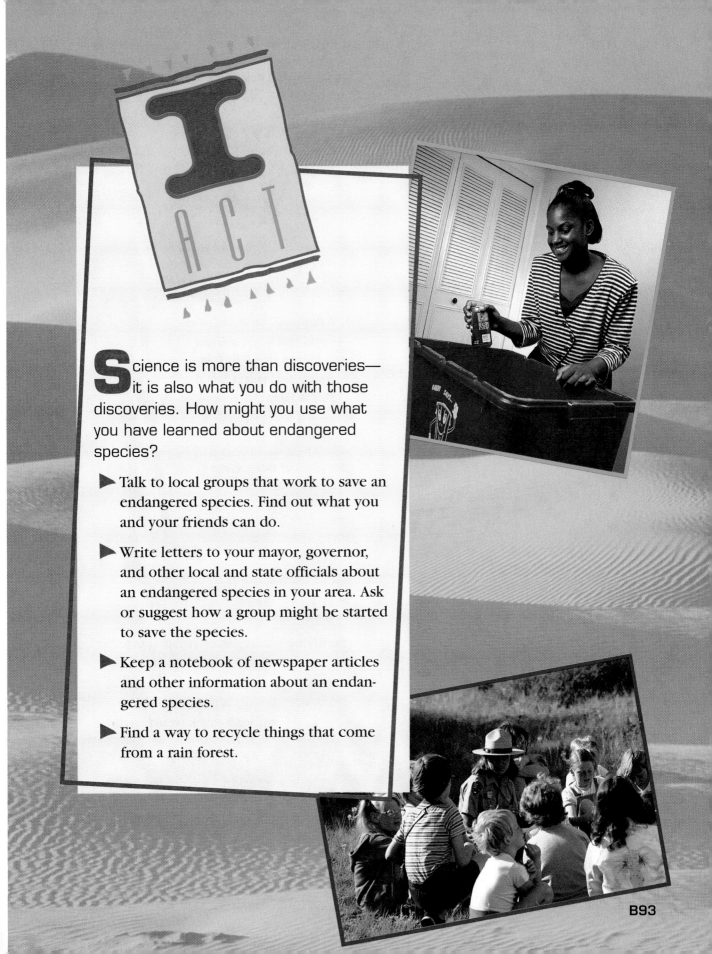

I ACT

Science is more than discoveries—it is also what you do with those discoveries. How might you use what you have learned about endangered species?

▶ Talk to local groups that work to save an endangered species. Find out what you and your friends can do.

▶ Write letters to your mayor, governor, and other local and state officials about an endangered species in your area. Ask or suggest how a group might be started to save the species.

▶ Keep a notebook of newspaper articles and other information about an endangered species.

▶ Find a way to recycle things that come from a rain forest.

THE LANGUAGE OF SCIENCE

The language of science helps people communicate clearly when they talk about endangered species. Here are some vocabulary words you can use when you talk about endangered species with your friends, family, and others.

adaptation—a change in structure or behavior that helps a living thing survive in its environment. **(B62)**

▶ **A flamingo's curved beak has combs that strain mud and sand from food it finds in water. Its long legs help it stay in the water without getting wet.**

animal—a member of a kingdom of living things that have many cells, do not make their own food, can move, and can sense their environment. **(B14)**

botanist—a scientist who studies plants and plant life. **(B14)**

classifying—arranging or grouping together things, based on similarities. **(B14)**

▼ **Passenger pigeon**

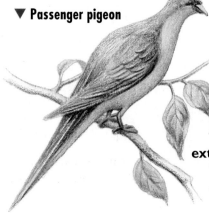

endangered—likely to become extinct. A plant or animal is endangered if it would die out in 20 years or less without special protection. **(B78)**

evolution—the process of change in living things that occurs over a long period of time. **(B69)**

extinct—no longer living or existing. The passenger pigeon is extinct. **(B68)**

◀ **Mushrooms (fungi)**

natural selection—a theory that explains how living things change. It states that the living things with the best features for their environment will survive and reproduce more living things like themselves. **(B62)**

plant—a member of a kingdom of living things that do not move about and that make their own food using a green substance called chlorophyll. **(B14)**

fungus—a member of a kingdom of living things that resemble plants but that do not have leaves or flowers or make their own food. A mushroom is a fungus. **(B24)**

habitat—the place where a plant or animal naturally grows or lives. **(B78)**

key—a guide for identifying living things, such as trees or grasses, by comparing them with similar groups of living things. **(B16)**

kingdom—the largest category in the classification system of living things. **(B14)**

moneran—a member of a kingdom of living things that have one cell with a very simple structure. Bacteria and some algae are monerans. **(B24)**

protist—a member of a kingdom of simple living things that resemble both plants and animals in some ways, but are not like either one. **(B24)**

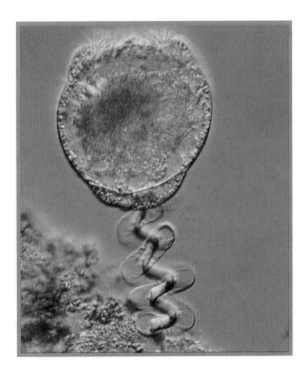

▲ **Ciliate (a protist)**

species—a group of living things that have certain like characteristics and can mate and produce fertile offspring. **(B15)**

threatened—likely to become endangered in 20 years or less. **(B78)**

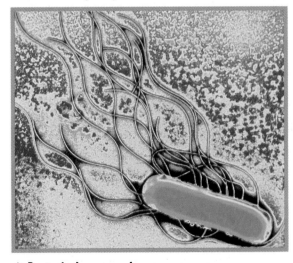

▲ **Bacteria (monerans)**

STAGE AND SCREEN

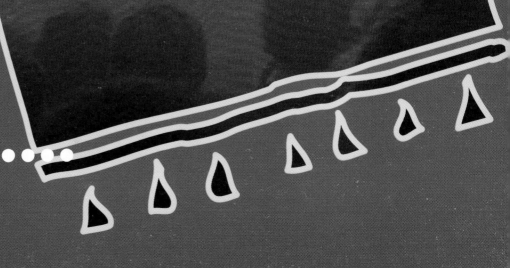

Unit C

Stage and Screen

Using Light and Sound

I WONDER

Colored lights flash. The deep sounds of the bass mix with the richness of the piano. What can you ask to find out how light, sound, and electricity are used to televise a concert? What can you ask to find out how these things are used for producing a news broadcast?

Work with a partner to make a list of your questions. Be ready to share your list with the rest of the class.

Recording studio's sound-mixing console
TV news crew

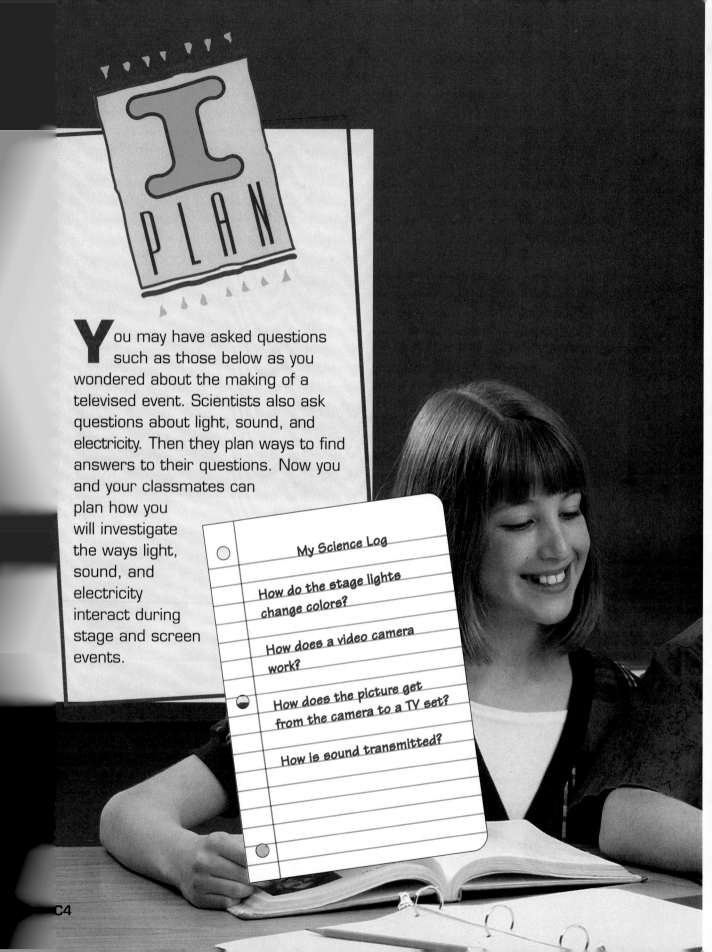

I PLAN

You may have asked questions such as those below as you wondered about the making of a televised event. Scientists also ask questions about light, sound, and electricity. Then they plan ways to find answers to their questions. Now you and your classmates can plan how you will investigate the ways light, sound, and electricity interact during stage and screen events.

My Science Log

How do the stage lights change colors?

How does a video camera work?

How does the picture get from the camera to a TV set?

How is sound transmitted?

With Your Class

Plan how your class will use the activities and readings from the **I Investigate** part of this unit. What other resources can you use?

On Your Own

There are many ways to learn about light, sound, and electricity. Following are some things you can do to explore light, sound, and electricity by yourself or with some classmates. Some explorations may take longer to do than others. Look over the suggestions and choose . . .

- **Places to Visit**
- **Projects to Do**
- **Books to Read**

PLACES TO VISIT

EXPLORE A TV STUDIO

Visit a local TV studio to see how a news program is produced with the latest equipment. Contact the studio's public relations department to arrange for a tour. Before you go, make a list of questions to ask. Find out all you can about the people who work together to put on a broadcast.

DISCOVER THE SCIENCE OF SOUND

Plan a visit to a local musical instrument store. Arrange for someone at the store to demonstrate both acoustic and electronic instruments. Find out how each instrument produces sound. Compare an electric guitar and a nonelectric guitar.

ATTEND A LIVE PERFORMANCE

Many communities have amateur or professional theaters. Check the schedule of a theater near you. Arrange to attend a play with friends or relatives. As you enjoy the performance, pay attention to how light and sound are used to help set the mood in the play.

PROJECTS TO DO

KEEPING AN EYE ON LIGHT

Make a drawing of one outdoor place at different times of day—even by moonlight, if you can. Notice how the shadows and the colors change. Explain why filmmakers need to use artificial light to change the way things appear. Describe how filmmakers might use artificial light.

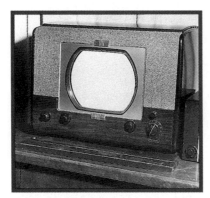

DISCOVERING OUR HISTORY

How many TV sets were in American homes in 1930? in 1940? How many are there today? Find out and make a graph to show the increase in numbers of TVs from 1930 through 1990. Then find out how TV has changed people's lives. Talk to an older relative or neighbor who remembers the time before TV. Share your discoveries with your class.

CHOOSE AN INVENTOR

Who was Lewis Howard Latimer? What did Philo Farnsworth and Vladimir K. Zworykin do? Science is about wondering and discovering. Find out about some of the people who have helped us learn more about light, sound, and electricity. Make a poster to share what you've learned.

BOOKS TO READ

by Harriet Berg Schwartz (Knopf, 1993).

This book introduces you to Clawdio the cat. It's a good thing he is backstage to make sure things for the play run smoothly. The play needs lighting, moving scenery, and even a flying Peter Pan. Putting it together takes a lot of work; special equipment; knowledge; and, of course, one cat to see that everyone does the job right.

Look Alive: Behind the Scenes of an Animated Film

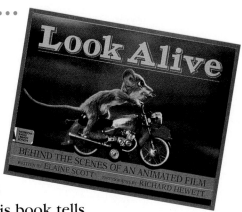

by Elaine Scott (William Morrow, 1992). Have you ever read Beverly Cleary's books about Ralph S. Mouse? Someone made a movie of one, *Ralph S. Mouse.* Could you train a mouse to act and to ride a motorcycle? Of course not. So the movie was photographed with actors for the human roles and a movable model for Ralph. The movie is great! This book tells how it was done.

More Books to Read

Mirrors: Finding Out About the Properties of Light

by Bernie Zubrowski (William Morrow, 1992), Outstanding Science Trade Book. Anyone who understands how light travels and who uses mirrors to reflect and bend the light can create many special effects and tricks. These effects can be used when putting on shows, playing tricks, or learning about light. This book shows you how this is done.

Exploring Electricity

by Ed Catherall (Steck-Vaughn, 1989). In this book, you will learn how electricity is made and how it is used. You will learn how to do simple experiments and some that are more difficult. You will find out how to make an electric motor, a battery with a lemon, and other projects. Electricity is important in our lives. We depend upon it in many ways.

Sound Waves to Music

by Neil Ardley (Gloucester Press, 1990). Sound is all around you. There are even sounds that you cannot hear. Sound can be so strong that it will make things move. Sound can be copied and stored. Sound can affect the way you feel. We can take pictures with sound. Read this book to find out why there is a lot more to sound than just hearing it.

The Chinese Mirror

by Mirra Ginsburg (Harcourt Brace, 1988). Suppose you were looking into a mirror for the first time. What would you think when you saw your reflection? This story, a tale from Korea, tells of the misunderstandings that occur when a man brings a mirror from China into his village. The people have never looked in a mirror before, and each person resents the stranger viewed in the glass. Read to find out what happens when the mirror is shattered.

To find answers to their questions, scientists read, think, talk to others, and do experiments. Their investigations often lead to new questions.

In this unit, you will have many chances to think and work like a scientist. How will you find answers to questions you posed?

▶ HYPOTHESIZING You form a hypothesis when you want to explain how or why something happens. Your hypothesis is an explanation based on what you already know. A hypothesis should be tested in an experiment.

▶ COMPARING When you compare objects or events, you look for what they have in common. You also look for differences between them.

▶ EXPERIMENTING You experiment to test hypotheses. In a test, you must control variables and gather accurate data. You also must interpret the data and draw conclusions.

Are you ready to begin?

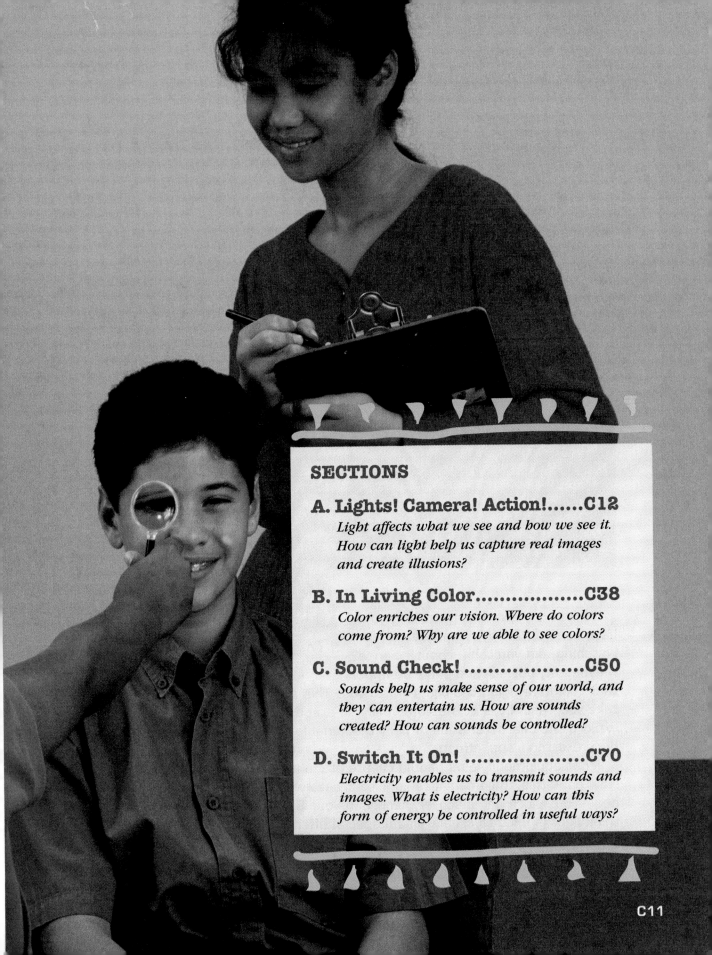

SECTIONS

SECTION A
Lights! Camera! Action!

▲ TV camera operator

Think about something exciting you have seen on TV. While you were watching, did you think about science? Maybe not, but science plays an important role in bringing the program to you. This section will take you behind the scenes of events on stage and screen. You'll explore the characteristics of light that enable us to see and to produce exciting visual effects.

What equipment helps people create stage and screen events? How does this equipment use light to create what we see? As you begin to explore and discover, record in your Science Log how you think light is used to create visual special effects you have seen.

1 BEHIND THE SCENES

The image on your TV set is the end of the long process of bringing a show from the stage to you. Light and images are carefully controlled to give the visual effects desired by the writers and producers. As you read, think about which part of the process you'd like to try.

PREPRODUCTION

PRODUCTION

▶ Every show begins with an idea. Producers and directors work together to plan how to present their ideas to an audience. Scriptwriters put the ideas on paper. These people are planning to produce a concert for TV.

▲ On the day of production, after many hours of setting up and rehearsing, the performers begin the show.

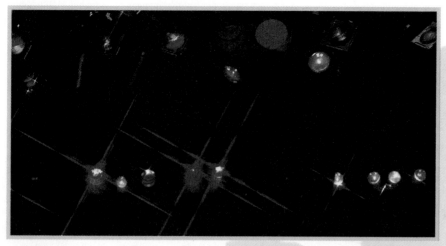

▲ Lights are used to light the stage and the performers, to create a mood, and to produce exciting special effects.

▶ The sound engineer listens as the sound is recorded from microphones placed on stage. The engineer uses the sound board to control the quality and level of the sound being recorded.

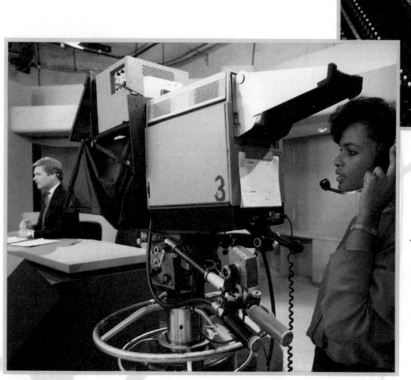

◀ At least one camera operator, or videographer, records the events on stage. The videographer controls the content and quality of the recorded image by adjusting the camera and its lens.

▲ The director watches the monitor to see what is being recorded on tape and gives each videographer directions. In a live show, the director works with an engineer to control which camera's picture is transmitted at each moment.

POST PRODUCTION

◄ The editors select and combine the best scenes to create the final program. The editors must pay attention to both the image and the sound. They may also put in special audio effects, such as a crowd cheering, or video effects, such as making an image spin onto the screen, for excitement.

▶ When the show is ready for transmission, it travels through cables as a series of electrical impulses. The cables carry the program to a transmitter, which sends signals to homes by way of antennas or another series of cables, or to a satellite for transmission around the world.

▼ Finally, the show reaches the TV in your home, where you can sit back and enjoy yourself. Today you're just a spectator, but in the near future, you will be able to use an interactive TV to interact with the characters in a program. TVs will become more like computers.

QUICK CHECK

LESSON 1 REVIEW
Make a list of all of the ways that light, sound, and electricity are used to bring a show from a stage to your TV.

2 LIGHT AND SHADOWS

The scene opens with the street in darkness. Suddenly, as the sun breaks out from behind the clouds, light and shadows mix. In this lesson, you will discover how light travels.

Beyond the Shadows

Creating images with light and shadows can turn science into entertainment. As you read, try to picture how light and shadows help create the show.

SHADOW PUPPETS OF INDONESIA

by **Marjorie Jackson** from *Cricket*

 After sundown in the island country of Indonesia, crowds gather in front of white screens to watch *wayang kulit* performances, the dramatic shadow puppet plays that have been a part of Indonesian culture for many hundreds of years. Cymbals clang and drums thump as fanged giants lumber across the screen. Everyone laughs to see clowns argue and bite each other's noses, or watch monkeys soar in wild games of leapfrog.

▲ Indonesian puppet

Wayang kulit is one of the most popular and entertaining arts of Indonesia. The plays are often staged in open courtyards, and once the music begins, the whole village stops to watch. Children perch in trees, and others sit on mats, but important guests are given chairs. Even today a *wayang* (the Indonesian word for shadow) performance is thought to work a special magic. A powerful *dalang*, or puppet master, is said to bring protection and good fortune to all who attend.

Each *wayang kulit* is a flat figure, cut out, hammered, and chiseled from dried water buffalo hide.

Today, a full set of *wayang kulit* might contain six hundred puppets, but usually only forty or fifty are needed at one performance. The *dalang* arrives wearing a printed sarong and headcloth. He sits cross-legged next to the screen, on the side away from the audience, and takes his puppets from their box. He then spreads incense over them. A bright coconut oil lamp hangs overhead to cast the puppets' shadows onto the screen. The light shimmers and makes the puppets' shadows come to life and move. Today an electric light bulb is often used instead. Since its

light is steady, the *dalang* gently shakes the puppets to make them move. The puppet master moves new characters quickly on or off stage so that his hands won't cast shadows. A figure appears to become smaller when he moves it toward the screen, and then it blurs when he pulls it away. At the moment of blurring, the *dalang* can exchange two puppets, giving the illusion of changing a beautiful maiden into an ogre, or a lion into a knight.

At sunrise the final gong is sounded. Some of the crowd are caught napping. The puppets fade from the screen and are folded into their box. Everyone has laughed and cried, and now they will go home content. The *wayang kulit* performance was a success. It has been "written in the world," as the Indonesians say, and its goodness will be lasting.

THINK ABOUT IT

How are the shadow puppet show and the TV concert alike? How are they different?

Shadow Play

The *dalang* entertains his audience with shadow puppets. Now, you can entertain your classmates with a shadow puppet show.

DO THIS

❶ Make a puppet by cutting a shape out of cardboard. Use tape to attach the puppet to a thin stick.

❷ Hang the sheet from the ceiling or over a doorway.

❸ Place the light about 2 m away from the back of the sheet.

❹ **CAUTION: Do not touch the hot light.** Turn on the light. Direct the beam toward the sheet.

❺ Darken the room by closing the shades and turning off most of the lights.

MATERIALS
- cardboard
- scissors
- tape
- sticks
- white sheet
- gooseneck lamp
- Science Log data sheet

❻ Do the following with a partner and record your observations.

- Hold the puppet behind the light. Is there a shadow?

- Hold the puppet between the light and the sheet. What happens?

- Take the puppet from between the light source and the sheet. Move the light source away from the sheet. What happens to the brightness and the area of the light?

- Move the light source closer to the sheet. What happens to the brightness and the area of the light?

THINK AND WRITE

How do light and a puppet create a shadow? Draw a labeled diagram to show your ideas.

How Does Light Travel?

Think about how the light and the puppet worked together to create the images in your shadow puppet theater. You can use a model to show this and to explain how shadows are cast.

Light travels in a straight line. Your puppet blocked the rays of light and cast a shadow on the sheet. A shadow forms when something blocks a source of light like a flashlight, a projector, or the sun. A *ray model* like the one below can help you see how the light traveled in your shadow theater.

In the diagram, notice how the rays spread out as they get farther away from the light source. When the rays are spread out, the light is less bright than when the rays are close together. You probably discovered that the light became brighter as you moved the light source closer to the sheet in your theater. How would the puppet's shadow look in bright light?

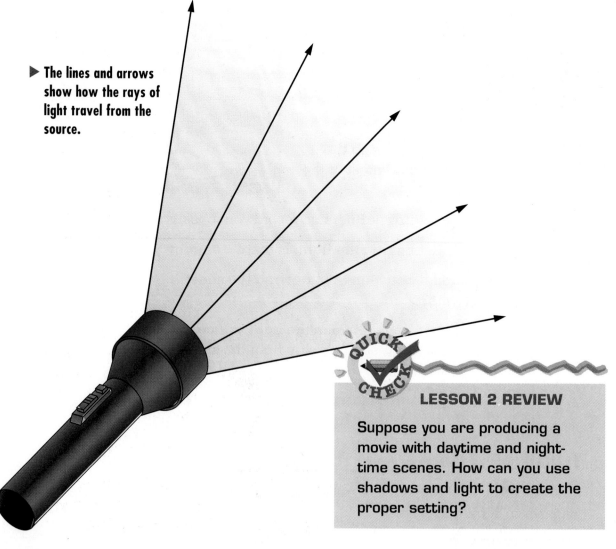

▶ The lines and arrows show how the rays of light travel from the source.

QUICK CHECK

LESSON 2 REVIEW

Suppose you are producing a movie with daytime and night-time scenes. How can you use shadows and light to create the proper setting?

HOW LIGHT IS REFLECTED

When you look in a mirror, you see yourself. This experience shows one way in which light behaves. In this lesson, you will discover how light is reflected.

Stage Lights

Stage and screen producers use behaviors of light to produce interesting visual effects. The following passage describes some of the ways people work with stage lighting.

from *Ramona: Behind the Scenes of a TV Show* by **Elaine Scott**

 The lights that illuminate the set can be adjusted in hundreds of different ways. During blocking, Doug decides how much light he wants and where he wants it, and then he asks the lighting gaffer, Gary Phipps, to trim the lights accordingly. The gaffer is the person who is in charge of the lights, and the lighting grip is the per-son who helps the gaffer by moving the lights from place to place.

When a camera operator talks to a gaffer, it is almost as if they were conversing in an alien language.

"Barn-door that inkie off the wall, will you, Phipps?" asks Doug, and Phipps turns to his grip and asks him to climb up on a kitchen cabinet to adjust a black reflector (that does

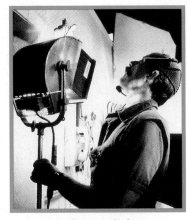

▲ **A grip adjusting lights**

indeed look a bit like a barn door) over the "inkie," a 750-watt light, until the light shines exactly where Doug wants it.

By carefully moving the reflectors, the gaffer can create shadows on walls and take shadows away from faces. Different-colored filters, called gels, can be placed over the lights to give the scene a different mood. Filters placed over the lens of the camera can also change the lighting. For example, a special filter on the camera can change the ordinary flame of a candle into a star-shaped glow.

THINK ABOUT IT

Briefly describe what a gaffer needs to know about using light.

ACTIVITY

Just Passing Through

You've just read how the gaffer on a TV production crew changes the look of a set by adjusting light in different ways. Try this activity to see how different materials allow different amounts of light to pass through.

DO THIS

1 Darken the room, and shine the flashlight down onto a tabletop. Observe how much light falls on the tabletop.

2 Place each material one at a time over the lens of the flashlight, and shine the beam in the same place as before. Observe how much light falls on the tabletop.

THINK AND WRITE

COMPARING Comparing involves telling how objects are alike and how they are different. Which of the materials from this activity are most alike? Which are most different?

Traveling Light Rays Different materials allow different amounts of light to pass through. If all of the light from a light source passes through, the material is *transparent*. If some light passes through, the material is *translucent*. If no light passes through, the material is *opaque*. Use these definitions to classify the materials you tested in the activity.

Bouncing Light Rays

When light hits the smooth, flat surface of a mirror, it bounces, or reflects. See if you can predict the direction in which light rays will reflect.

DO THIS

1 Attach the mirror to the wall at chest level or lower. Stand 1 to 2 m away from the mirror, off to one side. From this spot, you will be shining the beam of your flashlight toward the mirror. Before you turn the flashlight on, ask a partner to stand where you think the rays of light will be reflected by the mirror.

2 Darken the room, and shine the flashlight so that its beam hits the mirror. Do the light rays bounce to where your partner is standing? If not, have your partner move to where the light rays do reflect. Experiment with different locations for you and your partner.

3 For each trial, draw a ray diagram to show the path of light from the flashlight to the mirror to your partner.

MATERIALS
- small mirror
- flashlight
- Science Log data sheet

THINK AND WRITE

EXPERIMENTING When you experiment, you gather and interpret data and draw conclusions. Examine your ray diagrams. Describe how the angle at which light rays strike the mirror compares with the angle at which the rays reflect off it.

Multiply with Mirrors

You've discovered how mirrors reflect light. Now, in this activity, you will use mirrors to produce special effects.

MATERIALS
- 2 small, flat mirrors
- tape
- eraser or other small object
- Science Log data sheet

DO THIS

1 Tape the mirrors together side by side so that they can be folded to face each other.

2 Unfold the mirrors and stand them upright. Place the object so that it faces the unfolded mirrors in front of where they are joined. Count the reflections of the object.

3 Fold the mirrors slightly to form a very wide V shape. Count the reflections of the object.

4 Gently move the mirrors to make the V narrower. Observe how the number of reflections changes.

THINK AND WRITE

How would you explain the changes in the number of reflections as you folded the mirrors?

Take a Look at Yourself

Try this activity to see how differently shaped mirrors reflect light and form images.

DO THIS

Look at your reflection in each mirror, try the following, and record your observations.

MATERIALS
• flat mirror
• convex mirror
• concave mirror
• Science Log data sheet

- Describe the image in the mirror. Is the image smaller than, the same size as, or larger than your face? Is the image right side up or upside down?

- Describe where the image in the mirror appears to be: on the surface of the mirror or behind it.

- Move the mirror left, right, backward, and forward. What happens to the image?

- Touch your right cheek. Which cheek does the image in the mirror touch?

THINK AND WRITE

1. Compare the images formed by the three mirrors.

2. How might a convex mirror be used on a school bus? Explain how the image formed by the mirror fits the use.

Reflecting on Reflection

Here are the answers to some of the questions you might have about the activities you've done in this lesson.

Q: How can a gaffer tell where a ray of light will be reflected?

A: Think of light as traveling like a basketball. Basketball players know that once the ball hits the backboard, it must move at a certain angle to go into the hoop. A gaffer knows that when light hits something, like a mirror, it bounces in much the same way a ball would. The ray of light hits the mirror and bounces off at equal angles.

Q: Why can I see myself in a mirror?

A: When you look in a flat mirror, light rays bounce off your body to the mirror and back. Since the surface of the mirror is smooth, most of the rays are reflected back to your eyes in the same direction.

    Curved mirrors reflect images differently than flat mirrors do. That's why your images in the concave and convex mirrors look different from your image in a flat mirror. Concave mirrors are curved inward. Convex mirrors are curved outward.

Q: Why don't all objects reflect light as a mirror does?

A: Most objects are not smooth like a mirror. When light rays strike a rough surface, they are reflected back in different directions. That's why on a windy day, you can't see your reflection in a lake. The rough surface of the water scatters the light in many directions. On a calm day, though, a lake can act like a mirror, reflecting the rays of light back to you in a single direction.

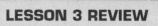

LESSON 3 REVIEW

Describe one "special effect" you could create using filters and each of these mirrors: flat, concave, and convex.

4 LIGHT AND LENSES

You've explored ways that light rays reflect in straight lines. Can light rays bend? Light rays and camera lenses produce some surprising sights.

ACTIVITY

How Lenses Bend Light

What kind of lens is used in a camera? This activity can help you find out.

MATERIALS
- light source
- convex lens
- meter stick
- sheet of white paper
- concave lens
- Science Log data sheet

DO THIS

1 Place the light source more than a meter away from where you are working. Turn on the light source. Hold the convex lens above the zero end of the meter stick so that light from the source passes through the lens.

2 Move the sheet of paper along the meter stick until the light rays form a pinpoint of light. This is the focal point.

3 Measure the distance between the center of the lens and the pinpoint of light. This is the focal length.

4 Hold the convex lens close to this page, at a distance less than the focal length. What do you observe? Where does the image appear in relation to the paper?

5 Hold the concave lens in the path of your light source, as in step 1. What happens to the rays of light?

THINK AND WRITE

Compare what convex and concave lenses do to light.

Can You Believe Your Eyes?

A movie character sees a mirage in a desert scene. What causes a mirage? Read and examine the pictures to find out.

Think about how it feels to walk through deep water. Your legs have to work much harder than usual, and you can't move as fast as on dry ground. When light rays travel from one medium to another, they change speed, too. This change sometimes causes the rays to bend, or *refract.*

Have you ever seen a mirage on a hot day? This is an example of refraction, too. Light refracts when it travels through air of different temperatures. If the air just above the ground is hotter than the surrounding air, the sunlight is refracted, creating an optical illusion on the surface. Refracted light may create images that surprise you, but refraction follows very predictable rules.

▲ One straw or two?

◀ Mirage

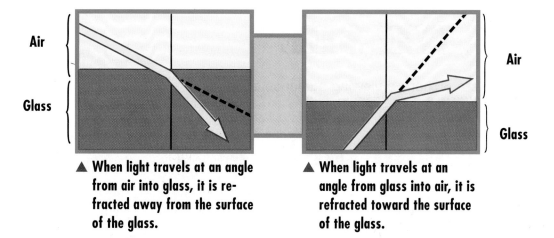

Air

Glass

▲ When light travels at an angle from air into glass, it is refracted away from the surface of the glass.

Air

Glass

▲ When light travels at an angle from glass into air, it is refracted toward the surface of the glass.

Understanding how light refracts has helped people create lenses to refract light in useful ways. Look at the instruments pictured here, and tell what each does.

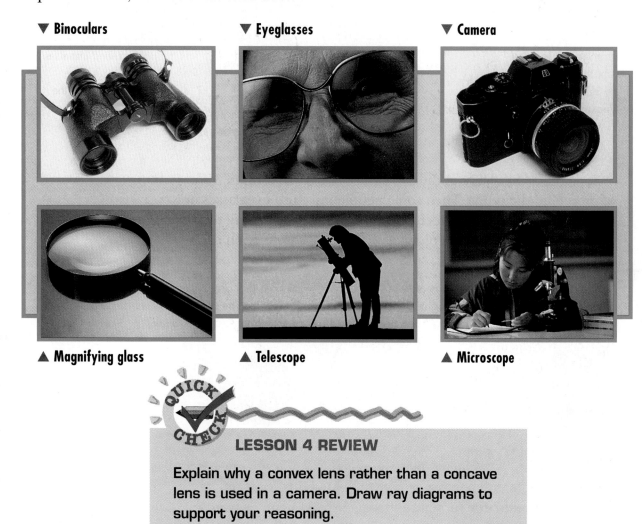

▼ Binoculars

▼ Eyeglasses

▼ Camera

▲ Magnifying glass

▲ Telescope

▲ Microscope

QUICK CHECK

LESSON 4 REVIEW

Explain why a convex lens rather than a concave lens is used in a camera. Draw ray diagrams to support your reasoning.

5 HOW WE SEE

No performance is complete without a viewing audience.
In this lesson, you will find out how people see.

Taking a Look at the Eye

You turn on the TV and watch your favorite program. Here is how you see it.

The lens refracts light rays to come together and form an upside-down image on the retina.

Light passes through the pupil and enters the lens. Muscles change the focal length of the lens by adjusting its thickness.

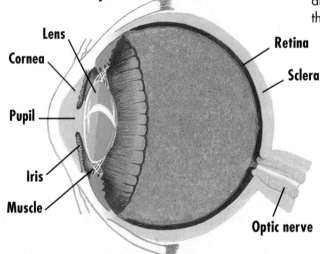

Lens
Cornea
Pupil
Iris
Muscle
Retina
Sclera
Optic nerve

The nerve cells of the retina send impulses to the brain. The brain interprets the image and you see it right side up.

Sometimes the shape of the eye causes images to form in front of or behind the retina. Then some people must use eyeglasses or contact lenses. Lenses correct vision problems by adjusting the refraction so that the rays come together at a focal point on each retina.

▼ Eyeballs that are too long form images in front of the retinas. The person is nearsighted and can't see faraway objects clearly.

▼ Eyeballs that are too short form images behind the retinas. The person is farsighted and can't see nearby objects clearly.

THINK ABOUT IT

What kind of lens, concave or convex, is used to correct for nearsightedness? for farsightedness? Explain your answers.

ACTIVITY

Eyeball to Eyeball

You look through your eyes at the world around you, but when was the last time you looked at your eyes?

DO THIS ⚠CAUTION

1 Look at your eye in a mirror. Use colored pencils to draw what you see. Label the pupil, sclera (white area), iris, and cornea.

2 Look at another student's eye from the side. Can you see the clear bulge of the cornea in the eye?

3 Use a hand lens to look at the other student's eye under magnification. Compare what you see with what you noticed in your own eye.

4 Look at the pupil of the other student's eye, first in a brightly lit part of the room and then in a dark part of the room. What do you observe?

5 **CAUTION: Be careful not to press against or jab at your closed eyelid.** Darken the room. Turn the penlight on, and place it against the outer corner of your closed upper eyelid. Gently but firmly wiggle the penlight back and forth. Do you see the blood vessels on the back of your retina? Add these to your drawing.

THINK AND WRITE

Why are you unable to see well for a few minutes when you walk from a well-lighted room into a dark room? Why does your vision gradually improve?

Create Your Own Picture Show

Did you know that a movie is really just a series of still images, or frames? You can make an animated feature of your own with just a little drawing ability and with a trick played on your vision by your eyes.

DO THIS

1. Decide what you want to show in your animated feature. Here are some suggestions: the sun rising, a ball bouncing, a bird flying.

2. On each card, draw a tiny step in the action you want to show.

3. Put the cards in order from last to first. Staple the cards together at the side to form a book.

4. Flip the pages of the book, starting with the last page, and watch your drawings in action. Share your animated book with your classmates.

THINK AND WRITE

What appeared to happen to your drawings as you flipped the pages of your book? Why do you think this happened?

Visual Images   The figures in motion pictures appear to be moving because of *persistence of vision*. The retina of your eye can retain an image for a brief amount of time. If the images move quickly enough, one image blends into the next and you don't notice the empty space separating the images. Stare at the picture of stars and circles for at least 30 seconds. Then, immediately look at a white sheet of paper. What do you see on the paper? Why do you see this?

LESSON 5 REVIEW

In a movie, a nearsighted character starts a fire with her eyeglasses. At the same time, she describes in detail the small insect crawling up her arm. Is this possible? Explain your reasoning.

CAMERAS AND MOVIES

So far in this section, you've explored some of the science involved in creating and seeing both still and moving images. Now take a closer look at the technology that helps bring it all together. As you find out more about still cameras and motion pictures, think about how you might use these tools to create images of your own.

The Birth of Photography

This article describes the beginnings of photography in America. As you read, try to imagine what it must have been like for people to see their own images captured permanently for the first time.

THE DAGUERREOTYPE IN AMERICA

by **June L. Sargent** from *Cobblestone*

 Joseph Nicéphore Niépce took the earliest existing photograph in 1826 in France. Other experimenters, like Thomas Wedgewood, had produced images, but Niépce was the first to make them permanent.

Louis Jacques Mandé Daguerre was a stage designer in Paris who coproduced the diorama, a highly successful picture show that used special light effects. In an effort to find a mechanical method of producing pictures, Daguerre became Niépce's partner in 1829. But before Niépce's heliographic (etched by sunlight) process could be perfected, Niépce died.

By 1837, Daguerre produced a permanent photographic image. The daguerreotype, a silver-coated copper plate (sensitized by fuming with vapors of iodine), recorded a sharp image within a half hour when exposed to sunlight. Although the daguerreotype was expensive and laborious to prepare, it produced amazingly fine details and became extremely popular, especially in America.

Making a daguerreotype took a long time. A person could be required to sit still for approximately three minutes (some sittings could be longer). Any slight movement could distort the daguerreotype's image. To ensure that a subject did not move, a chair was developed that held the neck securely with a vise (a clamping device). Sometimes wrists and ankles were also strapped to the chair. In full-length daguerreotypes, a metal base can be seen behind the subject's feet.

The daguerreotype was important in the cultural development of America. It also helped the country make the transition from an agricultural to a technological society. Families afraid of separation by death could now obtain permanent images of

▲ Louis Daguerre

themselves together. Portraits of such famous personalities as Andrew Jackson, Edgar A. Poe, Jenny Lind, and Tom Thumb made

▲ Daguerreotype from the 1850s

them more real to the public. With the aid of the camera, the average American family could now view such exotic and faraway places as Africa, China, and Japan for the first time. The daguerreotype also became the eye of history, recording many important events.

Frontier photographers, like Robert H. Vance, were pioneers in a double sense. They explored a wild and

unsettled country and practiced a new science. Their daguerreotypes (prints made from negatives on glass were also used) of frontier towns, riverboats, miners, and Native Americans captured and preserved the adventurous flavor of life in the American West. As a result, hundreds of thousands of people migrated westward in search of golden opportunities.

The work of daguerreotypists helped educate the American people about themselves, their society, and the world. These early photographers can be considered artists, scientists, and historians all at the same time.

THINK ABOUT IT

How have photographs and movies helped you understand something about your family or the world around you? Tell how you think this technology makes a difference in our lives today.

How a Camera Works

Still cameras and film have changed dramatically since the time of the daguerreotype. As you look at the diagram below, think about ways in which the camera is similar to the human eye.

The *shutter speed control* lets you decide how long the shutter should be open to let light into the camera. Slower shutter speeds let in more light. You'd need a slower shutter speed on a cloudy day. Faster shutter speeds work better on a sunny day.

The *viewfinder* lets you look at an image before photographing it.

The *pentaprism* has mirrors to reflect the image you are photographing so that you can see it right side up. (The image is inverted when the light rays are refracted through the lens.)

The *release button* opens the shutter to let light into the camera.

The *aperture control* lets you adjust the amount of light coming into the camera. On a cloudy day, you might set the aperture to use the full diameter of the lens and let in plenty of light. On a bright day, you'd set the aperture to use less of the lens.

The *film* is a piece of plastic treated with light-sensitive chemicals. The light rays form a pattern on the film that is later developed to show the image.

The *lens*, or more often a series of lenses, refracts the rays of light to converge in a focal point on the film.

THINK ABOUT IT

Suppose you photograph a dimly lit indoor scene and later photograph a speeding race car in bright sunlight. How might your aperture control settings and your shutter speed control settings change?

Rana Segal:
Cinematographer

What is it like to be behind the eye of a camera? As you read the following, think about how the job described balances creativity with an understanding of technology.

▲ **Rana Segal shooting a scene**

Rana Segal became a filmmaker ten years ago. Now specializing in cinematography, Segal expresses her ideas on film. "I like creating beautiful images," explains Segal, "and cinematography is creating visual art."

Long before the camera starts to roll, Segal is involved in planning the shoot. "We sit down and decide how we want to convey the story with images. We deal with whether a shot will be a moving shot; a zoom or a close-up; a medium shot or a wide shot," explains Segal. She and her co-workers also discuss lighting.

"When we go to production, we are applying what we've already decided," says Segal. The production crew carries out the plan. Segal enjoys "working with a group to bring the project together."

Segal also works with many people outside of the film industry. "My favorite projects involve working with people who explore other cultures through film," says Segal. "One of the things I like about filmmaking is that it seems like a good way to continue the learning process."

Segal has some advice for aspiring cinematographers. "When you go to the movies, pay attention. Look at the lighting and what the camera is doing. But most of all," says Segal, "you have to have persistence. If you really want to do it, keep working at it."

LESSON 6 REVIEW

Compare and contrast the human eye with a camera.

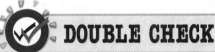

DOUBLE CHECK

SECTION A REVIEW

Suppose you film your own movie. Describe how you would use light and shadow, mirrors, lenses, and cameras.

SECTION B
In Living Color

How do colors affect what you see?
Why do you think some photographers choose to take photographs in color, some like to take them in black and white, and some prefer to use colored filters?

In this section, you'll explore how colors are formed and how photographers, filmmakers, and painters use color to share their views of the world. As you explore, use your Science Log to record some ways that you might use color in your artwork to share your view of the world.

1 LIGHT YOU CAN SEE

Perhaps you've walked home from school after a rainstorm and spotted a rainbow. In this lesson, you'll discover how sunlight is changed into a colorful rainbow.

ACTIVITY

What Color Is White Light?

Is white light white? Explore white light with a prism to find out.

MATERIALS
- clear plastic 2-L soda bottle
- water
- flashlight
- duct tape
- scissors
- Science Log data sheet

DO THIS

❶ Work with a partner. Fill the bottle two-thirds full of water. One partner squeezes the bottle to force the air out. The other partner tightens the bottle cap.

❷ Pinch one side of the bottle out as you push the other side down flat against the tabletop. Try to mold the bottle into a triangular shape.

❸ Place two pieces of duct tape across the flashlight lens to make a narrow (2-mm) slit.

❹ Darken the room and shine the flashlight onto the wall. What do you see?

❺ Now shine the light through different areas of your prism. Project the light on the wall. What do you see?

THINK AND WRITE

1. How did you turn your prism to get the best rainbows?

2. Were the colors always in the same order?

How Are Rainbows Formed?

There's something about rainbows that has inspired works of art and tales of fantasy. But what really causes a rainbow to form in the sky? This poem gives one person's view.

How Gray the Rain

by Elizabeth Coatsworth

How gray the rain
And gray the world
And gray the rain clouds overhead,
When suddenly
Some cloud is furled
And there is gleaming sun instead!

The raindrops drip
Prismatic light,
And trees and meadows burn
   in green,
And arched in air
Serene and bright
The rainbow all at once is seen.

Serene and bright
The rainbow stands
That was not anywhere before,
And so may joy
Fill empty hands
When someone enters
   through a door.

Rainbows are formed when the white light of the sun passes through raindrops. Each raindrop acts like a *prism*. The raindrop refracts, or bends, the light into the individual colors that make up the white light. These colors are the colors of the *visible spectrum*, the range of colors humans can see. Each color of the visible spectrum is refracted by a different amount. Red is refracted the most, followed by orange, yellow, green, blue, and finally violet, which is refracted the least. This series of refractions is what creates the bands of color that form a rainbow when the sun peeks through the clouds on a rainy day.

You may wish to write a poem about rainbows. Include in your poem at least one fact you have learned about rainbows.

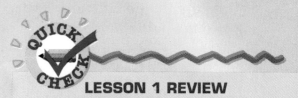

LESSON 1 REVIEW

Draw a ray diagram to show how white light is refracted through a prism. Include and label a different ray for each color of the visible spectrum.

2 BUILDING WITH COLORS

On a color TV screen, tiny bars of red, blue, and green combine to form all the brilliant colors you see as you watch a show. On these pages, you'll see how colors are created.

ACTIVITY

A Colored-Light Show

How do three colors combine to produce all the colors you see on TV? Do this activity to find out.

DO THIS

❶ Cover the lens of each flashlight with a different color of cellophane, and secure the cellophane with tape.

❷ In a darkened classroom, shine one flashlight at a time onto the white paper. Record what color you see.

❸ Shine the flashlights in combinations of two and three so the rays of light overlap on the paper. Make a chart to show the color each combination produces.

THINK AND WRITE

Describe how you would use primary-color filters on your flashlights to create special effects for a show.

Building Colors The colors of the tiny bars on a TV screen and the colored light beams of your flashlights are *primary light* colors. The colors created by combining primary light colors are *secondary light* colors.

Food-Color Kaleidoscope

Try this activity to see how products found in many kitchens and bakeries can be used to make a kaleidoscope of color.

DO THIS

1 Cover the bottom of the petri dish with 1 cm of milk.

2 Drip one drop of each food coloring onto the milk. The drops should be placed around the edge of the dish and should form the points of a square.

3 Place a drop of detergent in the center of the dish.

4 Observe the milk until the color movement stops. Record your observations.

5 Stir the colors together.

MATERIALS
- petri dish
- whole milk
- red, yellow, blue, and green food coloring
- liquid dish detergent
- dropper
- spoon
- Science Log data sheet

THINK AND WRITE

1. What new colors were made while the colors moved? What color did you observe after you stirred the colors together?

2. Why would it be helpful to know how to combine different-colored liquids to make new colors?

Testing Color Vision

You've explored how some colors are produced. Now it's time to investigate how your eyes see the colors around you.

MATERIALS
- meter stick
- several different-colored pieces of paper (each about 10 cm square)
- Science Log data sheet

DO THIS

1 One group member sits in a chair and looks straight ahead. A second group member holds the meter stick as shown. The zero mark should be beside an ear of the seated student.

2 Another student selects one of the pieces of colored paper. This student holds the paper alongside the meter stick. Next, this student moves the piece of paper along the meter stick until the seated student identifies the color. Record the point on the meter stick at which the student recognizes the color. Repeat this step for each color.

3 Repeat the experiment with another group member seated in the chair. Compare and discuss the results in your group and with other groups.

THINK AND WRITE

COMPARING You compared the distances at which each student could first see different colors through his or her peripheral vision. (*Peripheral* means "at the edges.") According to your comparison, was one color seen sooner— more easily—than the others? Explain.

How Do We See Color?

In Section A, you discovered some of the similarities between the lenses of your eyes and the lens of a camera. As you follow the path an image takes through a color TV camera and TV set to you, look for other similarities between TV equipment and your eyes.

What you see on a color TV set starts with an image. Prisms inside a color TV camera refract the light from the image in front of it into the primary light colors: red, green, and blue. Three camera tubes, one for each color, produce signals that communicate the image's color and brightness.

These signals are received by antennas or satellite dishes and are then broadcast to the receiver on a color TV. These signals carry all the information needed so the TV set can reproduce the image and the sound recorded by the camera. The TV receiver sends the signal to the TV picture tube.

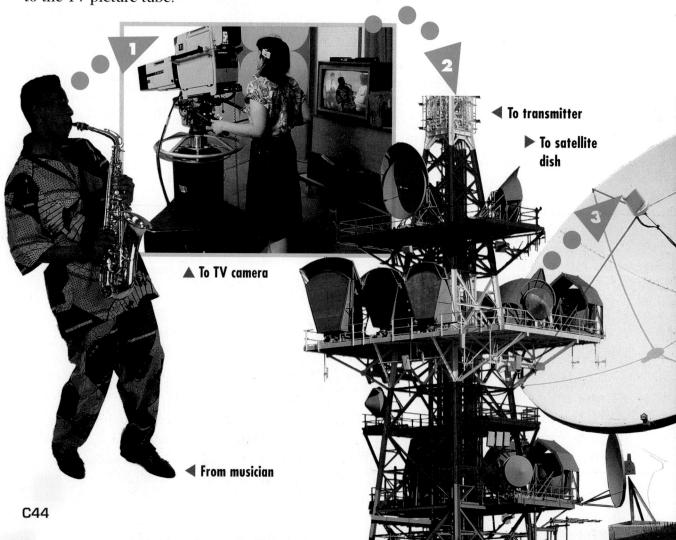

◀ To transmitter

▶ To satellite dish

▲ To TV camera

◀ From musician

The picture tube sends signals to the screen. The combination of color bars in red, green, and blue reproduces the original image in all of its many colors and degrees of brightness.

The color image is then reflected from the TV screen to your eyes. In each eye, the image passes through your pupil and lens and onto your retina.

When light hits your retina, two kinds of cells—rods and cones—are stimulated. *Rods* are not sensitive to color, but they help you see in very dim light. *Cones*, which are sensitive to color, need good light to work. There are three types of cones, each type sensitive to either red, green, or blue light. Cones work together to send information about the image's colors through your optic nerve.

The optic nerve for each of your eyes carries the information in the form of impulses to your brain. Your brain "translates" the information into a color image for you to see.

◀ To TV set

▼ To your eyes

5

4

QUICK CHECK

LESSON 2 REVIEW

❶ List how your eyes are like a TV camera. Compare your list with a classmate's.

❷ You're in charge of the lights for a stage show. You can use only three white lights and filters of any three colors. Tell what three colors you would choose and why.

3 WHY OPAQUE OBJECTS HAVE COLOR

You'd probably be surprised to see a black tomato or a red cucumber. But why do things appear to have a certain color? In this lesson, you'll discover why opaque objects have colors and how their colors can appear to change.

ACTIVITY

By Any Other Light

Can the color of light in which an object is seen affect the color the object seems to be? Do this activity to find out.

DO THIS

1 Cover the lens of each of three flashlights with either red, blue, or green cellophane, and secure the cellophane with tape. The light from the fourth flashlight will remain white.

◀ Tomato—white light

▼ Tomato—blue light

▼ Tomato—green light

▼ Tomato—red light

C46

❷ You'll be testing the color of opaque objects as you shine different colors of light on them. Make a table like the one below on which to record your results. Title your table.

white light								
red light								
blue light								
green light								

❸ Darken the room, and shine each color of light on each object. Record the color the object appears to be each time.

THINK AND WRITE

1. When you looked at an opaque object under white light, the color you saw was the color reflected by the object. All other colors were absorbed. For each object in your table, tell under each color of light which colors were absorbed and which were reflected.

2. Why do you think a red object appears black under green light?

3. Black objects *absorb* nearly all light. White objects *reflect* nearly all light. Tell why you think it's a good idea to wear white clothes on a hot, sunny day.

4. Add a new object to your chart. Predict what color it will be under each color of light. Test your predictions.

How Artists Create Color

Look through any collection of paintings in a museum or in a book, and you'll notice a tremendous variety of colors. How do you think artists create the many different colors for their paintings?

◀ **Sunday Afternoon on the Island of La Grande Jatte by Georges Seurat**

You've explored how red, blue, and green light can be combined to create color images for films and TV. Painters also combine colors to create new colors. But since they are working with paints, not light, they use a slightly different technique.

Paints are opaque—the colors we perceive are created by the light reflected by the paints. Each pigment, paint, and dye is made of materials that are especially good at absorbing light so that each reflects only one very specific color of light.

The *primary pigments*, like the primary colors of light, are colors that can be combined to create every other color. The primary pigments are yellow, magenta, and cyan.

Mixing pigments in different combinations will change the colors of light that are absorbed and reflected. That's why mixing pigments makes it possible to create thousands of different colors.

THINK ABOUT IT

Look at the notes you made when you overlapped primary colors of light. Do you think there is a relationship between the secondary light colors and the primary pigments? Explain.

Experimenting with Pigments

Painters must learn how to mix paints to create colors that are just right for their projects. Try your hand at mixing colors as you create some artwork.

DO THIS

1 Choose something you would like to create with paints.

2 Make a table like the one shown to record colors you might want to use for your project.

Possible Colors for my Project	
Colors Combined	Results
1 part cyan 1 part yellow	

3 Use a spoon to measure equal parts of two of the primary pigments, and mix them in a cup. Record your results on your table. Repeat the procedure, mixing equal parts of each possible combination of two primary pigments. Then combine equal parts of all three pigments. Record your results.

4 Continue experimenting with different proportions of primary pigments. Record your results.

5 Select appropriate colors and complete your art project.

THINK AND WRITE

How many different colors were you able to create from just three pigments?

LESSON 3 REVIEW

Mixing the three primary pigment colors in equal parts creates black. Explain why.

✔ DOUBLE CHECK

SECTION B REVIEW

1. How are the primary colors of light and the primary pigments alike? How are they different?

2. Why do you think many people wear black or other dark-colored clothing during winter to keep themselves warmer?

SECTION C
Sound Check!

▶ Tuning forks

Think of a concert you have attended or seen on TV. Lighting and special effects might have made it more exciting to watch, but listening to the music was probably more important to you. Sound effects in movies and TV shows often set the mood for the story. Just listen—sounds are all around you.

In this section, you'll explore some of the characteristics of sound and have a chance to create sounds of your own. What characteristics of sound are important to consider when preparing for and performing in a concert? In your Science Log, describe how sounds are produced and controlled during a concert.

1 TUNING IN TO SOUND

You're listening to a recording of your favorite group. You turn up the volume and begin to sing along. How are music and other sounds produced? How does sound travel? You'll find answers to these questions in this lesson.

Sound Out

Take some time to think about how sound is a part of your world. Here are some ideas to get you started.

Keep a Sound Log

Carry your Science Log with you for at least a day, and write down the sounds that you hear. Compare your list to a classmate's. Discuss what or who made each sound. Were you surprised at any of the sounds you heard? Do you think people living 200 years ago would have had the same list of sounds? Explain.

Write a Sound Poem

Buzz, crackle, clang, and *zap* are examples of words that sound like what they are describing. Writers use words like these to help readers "hear" the sounds being described. Make a list of words that describe sounds you hear during your day. Use those words in a poem.

Talk About Sound

Ask family members to describe one sound that they think is unpleasant and one sound they think is pleasant. Did you all have the same opinions about sounds? Explain your answer.

▲ Sound is all around.

THINK ABOUT IT

What are some other ways you can tune in to sounds?

What Happens When a Sound Is Made?

Hearing is one way of experiencing sounds. But you can also feel and see the effects of sounds. In this activity, what you see and feel will help you form a hypothesis about sounds.

MATERIALS
- coffee can
- plastic wrap
- rubber band
- salt
- pencil with eraser
- radio
- Science Log data sheet

DO THIS

1 Make a drum by stretching a piece of plastic wrap across the open end of an empty coffee can. Use the rubber band to hold the wrap tightly in place. Sprinkle a small amount of salt on top of the plastic wrap.

2 Gently tap the metal bottom of the coffee can with the eraser end of a pencil. What do you observe?

3 Now gently strike the plastic wrap, as if you were playing a drum. What do you observe now?

4 Place the coffee can on the radio, and turn the volume up. Observe the salt on the plastic wrap. Place your hands on the radio while the volume is turned up. What do you feel now?

5 Place your fingers gently on your throat while you hum a tune or say a few words. What do you feel?

THINK AND WRITE

HYPOTHESIZING You form a hypothesis to explain how or why something happens. Make a list of what you saw or felt for each sound you heard. Use your observations to write a hypothesis to explain how sounds are produced and transmitted.

Make a Telephone

Of all the sounds you hear throughout the day, the most common just might be a human voice. As you explore one way you can hear a voice, keep in mind the hypothesis you wrote after the last activity. See if your hypothesis is supported by what you discover.

MATERIALS
- pencil
- 6 small paper cups
- 6 small foam cups
- string, yarn, fishing line (each 6 m long)
- 12 paper clips
- Science Log data sheet

DO THIS

1 Use a pencil point to make a small hole in the center of the bottom of two paper cups.

2 Insert one end of a piece of string through the hole from the outside of one cup. Tie a paper clip onto the end of the string, and pull the clip and excess string back into the cup. Repeat this process with the other end of the string and another cup.

3 Hold one cup and give the other cup to a partner. Move apart until the string is stretched tight.

4 Talk into your cup while your partner holds the other cup over his or her ear. Take turns talking and listening through the paper-cup telephones. Try whispering. How well can you hear each other? Gently touch the string while you are talking. What do you feel?

5 Make new paper-cup telephones with lines made of yarn and of fishing line. Repeat steps 3 and 4.

6 Repeat steps 1–5, using the foam cups.

THINK AND WRITE

Compare the quality of sound you heard over each telephone. Which cup and telephone line were the best transmitters of sound?

Listening to Underwater Sounds

Most of the sounds you hear probably travel through air or solids. This passage tells about an animal that depends on its keen ability to hear underwater. Read the passage, and then do the next activity. Think about why dolphins and other whales depend on hearing, rather than sight, in their lives underwater.

Dolphins: Our Friends in the Sea

from *Dolphins: Our Friends in the Sea* by **Judith E. Rinard**

LITERATURE

In whales, hearing is the most highly developed sense. It helps them communicate, navigate, and find food in the ocean. They use a system of sound waves called echolocation. The dolphin's brain shows the greatest development in the areas devoted to hearing.

To echolocate, dolphins send out high-pitched clicking sounds—as many as 1,200 a second. The clicks may be seven to eight times higher than sounds humans can hear.

As a dolphin swims through the water, it moves its head back and forth to scan for objects ahead. When the clicking sounds hit an object, such as a rock or a fish, the sounds bounce back as echoes. Scientists hypothesize that these echoes travel through the dolphin's lower jaw to the inner ear.

▲ Above water, dolphins make sounds through air cavities.

Then they are transmitted to the brain. Much like a computer, the brain analyzes the echoes and tells the dolphin the location, size, and shape of the object.

In experiments designed to test the dolphin's ability to echolocate, scientists have found that a blindfolded dolphin can tell the difference between a dime and a nickel when both are thrown into the dolphin's pool!

THINK ABOUT IT

Describe any times when you have heard sounds underwater or when you have heard your voice echo, or bounce back to you.

A C T I V I T Y

The Medium Matters

Which is a better medium for carrying sound—air or water?
Do this activity to find out.

DO THIS

1 Work with a partner. Fill two balloons with water. Tie each closed with a piece of string. Take a balloon, and stand across the room from your partner.

2 Ask another student to strike a coat hanger with a wooden dowel. Describe what you hear.

3 Extend a long string between your water balloon and your partner's balloon as you hold your balloons against your ears. The string should be fairly taut.

MATERIALS
- several balloons
- water
- string
- I metal coat hanger
- wooden dowel
- Science Log data sheet

4 Have the third person hang the coat hanger on the string and strike it again. Have someone move the coat hanger to different parts of the string, and listen to how the sound changes when the coat hanger is struck. Record your observations.

5 Repeat steps 2 through 4 with balloons filled with air.

THINK AND WRITE

Does sound travel better in water or in air? Explain.

Taking a Closer Look at Sound

As you've discovered, every day you hear many different sounds from many different sources. But, as you will read below, all of the sounds you hear have one thing in common. Not sure what that thing is? Here's a hint: Think about what a guitar string does after it is plucked.

Sound waves are formed by an object's **vibrations**. The vibrations cause the molecules around the object to first press closer together and then to separate—again and again. This is like the action of pushing a long coiled spring forward, compressing the coils, and then pulling back, separating the coils. The energy of a vibration moves through the medium around an object in the same way as it moves down the length of the coiled spring.

The sound from a vibrating drumhead spreads outward in all directions. The pressure waves, formed by the compressing and separating of the air molecules, are like ever-enlarging spheres coming from the sound source at the center. The distance between two waves is one **wavelength**. As each wave moves outward, its energy is spread out more thinly. This is why a sound becomes softer as you move farther away from the source. The **frequency** of a sound tells how often a wave is produced.

Sound waves can travel through liquids, gases, or solids. In Section A, you read that light changed speed when it passed from one medium to another. A change in medium affects the speed of sound waves, too.

At sea level, sound travels through air at about 340 meters (1,115 feet) per second.

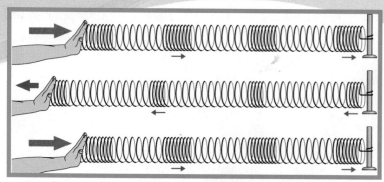

▲ Sound waves, like coils in a spring, move back and forth.

▲ Sound waves spread outward in circles.

▲ Sound travels through water, a liquid.

Sound travels through water at about 1,500 meters (4,921 feet) per second.

Sound travels through wood at about 3,800 meters (12,467 feet) per second. Denser materials, such as steel, carry sound even faster, at more than 5,000 meters (16,404 feet) per second.

Why do you think sound travels faster in solids than in liquids or gases? Here's a hint: In a solid, the molecules are closer together than they are in a gas or a liquid. Now think again about why the type of medium affects the speed at which sound travels.

▲ Sound travels through air, a gas.

▲ Sound travels through wood, a solid.

LESSON 1 REVIEW

Explain in your own words how sound is produced and how it travels.

2 HOW WE HEAR SOUND

Have you ever cupped your hand to your ear to help you hear a faint sound? If so, you've already discovered the first step in the path a sound takes on the way to being heard by you. Read on to find out more.

The Ears Have It

Have you ever thought about why your ears are shaped as they are? How are your ears different from the ears of other animals?

▲ Cupping an ear helps gather sound waves.

▼ Some animals, such as deer, dogs, and bats, can move their ears to help gather sound waves.

The curves and ridges of the human ear serve an important purpose. They collect the sound waves that travel into your ear.

Many animals have ears adapted to collect sound waves, too. Compare the animal ears pictured and your own. Why do you think it would be an advantage to have large ears that can move and turn?

Once the sound is collected by the outer ear, a chain of events enables you to hear the waves in the form of a sound. Look at the diagram to see what happens.

Listen to the sounds around you. Now try covering your ears with your hands. You can still hear some sound, although perhaps less clearly. Why? Sound waves hitting your skull cause it to vibrate. These vibrations cause the cochlea to vibrate, and the process continues as if the sound waves had entered through the ear.

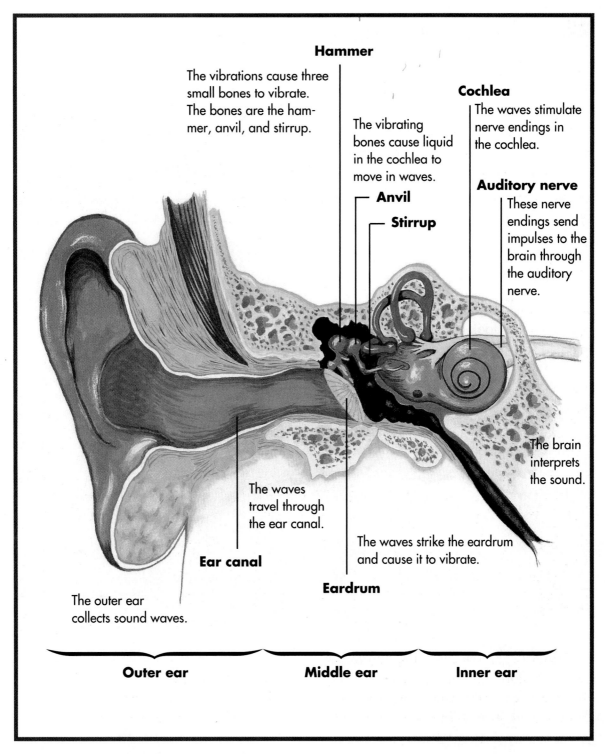

Hammer

The vibrations cause three small bones to vibrate. The bones are the hammer, anvil, and stirrup.

Cochlea

The waves stimulate nerve endings in the cochlea.

The vibrating bones cause liquid in the cochlea to move in waves.

— **Anvil**

— **Stirrup**

Auditory nerve

These nerve endings send impulses to the brain through the auditory nerve.

The brain interprets the sound.

The waves travel through the ear canal.

Ear canal

The waves strike the eardrum and cause it to vibrate.

Eardrum

The outer ear collects sound waves.

Outer ear   **Middle ear**   **Inner ear**

THINK ABOUT IT

Why do you think it is helpful to have an ear on each side of your head? Discuss with a partner some of the advantages and disadvantages of the placement and shape of human ears.

Hearing in Different Ways

The passage below is from a book about Amy Rowley, who has been hearing-impaired since birth. As you read, look for devices and skills Amy uses to communicate with hearing people.

Amy: THE STORY OF A DEAF CHILD

by **Lou Ann Walker,** with photographs by **Michael Abramson**

 I love to climb trees. I also like to take care of my pets—my rabbit Brown Eyes, my cat Checkers, and my parakeet Garfield. Also my fish. If you look closely at this picture, you can see my hearing aid. My mom and dad are deaf, too. My brother John is hearing. He's thirteen. I'm eleven.

In the mornings, my alarm clock has a flashing light to wake me up. I like it better when my mom comes to get me out of bed.

▲ Amy with a "friend"

▲ Amy's body aid helps her understand another student.

Our house also has lights that flash when someone rings the doorbell.

I can hear myself talking right now. I can hear some sounds, but I can't understand everything. Say I heard an ambulance go by. I wouldn't know what it was unless I saw it.

All the other kids who go to my school are hearing. I'm the only deaf person at Furnace Woods School.

When I'm in school, I wear a body aid: a big hearing aid that fits on my belt. My teachers wear microphones that send signals to the body aid.

Reading lips helps me understand what people are saying. But I can't really understand the noises I hear from my body aid without looking at people's mouths.

If I can't figure out what the teacher is saying, I ask "What?" Then he repeats it, and I look closer at his mouth. I probably say "What?" more than most people do, but I want to know everything that is going on. Sometimes kids don't understand what I say, and so I have to repeat myself, too.

Some people shout at me. They think I'll be able to hear them better. It's harder to understand them, though, because shouting makes their mouths look strange so that I can't even lip-read.

▲ Amy and a friend are finger-spelling.

Lots of hearing people ask me what it's like to be deaf, but I never ask them what it's like to be hearing.

I think deafness feels like peace. Hearing people have to hear all sorts of things they don't want to hear. I don't.

LESSON 2 REVIEW

❶ Suppose Amy is coming to your school. What can be done to make sure Amy is able to attend the same classes and do the same activities as hearing people?

❷ How can a person who can't hear make up for the impairment by using his or her other senses? Make a list of your ideas.

❸ List three new things you have learned about hearing.

3 COMPARING SOUNDS

You've discovered that all sounds have one thing in common: They are caused by vibrations that form sound waves. But all sounds don't sound the same, do they? As you do the activity and read the information on this and the following pages, look for ways to describe the sounds you most like to hear.

A C T I V I T Y

Make Your Own Music

You don't need to buy a musical instrument to create sound. All you need are a few ordinary objects and a little bit of creativity. Try it!

DO THIS

1 Make a table to keep track of each sound you discover and to tell how it is made. On your table, record any observations you make about the sound and its characteristics. The next page shows one way you might organize your data.

2 Work in a group to make a variety of sounds, using your materials. Combine materials to make musical instruments. Strike different objects with spoons. Strike gently if the object is glass. Instruments you've seen, such as drums or guitars, might give you some ideas. Try to invent new ways of making sound, too.

MATERIALS
collection of readily available objects, such as
- plastic and metal containers with lids
- marbles
- cardboard boxes
- plastic wrap and wax paper
- rubber bands of different sizes
- pieces of wood
- drinking straws
- string or fishing line
- glass bottles filled with water
- metal and plastic pipes
- wooden, metal, and plastic spoons
- Science Log data sheet

Materials	What We Did	Observations
wood blocks rubber bands and shoe box		

3 As you make your observations, consider the following questions:

- Is the sound loud or soft?

- Which materials make the highest sounds?

- What can you do to change a sound without changing the materials used?

THINK AND WRITE

1. What, of anything you tried, made a sound you could barely hear? Why do you think that happened?

2. What variables affect the characteristics of a sound?

3. **COMPARING** Comparing provides you with an opportunity to determine the characteristics of each instrument in the activity. Describe how you determined which instrument made the highest sound.

Qualities of Sound

A TV show or a concert wouldn't be very interesting if it weren't for the great variety of the sounds that we can hear. As you read, look for ways to describe the sounds you created in the last activity.

▲ Tuba

◄ School band

▲ Flute

Sounds can be described as having pitch and volume. *Pitch* describes how high or low a sound is. *Volume* describes how loud or soft a sound is. First let's take a closer look at pitch.

You've discovered that a sound is made by vibrations. Think about how a guitar string vibrates when it is plucked. The speed of the string's vibration, or its *frequency*, affects the pitch. Frequency is measured in number of vibrations per second, or *hertz*. Humans hear sounds ranging from about 20 hertz (a very low pitch) to 20,000 hertz (a very high pitch).

A tuba has a lower pitch than a flute. A violin has a higher pitch than a bass. Think about the instruments you made in the last activity. Which instrument had the lowest pitch? Which had the highest pitch?

Pitch is affected by the amount of matter that is vibrating. In stringed musical instruments, a longer or thicker string has a lower pitch than a shorter or thinner string. In wind instruments, a larger column of air produces a lower pitch than a smaller column of air. The more material there is to vibrate, the lower the pitch will be.

▶ Violin

▲ Bass

C64

Tension affects pitch, too. A tighter string produces a higher pitch than a looser string.

Most musical instruments can play a range of pitches. These pitches are called tones. Tones form a musical scale, and a scale with eight tones is called an *octave*.

The letters on this staff represent the tones in one octave. The pitch of the tones gets higher as you move up the scale.

Pitch isn't the only thing that affects how something sounds. Use your hand to strike a table or desk gently. Now use the same part of your hand to strike the table harder. You haven't changed the pitch of the sound, but you have changed the volume.

When you hit the table the second time, you used more energy and increased the sound's volume. A sound's volume is measured in *decibels*.

Sounds that are louder than 100 decibels can permanently damage your ears. Many construction and factory workers and people working on airport runways must wear ear protectors. Listening to any sound at a high volume, such as music or noise from a TV, can damage your ears if you do it over a long period of time.

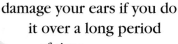

▼ TV, 60 decibels or more

▲ A whisper, 20 decibels

▲ Jet airplane, 140 decibels

QUICK CHECK

LESSON 3 REVIEW

❶ What is the difference between pitch and volume?

❷ How can a sound's pitch and volume be changed?

4 CONTROLLING SOUND

Have you ever been told to turn down loud music at home?

Have you ever had trouble hearing a speaker in an auditorium?

As you read, think about times that sound volume needs to be controlled.

ACTIVITY

Throwing Your Voice

Sound engineers can control sound in many ways. In this activity, you will become a sound engineer by directing sound.

DO THIS

❶ Stand back-to-back with a partner.

❷ Hold an open umbrella to one side. Talk in a normal voice as you slowly move the umbrella until it is in front of your face. Ask your partner to listen for any changes in the way your voice sounds. Can your partner guess when the umbrella is directly in front of your face?

❸ Give your partner the other umbrella. Stand back-to-back again, and hold your umbrellas in front of your faces. Speak again while your partner listens. Can your partner tell the difference between your voice now and when there was just one umbrella?

4 Line the inside of the umbrellas with foil and try steps 2 and 3 again. Can you notice a difference in the sound?

THINK AND WRITE

Draw diagrams to show how the sound waves traveled in steps 2 and 3. Use your diagrams to explain the difference made by the second umbrella. What effect did the foil have?

Testing for Sound

If your favorite band came to your school, where would its music sound the best? Do this activity to find out.

DO THIS

1 Describe each room. How large is it? What materials are on the floor, ceiling, windows, and walls? What kind of furniture is there?

2 In each room, place the tape player on the floor. Always play the same song at the same volume.

3 Listen from several locations within the room. Describe how the music sounds. Can you hear echoes?

THINK AND WRITE

In which room did the music sound best? What conditions in that room might have helped make it a good room for listening to music?

MATERIALS
- several rooms in your school
- tape player and music tape of your choice
- Science Log data sheet

Sounding Good

In the last activity, you identified rooms that were good places to listen to music. Now read to find out why sound carries better in some rooms than in others.

Acoustics is the science of sound. One important application of acoustics is in the design of buildings.

You've discovered that sound is produced by vibrations that form waves. Understanding how the sound waves can be reflected or absorbed is important to a knowledge of acoustics.

For a place like a concert hall or an auditorium, "good acoustics" would mean that music or other sounds can be heard clearly anywhere in the room. The shape of an auditorium is important for good acoustics. A curved ceiling, for example, can help reflect sound waves from the stage to the audience. Acoustics can even be affected in an outdoor performance area. How do you think the backdrop of the outdoor theater shown on the next page reflects sound?

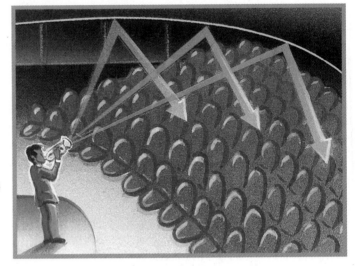

Sometimes you hear echoes when sound is reflected. *Echoes* are reflected sound waves. They occur when sound waves are reflected from a distant source, like the wall of a canyon. If a sound is reflected from several different points, you hear *reverberation,* a quick series of echoes.

Sometimes rooms are designed to absorb sound instead of reflecting it. Soft materials, like carpets and drapes, help absorb sound waves. Acoustical tile, a soft tile with tiny holes in it, is used in ceilings and walls of recording studios and other places where people do not want sound to be reflected.

Factories often need to soundproof areas where noisy machinery is used. Walls, floors, and ceilings are constructed with materials that absorb sound so that the noise does not travel to other parts of the building.

Acoustics are important in homes, too. Carpeting and insulated walls can help keep sound from traveling from one room to another.

▲ Hollywood Bowl

▲ Food court

▲ Printing press

▲ Recording studio

▲ Canyon

▲ Home

▲ Library

QUICK CHECK

LESSON 4 REVIEW

Design a recording studio for your school, and tell what materials you would use to build it.

DOUBLE CHECK

SECTION C REVIEW

Think of a concert you have attended or of a place where you have listened to music. Describe how different instruments produced sound. Tell about the acoustics of the site.

SECTION D
Switch It On!

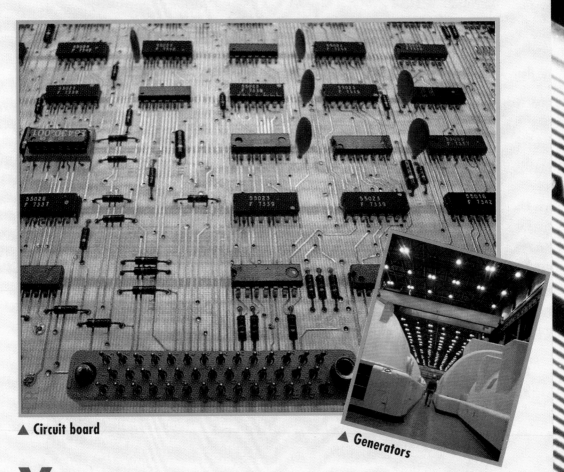

▲ Circuit board

▲ Generators

You've seen how light and sound each play a role in the creation and recording of much of what you see in a live performance or on TV. But there's one key ingredient that helps bring it all together: electricity.

How is electricity used in creating, recording, and transmitting stage performances? As you explore ways that electricity can be controlled, research ways in which electronics is used to create music. Describe types of musical performances that depend on electronic sound. Record the results of your research in your Science Log.

1 LET THE CURRENT FLOW

How does electricity "know" where to go when you plug in an electric guitar and switch it on? In this lesson, you will discover how the flow of electricity is controlled.

The Electronic Stage

You may have enjoyed a concert like this one in person or on TV. Now take a look at the equipment that uses electricity during the show.

Sounds from the electric guitar can be amplified so they are heard throughout the auditorium. The microphone turns the singer's voice into electronic impulses that can be amplified and recorded. Electronic synthesizers can produce any sound you can think of. Speakers amplify and direct the sounds.

Backstage, an engineer uses an electronic soundboard to control the volume and balance of the sounds. Even if you miss the show, you can enjoy it later. Video and sound equipment can record the show for broadcast.

THINK ABOUT IT

How is electricity used during a concert?

ACTIVITY

Your Own Circuit

You began your investigations in this unit by wondering about what goes into staging and recording a musical performance. Do this activity to investigate how electronic equipment really works.

DO THIS

1 Work with the bulb, battery, and wires until you get the bulb to light. Draw a picture to show exactly how you arranged the materials to turn on the light.

2 Connect the materials to light the bulb in as many other ways as possible.

THINK AND WRITE

1. Draw a diagram to represent each of your arrangements. Use the symbols for the battery, wire, and light as shown on the diagram below.

2. Look at your diagrams. Compare your successful and unsuccessful attempts to light the bulb. What was needed to produce a successful circuit?

Simple Circuit Each time you arranged your materials to light the bulb, you created an electric circuit. An **electric circuit** is a closed pathway for electricity to follow. Scientists use circuit diagrams like this one to show what is happening in an electric circuit.

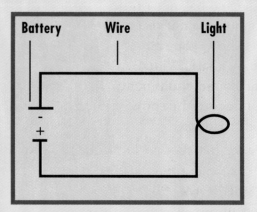

A Water Circuit

What images come to mind when you think of current flowing through an electric circuit? Since you can't see electric current, take a moment to think about a circuit you can see. Look for similarities between the water circuit described and the electric circuits you created.

▼ The pump rotates, creating a pressure difference to drive the water. A stronger pump would push the water through faster.

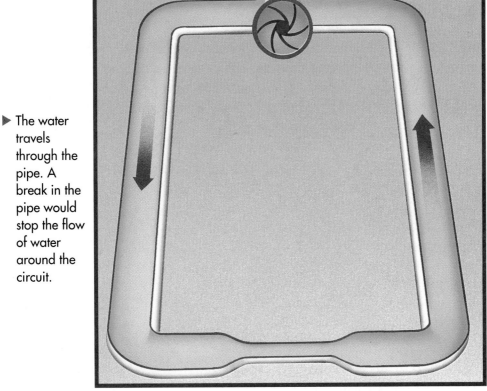

▶ The water travels through the pipe. A break in the pipe would stop the flow of water around the circuit.

◀ The water returns to the pump, and the cycle continues.

▲ The narrowed pipe slows the flow of water passing through the pipe.

THINK ABOUT IT

Compare the water circuit described above with the electric circuits you made. Which parts of an electric circuit function like the water pump and pipe? Which part of an electric circuit would affect the flow of current, just as the narrowed water pipe slows the flow of water?

▶ A battery's negative terminal has more negative charges than positive charges.

▲ A battery's positive terminal has more positive charges than negative charges.

What Is an Electric Circuit?

Whether you are using electricity to light a single bulb or to fill an auditorium with sights and sounds, the principles of electric circuits remain the same. As you continue to explore electric circuits, keep in mind the model of the water circuit.

Resistance is a measure of how much a material opposes the flow of electricity. The wire inside the light bulb resists the flow of electricity. The resistance causes the filament to heat up and glow.

Current is the flow of negatively charged atomic particles called *electrons*.

THINK ABOUT IT

Why does an electric light bulb glow?

◀ An electric circuit is the path from one terminal to the other along which electricity flows.

▶ Wire provides the pathway along which electrons flow from the negative terminal to the positive terminal.

How Strong Are Your Batteries?

Earlier in this section, you used a battery to light a light bulb. In this activity, you'll explore ways to increase the amount of energy in a system.

DO THIS

1 Make a circuit by using one battery, the wire, and the bulb. Observe the brightness of the light.

2 Add a second battery to your circuit by placing the positive end of one battery against the negative end of the other battery. Observe the brightness of the light. How does it compare with the light produced by one battery?

3 Repeat step 2, adding a third and then a fourth battery.

THINK AND WRITE

1. Describe the relationship between the number of batteries and the brightness of the bulb.

2. EXPERIMENTING When you experiment in an activity, you are comparing the effects of variables. How might your experiment have been affected if you had used two light bulbs?

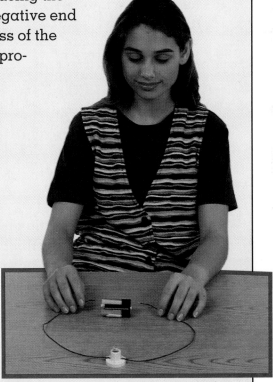

Conductor or Insulator?

Can the materials used in an electric circuit affect the flow of electric current? As you do this activity, think about when it might be useful to prevent the flow of current altogether.

DO THIS

1 Make a table with the headings *Conductors* and *Insulators*.

2 Put the bulb, the battery, and two pieces of the wire together so that the bulb lights.

3 Add a third piece of wire to your circuit. One end of two of the wires should not be attached to anything. When you touch the two unattached ends of wires together, your bulb should light.

MATERIALS
- light bulb and holder
- battery and holder
- 3 10-cm pieces of insulated wire, with 1 cm of bare wire on each end
- a collection of materials such as paper cups, nails, screws, toothpicks, plastic and metal spoons, rubber erasers, and cloth
- Science Log data sheet

4 Look over your collection of materials. Predict which items will make the bulb light when the item is touched by the loose ends of the two wires.

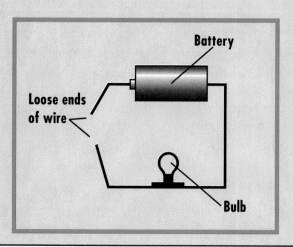

Battery

Loose ends of wire

Bulb

5 Choose one item from your collection of materials. Place the free end of each wire 1 cm apart on the material. If the bulb lights, write the name of the item under the column heading *Conductors*. If the bulb does not light, write the name of the item under the column heading *Insulators*. Repeat this step for each of the materials you collected, and record the results in your table.

THINK AND WRITE

1. Based on your observations, define the terms *conductor* and *insulator*.

2. Describe one way you might use an insulator in an electric circuit.

Superconductors Materials that allow electricity to pass through them are called *conductors*. Materials through which electricity will not pass are *insulators*.

Some materials, such as tin and lead, allow electricity to pass very easily when they are cooled to a very low temperature. When this happens, such a material becomes a *superconductor*. Superconductors can carry more electricity faster and farther. They can be used to make faster computers and more efficient motors.

The Amazing Tesla

Electric appliances require a great deal of electricity. Read about the man who made this widespread use of electricity possible.

REDISCOVERING TESLA

by **Bill Lawren** from *Omni*

Nikola Tesla insisted on having exactly 18 napkins before him at every dinner, regardless of the number of guests, and would not stay in the same room with a woman wearing pearl earrings. His startling lab demonstrations were considered better entertainment than an evening at the theater.

But there was a good deal more to Tesla than parlor magic. By 1898 he had already created two inventions that would change the world: alternating current, which made the widespread distribution of electricity possible; and the high frequency coil, which helped lay the groundwork for every broadcasting system from radio to radar. His radical and imaginative thinking foreshadowed and, to some degree, provided the conceptual basis for a remarkable variety of modern technologies.

By the middle of this century, however, Tesla had been all but forgotten. Many of his inventions were attributed to others, and his ideas were often dismissed as the ramblings of a madman. Now, Tesla and his more futuristic ideas are enjoying a revival. His work has been taken up by a new generation of inventors, researchers, and tinkerers. Like Tesla himself, they defy easy classification: They seem to run the gamut from hardheaded, practical engineers to wild-eyed fanatics. The range of their ideas is equally broad. They are working on everything from more efficient pumps and more powerful jet engines to the secret of time travel.

Tesla was born in 1856 in the tiny village of Smilijan, Croatia. From his childhood on, he demonstrated a fondness for outrageously ingenious ideas. As a student he dreamed of sending intercontinental mail via a huge sub-Atlantic tunnel. By age twenty-eight, he had already designed a prototype for the motor that would change the world.

In the 1800s, electricity was direct current, or DC, and was a purely local phenomenon. Without expensive generators to boost power over long distances, electricity could be

◀ Nikola Tesla

▼ Generating artificial lightning
in Tesla's laboratory

transmitted only a few miles. Tesla designed a generator that produced current in alternating impulses. These could sustain high-voltage transmission over long distances. With this alternating current, or AC, system, electricity could be sent cheaply anywhere wires could be strung.

After a brief and stormy partnership with Thomas Edison, Tesla enlisted the support of industrialist George Westinghouse to develop a model for his AC system that revolutionized the use of electricity. He later developed the "Tesla Coils," an invention that led to the wireless transmission of electromagnetic waves: the radio. 📖

QUICK CHECK

LESSON 1 REVIEW

1 How are conductors and insulators useful in everyday life?

2 Do you think that Tesla's characteristics helped make him a good scientist? Explain.

2 SERIES AND PARALLEL CIRCUITS

If you were watching a concert and one of the stage lights burned out, would you expect every other piece of electronic equipment to stop working? Of course not! In this lesson, you'll explore different ways to construct an electric circuit and how to choose the best way.

ACTIVITY

Different Circuits

You've already shown how you can combine wire, a bulb, and batteries to make a bulb light. Is every circuit that lights a bulb identical? Do this activity to find out.

DO THIS

❶ Make a table to record your data. Set up circuit 1 as shown. Touch both screws on the bulb holder with the wires from the voltmeter. Record the reading on the voltmeter. Remove one battery from the circuit, and record the new reading.

❷ Set up circuit 2 as shown. Test the bulb with the voltmeter, and record your results. Remove one battery, test the bulb, and record your new results.

MATERIALS
- 2 batteries
- 2 battery holders
- 2 light bulbs
- 2 bulb holders
- voltmeter (0–3 V)
- 4 20-cm pieces of insulated copper wire, with 1 cm of bare wire on each end
- Science Log data sheet

3 Set up circuit 3 as shown. Test each bulb with the voltmeter. Record your results. Unscrew one of the bulbs. Test both bulbs with the voltmeter, and record your new results.

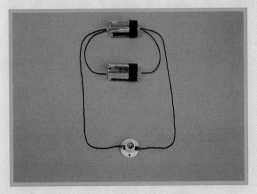

▲ **Circuit 1**

4 Set up circuit 4 as shown. Test both bulbs with the voltmeter, and record your results. Unscrew one bulb, test the remaining bulb, and record your results again.

THINK AND WRITE

1. Which circuit's bulb produced the brightest light? Which circuit's voltmeter reading was the highest? the lowest?

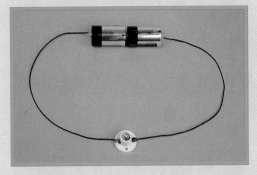

▲ **Circuit 2**

2. Which circuits were not affected by removing a battery? by removing a bulb?

3. Which circuit do you think has the most advantages and the fewest disadvantages?

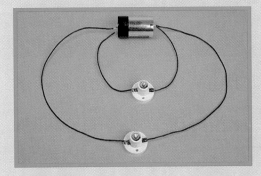

▲ **Circuit 3**

▲ **Voltmeter**

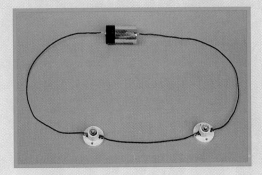

▲ **Circuit 4**

Comparing Circuits

As you observed in the previous activity, the way you wire a circuit affects how it works. Take a closer look and compare two different kinds of circuits.

▼ In the circuit shown below, the current has only one path to follow. If one bulb is removed, the circuit is broken, and no bulbs will light. This is a *series circuit*.

▼ In this circuit, the current has more than one path to follow. If one bulb is removed, there is still a complete circuit to light the other bulb. This is a *parallel circuit*.

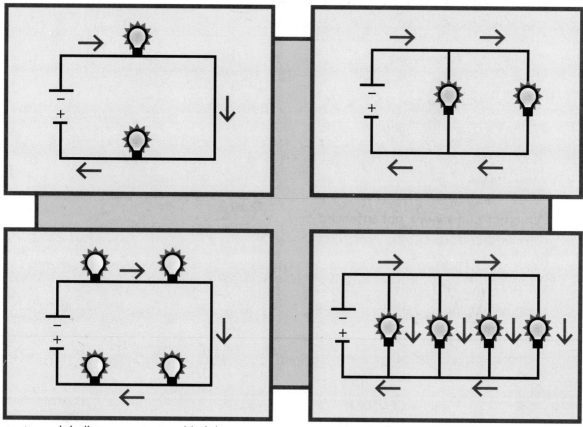

▲ As each bulb in a series is added, less energy is available to light each bulb. All the bulbs become dimmer.

▲ Adding bulbs to a parallel circuit does not affect the bulbs' brightness. Each circuit carries current to only one bulb.

THINK ABOUT IT

How would adding an extra bulb affect a series circuit? a parallel circuit? Explain.

ACTIVITY

Which Batteries Last Longer?

Have you ever discovered that your flashlight didn't work when you needed it? Has your portable radio faded out in the middle of your favorite song? Then you know the importance of helping batteries last as long as possible. In this activity, you'll use water flowing from a bottle as a model of current flowing from a battery.

DO THIS

1 Working with a partner, stick a strip of masking tape around the middle of one bottle to separate it into two halves. Then completely fill the bottle with water.

2 Fill each of the other two bottles half full of water.

3 Begin emptying one half-full bottle of water at the same time your partner begins emptying the full bottle. When your first bottle is empty, immediately begin emptying your second bottle.

MATERIALS
- 3 1-L plastic bottles
- masking tape
- water
- Science Log data sheet

THINK AND WRITE

1. Did the full bottle or the two half-full bottles empty first?

2. Which bottle or bottles could represent two batteries connected in series? in parallel?

3. **HYPOTHESIZING** When you hypothesize, you base your explanation on what you already know. Use your observations from this activity as a basis for hypothesizing which would completely use up its energy first: two batteries connected in series or two batteries connected in parallel. Describe how you could test your hypothesis.

Using the Right Circuit

You've explored the differences between series and parallel circuits. How can this understanding be applied?

Homes and offices are wired in parallel circuits. Suppose that your home were wired in a series circuit: Every appliance and light would have to be on or off at the same time. But a switch is wired in series with the appliance it controls.

▲ Parallel circuits make productions possible, allowing the producers to use a variety of multi-media equipment.

QUICK CHECK

LESSON 2 REVIEW

❶ How could you determine whether a string of lights is connected in a series circuit or in a parallel circuit?

❷ Describe when and why you would use a parallel circuit.

3 CREATING WITH ELECTRONICS

Now that you understand how electricity works, you can think about how it can be used. Read this article about how one man's understanding of electricity—and his curiosity—led to one of the most common home appliances.

TV Pioneer

Today TV is common. Almost every home has a TV. Some have two or three! Your grandparents probably remember when that was not so.

PHILO FARNSWORTH: Forgotten Inventor

by Jeanne Field Olson from *Cobblestone*

 Modern television began the day young Philo Farnsworth looked back over the Idaho field he was harrowing. The pattern of the soil, shaped into rows by the harrow's disks, inspired Farnsworth's creation of the first all-electronic television system. Farnsworth believed that television could be transmitted electronically and had been trying to figure out a way to do it. Looking at the rows in the field, he realized that he could use an electron beam to scan an image line by line to turn it into an electrical pulse. That pulse could then be sent to a television receiver.

Philo Farnsworth was born in a log cabin in Utah in 1906. He was thirteen when his first invention, a "thief-proof" auto lock, won a national contest. He soon lost interest in mechanical inventions, however, and became fascinated with electricity and electrons after his family moved to Idaho, where his uncle managed a ranch that had a power plant. Philo watched the repairman who came whenever the power plant broke down and was soon able to fix it himself.

▲ Harrowed field

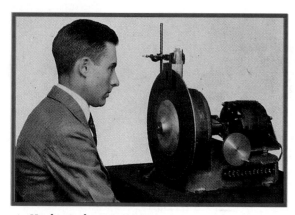

▲ **Mechanical transmission system**

A generator supplied electricity to the Farnsworths' Idaho home. Philo took apart and reassembled this generator many times. He added electric motors to his mother's hand-cranked washing machine and foot-powered sewing machine.

Farnsworth read everything he could find about electricity. He even drove a horse-drawn school wagon to earn money to buy books on the subject. Reading about early mechanical television experiments using spinning disks interested him in the idea of television. Even then he was convinced that only an all-electronic television system could succeed.

Justin Tolman, Philo's science teacher at Rigby High School in Idaho, recognized his pupil's interest and rare scientific ability and tutored him outside of class. One day after school in February 1922, fifteen-year-old Philo drew diagrams for Tolman on the school blackboards explaining his theories of an "image dissector" television camera tube and an all-electronic television system.

The next fall the Farnsworth family moved back to Utah, and Philo had to leave school. He worked at a variety of jobs from janitor to railroad electrician while taking correspondence courses in electricity and briefly attending Brigham Young University. He continued his television experiments in the college labs.

Philo met George Everson, a professional fund raiser, while both were working on a Salt Lake City Community Chest campaign. Philo was normally quiet and shy, but his enthusiasm and knowledge of electronics convinced Everson to invest six thousand dollars of his own savings in Philo's research. He also agreed to contact potential investors in California.

The conservative California bankers Everson contacted invested twenty-five thousand dollars and gave Philo Farnsworth one year to prove that his electronic camera tube could transmit a picture. He began working behind drawn blinds in a simple lab above a garage at 202 Green Street, San Francisco. His bride, Pem, learned to spot weld and helped with drafting and secretarial work.

▼ **Philo Farnsworth**

▲ First TV transmission (about 1934)

Cliff Gardner, Farnsworth's best friend and Pem's brother, was his assistant, learning glass blowing to create the special glass tubes needed.

In less than a year, Farnsworth succeeded. He was barely twenty-one when his television camera transmitted the world's first completely electronic picture on September 7, 1927. After another year's work, Farnsworth was able to transmit a much-improved picture.

THINK ABOUT IT

What made Philo Farnsworth a scientist? Describe character traits and actions he took that enabled him to realize his dream.

Putting It All Together

You've done a lot of exploring to discover how light, sound, and electricity work. Now is your chance to put your knowledge to use. Follow these guidelines for planning, recording, and sharing your own multimedia presentation.

START WITH AN IDEA

Decide what kind of show you will video-tape. A concert? A music video? A play? Figure out how to use your best talents.

FIND OUT WHAT EQUIPMENT YOU HAVE

Find out what you can borrow from your school, family members, or other people in the community.

⚠️ **CAUTION:** Find out what you need to know about using equipment safely before you begin. Ask an adult to help you with any piece of equipment that is new to you.

ASSIGN JOBS

Each member of the group should have a job to do. You'll need people to—

- write the script and plan the show.
- run the camera, lights, and any other equipment.
- perform in the show.
- plan and advertise the presentation.

GET SUPPORT

Involve people outside the school in your efforts. A local video store might lend equipment or donate supplies. Parents might help make any needed costumes or props.

KEEP A RECORD

Make a behind-the-scenes record of the process, using photographs or a video camera. Use what you've learned about sound, light, and electricity to help explain what is happening at each step.

ON WITH THE SHOW!

Share your video with as many people as possible. Show it in the school auditorium or the public library. See whether a local cable-access channel will let you broadcast your show.

LESSON 3 REVIEW

When putting on a show, you may be a director or a camera person, but how are you a scientist?

DOUBLE CHECK

SECTION D REVIEW

Using what you learned in this section, explain how science is a part of our everyday lives. Include at least five new things you learned about light, sound, and electricity.

I REFLECT

I t's time to think about the ideas you have discovered during your investigations. Think, too, about your many accomplishments.

SUMMARIZE

Answer the following in your Science Log.

1. What **I Wonder** questions have you answered in your investigations, and what new questions have you asked?

2. What have you discovered, and how have your ideas changed?

3. Did any of your discoveries surprise you? Explain.

CONNECT IDEAS

1. Describe one way in which light, sound, and electricity interact.

2. Think about the people you have read about and the experiences you have had in this unit. Tell what you think makes a good scientist.

3. How have advances in audio and visual technology affected our lives?

4. Think about the different jobs involved in planning and recording a televised event. Describe a job that interests you, and tell why you chose it.

SCIENCE PORTFOLIO

1 Complete your Science Experiences Record.

2 Choose several samples of your best work from each section to include in your Science Portfolio.

3 On A Guide to My Science Portfolio, tell why you chose each sample.

Scientists share their discoveries and ideas and learn from one another. How can you share what you've learned?

Decide

► what you want to say.

► what the best way is to get your message across.

Share

► what you did and why.

► what worked and what didn't work.

► what conclusions you have drawn.

► what else you'd like to find out.

Find Out

► what classmates liked about what you shared—and why.

► what questions your classmates have.

SHOW OF THE YEAR!

featuring
the music of the Zip Tops
comedy acts

TUESDAY MAY 10
3:00 P.M.
Parker School Auditorium

Watch us again on cable 43!
May 20 at 7:00 P.M.

I ACT

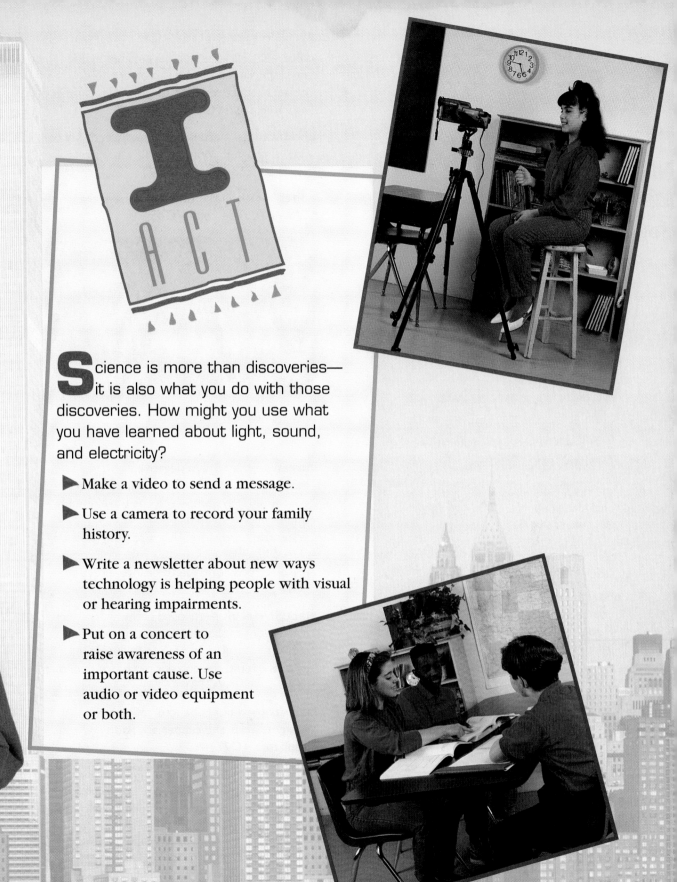

Science is more than discoveries—it is also what you do with those discoveries. How might you use what you have learned about light, sound, and electricity?

▶ Make a video to send a message.

▶ Use a camera to record your family history.

▶ Write a newsletter about new ways technology is helping people with visual or hearing impairments.

▶ Put on a concert to raise awareness of an important cause. Use audio or video equipment or both.

THE LANGUAGE OF SCIENCE

The language of science helps people communicate clearly when they talk about light, sound, and electricity. Here are some vocabulary words you can use when you talk about light, sound, and electricity with your friends, family, and others.

acoustics—the science of sound. Acoustics is applied to the design of buildings. **(C68)**

aperture—an opening through which light comes into a camera. The size of the aperture is adjusted to let in different amounts of light. **(C36)**

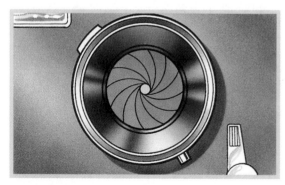

▲ **Aperture**

color—a characteristic determined by the rays of light reflected by an object. Red objects reflect red light. White objects reflect nearly all light. **(C46)**

conductor—matter that allows electricity to flow through it. Wire and salt water are excellent conductors. **(C77)**

cones—cells in the retina of the eye that allow us to see color. **(C45)**

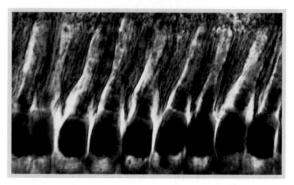

▲ **Cones and rods**

current—the flow of negatively charged atomic particles called *electrons*. In a *direct current* (DC) system, electrons travel in only one direction. In an *alternating current* (AC) system, electrons travel in a rotating wire coil placed in a magnetic field. As the coil rotates, the electrons continue to change direction. **(C74)**

electric circuit—a closed pathway for electricity to follow. In a series circuit, the current has only one path to follow. In a parallel circuit, the current has more than one path to follow. **(C72)**

insulator—a nonconductor of electric current. Glass and rubber are good insulators. **(C77)**

opaque—not allowing light rays to pass through. *Translucent* objects allow some light to pass through. *Transparent* objects allow all light to pass through. **(C22)**

persistence of vision—the holding of an image on the retina for a fraction of a second, making it possible for us to see a series of still images as motion. **(C33)**

pitch—the sound quality determined by the number of vibrations per second, measured in *hertz*. In music, different tones have different pitches. **(C64)**

primary colors of light—red, blue, and green, which can be combined to produce all other colors of the visible spectrum. **(C41)**

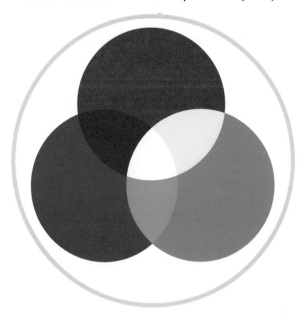

prism—a piece of glass with triangular bases that refracts white light into the visible spectrum: red, orange, yellow, green, blue, violet. **(C40)**

ray model—a way for scientists to show how rays of light travel. **(C20)**

▲ **Ray model**

reflection—the bouncing of light rays. A smooth surface such as a mirror provides a clear reflected image that you can see. **(C23)**

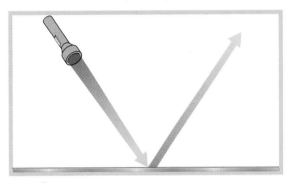

▲ **Reflection**

refraction—the bending of light rays. **(C28)**

◀ **Raindrops act as tiny prisms, refracting sunlight to form a rainbow.**

resistance—the property of matter that causes it to oppose the flow of electricity. The filament in a light bulb heats up and glows because of resistance. **(C74)**

rods—cells in the retina that help a person see in dim light. **(C45)**

volume—the loudness or softness of sounds. Volume is measured in decibels. Continued exposure to sounds of 100 decibels or more can damage the ears. **(C64)**

SEABASE NAUTILUS

SeaBase Nautilus

Exploring the Oceans

I WONDER

Waves crash onto a rocky shore. A scuba diver uses an underwater camera to capture the beauty of life on a coral reef. What do you wonder about when you see ocean scenes like these?

Work with a partner to make a list of questions about the ocean. Be ready to share your list with the rest of the class.

◀ Ocean waves

▼ Exploring the ocean

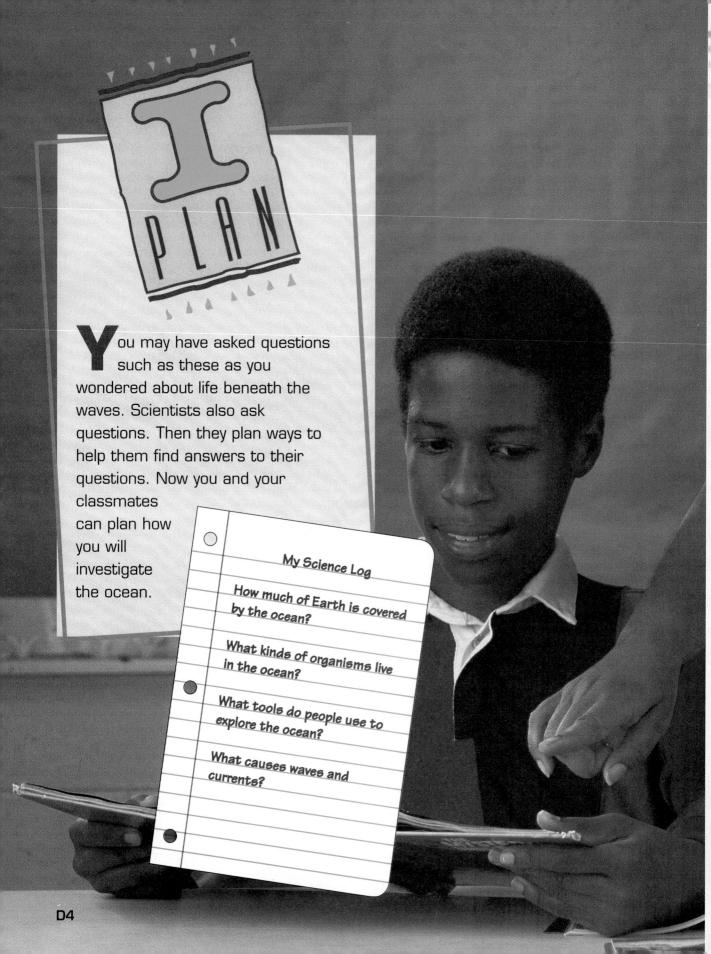

I PLAN

You may have asked questions such as these as you wondered about life beneath the waves. Scientists also ask questions. Then they plan ways to help them find answers to their questions. Now you and your classmates can plan how you will investigate the ocean.

My Science Log

How much of Earth is covered by the ocean?

What kinds of organisms live in the ocean?

What tools do people use to explore the ocean?

What causes waves and currents?

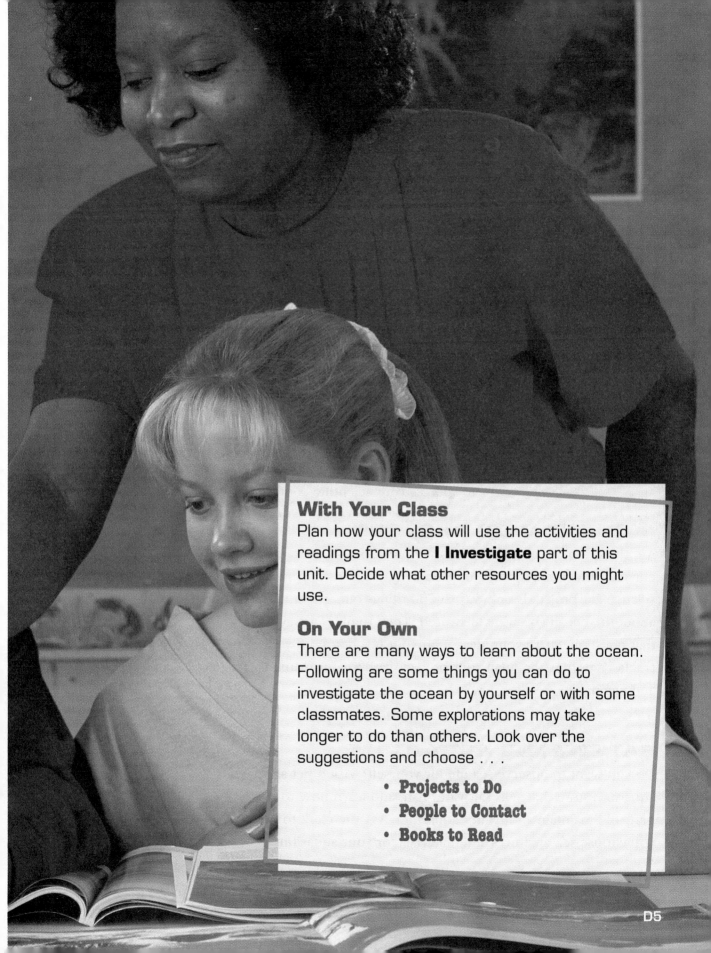

With Your Class

Plan how your class will use the activities and readings from the **I Investigate** part of this unit. Decide what other resources you might use.

On Your Own

There are many ways to learn about the ocean. Following are some things you can do to investigate the ocean by yourself or with some classmates. Some explorations may take longer to do than others. Look over the suggestions and choose . . .

- **Projects to Do**
- **People to Contact**
- **Books to Read**

PROJECTS TO DO

HALL OF MURALS

With your teacher's permission, cover the wall of a hall-way with butcher paper or craft paper. Cut the paper to fit around doors along the hallway. Use a variety of art supplies and pictures to produce a giant sea mural that seems to stretch forever—like the ocean!

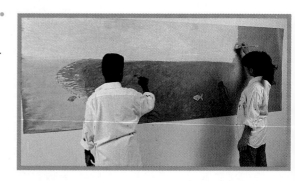

SAVING THE SEAS—A STUDENT CONFERENCE

Invite other students to submit papers, videos, artwork, or other projects to be presented at a student conference called Saving the Seas. Review the projects, and choose the most interesting ones to be presented. Issue a program that includes biographies of the participants along with the names of the projects. You may wish to invite a guest speaker to address your scientific conference.

SCIENCE FAIR PROJECT

Are there topics you want to know more about—for example, how currents affect temperature on land or how and why waves move? A science fair project is one way to find things out. Think of a question about the ocean you want answered. Then think of a way to answer that question. Share your ideas with your teacher. With your teacher's permission, plan your project, gather your materials, and begin.

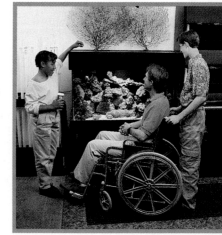

SALTWATER AQUARIUM

Do you want to observe sea life for yourself? Visit a pet shop or aquarium store that sells saltwater fish, and learn how to pre-pare and maintain a saltwater aquarium. Ask the clerk to help you choose sea creatures and materials for your aquarium.

PEOPLE TO CONTACT

IN PERSON

Do you know people who live near the ocean? Ask them about the joys of a day at the beach, such as digging their heels into the sand during a race, feeling the wind blow their hair into tangles, and tasting the salt on their lips after a swim. Ask them about any changes they may have noticed in the shoreline and about the sea organisms they have seen on the coast or in the water. Think of an interesting way to share the information with your classmates.

BY TELEPHONE

Interview people who have been to sea. You might contact people who go fishing, scientists who study sea life, or members of organizations that try to protect the sea and its communities. Ask them to tell you about their most exciting shipboard adventures—an ancient tradition among seafarers! You may want to contact some of the organizations below to learn more about the ocean.

- Earth Island Institute
- The National Coalition for Marine Conservation
- The National Oceanic and Atmospheric Administration
- The World Resources Institute

BY COMPUTER

Use a computer with a modem to connect to on-line services or bulletin boards. You can look for information about the ocean and talk with others to find out what they know about the oceans in their parts of the world.

Perhaps the computers at your school are connected to Internet, an international network of computers. Internet links computer users in more than 40 countries. Contact students in several parts of the world. Ask them to trade information about the ocean with you.

BOOKS TO READ

The Sign of the Seahorse:
A Tale of Greed and High Adventure in Two Acts

by Graeme Base (Harry N. Abrams, Inc., 1992). It was love at first sight for Pearl, the beautiful trout, and Bert, the handsome, dashing crab. Their travels take them past an evil grouper, sharks, and a swordfish. But worst of all, they have to face the poison oozing from barrels that fall from above. Can Bert save the day? Read to find out.

Marine Biology

by Ellen Doris (Thames and Hudson, 1993). Marine biology is the study of organisms that live in the ocean. With this book, you can learn about zonation and classification, as well as about jellyfish and seaweed. You will learn how to set up a saltwater aquarium and how to press seaweed. Share this book with a friend, or read it alone. Either way you'll have a great day.

More Books to Read

Swimming with Sea Lions and Other Adventures in the Galápagos Islands

by Ann McGovern (Scholastic, 1992), Outstanding Science Trade Book. Would you like to feed giant tortoises, have sea lions come right to you, and see many strange animals and plants? This is the diary of a girl who traveled to the Galápagos Islands with her grandmother. As you read, you will learn much about these islands. Maybe someday you can visit there, too.

The Diving Bell

by Todd Strasser (Scholastic, 1992). The Spanish came to Mexico for gold. Many of their ships were overloaded and sank with fabulous treasures. This is the story of Culca, a Native American girl who shows the Spanish how to use a diving bell to recover their gold.

Window on the Deep: The Adventures of Underwater Explorer Sylvia Earle

by Andrea Conley (New England Aquarium/Franklin Watts, 1991), Outstanding Science Trade Book. In this book, you can dive with Dr. Sylvia Earle, aquanaut and scientist, as she explores the ocean's depths. She wants us to learn as much as possible about the oceans, so that we can keep them healthy.

The Desert Beneath the Sea

by Ann McGovern and Eugenie Clark (Scholastic, 1991). Join scientists scuba diving in the Caribbean. Discover many forms of life on the desertlike sand around a coral reef. Study eels that stand upright in the sand and fish that carry things in their mouths.

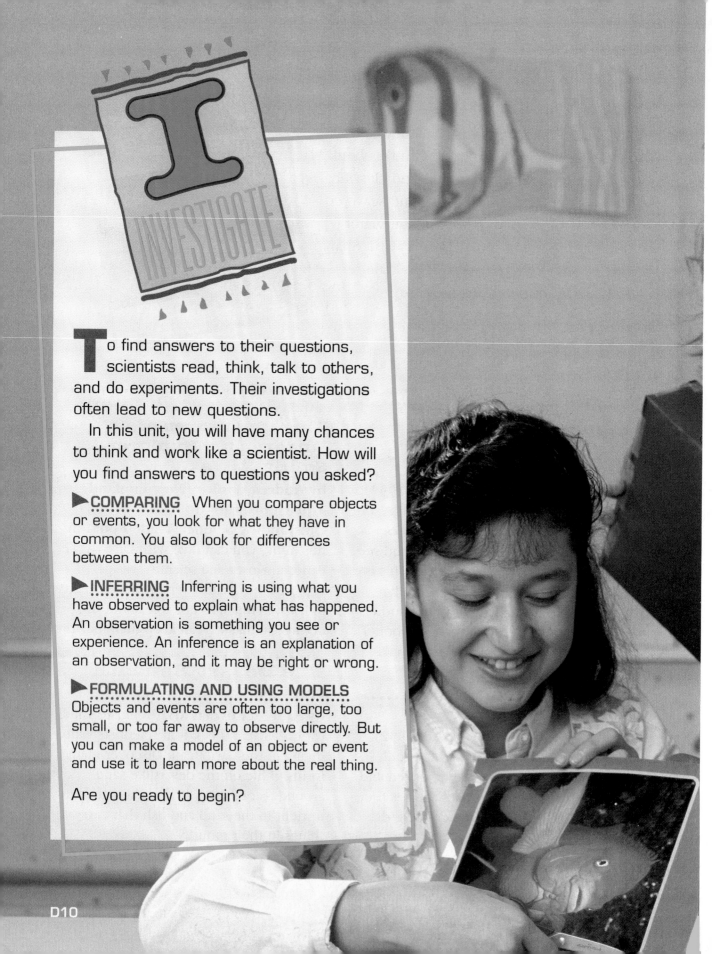

INVESTIGATE

To find answers to their questions, scientists read, think, talk to others, and do experiments. Their investigations often lead to new questions.

In this unit, you will have many chances to think and work like a scientist. How will you find answers to questions you asked?

▶ **COMPARING** When you compare objects or events, you look for what they have in common. You also look for differences between them.

▶ **INFERRING** Inferring is using what you have observed to explain what has happened. An observation is something you see or experience. An inference is an explanation of an observation, and it may be right or wrong.

▶ **FORMULATING AND USING MODELS** Objects and events are often too large, too small, or too far away to observe directly. But you can make a model of an object or event and use it to learn more about the real thing.

Are you ready to begin?

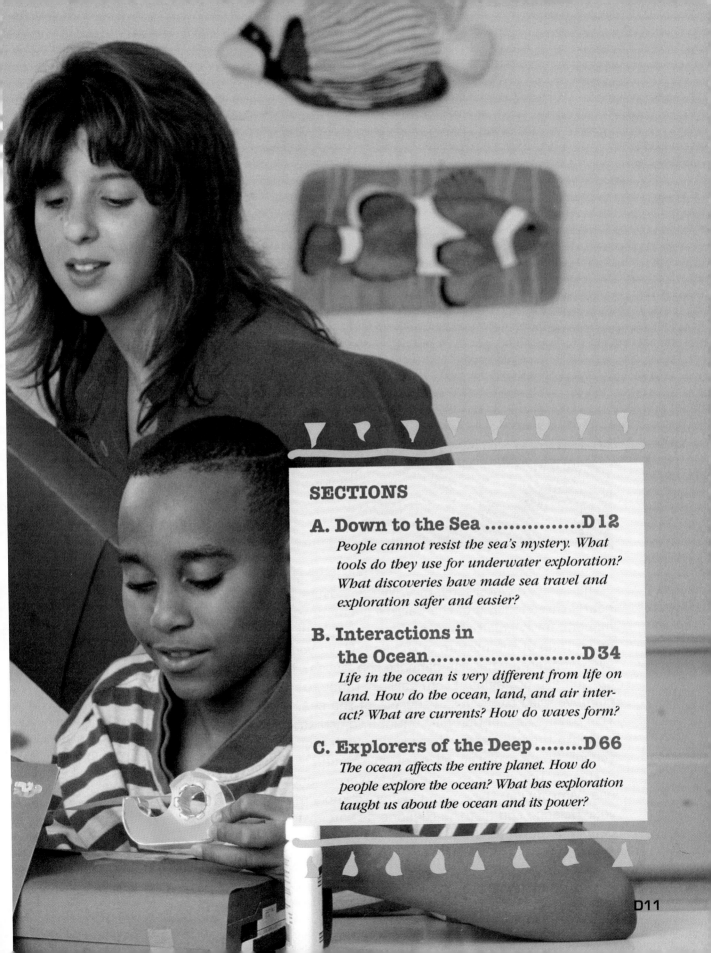

SECTIONS

Down to the Sea

▶ **Modern research submarine**

The sea is a watery mystery. Water covers nearly three-fourths of the Earth's surface, yet humans have explored more of the surface of the moon than of the bottom of the sea. Have *you* ever wondered what lies beneath the waves? If so, you are not alone. From earliest times, people have tried to learn the secrets of the sea. This deep blue frontier will continue to attract explorers well into the future, for there is so much more to know. In this unit, you will be an explorer, for to study the sea is to explore it.

This section discusses the sea explorers and the equipment they use. Why do you think people want to know more about the sea? In your Science Log, list the reasons as you investigate why, and how, people go down to the sea.

1 FEEL THE POWER

Almost everyone who looks at waves—on a beach or in a painting—would probably say the sight is inspiring. Some of the world's greatest stories express strong feelings about the sea. But writers aren't the only ones who have such feelings. In the activities and readings that follow, you will discover scientists and explorers with equally strong feelings about the sea.

Writers Who Loved the Sea

You will need: poster board and markers

Read the words below of some famous people who loved the sea. Then, using poster board and markers, draw a picture that illustrates your favorite sea story or poem. You might want to include words from the story or poem, as in the sample below.

Why is almost every robust healthy child with a robust healthy soul in him or her, at some time or other crazy to go to sea?

from *Moby Dick* by Herman Melville

Beginnings are apt to be shadowy, and so it is with the beginnings of that great mother of life, the sea.

from *The Sea Around Us* by Rachel Carson

The sea actually conditions all human activities, generating rain, floods, or droughts, bringing about constant changes. . . . Our "liquid future" depends upon the foresight, the care, and the love with which we will manage our only water supply: the oceans.

from *The Ocean World* by Jacques Cousteau

Worth the Risk?

Like the children pictured on the preceding page, explorers of the sea often face danger. However, explorers like photographer David Doubilet often consider the risk worth taking. As you will see in the following story and photographs, the love of adventure often outweighs any fears.

DEEP TROUBLE

from *Disney Adventures*

▲ Barracudas circle a daring diver named Dinah.

LITERATURE Being attacked by a barracuda isn't David's idea of a good time, but it makes for a great scary adventure. He was diving in the Bahamas, and a 5-foot-long fish slammed into his air tank. "I felt a hard push behind me, turned around, and saw this huge barracuda," says David. "He'd hit my tanks so hard that all his front teeth came out. But if he'd hit me an inch to the right or left, I would have been hurt."

Sometimes, though, the shot is worth the danger. "I shot this picture near Kavieng Island near Papua New Guinea," David says. "I swam into a school of probably 1,000 barracudas. Suddenly, they began to circle me."

David wanted a picture of the barracuda circle with someone floating inside it, so he swam back to the boat and got another diver, Dinah, to jump in.

"I crossed my fingers and hoped the barracudas would still be there," David says. "They were, so I dove to the bottom and rolled on my back. Dinah

swam right into the school and they began circling her. They circled around her three times and then disappeared."

David shot an entire roll of film in less than 30 seconds. "It's very difficult to get a human involved in a pattern of fish," David says. "You can watch them from a distance, but when you get near them, they scatter."

THINK ABOUT IT

Why do you think people overcome their fears to explore the sea?

Deep, Dark, and Dangerous

Why is exploring the ocean dangerous work? In this activity, you will discover some answers to this question by creating a mini-ocean—right at your desk.

DO THIS

1 Work with a partner. Cover the outside of the aquarium with black construction paper. Then fill the aquarium about three-quarters full with cold water.

2 Close your eyes and drop a golf ball into the aquarium. It represents a USO—an unidentified sunken object—to be retrieved later.

MATERIALS

- small aquarium
- black construction paper
- water
- golf ball
- sand and pebbles
- blue food coloring
- wooden spoon
- ice cubes
- rubber gloves
- Science Log data sheet

3 Put a lot of sand and various-sized pebbles into the aquarium, and let them settle to the bottom.

4 Add blue food coloring to the aquarium as you gently stir the water with the wooden spoon. Continue adding food coloring until the water is too dark to see through.

5 Add 10–20 ice cubes to the water. Let them melt just a little.

6 Put on the rubber gloves. With your partner, take turns reaching straight into the water, trying to find the USO. Make sure you reach straight down into the water. Don't move your hand across the bottom to search for the USO.

THINK AND WRITE

Most of the ocean is very deep. What are some problems associated with diving in deep water?

Density Deep water is very cold and dark because the sun's light can't penetrate it. And sea water is very dense—thick and heavy—because of the cold temperature and the salt. Since sea water is denser than fresh water, things float better in sea water. Early divers had to invent a way to solve this problem—the tendency to float. In the next activity, you can learn how they did this.

ACTIVITY

Weigh Me Down

Early divers would not have had the strength to dive very deep or the time to do anything underwater if they had not used the method you will discover in this activity.

DO THIS

1 Fill the aquarium nearly to the top with water. Use the ruler to measure the depth of the water. Then cut a piece of string half as long as the depth of the water.

2 Drop one of the feathers into the water. The feather represents a diver.

3 Tie one end of the string to the weight. Tie the other end to the second feather. Drop the weight into the water.

4 With your scissors, reach into the water and cut the string, just under the feather.

THINK AND WRITE

1. What happened to the weighted feather when the string was cut? Why do you think this happened?

2. Early divers once tied weights to their feet before jumping into the water. How did this help them reach the bottom?

3. **INFERRING** In the activity, you were asked to infer information about early divers. Inferring is using what you have observed to explain what has happened. From this activity, what can you infer about the diver's weight belt pictured here?

MATERIALS
- small aquarium
- water
- ruler
- scissors
- string
- 2 feathers
- fishing weight
- Science Log data sheet

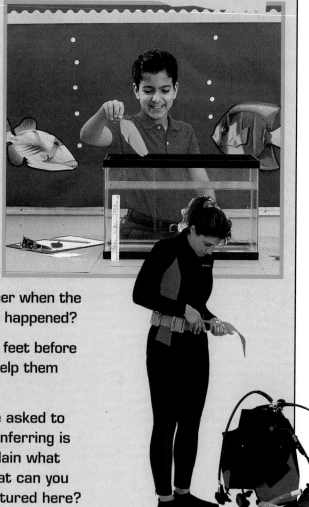

Daring Divers

The first ocean divers had few tools to make their work easy or safe. Who were these early divers? How deep could they go? And what were they looking for? Continue reading to discover how early divers turned deep-sea diving into an art.

▲ An oyster containing several pearls

▲ Pearl divers

The photograph above shows the ancient Japanese art of pearl diving. Pearl divers look for their "sunken treasure" in the Red Sea, the Persian Gulf, and the South Pacific Ocean. In ancient times, such divers served royalty. Now, they supply commercial jewelers. Their methods of diving are thousands of years old. Using no breathing equipment, pearl divers reach depths of 43 meters (141 feet)—a long way down, even for modern scuba divers. Pearl divers work hard for a very small yield. In nature, only one oyster in a thousand may contain a pearl. The following story is about a 12-year-old pearl diver in the South Pacific.

▲ Inspecting the quality of pearls

My name is Lo. I live in the Tuamotu Archipelago. An *archipelago* is a string of islands. All the islands here are on coral reefs. My island is an *atoll*—a circular island surrounding a calm lagoon. After school, I sometimes dive for pearls with my older sister in the lagoon. Come with us on a dive.

Look, some of my friends are harvesting coconuts. Our island exports copra, or dried coconut meat, as well as pearls. The kids earn a little spending money by helping with the harvest.

I've seen pictures of the waters around my island, but they don't capture its true beauty. The water is always warm, and the trade winds keep the weather from getting too hot. I feel lucky to live here. There's my sister now; let's go!

First we row out into the lagoon. The best oyster beds are in water about 15 meters (49 feet) deep. Then we sit quietly; we must concentrate fully on our dive. There are sharks and moray eels in the water. But if we keep our minds on what we are doing, we will be safe.

It's my turn first. The youngest diver always goes first. If I need help, my sister, who has been diving for many years, can come to my aid.

No one ever dives alone—it wouldn't be safe.

I take several deep, quick breaths, whistling as I breathe out. I wrap my toes around a rope tied to a weight. My sister tosses the weight overboard. I follow quickly, feet first.

I drop to the bottom; that's the easy part. Wearing a glove and carrying a basket, I grab all the oysters I can. It's a rich bed! I'll return to it many times today, until I've collected 200 or so oysters.

When my basket is full, I untangle my toes from the rope, for I am running out of air and must surface. I've been underwater two minutes! I swim toward the sun, thankful that the salt water helps me reach the surface quickly.

My sister surfaces a moment later, and we compare baskets. If we find even one pearl, we will be lucky.

LESSON 1 REVIEW

What are the risks associated with ocean diving? How do pearl divers minimize the risks in what they do?

2 TECHNOLOGY AT YOUR SERVICE

In recent years, sea explorers have overcome some of the risks by discovering ways to make their work safer. One way to make ocean explorations safer is by using robots. Robots can explore places that are too dangerous for people. In this lesson, you will hear from Nautica, a robot that specializes in sea safety. Nautica will tap into its data bank for information on the dangers of ocean exploration as well as on modern equipment used to explore the sea. As you work through the activities, notice how "safety first" is a big part of ocean exploration.

Buoyancy and Water Pressure

Hi, I'm Nautica. Lo asked me to talk to you about buoyancy and pressure. Pearl divers experience difficulty in getting to the ocean bottom because of the water's buoyancy. On the other hand, divers using modern equipment must deal with a different problem—the tremendous pressure water exerts on their bodies. The diagrams will help me explain buoyancy and pressure to you.

You know that many things float in water. This is due to buoyancy. **Buoyancy** is water's ability to support objects. An object underwater is buoyed, or held up, by a force equal to the weight of the water the object displaces. As Lo's dive showed, buoyancy can work for, and against, a diver.

▲ **Positive buoyancy**   ▲ **Neutral buoyancy**   ▲ **Negative buoyancy**

If the diver weighs less than the water he or she displaces, the diver will float. This is called *positive buoyancy*. If the diver weighs the same as the water he or she displaces, the diver will be suspended in the water. This is *neutral buoyancy*. If the diver weighs more than the water he or she displaces, the diver will sink to the bottom. This is *negative buoyancy*.

Divers can overcome buoyancy problems by wearing a weight belt. The proper amount of weight gives a diver neutral buoyancy.

Water pressure is a much bigger problem for divers. As you probably know, water is much heavier than air. As divers go deeper, the pressure, or weight, of the water increases. Since a diver's lungs are filled with air, they become squeezed. Underwater, air must be forced into a diver's lungs to overcome this pressure. Modern diving equipment does this so the diver can breathe normally underwater.

As a diver surfaces, the water pressure decreases quickly, causing the air in the lungs to expand. Divers who breathe underwater must exhale as they surface, or their lungs will burst.

THINK ABOUT IT

Why don't pearl divers have to exhale as they return to the surface?

Under the Sea

So many advances have occurred in underwater ocean exploration over the years that in order to keep track of them, I've organized the information in SeaBank—my data bank. As we move from one advance to the next, I'll provide both facts and pictures. Let's look at personal diving equipment first.

Personal Diving Equipment

▲ In 1689 Denis Papin invented the diving helmet. It was worn over the head, and air was pumped through a line from the surface. Diving helmets led to the development of diving suits, which allowed divers to go deep but greatly restricted their movement. Diving helmets are back in use today. A modern version is used by tourists who want to "walk on the ocean floor" in resort areas.

▲ Divers can't breathe water. Snorkels let them breathe air from the surface. *Snorkel* comes from a German word for "snout."

▼ The freedom to move around while diving at greater depths was made possible by *scuba* (*s*elf-*c*ontained *u*nderwater *b*reathing *a*pparatus). The inventor, Jacques Cousteau, understood that the pressure of the air inside the lungs must equal the water pressure acting on the diver. Since water pressure increases with depth, the equipment has a regulator to match air pressure and water pressure.

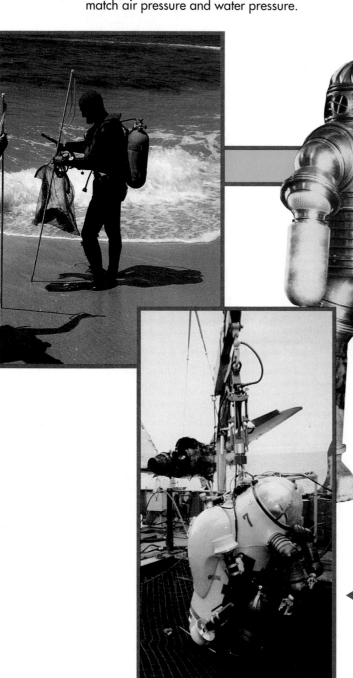

▲ Since the time of Leonardo da Vinci, people have tried making underwater "armor" that is able to withstand the tremendous deep-sea water pressure and is comfortable. A very heavy version, called a JIM suit, was tested in the 1970s. It had oiled joints, mechanical arms, and a communication line to the surface.

◀ An improvement on the JIM suit, this flexible apparatus, part suit and part bubble, has been in use since the 1980s. Its user can reach depths of 1,600 meters (5,250 feet). The diver guides its crablike arms as they work on the sea floor. Cousteau and his crew named the suits *puces*, a French word meaning "fleas."

Wow, personal diving equipment has sure come a long way. But if you think those advances were something, take a look at what has happened to *submersibles*—underwater vehicles.

Submersibles

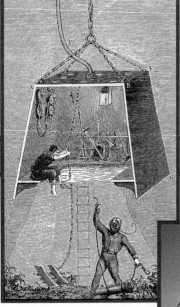

▲ Alexander the Great lowered glass-windowed barrels into the water to watch divers disabling underwater war gear. These were the first submersibles.

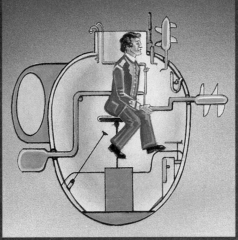

▲ An early submarine, the *Turtle*, was used during the Revolutionary War. Invented by David Bushnell, it was oblong and powered by hand. A person inside the sub turned cranks, which were connected to outside propellers.

▲ Invented in 1930 by William Beebe and Otis Barton, the first bathysphere plunged deeper than any vessel ever had—923 meters (3,028 feet). Its pilots were the first to see the "deep black sea." Because its cable restricted the depth to which the bathysphere could dive, the bathysphere could have broken in rough seas.

▲ Swiss balloonist Auguste Piccard applied his aeronautical skills to the exploration of the sea with the invention of the bathyscaphe in 1948. It enabled scientists to cut the cord—the line to the surface. Free-floating, the bathyscaphe had piped-in air, so scientists did not have to carry air tanks. Later models included *Trieste*, which set a world record by diving almost 11,000 meters (36,100 feet) into the Mariana Trench—the deepest part of the ocean.

▲ In the last three decades, underwater labs have enabled scientists to live and work under the sea for weeks at a time. The parts of this lab, called *Conshelf*, included Starfish House, the main room; a "garage" for scooters and tools; and a dry bubble for parking the diving saucer. Underwater labs also use robots—like me, Nautica—when necessary.

THINK ABOUT IT

How have advances in the equipment used for diving increased our knowledge of the sea?

While on the Surface . . .

Nautica would have you believe that the only way to explore the oceans is by going underwater. However, there was, and still is, a lot of ocean exploration taking place from the surface. Surface explorers just use different equipment. Continue reading to discover how they explore the sea and what they have learned about it.

The explorers who sailed the seas looking for new worlds on land were the first to collect data on the watery world around them. Using tools like the sextant and chronometer, they were the first to map the globe, complete with oceans and seas. Early explorers' knowledge of winds, waves, and currents made maps more accurate and complete. Ships' crews also used scoops attached to ropes to take deep-sea samples of bottom mud. Modern ships still do similar samplings.

Modern ships, such as the *Glomar Challenger,* also use sophisticated depth-finding devices called *sonar—so*und *nav*igation and *r*anging— which measure the time it takes for sound to travel to the ocean bottom and back. The data goes into a computer that then draws

▼ **Sextant**

◀ **Chronometer**

▼ *Glomar Challenger*

a picture of the ocean bottom, based on the distances calculated by the sonar. This is a far cry from one of the first depth finders—a weight on a long rope!

The cost of keeping a ship at sea makes surface exploration expensive. Bad weather often makes it dangerous. So scientists now depend on *remote sensors*—anchored buoys that take readings and relay them electronically to shore. A fleet of sensors in use today is named *NOMAD,* for *n*aval *o*ceanographic and *m*eteorological *a*utomatic *d*evices.

THINK ABOUT IT

How do sonar and NOMAD help scientists explore the sea?

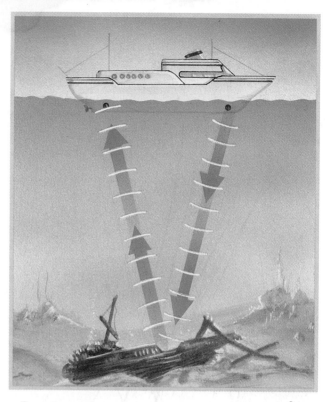

▲ Sonar

▼ NOMAD

Above the Water

One of the best places from which to explore the oceans is high above them, flying in the atmosphere or orbiting in space. What kind of equipment is used for sea exploration from the sky and from space?

▼ **Hawaiian rainbow**

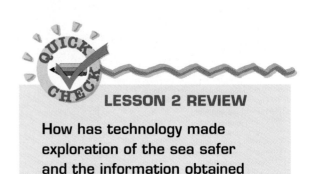

Mesoscale Variability of Sea Surface Height (cm)
Oct 3 - 12, 1992

▶ **Satellite photo of wave heights**

A photograph taken from an aircraft provides a real bird's-eye view of the sea. In the photo above, you can see a rainbow off the coastline of Kohala, Hawaii. The connection between land, air, and sea is dramatically evident on film.

Satellites have taken sea photography to a new level. Employing advanced technologies, such as lasers, microwaves, radar, and computers, satellites enable scientists to "see" straight into the sea.

QUICK CHECK

LESSON 2 REVIEW

How has technology made exploration of the sea safer and the information obtained more accurate?

3 MAPPING THE OCEAN

Even if you live thousands of kilometers from the sea, you have something in common with people who see the ocean every day. Everyone on Earth is an islander. From the tiniest shoals to the largest continents, all land on Earth is surrounded by ocean. Much remains to be learned about the ocean because there is so much territory to cover—both in width and in depth.

One Ocean

The surface of Earth is one vast ocean, covering nearly three-fourths of the planet. Scientists have divided Earth's ocean into four smaller oceans and many seas.

Oceans have surface areas of at least 12 million square kilometers (4.6 million square miles). *Seas* are bodies of salt water having surface areas of less than 3.6 million square kilometers (1.4 million square miles). Some seas are connected to oceans by a thread of water. Chains of islands form boundaries between other seas and oceans.

▼ Earth's oceans and seas

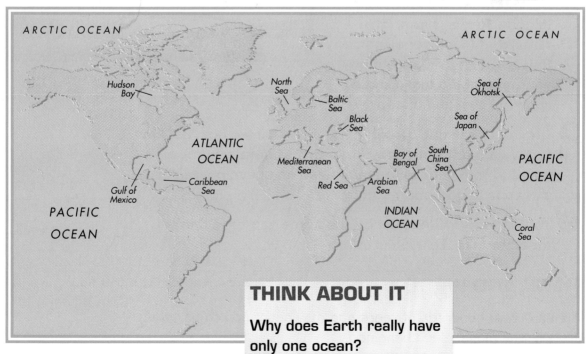

THINK ABOUT IT

Why does Earth really have only one ocean?

ACTIVITY

Ocean Atlas

Explorers and scientists have worked together for hundreds of years to make accurate maps of the oceans and seas. As we learn more, the maps become more accurate. In this activity, you will study a body of water and become an "expert" on this ocean or sea. Then you will draw an accurate map of it. When you combine your map with those of your classmates, you will have an ocean atlas.

MATERIALS
- atlas
- large sheet of paper
- colored pencils
- encyclopedia
- almanac
- Science Log data sheet

DO THIS

1 Your teacher will assign you an ocean or a sea to investigate.

2 Find the body of water in an atlas, and draw its boundaries on a large sheet of paper.

3 Draw and label countries, islands, towns, cities, currents, and whatever else you find in the atlas. Then color your map and make a scale showing size and distance.

4 Draw a box in one corner of the paper. In the box, list key facts, such as depth, area, and any other information you find interesting. You may need an encyclopedia or almanac to find information.

5 Your teacher will collect all the maps and bind them together to make a class atlas.

THINK AND WRITE

A map drawn hundreds of years ago may seem odd to us today. Explain why maps keep changing.

Ocean Architects

Like the land, the ocean floor has mountains, valleys, trenches, and plains, which all formed over millions of years. Scientists have named many of the areas they have identified. In this activity, you will make a model of the ocean floor.

DO THIS

1. Work with a small group. Choose one part of the ocean floor to model.

2. Mold a piece of clay the size of a sheet of notebook paper into a block resembling that part of the ocean floor.

3. When you finish, put your block on a large table, next to the blocks of others in your group.

4. When the ocean floor model is finished, your group can paint and label plains, ridges, trenches, valleys, and islands. Make up any names you like.

THINK AND WRITE

1. In what ways is the ocean floor like the land of the continents?

2. **FORMULATING AND USING MODELS**
   Scientists use models to help them picture things that cannot be observed directly. How does making a model of the ocean floor help you form a picture of its structure?

QUICK CHECK

LESSON 3 REVIEW

How do you think scientists might use maps of the ocean floor?

 DOUBLE CHECK

SECTION A REVIEW

1. Identify three important advances in ocean exploration, and tell how each has been made safer.

2. How have accurate maps helped ocean explorers?

Interactions in the Ocean

▶ Butterfly fish

Picture a breezy day at the shore, where the ocean and the land meet. Sea spray dampens your face, and you can't resist taking a salty taste. The waves whip the water into foam, and you can almost feel the water surging past. You notice that the land here is sandy, but there are other places where the shore is rocky or grassy. You wade into the water. As you get your arms wet and your feet sandy, you begin to interact with the ocean—you become a true ocean explorer. You begin to have a sense of what life must be like in the sea.

In this section, you will discover ocean life, and you will see how land, air, and water interact. As you work through the investigations that follow, list some of these interactions in your Science Log.

1 TAKE A CLOSER LOOK

While snorkeling or riding in a glass-bottomed boat, you can see a fabulous underwater show featuring colorful organisms of the ocean. You might see a fish swimming near what appears to be a flower. But take a closer look. It's a clown fish and a sea anemone (uh NEM uh nee). Both are animals. Back on the beach, the sand seems to be alive. Take a closer look. There's a ghost crab, barely visible against the sand.

In the activities and readings that follow, you will journey from the shore to the depths. If you stop to take a closer look, you will discover that the ocean is a wonderful world of living creatures.

Field Notes

One way to take a closer look at ocean life is to study an animal in its natural environment and take notes on what you observe. Scientists always take notes as they work "in the field." Field notes contain data such as time and place of observations, feeding habits and other behaviors, and environmental conditions.

▲ Clownfish

You will need: Science Log, reference books

Choose an animal that lives in the ocean. Try to observe the animal in a natural setting, which you may find at a public aquarium, in a pet store, or in a nature video. Take notes that tell when and how you studied the animal. In your notes, describe where the animal lives, what it eats, how it behaves, and any other important information you discover. Use reference books to research additional information.

Share your notes with other students. Ask your classmates what else they would like to know about your animal. Find answers to their questions by continuing your research and adding to your notes.

▲ Ghost crab

Knee-Deep

Every year at Galveston Bay, on the Gulf of Mexico, a camp is held to introduce students—like you—to the ocean. In eight years, the camp has involved more than 2,000 young explorers with a hands-on study of ocean life. In the newspaper article that follows, you will discover how some of the campers reacted to this experience. As you read the article, think about how you might react to Sea Camp.

FIELD DAYS IN THE MARSH

by **Kevin Moran** from *The Houston Chronicle*

For many adults, there's nothing more relaxing than getting into the old waders and wetting a line in the shallow waters on the back side of a Texas barrier island.

The same places beckon to the 460 children who come to Texas A&M University at Galveston's Sea Camp program each summer, but peace and relaxation aren't exactly what they have in mind.

For them, there's nothing more exciting than getting their tennis shoes soaked and full of mud while slogging through a salt marsh, netting shrimp, crabs, and a host of

other creatures just starting their lives in a little corner of Galveston Bay along the back side of Galveston Island.

"I think the marsh is really fun," Daniel Krohn, 11, said after helping drag a seine net through a marsh area. "You get to do a lot of really neat stuff here."

Daniel and a gaggle of his Sea Camp mates crowded around a net one recent morning, eagerly snatching up bay creatures for a closer look at their squirmy anatomies. Far from squeamish, the children vied with each other for better views of their catch.

"This is probably my favorite thing," Collin Crea, 11, said as he squatted in the marsh mud. "You find neat things in the water and you slip up in the mud."

On the day before, Collin said, he had helped haul squid, jellyfish, and other sea creatures into the A&M vessel *Roamin' Empire* during a floating field day on Galveston Bay.

At least one of Collin's young camp mates was already looking well beyond her week on Galveston Bay, planning to put into practice some of the things she learned there.

"I want to be a marine veterinarian when I grow up," said Deborah Horwitz, 11. "I like dolphins and seals and whales and things and I don't mind gross stuff."

"The program is mostly hands-on, outdoor activities," said Judy Wern, assistant Sea Camp director. "The laboratory is the Galveston Bay estuary system. That's what Sea Camp is."

▲ Hermit crab in a "borrowed" shell

◀ A day at Sea Camp

LESSON 1 REVIEW

How do you think a week at Sea Camp might help you take a closer look at life in the ocean?

LIFE ON THE EDGE

You may recall that an ecosystem is a community of living things and the environment they interact with. Places where one ecosystem meets another are called *ecotones.* Shorelines are ecotones. Nautica is going to guide you on a walking and wading tour of several shoreline ecotones. But first, let's make some models of shorelines.

ACTIVITY

All Ashore

The shoreline of Galveston Bay is marshy and calm, while the shoreline of Maine is rocky and wild. The way the land and the sea come together affects the plants and animals that live there. In this activity, you will model several types of shorelines.

MATERIALS

- damp sand and gravel mixture
- rectangular baking pan
- paper clip
- water
- wooden block
- stopwatch
- large pebbles
- 2 blocks of wax
- thin strips of carpet
- Science Log data sheet

DO THIS

1 Place the damp sand and gravel mixture in one end of the baking pan. Use only that end, about $\frac{1}{3}$ of the pan, for the mixture. Hide a paper clip about 2 cm deep in the sand. Then pack the sand firmly with your hands.

2 At the other end of the pan, slowly add water to a depth of about 3 cm. Try not to disturb the sand.

3 Float the wooden block in the water end of the pan. Move the block up and down, making waves that break on the "beach." Time how long it is until you can see the paper clip again.

4 Remove the water, and rebuild the beach as in step 1. This time, edge the beach with pebbles. Repeat steps 2 and 3. Again time how long it is before you can see the paper clip.

5 Remove the water, sand, and pebbles. Rebuild the beach as in step 1. Place the wax blocks 4 cm apart across the center of the pan. Repeat steps 2 and 3, noting where beach damage occurs. Time how quickly the paper clip reappears.

6 Remove the water and the wax blocks, and rebuild the beach as in step 1. This time, partially bury the carpet strips so that the fibers look like beach grass. Repeat steps 2 and 3, noting what happens to the beach, the paper clip, the "grass," and the water.

THINK AND WRITE

1. What happened to the sand as the waves broke on the different beaches? How long did it take for the paper clip to reappear on each beach?

2. How did the pebbles change the waves striking the beach?

3. How would the sand on a real beach be affected by grass growing on the beach?

4. **FORMULATING AND USING MODELS** Formulating models helps scientists study things that are hard to observe in nature. Using the models in this activity helps you understand the effects of waves on different types of beaches without leaving the classroom. How were the effects of the waves different in each model? Why do you think people sometimes build rock walls along the shore?

Crash! Smash! Splash!

The waves pound on the rocks and then surge back out to sea. What kind of environment does a rocky ecotone provide for plants and animals? Let's start our tour with Nautica.

Notice the rough seas and huge rock formations. A rocky coast is a natural artwork in progress. Wind and water erode the rocks into new shapes. Life on a rocky shore is hard. Waves slam into you. Tides flood your space and then leave you high and dry—twice a day. The hot sun scorches you in summer, and the cold air chills you in winter.

We're in luck! We've found a *tide pool,* a calm pool formed where rocks trap tidewater. Most creatures in a tide pool are simple plants and *invertebrates,* animals without a backbone. Each one is adapted to the harsh conditions of intertidal life. For example, to prevent water loss during times of low water level and drying heat, mussels and periwinkles hold water in their shells. Crabs and sea stars hide in seaweeds to stay moist. And seaweeds anchor themselves to the rocks.

▲ **Rocky coast**

▼ **Tide pool**

Starfish

Vorticellids

Hydroids

Gooseneck barnacles

Rock weed

Mussels

Sea urchin

Anemone

Sea creatures are great adventurers. They scout the shoreline for new places to settle. If a storm knocks down a sea wall, or if a new rock pier, or jetty, is built, sea life rushes in to take up residence.

Within hours, bacteria land on the rock, coating it with a clear film. Soon one-celled protists move in. Some have hairlike projections called *cilia*. The cilia make whirlpools in the water to trap food.

Anemones come next. Their strange tentacles attract both attention and food.

Once the new site is established, algae begin to show up. The cells soon sprout into green and brown seaweeds. Floating larvae of mussels and barnacles find their homes next, where they attach themselves for life. Starfish, the only mobile residents, move in and out with the changing tides.

THINK ABOUT IT

How are various organisms adapted to the hardships of life in a rocky ecotone?

Swish! Slosh! Wash-sh!

The rocky shore is one kind of ecotone. Sandy beaches are another. How is beach life different from life on rocks? Let's continue our tour with Nautica and find out.

It's more peaceful here. The waves are slower and gentler than those on a rocky shore. I'm sitting on a sand dune now, looking out over the wide, sloping beach. There's more room for animals to roam here. And they don't have to cling tightly to wet rocks.

Like plants and animals on rocky shores, organisms that live on sandy beaches are adapted to survival there. To escape the drying sun and to find hidden pools of water, beach animals dig into the sand. Sandy hide-aways also protect them from predators above, such as birds. Some animals have eyes on stalks, like periscopes. The eyes can check for danger before the animal crawls from its burrow. Others come out only at night, when the drying sun and predators are gone.

▶ **Sandy shore**

▲ Sand dollar

▲ Hermit crab

▲ Ghost crab

To protect its soft body, the hermit crab climbs into an empty shell. A sand dollar lives partly buried in the sand in shallow water. If you see the sand moving, take a closer look—you just might see a ghost crab. The ghost crab's pale colors help it blend with the sand.

The lugworm burrows deep into the sand, where it feeds on decaying material. Lugworms may grow as long as 30 centimeters (12 inches). You might see if you can spot some lugworm burrows in the sand. These animals make good bait for surf fishing.

THINK ABOUT IT

How is a beach ecotone similar to and different from a rocky ecotone?

▲ Lugworm and burrow (above) and lugworm cast (right)

Water to Water

You've seen two environments where the ocean meets the land. Now let's take a look at two ecotones where the ocean meets fresh water. As you finish touring with Nautica, think about how conditions in these ecotones differ from conditions on a rocky shore and sandy beach.

This is where the Mississippi River meets the Gulf of Mexico. These bands of water at the mouth of the river form an estuary. An **estuary** is an area where fresh water and salt water mix.

▲ Mississippi Delta—an estuary

▲ Flounder

▲ Oyster

▲ Crab

▲ Clams

▲ Shrimp

Estuaries are important ecotones. Estuaries serve as nurseries for a variety of fish, clams, crabs, oysters, and shrimp. In an estuary, waves don't crash on the shore, and the salt content of the water is usually lower than it is on a rocky shore or sandy beach. These conditions allow the young of many marine animals to grow up in safety.

▲ Salt marsh

Do you smell what I smell? That strong odor means that a salt marsh is nearby, working for the good of the entire coastal area. Tourists on their way to more appealing beaches often pass, but rarely visit, salt marshes. But scientists know that salt marshes are well worth exploring.

You might think of a salt marsh as a natural "soup," full of healthful nutrients. The soup contains algae and grasses, which are eaten by the animal residents. A salt marsh also contains waste from animals and decaying plants, because animals eat only 10 percent of the plant life. In the marsh mud, bacteria break down the waste and the decaying materials, releasing nutrients back into the marsh for the live plants to use. Excess nutrients are carried into the ocean, where other bacteria and larger organisms feed on them. Plankton, which are the first step in the ocean food chain, thrive on these nutrients.

A large variety of animals live in these watery fields of salt hay, or marsh grass. Insects, birds, muskrats, crabs, turtles, and fish find a lush paradise here. But there may be trouble in paradise, as the poem on the next page explains.

THINK ABOUT IT

Why are estuaries and salt marshes important to life in the ocean?

Shrimp Don't Need Soap!

In recent years, life has not been easy for shoreline plants and animals. They are threatened by a new hardship—development. When people move into coastal areas, there may be problems for beaches, estuaries, and salt marshes. And, as the following poem describes, the problems don't easily go "away."

Away on the Bay

from *Ranger Rick's NatureScope® Pollution: Problems & Solutions*

This is the tale of a town called **Away**—
A town that was built on the shore of a bay,
A town where the folks didn't think much about
What they dumped in their water day in and day out.

⋯⋯

For one thing, a sink was an excellent place
To get rid of messes and not leave a trace.
Cleansers and cleaners and yesterday's lunch
Went **away** down the drain with a gurgly crunch.

⋯⋯

At everyone's house there was laundry to do.
Day after day, how those laundry piles grew!
Load after load was washed, rinsed, and spun
And **away** went the water when each load was done.

⋯⋯

On Main Street each day there were sidewalks to sweep.
The litter and dirt were swept into the street.
And then when it rained, everything washed **away**
Into drains in the road that dumped into the bay.

⋯⋯

A mill there made "stuff" for the town-folks to use,
But a pipe from the mill churned out oodles of ooze.
And the ooze, well it goozed from the pipe to the bay
Where it bubbled and glubbed as it drifted **away.**

⋯⋯

When the weather was warm, it was always a treat
To sail on the bay and bring picnics to eat.
But when folks were finished, they'd toss all their trash
Overboard and **away** with a plop and a splash.

⋯⋯

Then folks started seeing that things weren't quite right;
The bay had become an unbearable sight.
Beaches were covered with garbage and glop
That rolled in with the waves—and the waves didn't stop.

⋯⋯

The fish in the bay all seemed sluggish and sick,
The algae was everywhere—slimy and thick.
The birds near **Away** were all suffering too,
'Cause the fish they were eating were covered with goo.

⋯⋯

So a meeting was called to discuss the
   sick bay
And townspeople came from all parts of
   Away.
And during the meeting one person
   proclaimed,
"I know who's at fault: We *all* should be
   blamed."

· · · · · ·

"For years we've washed chemicals, dirt,
   and debris
Down our sinks, off our streets, and out
   pipes—so you see,
Although we all thought that our waste
   went **away,**
It all ended up going into the bay."

· · · · · ·

"Now the bay is a mess—full of trash,
   soap, and goop,
The water's turned green—like a bowl
   of pea soup.
And our wildlife is sick from the garbage
   and grime;
The bay needs our help, right now while
   there's time."

· · · · · ·

The folks were all silent—they knew it
   was true.
And they realized now what they all
   had to do.
It was time to get busy—the bay couldn't
   wait.
If they didn't act now, it might soon be
   too late.

· · · · · ·

So they signed an agreement that very
   same minute
To take care of the bay and to stop putting
   in it
The stuff that had made the bay icky
   and ill,
Like soaps that pollute and the ooze
   from the mill.

· · · · · ·

They also agreed to stop dumping their
   trash
Overboard and **away** with a plop and a
   splash.
And all of their efforts have been a success:
Today the bay's clean and no longer
   a mess.

· · · · · ·

And that is the tale of a town called **Away**—
A town where the people, to this very day,
Remember a saying that's simple and plain:
Nothing just goes **away** when it's washed
   down the drain.

· · · · · ·

THINK ABOUT IT

**Why does development present
problems for organisms living in
shoreline ecotones?**

Water, Water Everywhere . . .

You probably know that all the water on Earth—including rivers, lakes, and glaciers—ends up in the ocean. If you think about this, you will probably realize that water must somehow leave the ocean and return to the land. This happens through the *water cycle*.

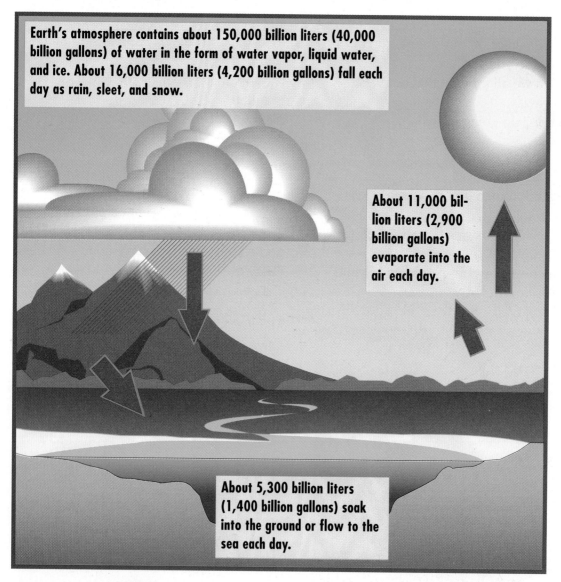

Earth's atmosphere contains about 150,000 billion liters (40,000 billion gallons) of water in the form of water vapor, liquid water, and ice. About 16,000 billion liters (4,200 billion gallons) fall each day as rain, sleet, and snow.

About 11,000 billion liters (2,900 billion gallons) evaporate into the air each day.

About 5,300 billion liters (1,400 billion gallons) soak into the ground or flow to the sea each day.

THINK ABOUT IT

What would happen to the water level in the ocean if the amount of evaporation doubled each day?

...But Hardly a Drop to Drink

Since most of Earth's water is in the ocean, most of Earth's water is salt water. Plants and animals need fresh water to survive. So just how much of Earth's water is available for plants and animals to use? You can find out in this activity.

MATERIALS
- 7 large jars
- wax pencil
- water
- 1-L graduate
- dropper
- Science Log data sheet

DO THIS

1. Set the jars in a row. Use the wax pencil to label them *1, 2, 3, 4, 5, 6,* and *7.*

2. Put 1 L of water in jar *1.* Label it *All the Water on Earth.* Put 972 mL of water in jar 2. Label it *Water in the Ocean.* Put 28 mL of water in jar 3. Label it *Fresh Water.* Put 23 mL of water in jar 4. Label it *Water Locked Up as Ice.* Put 4 mL of water in jar 5. Label it *Underground Water.* Put 2 drops of water in jar 6. Label it *Surface Water.* Put 1 drop of water in jar 7. Label it *Water in Soil and Air.*

THINK AND WRITE

1. How does the amount of fresh water on Earth compare with the amount of salt water?

2. From your observations, why do you think it is important to conserve water?

QUICK CHECK

LESSON 2 REVIEW

1. List three reasons why life is hard for plants and animals in coastal ecotones.

2. Which hardship may present the greatest threat to coastal sea life? Explain.

3 LET'S DIVE!

Shoreline ecotones contain a wide variety of plant and animal life. But some of the most interesting organisms are found away from the shoreline—at great depths. Deep-water explorer William Beebe often surfaced in a daze, amazed by what he had seen beneath the surface. Now it's your turn to discover the wonders of the deep. You will be traveling in a minisub, and Nautica will be your guide.

Life Zones

On board the research ship, you step into the minisub that will take you on your adventure. The sub will descend from the surface to the bottom of the ocean. What kinds of life will you see? Will the organisms at the bottom be the same as those near the surface? Let's find out!

▲ Minisub

Photosynthetic Zone

What a splash! Sea and sun meet here, at the silvery surface. This zone is more than pretty. It's pretty important. Scientists call this sunlit zone the *photosynthetic zone.* There's a reason. *Phytoplankton,* the tiny plantlike organisms that you see as green, floating stuff, use the sun's light to make food. *Zooplankton,* tiny animal-like organisms, feed on the phytoplankton.

▲ **Photosynthetic zone**

This zone goes down to about 200 meters (656 feet). Right now we're passing through a maze of shimmering jellyfish. And over there is a school of herring. Some schools of fish are more than 100 meters (328 feet) thick! With that many fish, there are probably predators nearby, such as bluefish or sharks. See if you can spot one.

Well, it's time to turn on our spotlights. The sun's still blazing above, but we're about to descend to a place where it never looks like daytime.

Middle Zone

We're entering a place where it's forever dusk. In this middle zone of the sea, which reaches to a depth of 1,000 meters (3,280 feet), light goes from a faint glow to nothing. Dr. Sylvia Earle, a famous diver you'll hear more about later, describes the loss of light this way: "First the water looks blue, then blue-black, then black-blue, and finally black." However, this is no deserted seascape. Like a city skyline, it has lights. But they're not electric lights.

▼ Red clownfish

You've heard of fireflies. Well, you're looking at "fireflies of the sea." About 80 percent of all deep-sea creatures make their own light. It's called *bioluminescence.*

For sea creatures, light is more than just light. It's a tool. Some species use it to attract prey. The anglerfish, for example, dangles a glowing lure at the end of a long, fleshy line. The other end of the line is attached, conveniently for the anglerfish, right next to its large mouth. Smaller fish take the false bait, and the anglerfish takes its meal.

▼ Flag-tail surgonfish

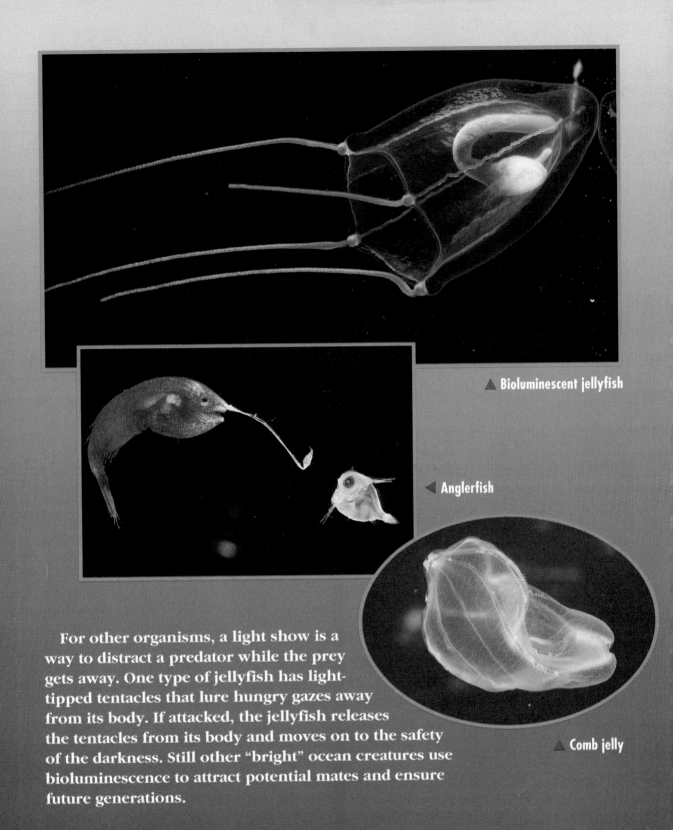

Bioluminescent jellyfish

Anglerfish

Comb jelly

For other organisms, a light show is a way to distract a predator while the prey gets away. One type of jellyfish has light-tipped tentacles that lure hungry gazes away from its body. If attacked, the jellyfish releases the tentacles from its body and moves on to the safety of the darkness. Still other "bright" ocean creatures use bioluminescence to attract potential mates and ensure future generations.

Abyss

At the bottom of the ocean, tons of water press down hard from above. Total darkness covers all—sunlight is a distant memory 4,000 meters (13,100 feet) away. Volcanoes shoot lava and minerals into the water, which changes from a nutrient-rich soup to a foul brew that few would find appetizing.

Out of the corner of your eye you see shadows with huge jaws. You begin to feel like a stranger in a strange land, and you are, for this is the *abyss*.

▽ Snipe eel

▲ Rat fish

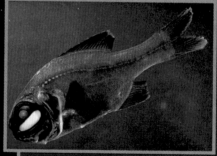

▲ Flashlight fish

▲ Swallower

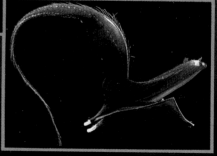

▲ Deep-sea gulper

Bottom Dwellers

Venus's flower basket

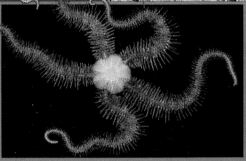

Brittle star △   ▽ Sea cucumber

Yellow sea fan △   ▽ Sponges

On the ocean floor is a different world—a dark world of flowerlike organisms with small, almost delicate bodies and beautiful colors. However flowerlike these creatures appear, though, there are few plants here. These organisms, with names like sea cucumber, Venus's flower basket, and sea fan, are all animals.

THINK ABOUT IT

How do organisms differ from one life zone to another?

▲ Crinoid

ACTIVITY

Ocean Overlay

Now that you've made your dive to the ocean bottom, how can you compare the organisms that live in shallow water with those that live in deep water? One way to compare them is by making an ocean overlay.

DO THIS

1. Punch two holes on the top of each transparency sheet. Thread yarn through the holes, and tie the ends to bind the sheets into a booklet.

2. At the top of the first sheet, draw animals found in the shallows. In the middle of the second sheet, draw animals found at middle depths. At the bottom of the third sheet, draw animals found in the lowest depths.

THINK AND WRITE

1. When you finish drawing and putting the sheets together, the layers of ocean life will appear in order. Why do you think ocean life is different in each layer?

2. **COMPARING** One of the things scientists can do with observations they make is compare one group of organisms with another. How did the overlay help you compare organisms from different life zones?

QUICK CHECK

LESSON 3 REVIEW

1. Why are most organisms found in only one layer of the ocean?

2. Why do some animals that live in total darkness produce their own light?

4 OCEAN MOTIONS

How would it feel to live with the floors, walls, and ceilings of your home constantly swirling around you? Sea creatures live in water that is always moving. Tides rise and fall, waves break, currents flow—the ocean is never still. In the activities that follow, you will investigate some of the forces that keep the ocean moving.

ACTIVITY

Moon Pull

Twice a day the water level of a tide pool rises and falls with the tides. What causes tides? You can find out by doing this activity.

MATERIALS
• Science Log data sheet

DO THIS

❶ Four students should join hands in a circle to represent the Earth. Ten students should join hands in a circle around the first circle to represent ocean water covering the Earth.

❷ One student should represent the sun, and another the moon. Have the "moon" pull gently on the side of the "ocean" closest to him or her. This represents the moon's gravity pulling on the ocean. Note how the shape of the ocean changes.

❸ Now have the "sun" stand behind the moon and gently pull the moon as the moon, in turn, pulls the ocean. Again, notice how the shape of the ocean changes.

THINK AND WRITE

1. What parts of the circle represent high and low tides?

2. When the moon and the sun join forces, what happens to the tides?

Tidal Power

In the last activity, you observed how the ocean is pulled toward the moon and the sun. This produces *tides*. But why do ocean tides change twice a day? The diagrams below should help you figure it out.

▲ High and low tides

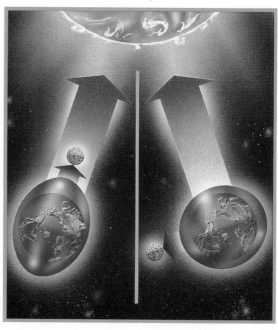

▲ Spring tide (left) and neap tide (right)

The moon pulls on the ocean, causing it to bulge up on the side of the Earth that is closest to the moon and also on the opposite side of the Earth. This produces two high tides. At the same time, there are two low tides, at locations midway between the two high tides. The moon's position relative to the Earth remains about the same from one night to the next. So in 24 hours, the Earth has two high tides and two low tides as it rotates.

Actually, the moon's position does change slightly. Have you noticed that the moon seems to rise about 50 minutes later every day? Because of this, high tides and low tides occur about 50 minutes later every day.

Spring tide has nothing to do with the season. Spring tides are very high and very low tides that occur when the moon and the sun line up and their pulls combine, as you demonstrated in the last activity. *Neap tides* occur when the moon and the sun are at right angles to each other. Their pulls cancel each other somewhat, producing smaller than average tides.

THINK ABOUT IT
How often will spring tides and neap tides occur?

ACTIVITY

Surf's Up, Dude!

In addition to dealing with changes in water level caused by tides, shoreline creatures have to contend with crashing waves. In a breaking wave, water rushes onto the shore. But what about the water in a wave on the open ocean? In this activity, you can discover how water in ocean waves really moves.

MATERIALS
- small aquarium
- water
- cork
- Science Log data sheet

DO THIS

1 Fill the aquarium about $\frac{2}{3}$ full of water.

2 Place the cork on the water.

3 Paddle your hands in the water at one end of the aquarium to make waves.

4 Observe the motion of the cork.

THINK AND WRITE

1. How did the cork move?

2. What does the movement of the cork suggest about the movement of water in a wave?

A Very Moving Story

Have you ever wondered where waves come from? Nautica has made a video titled *Ride the Wave Train.* Here are some frames from the video that were stored in Nautica's SeaBank.

FRAME 1

Wind blows across the water, producing a *ripple.*

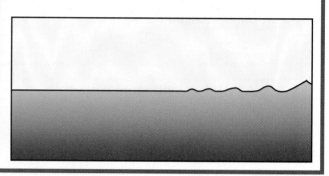

FRAME 20

As the wind continues to blow, it pushes on the sides of the ripple, setting a small circle of water in motion.

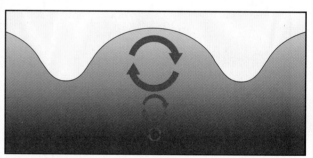

FRAME 40

No matter how hard the wind blows or how big a wave gets, the water stays in one place. Only the energy producing the wave moves forward.

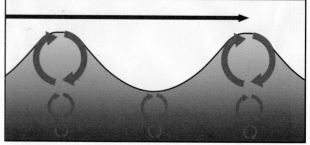

FRAME 60

As more energy is transferred from the wind to the water, the waves grow. Ripples become *swells*.

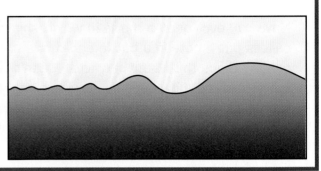

FRAME 100

As swells get near a shore, they become *breakers*.

FRAME 120

As waves break on shore, the circular water paths become flat. We feel the energy as *surge,* the back-and-forth flow of water near the beach.

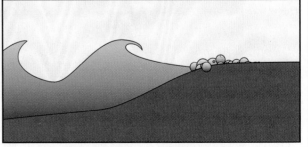

THINK ABOUT IT

Explain why waves break on most beaches, even when the wind isn't blowing.

Current Data

Have you ever seen a movie in which shipwrecked sailors put a note in a bottle and throw it into the ocean? Since the water in waves doesn't actually move forward, how can the survivors expect to be rescued? You can get a clue by doing the next activity.

MATERIALS
- rectangular baking pan
- water
- cork
- straw
- Science Log data sheet

DO THIS

1 Fill the baking pan with water, and float the cork at one end.

2 Blow gently across the surface of the water. Observe the movement of the cork.

3 Now, blow a steady stream of air through the straw across the surface of the water. Again, observe the movement of the cork.

THINK AND WRITE

What did the steady stream of air do to the movement of the cork?

A Chilling Experience

In the last activity, a steady flow of air created *surface currents* that moved the cork. But wind is not the only force that can produce currents. In this activity, you'll get the cold facts on *underwater currents*.

MATERIALS
- glass baking dish
- 2 glasses
- tap water, warm water, ice water
- red and blue food coloring
- spoon
- Science Log data sheet

DO THIS

1 Fill the baking dish with tap water. Fill one glass with very warm water and the other glass with cold water. Melt ice to get the water really cold.

2 Drop red food coloring into the glass of warm water and blue food coloring into the glass of ice water. Use the spoon to mix the food coloring with the water in each glass.

3 Pour the warm water very slowly into one end of the baking dish. Pour the cold water slowly into the other end of the dish. Observe the movement of the red and blue colored waters as they mix with the water in the dish.

THINK AND WRITE

1. Cold water is heavier than warm water. How does this fact explain the movement of the blue water?

2. How would cold water create an underwater current in the ocean?

3. **COMPARING** When you compare, you look for things in common. Which kind of current, a surface current or an underwater current, is more likely to carry off that note in the bottle? Explain.

Ocean Rivers

You may recall that *currents* are produced by steady winds blowing across the surface of the ocean, or by differences in water temperature. Early European explorers used wind and currents to speed up their trips to and from the Americas. To discover more about ocean currents, study the map of surface currents and answer the questions below.

On the map, warm currents are shown in red, while cold currents are shown in blue. What currents affect the eastern and western coasts of the United States? Where do most warm currents begin? On which sides of the oceans are most cold currents found? What cold current completes the circle started by the warm Gulf Stream?

In addition to helping navigation, currents affect the Earth's climate. The Gulf Stream, for example, moves heat from the warm, tropical Caribbean Sea to the cold North Atlantic. Its waters move north along the east coast of the United States and then east across the Atlantic Ocean toward Europe. Europe would be much colder if the Gulf Stream did not carry warm water its way.

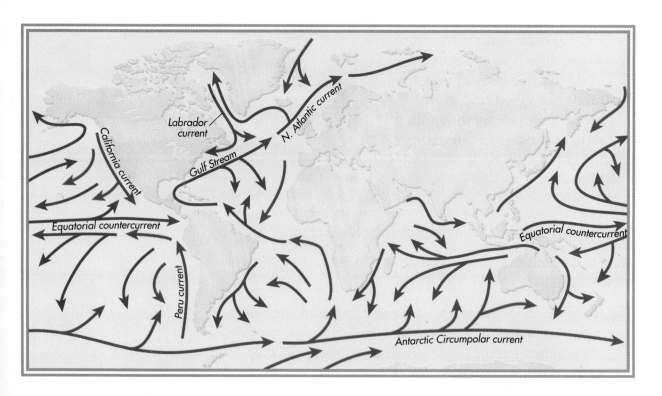

Changes in the normal pattern of currents can be disastrous. Every year in December, a current called *El Niño* arrives and warms the cold waters off the coast of Ecuador.

In some years, the warming effects of *El Niño* are much greater than usual, leading to storms and floods as far away as North America and Africa.

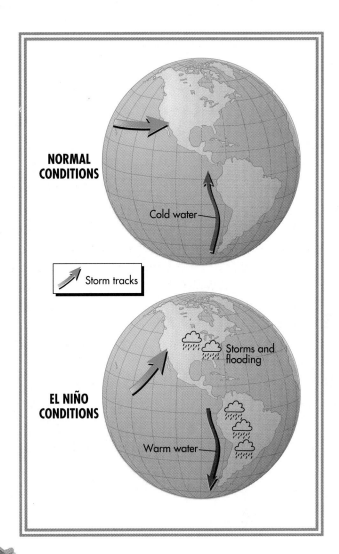

NORMAL CONDITIONS

Cold water

Storm tracks

EL NIÑO CONDITIONS

Storms and flooding

Warm water

LESSON 4 REVIEW

❶ Describe two ways that wind can affect ocean water.

❷ Why are ocean currents important to life on Earth?

DOUBLE CHECK

SECTION B REVIEW

1. How do land, air, and sea interact?

2. Describe several threats to the water cycle and to ocean life.

SECTION C
Explorers of the Deep

"I cannot believe my eyes. From the abyss two-and-a-half miles beneath the sea, the bow of a great vessel emerges in ghostly detail. I have never seen the ship—nor has anyone for 73 years—yet I know nearly every feature of her. She is S.S. Titanic, the luxury liner lost after collision with an iceberg in 1912, at a cost of 1,522 lives."

▲ Alvin

With these words, Dr. Robert Ballard introduced the world to perhaps the greatest ocean exploration adventure of all time. In this section, you will meet Dr. Ballard and other scientists who have devoted their lives to exploring the ocean.

As you work through the investigations, you may discover ways in which you can join them. In your Science Log, list some of the ways you might like to contribute to ocean exploration.

1 ADVENTURE AHEAD

Ocean exploration depends on technology just as much as space exploration does. And it carries many of the same risks. You probably know the names of famous spacecraft, such as *Apollo* and *Voyager,* but have you ever heard of *Alvin*? In this lesson, you'll discover how *Alvin* has advanced ocean exploration and helped scientists discover new species of organisms on the ocean floor.

Heeeere's *Alvin!*

Nautica wants us to meet a famous friend of hers—*Alvin.*
Let's join Nautica at SeaBase Nautilus for the introduction.

Hello again, and welcome to SeaBase Nautilus. This is where I live when I'm not out exploring the ocean or talking to classes like yours. Right now, I'm here for my 20,000-leagues-under-the-sea checkup. Soon, I'll be joining my good friend *Alvin* on one of its fantastic underwater adventures. I don't know where we're going yet, but with *Alvin,* there's never a dull moment! Let's head over to the docks, and I'll introduce you.

On the way, let me tell you a little about *Alvin*'s history. Back in the 1950s, just about the same time the space program was starting up, a group of scientists was meeting to discuss the future of ocean exploration. The scientists knew they were going to need a unique vehicle to explore the ocean.

Like space, the deep ocean is a pretty hostile place. The temperature is barely above 0°C (32°F). It's always dark, and the pressure is enough to squash a foam cup into something smaller than a thimble. So, like a spacecraft, a deep ocean submersible would need powerful lights, a heated, pressurized crew compartment, and a communications system—to keep in touch with the surface. The result of the scientists'

efforts to build such a submersible was *Alvin*.

Alvin was built for the United States Navy in 1964. Now it's operated and maintained by our sister base, the Woods Hole Oceanographic Institution in Massachusetts. *Alvin* is about 2.4 meters (8 feet) wide and 6.7 meters (22 feet) long. But its interior is only large enough for a pilot and two scientists. *Alvin* can dive as deep as 4,000 meters (13,000 feet), so its manipulator arm can scoop up samples or retrieve objects from the ocean floor.

▼ **Meet *Alvin*!**

As versatile as *Alvin* is, it seldom dives alone. On some of its most famous adventures, a robot submersible, Jason Junior, or JJ, went along. Because of its small size, JJ could get into places that were too small for *Alvin*.

Describing all of *Alvin*'s accomplishments would fill this book, so we'll just concentrate on a few of them. In 1977, for example, scientists using *Alvin* discovered warm-water vents along the Galápagos Rift, off the coast of South America. These vents are really cracks in the ocean floor along a boundary between two tectonic plates. The warm, mineral-rich water from these vents supports a community of sea life that scientists had never seen before. So far, more than a hundred new species of organisms have been identified.

▲ Sea life near a warm vent

THINK ABOUT IT

Why was finding the underwater vents important to scientists?

A Close Call!

Not every day aboard *Alvin* is filled with new discoveries. The little research submersible has made thousands of dives, but as you will see in the story that follows, some days are more exciting than others.

It was August 12, 1991. *Alvin* was diving off the coast of Oregon. The researchers were trying to find out more about the vent animals that had been discovered nearly 15 years earlier. The day before, they had delivered only one clam to the lab on board the companion ship *Atlantis II.* Because it costs $30,000 a day to operate *Alvin,* the crew had nicknamed the lone creature "the 30,000-clam clam." Jokes aside, the crew were concerned and determined to find something more exciting on this, their last day of diving.

A normal dive lasts about nine hours. Although *Alvin* carries enough food, water, and air for three days, the crew would probably freeze before that in the ice-cold water. After two hours of sliding down a muddy slope, pilot Cindy Van Dover tried to engage the lift propellers. However, the submersible didn't respond.

Van Dover calmly radioed the surface, "I think we may be snagged on something." For what must have seemed like forever to the stuck crew, experts tried to figure out what *Alvin* was stuck on. Then the talk shifted to rescue plans. There were several choices:

Plan A—Drop weights from *Alvin*. This was risky, because if the sub was snagged by a net or a cable, dropping weights would put it nose down, making "the last resort" impossible.

Plan B— "Go fishing." Attached to the sub was a long line with a float attached.

▶ Starting a dive

The surface ship could try to snare the float and reel in *Alvin*. All agreed this was a long shot. Besides, it had never been tried before.

Plan C—Call for help. A French ship with another submersible was about a day away. But if its submersible couldn't free *Alvin*, too much time would have been wasted.

Plan D—Try the last resort. Van Dover could release the crew cabin, sending it bobbing to the surface. However, if this worked—and it had never been tried— the rest of *Alvin* would sit worthless on the ocean bottom.

The crew decided to try releasing weights one at a time. Weight after weight was dropped, all with the same result—nothing. Finally, the last weight was dropped. If this didn't work, they would have to try another, riskier plan.

A few long moments later Van Dover again radioed the surface. "We have lift-off. The sub is free." An hour later, *Alvin* reached the surface, and the crew on the deck of *Atlantis II* solved the mystery. Mud poured from the bottom of the sub. *Alvin* had picked up over 270 kilograms (600 pounds) of mud while sliding down the slope. A few kilograms more, and the sub may have been stuck forever on the ocean bottom.

No clams again, but at least *Alvin* would be around to dive again another day. And pilot Van Dover earned a new nickname—"Scoop."

▲ *Alvin* returns!

LESSON 1 REVIEW

How is exploring the deep ocean a lot like exploring space? How is it different?

2 THEY FOUND THE *TITANIC!*

As scientifically important as the discovery of the underwater vents was, *Alvin's* most famous adventure was probably finding the *Titanic,* an ocean liner that hit an iceberg and sank in the North Atlantic Ocean in 1912. The ship lay at the bottom of the ocean for nearly 75 years, until a team of scientists found her and spent several days using *Alvin* to explore her. But before we learn the details of this adventure, let's see why the North Atlantic can be a dangerous place for ships.

ACTIVITY

Hidden Dangers

A crew member spots an iceberg and sends an alert to the bridge. The bridge responds, and the ship is steered away from a huge mountain of ice. Is the ship out of danger? This activity will help you answer that question.

MATERIALS
- small aquarium
- water
- blue food coloring
- plastic spoon
- small plastic bag of ice
- Science Log data sheet

DO THIS

❶ Fill the aquarium with water, and drop in food coloring until the water turns dark. Use the spoon to spread the food coloring throughout the water.

❷ Your teacher will float a bag of ice in the water. Make a sketch to show how much ice you estimate is above the surface of the water and how much ice you estimate is below the surface of the water.

❸ Remove the bag of ice and pour the colored water out of the aquarium. Refill the tank with fresh water, but don't add food coloring this time.

4 Refloat the bag of ice in the water. Make a sketch to show how much of the ice is actually above the surface of the water and how much is actually below the surface of the water.

THINK AND WRITE

1. How did your estimate of the amount of ice above and below the surface of the water compare with your observation?

2. From your observations, why do you think icebergs can be dangerous for ships passing nearby?

3. **INFERRING** Scientists must often infer something they cannot directly observe. In question 2, you were asked to infer something about the danger of icebergs to ships. From what observation could you make this inference?

A Hard Lesson

For its time, the *Titanic* was a marvel of technology. It had the latest in radio and navigational equipment and powerful, smooth-running engines. It was, according to its designers, unsinkable. But on its first voyage, something went terribly wrong. The *Titanic* struck an iceberg and sank. You can learn the details by reading the following story.

A SHIP OF DESTINY

On April 14, 1912, the pride of Britain's White Star Line was on her maiden voyage from Southampton, England, to New York. She was the most luxurious ship afloat.

And the biggest. The 46,000-ton *Titanic* was four blocks long and eleven stories high. When launched, she was the largest object ever moved.

Newspapers called her "the Wonder Ship," a crowning achievement of a century of rapid technological development. People looked at a floating palace like the *Titanic* and felt that, now, nothing was impossible.

She was the most glamorous of three sister vessels White Star hoped would dominate the profitable North Atlantic market. The *Olympic* was already in service; the *Britannic* was under construction.

The *Titanic*'s crew of more than 900 promised a pleas-

THE
Titanic
HAS
GONE
DOWN

by John C. Halter
from *Boys' Life*

ant voyage. First-class passengers enjoyed an indoor swimming pool (the first on a passenger liner), a gymnasium, a squash court, a sauna, and a library. They could eat in a 500-seat dining salon, a smaller private restaurant, or a French sidewalk cafe.

Even third-class passengers, used to cattle-car conditions in earlier ships, had four-bunk cabins, a dining hall, a lounge, and a promenade deck.

The 325 first-class passengers occupied 60 percent of the ship. Some were society celebrities; others were noted millionaires. Many brought personal servants. A one-way, deluxe first-class suite cost $1,300—about $13,000 in today's money.

Several decks below the first-class accommodations, the 700 third-class passengers were confined to the ship's forward and rear areas. They had paid just $32 for their one-way tickets.

THE "UNSINKABLE" SHIP

The *Titanic* had everything—except enough lifeboats.

The ship didn't need them, her designers said, because the *Titanic* was "practically unsinkable." Her hull had a double bottom and 16 "watertight" compartments.

Her captain, the 62-year-old White Star veteran Edward J. Smith, had confidence in the new technology. "I cannot imagine

R.M.S. "TITANIC

APRIL 14, 1912.

LUNCHEON.

CONSOMMÉ FERMIER   COCKIE LEEKIE
FILLETS OF BRILL
EGG À L'ARGENTEUIL
CHICKEN À LA MARYLAND
CORNED BEEF, VEGETABLES, DUMPLINGS
FROM THE GRILL.
GRILLED MUTTON CHOPS
MASHED, FRIED & BAKED JACKET POTATOES.

CUSTARD PUDDING
APPLE MERINGUE   PASTRY
BUFFET.
SALMON MAYONNAISE   POTTED SHRIMPS
NORWEGIAN ANCHOVIES   SOUSED HERRINGS
PLAIN & SMOKED SARDINES
ROAST BEEF
ROUND OF SPICED BEEF
VEAL & HAM PIE
VIRGINIA & CUMBERLAND HAM
BOLOGNA SAUSAGE   BRAWN
GALANTINE OF CHICKEN
CORNED OX TONGUE
LETTUCE   BEETROOT   TOMATOES
CHEESE.
CHESHIRE, STILTON, GORGONZOLA, EDAM,
CAMEMBERT, ROQUEFORT, ST. IVEL,
CHEDDAR

▲ *Titanic* **luncheon menu**

any condition which would cause a ship to founder," he had said a few years earlier. "Modern shipbuilding has gone beyond that."

British regulations, last updated in 1898, said ships of more than 10,000 tons only needed lifeboats for 980 persons. No problem there. The *Titanic*'s 20 boats would hold 1,178, almost 200 more than required.

But the ship held no lifeboat drills for passengers or crew. And most of the 1,320 passengers weren't aware she didn't have boats for everyone. Four days out of Southampton, however, the *Titanic* had experienced no major problems.

WARNING: ICE HAZARDS

An ice field lay ahead. Other ships had radioed alarms, and Captain Smith alerted his crew to keep a sharp eye out.

But he didn't slow the ship. No ship reduced speed until ice was sighted. Why should the *Titanic*?

The sun set, and the stars of a clear, moonless night came out. The outside temperature dropped steadily, to 43 degrees by 7 P.M., and passengers retreated inside.

By 11 P.M. the temperature was near freezing. In the radio room, the chief operator struggled to send out a pile of passenger ship-to-shore messages. In his haste, he brushed aside an interruption. The *Californian,* some 19 miles to the northwest, was

reporting that ice had forced her to stop for the night.

Forty minutes later, lookout Fleet saw an iceberg looming ahead. At his warning, the *Titanic* reversed engines and turned sharply to port. But not in time.

She scraped the giant iceberg, which stood as high as the top deck.

Below the surface, the rock-solid ice popped rivets and opened metal plate seams. Water poured into the first five compartments along a narrow, 300-foot-long area.

The ship slowed to a stop, and her engines shut down. Crew members reassured passengers that nothing was wrong.

A DEADLY WOUND

The damage, however, was fatal. The ship could float with her first four compartments flooded. But now water was filling the first

▶ *Titanic* **under construction**

▶ **Lifeboats away.**

five. As this weight pulled the bow down, water would soon spill into the remaining compartments. The ship would sink within hours.

The *Titanic* began sending the traditional CQD distress signal, as well as a brand new one—SOS. But on the *Californian,* just 20 miles away, the radio operator and captain had gone to bed. And her crew didn't understand why the *Titanic* was firing rockets.

Some 58 miles to the south, the 13,564-ton *Carpathia* picked up the SOS. She turned north, but at her 17-knot top speed, she would take four hours to reach the *Titanic.*

Captain Smith told the crew to begin loading the lifeboats. But—to avoid panic—he made no general announcement. The first boat—capacity 65—went into the water at 12:45 A.M. carrying only 28 persons. Passengers wouldn't leave the huge, brightly lit ship. They saw more danger in being lowered 60 feet in a wooden boat into the cold, dark sea.

And even though passengers became less hesitant as the ship's list increased, the inexperienced crew lowered many boats only half full. Just seven carried more than 50 passengers and only three were filled to capacity.

Many third-class passengers never had a chance at a lifeboat. The crew restrained them below deck during the early loading. Then, as the boats dwindled, more passengers surged to the boat deck. Panic threatened the loading, and an officer held them back with a revolver.

DRAMA ON COLLAPSIBLES A AND B

By 2:05 A.M. only collapsible rafts A and B remained. Assistant radio operator Harold Bride joined some crewmen struggling to release the two boats.

Too late. Water swept the boat and men overboard. Collapsible A landed upright but half swamped. Collapsible B landed upside down near the *Titanic*'s raised stern.

Harold Bride came to the surface underneath the overturned boat. More than three dozen other desperate swimmers struggled aboard or clung to the two collapsibles.

At 2:20 A.M. the *Titanic*'s stern rose into the air. Then the darkened hull slid beneath the surface. The great ship was gone.

Two hours later, in the gray light of early dawn, 705 survivors in the lifeboats saw the *Carpathia* steam into view. A woman in the nearest lifeboat screamed the dreaded news: "The *Titanic* has gone down with everyone aboard!"

THINK ABOUT IT

Why do you think the crew of the *Titanic* was unprepared for this disaster?

ACTIVITY

It's How Deep?

In the area of the North Atlantic where the *Titanic* went down, the ocean is about 3,750 meters (12,300 feet) deep. How can water that deep be measured? In the activities that follow, you will discover two methods—an old one and a modern one.

DO THIS

1. Work with a partner. Cover the aquarium with the construction paper, and pour sand and pebbles into it. Without looking, scatter several small rocks on top of the sand and pebbles. Then fill the aquarium with water.

2. Tie the fishing weight to a piece of string about twice as long as the aquarium is deep.

3. Without looking, one partner slowly lowers the weighted end of the string into the left side of the aquarium until the weight just touches the bottom. The other partner pinches the string at a point even with the top of the aquarium.

4. Measure the length of the string from the weighted end to the point where it is being held. This measurement will be the depth of the water on the left side of the aquarium.

5. Repeat steps 3 and 4 for the middle section and the right side of the aquarium.

MATERIALS

- small aquarium
- black construction paper
- sand, pebbles, small rocks
- water
- string
- fishing weight
- ruler
- Science Log data sheet

THINK AND WRITE

If a similar procedure were used to measure the depth of the ocean, what problems would occur?

Boing . . . Boing . . . Boing

Scientists used to measure the depth of the ocean by throwing a weighted rope off the side of a ship. The rope had knots tied at regular intervals. When the weight touched the bottom, they pulled the rope in and counted the knots. Today, scientists use sounding, or *sonar*, which you read about earlier, to determine ocean depth. In this activity, you will learn how to calculate depth by using sounding data.

MATERIALS
- calculator
- Science Log data sheet

DO THIS

1 Use the calculator to multiply the first *Time* from the data table by 1,500 m/sec (the speed of sound in water).

2 Divide the product by 2. This number will be the depth of the water in meters at the first *Location*. Record the depth.

3 Repeat steps 1 and 2 for each of the other locations in the data table.

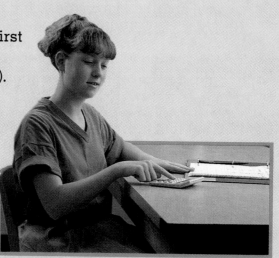

THINK AND WRITE

1. Why was it necessary to divide each product by 2 to calculate the depth of the water?

2. How could the sounding method be used to locate large objects on the ocean floor?

SOUNDING DATA		
Location	Time (sec)	Depth(m)
1	1.2	
2	2.0	
3	3.6	
4	4.8	
5	5.3	
6	2.3	
7	3.1	
8	4.5	
9	5.0	
10	5.1	

Alvin and Company

Now that you know a little more about finding objects in deep water, let's finish the story of the *Titanic*—its discovery and its exploration.

 Summer 1973: For decades the *Titanic* has rested two and a half miles down on the bottom of the North Atlantic. But with the passing years, her growing legend has captured the imagination of many people.

One who falls under her spell is professional oceanographer and former Life Scout Dr. Robert Ballard. He has long dreamed of finding the lost ship. Now, he begins organizing an expedition to find it.

August 1985: Dr. Ballard's team of scientists from the Deep Submergence Laboratory at the Woods Hole Oceanographic Institution in Massachusetts begins its search. The scientists join a French group already searching the ocean floor. The French use a powerful sonar they've developed. But its electronic sound waves bouncing off the ocean floor find nothing near the reported site of the sinking.

The searchers switch to video cameras on the Argo, a steel sled they tow by cable

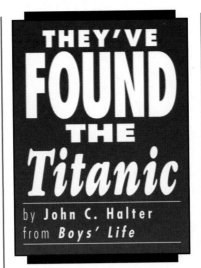

THEY'VE **FOUND** THE *Titanic*

by **John C. Halter**
from ***Boys' Life***

just above the ocean floor. They look for the thousands of small objects that fell from the *Titanic* as she sank.

Aug. 31, 1985: Only five days left before the expedition must return. Dr. Ballard feels "a rising panic." He begins to face "total defeat." Day after day, around the clock, the team sees "mud and more mud, endless miles of nothing" on the video monitors.

Just before 2 A.M.: "There's something," one of the crew says. On the screen, bits of wreckage stream past.

And then a massive round object. It's one of the *Titanic's* giant boilers. The gigantic hull lies nearby.

Crew members cheer, shake hands, and pound each other on the back.

They've found the *Titanic*!

Despite rough seas, they carefully scan the hull with Argo and another sled, ANGUS, that takes still pictures. These reveal that the *Titanic's* stern is missing. So are her four enormous smokestacks.

Sept. 9, 1985: A cheering crowd welcomes the team back to Woods Hole. Once again the *Titanic* is front-page news around the world.

A CLOSER LOOK

July 1986: The scientists return to visit the wreck. Crammed into their tiny titanium submarine, *Alvin,*

▲ **Argo**

▲ **Alvin and Dr. Ballard**

"like three sardines in a spherical can," Dr. Ballard and two others descend into the freezing blackness. They listen to classical music during the two-and-a-half-hour dive to the bottom.

On the *Titanic*, they discover that deep-sea worms have eaten away most of the ship's wood. They are surprised to find huge, bacteria-formed, powdery rust formations all over the hull. To Dr. Ballard they look like long icicles. He gives them the name "rusticles."

Their remote camera, a "swimming eyeball" called Jason Jr., or JJ, peers into the first-class cabins on the boat deck. It slithers down the grand stairway into the ship, where it photographs a light fixture still hanging from the ceiling.

Alvin also explores the 2,000 feet of debris between the bow and stern sections of the ship. Thousands of perfectly preserved objects lie on the ocean floor. The explorers see a rusty metal drinking cup sitting on top of a giant boiler.

The ship's stern section is badly damaged. Its huge propellers are buried in 45 feet of mud.

Before *Alvin* leaves for the last time, the scientists place a plaque on the *Titanic*'s stern, in memory of the more than 1,500 persons who had died when she sank.

SOME ANSWERS AND SOME NEW QUESTIONS

The expeditions answered many questions about the *Titanic*.

They confirmed that the ship had broken in half while sinking (as many survivors had reported). They concluded that the iceberg had probably popped open steel plates rather than ripped a lengthy gash in the ship's hull (as long believed).

The scientists discovered that deep-sea organisms had removed most organic material, including wood, food, clothing, and human remains. And the ship's metal parts are slowly rusting away too.

Living survivors Ruth Blanchard and Eva Hart, two of the last people to see the *Titanic*, and Dr. Ballard, the first to see her again, all hope the world will leave the ship in peace, a memorial to those who died with her. They were saddened when a French expedition returned in 1987 to retrieve objects from the debris field.

We can still learn from the *Titanic* disaster, Dr. Ballard believes.

"Too much confidence was placed in technology," he says, "and the power of nature was overlooked."

THE END OF AN ERA

The *Titanic* disaster rocked society's belief in relentless (and often unplanned) progress. The ship was supposed to be a triumphant symbol of technology, but less than three hours after hitting the iceberg, she was gone.

In our own time, the explosion of the space shuttle *Challenger* in 1986 had a similar impact. A sudden, unexpected disaster exposed the flaws in our vaunted technology. Such events in history remind us that the price of progress is often tragically high. ◪

THINK ABOUT IT

Why does Ballard say we place too much confidence in technology?

Up Close and Personal

The *Titanic* lay at the bottom of the North Atlantic for nearly 75 years. In 1986 *Alvin,* a free-floating submersible with a crew of three, and Jason Jr., JJ, a robot submersible attached to *Alvin* by a 61-meter (200-foot) cable, spent several days exploring the *Titanic,* which lay in 3,750 meters (12,300 feet) of water at the bottom of the North Atlantic. Now that you've read about what they did, let's take a closer look at *Alvin* and JJ.

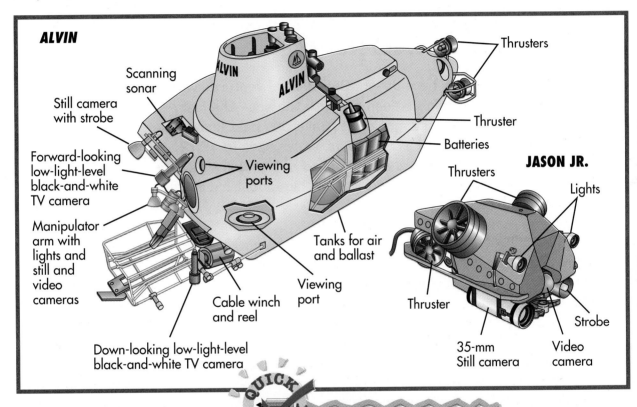

ALVIN

Thrusters

Scanning sonar

Still camera with strobe

Forward-looking low-light-level black-and-white TV camera

Viewing ports

Manipulator arm with lights and still and video cameras

Thruster

Batteries

JASON JR.

Thrusters

Lights

Tanks for air and ballast

Cable winch and reel

Viewing port

Thruster

Down-looking low-light-level black-and-white TV camera

35-mm Still camera

Video camera

Strobe

QUICK CHECK

LESSON 2 REVIEW

1 What might have been done to prevent the great loss of life on the *Titanic*?

2 Do you agree with Dr. Ballard's statement about the most important lessons to be learned from the *Titanic*? Why or why not?

3 How did technological advances help solve the mysteries surrounding the sinking of the *Titanic*?

3 JOIN THE CREW

In the years to come, more and more people will explore the ocean. Some may explore from a classroom or from an armchair at home. Others will explore from the deck of a research ship or the inside of a submersible like *Alvin.* In this lesson, you will meet two people who will share their explorations.

Meet Bob Ballard

Like the ancient Greek hero Jason, Bob Ballard ventures where few dare to go. He explores deep beneath the sea—the last frontier on Earth. A marine geologist, Ballard is best known for finding the wreck of the R.M.S. *Titanic,* which sank in 1912. Clay Sellers, 15, of Linville, Virginia, joined one of Ballard's projects as a student observer and talked to him about his lifelong interest in the sea.

▲ Clay Sellers and Bob Ballard

▲ Before a dive

Aboard the Research Ship *Laney Chouest*

from *National Geographic World*

CLAY: *What will you be studying during this expedition that we're on now in the Gulf of California?*

BALLARD: My team and I will be studying the ocean floor by using remote-controlled vehicles that can dive more than a mile deep. We'll look at smokers and the weird creatures that live near them.

CLAY: *Smokers? What are they?*

BALLARD: Smokers are hydrothermal vents, or hot springs. The vents spit out plumes of water loaded with black, gray or white minerals. They look like smoke. If those vents were on land, they'd be considered toxic waste dumps. But many sea creatures need the minerals to survive.

CLAY: *When did you first see hydrothermal vents?*

BALLARD: During the expedition we made to the Galápagos Rift, in the Pacific Ocean. That was back in 1977. It was the most exciting discovery of my career. Just imagine being the first human being to see all those strange sea creatures living near the vents!

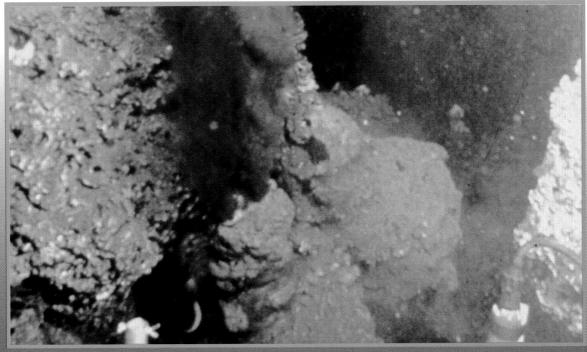

▲ Smokers

CLAY: *Were you surprised to find so many weird kinds of animals living there?*

BALLARD: I was flabbergasted. It was like traveling back in time to a world of primitive creatures. Animals like those have been around for millions of years. We saw white crabs, six-foot-long worms, and snails with sharp teeth.

CLAY: *Is there another discovery that was as exciting?*

BALLARD: It was thrilling to find the *Titanic* and explore it with the remote-controlled robot Jason Jr. Its camera filmed a small room where a chandelier was still hanging. You'd think it would have shattered after the ship hit an iceberg, broke in half, and sank 12,000 feet.

CLAY: *Would you explain how you find something like the* Titanic *on the ocean floor?*

BALLARD: Lots of homework. It's like being a detective. First I gather as much information as possible so I can narrow the search area to about ten miles long by ten miles wide. Then our ship sweeps back and forth over the area, kind of the way you do when you mow a lawn.

CLAY: *Do you have any plans for building new deep-sea research vehicles?*

BALLARD: No. Now I'm interested in setting up underwater museums. My first project will be the *Lusitania*, a British ocean liner that was torpedoed by

◀ **A chandelier on the *Titanic* before the ship sailed**

◀ **Same chandelier on the *Titanic* filmed by JJ**

▲ **Passengers walking on the deck of the *Titanic* before it sailed**

Germany during World War I. It sank in 310 feet of water off the west coast of Ireland. I want to turn the *Lusitania* into a museum that people can visit by using remote-controlled robots, the way kids now take part in expeditions for the JASON Project.

CLAY: *How did you get interested in oceanography?*

BALLARD: I grew up in San Diego, California, near the ocean. The sea was always part of my childhood. I spent a lot of time walking on the beach, fishing, and body surfing. But I was more interested in the bottom of the ocean. I wanted to scuba dive. Even if I was in a swimming pool, I'd go to the bottom just to look around.

CLAY: *What would you tell Junior Members who want to become oceanographers?*

BALLARD: The key is to get a broad education so you can do just about anything. Take math and lots of science: chemistry, biology, geology, and especially physics.

CLAY: *Do you know of any opportunities for high school students to get experience in oceanography?*

BALLARD: There's a summer program at the Woods Hole Oceanographic Institution in Woods Hole, Massachusetts, where I'm based. Many universities also have summer programs; check with schools near your home.

CLAY: *What kinds of people besides oceanographers work on a research ship?*

BALLARD: People from all walks of life work together as a team aboard a ship. There's room for everybody. Those who are in the United States Navy have leadership skills. Some people went to trade schools. Others have computer skills or a college degree in science.

CLAY: *Why is it important to learn about the ocean?*

BALLARD: Someday people will live at sea, but we have explored less than one tenth of one percent of the deep sea. Much of what we study in the JASON Project has never been seen by human beings. We need to learn to live together, the way the creatures of the ocean do.

THINK ABOUT IT

Why is being an ocean explorer a lot like being a detective?

◀ **Mission Bay, San Diego**

The JASON Project

After finding the wreck of the *Titanic,* Dr. Ballard received thousands of letters from students asking him to describe the adventure. In response to those letters, Dr. Ballard created the JASON Project so students could join him on underwater explorations.

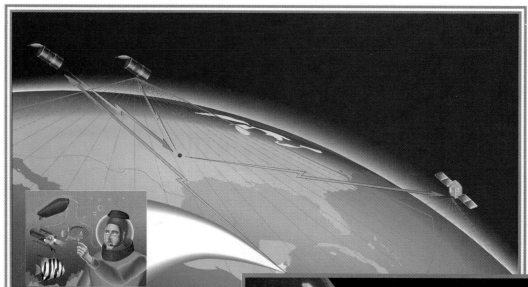

▲ JASON Project: Voyage V

The diagram is of the fifth JASON Project, which began in February 1994. During this project, as with the previous four, hundreds of thousands of students across North America watched live TV broadcasts of Dr. Ballard and other scientists working in Belize, a country in Central America.

A few students got to sit at control panels, where they talked to scientists and even helped control a robot submersible called ROV— short for *r*emotely *o*perated *v*ehicle. As the students worked at the ROV control panel, signals went

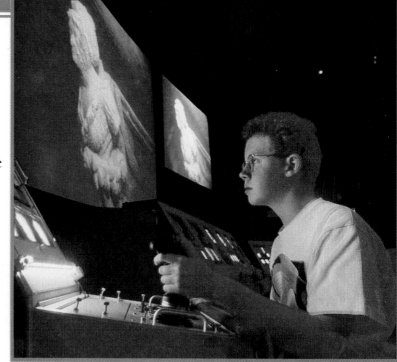

▲ Student guiding JASON

up to a satellite and then down to ROV, which was exploring a coral reef off Belize.

Since 1989, more than 1.5 million students have joined scientists on various JASON Projects. The following is a summary:

Voyage I—May 1989. On the bottom of the Mediterranean Sea a robot photographed hot springs and the wreck of a Roman trading ship that sank 1,600 years ago.

Voyage II—May 1990. A robot mapped the wrecks of two ships that sank in Lake Ontario during the War of 1812, a conflict between Britain and the United States.

Voyage III—December 1991. Scientists studied the wildlife of the Galápagos Islands, both on land and in the Pacific Ocean.

Voyage IV—March 1993. A robot and the three-person submarine Turtle photographed six-foot-long tube worms and other sea creatures in western Mexico's Gulf of California. Scientists also watched migrating gray whales.

Voyage V—February–March 1994. Scientists studied wildlife and an ancient Maya city in the rain forest of Belize, while a robot explored the largest barrier reef in the Western Hemisphere.

THINK ABOUT IT

Why do you think the JASON Projects are important to the future of ocean exploration?

▲ JASON students get a crash course in navigation.

▲ Towed camera-sled MEDEA photographing JASON inspecting marine life

▲ Artist's rendition of the completed Argo/JASON system

Dr. Sylvia Earle:
Deep-Ocean Explorer

Dr. Ballard has done much of his ocean exploring from the cabin of *Alvin*. On the other hand, the scientist you are about to meet gets just a little closer to her work. Read the following article about Dr. Sylvia A. Earle and her walk on the ocean floor in a personal submersible called the *JIM suit*.

A Walk in the DEEP

by **Sylvia A. Earle**
from ***National Geographic***

▲ **Getting ready to dive**

 Encased in a bizarre space-age diving suit, I stand strapped to the bow of a small research submarine like some ponderous figurehead. In the submarine behind me pilot Bohdan Bartko and team leader Al Giddings can observe me and maintain voice contact via a slender communications cable connected to the inside of my diving helmet.

By means of a simple control Al can disconnect the safety belt that holds me securely to the deck of the submarine. Plans call for him to release me when we reach the seafloor, allowing me to walk about at will.

At a depth of 1,150 feet the submarine gently touches down, and Boh switches on the submarine's lights. "Hang on for a while, Sylvia," Al advises. "Boh is going to try and find deeper water."

"Are you ready to take a walk?" Al asks over the communications line. Nothing in his voice betrays concern, though the step we are about to take is final. Once released from the submarine, I cannot climb back aboard and refasten the safety belt. Nor can Al or Boh swim out of the sub to help me in an emergency.

"Anytime," I answer Al's query. The belt drops free. As I step down onto the ocean floor, I am aware that I am entering terrain in some respects similar to a lunar landscape.

The suit is large enough for me to withdraw my hands from the metal arms to record my observations in a notebook. As I write down a few conclusions and numerous questions, I keep a running conversation with Al. At twelve o'clock he announces, "You've been out there two and a half hours. It's nearly time to surface."

As I rise slowly from the seafloor, I reflect on the dive—the deepest solo exploration of its kind ever made, and the work of a team of highly trained people.

The average depth of the ocean is 10,000 feet, and the deepest place in it nearly seven miles down. Clearly we still have far to go and much to do, but on this day we have taken an exciting step.

▲ Fastened to the sub

▲ On the surface again

QUICK CHECK

LESSON 3 REVIEW

❶ How are all ocean explorers alike? How are they different?

❷ Why is it important for ocean explorers to share their observations with us?

DOUBLE CHECK

SECTION C REVIEW

1. Based on the stories about *Alvin*, how has technology advanced our understanding of the ocean?

2. What do you think explorers such as Ballard and Earle hope to accomplish?

I REFLECT

It's time to think about the ideas you have discovered during your investigations. Think, too, about your many accomplishments.

SUMMARIZE

Answer the following in your Science Log.

1. What **I Wonder** questions have you answered in your investigations? What new questions have you asked?

2. What have you discovered about the ocean? How have your ideas changed?

3. Did any of your discoveries surprise you? Explain.

In the water cycle water goes from the air to the land and the sea and back to the air again. I was surprised to learn that more than 90 percent of the Earth's water is ocean water.

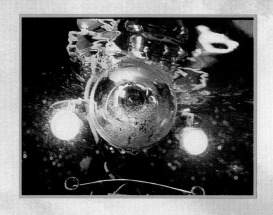

CONNECT IDEAS

1. Name two ways in which tide-pool organisms are different from beach organisms.

2. How have technological advances such as *Alvin* helped scientists gain a greater understanding of the ocean?

3. Why wouldn't you find phytoplankton in the abyss?

4. Explain the relationships between the sun, the moon, and the tides.

5. Why are weights needed by scuba divers and by submersibles like *Alvin*?

6. Why is it dangerous to trust technology as much as the *Titanic*'s designers did?

SCIENCE PORTFOLIO

1 Complete your Science Experiences Record.

2 Select several samples of your best work from each section to include in your Science Portfolio.

3 On A Guide to My Science Portfolio, tell why you chose each sample.

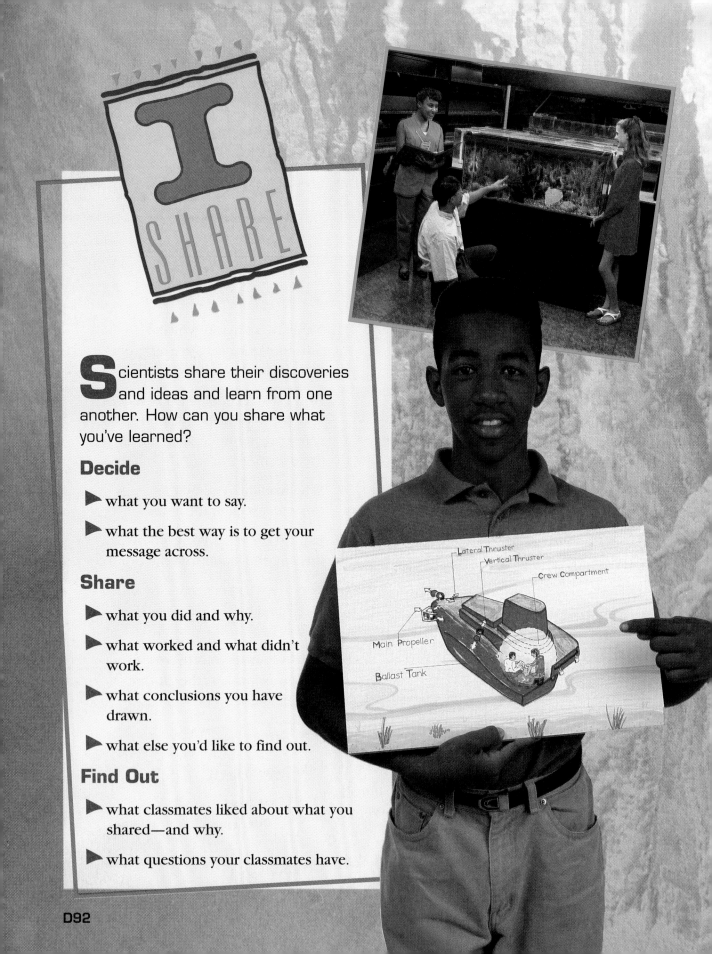

I SHARE

Scientists share their discoveries and ideas and learn from one another. How can you share what you've learned?

Decide

► what you want to say.

► what the best way is to get your message across.

Share

► what you did and why.

► what worked and what didn't work.

► what conclusions you have drawn.

► what else you'd like to find out.

Find Out

► what classmates liked about what you shared—and why.

► what questions your classmates have.

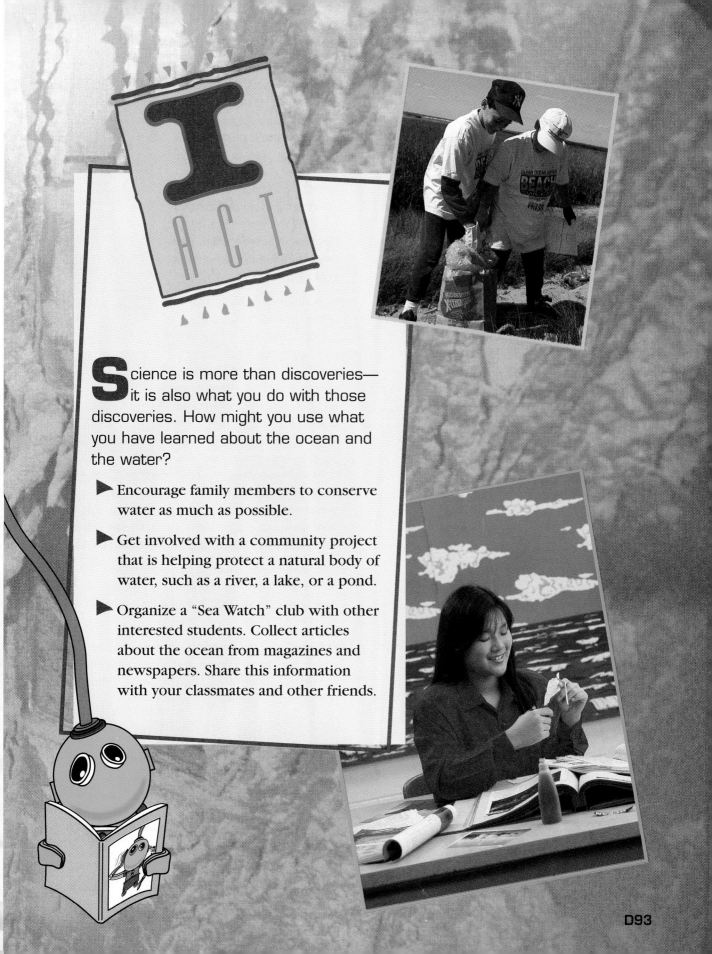

I ACT

Science is more than discoveries—it is also what you do with those discoveries. How might you use what you have learned about the ocean and the water?

► Encourage family members to conserve water as much as possible.

► Get involved with a community project that is helping protect a natural body of water, such as a river, a lake, or a pond.

► Organize a "Sea Watch" club with other interested students. Collect articles about the ocean from magazines and newspapers. Share this information with your classmates and other friends.

THE LANGUAGE OF SCIENCE

The language of science helps people communicate clearly when they talk about the ocean. Here are some vocabulary words you can use when you talk about the ocean with your friends, family, and others.

abyss—the deepest part of the ocean, occupying three-fourths of the ocean floor. **(D54)**

atoll—circular coral island that surrounds a calm lagoon. Atolls are built-up reefs, stonelike underwater structures made up of the skeletons of invertebrate animals, such as corals. Reefs provide a rich environment for many kinds of ocean organisms. **(D20)**

bioluminescence—light made by living organisms. Many of the creatures of the deep, dark ocean use light lures to attract prey. **(D52)**

buoyancy—water's ability to support objects. An object that weighs less than the water it displaces has *positive buoyancy,* and it floats. An object that weighs more than the water it displaces has *negative buoyancy,* and it sinks. An object that weighs the same as the water it displaces has *neutral buoyancy,* and it can be suspended in the water. **(D22)**

currents—streams of moving water within the ocean. *Surface currents* are caused by wind continuously blowing from one direction. Surface currents may be warm or cold and can affect the climate of any land they flow near. *Underwater currents* are caused by differences in the density, or weight, of certain bodies of water. Cold water is denser than warm water, so cold water sinks and flows along the bottom. Salt water is denser than fresh water, so salt water also sinks and flows along the bottom. **(D64)**

ecotone—a place where one ecosystem meets another. The shoreline, where the ocean meets the land, is an example of an ecotone. **(D38)**

estuary—an area where fresh water and salt water mix. For example, the area where the Mississippi River flows into the Gulf of Mexico is an estuary. **(D44)**

▼ Buoyancy

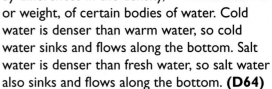

▲ Estuary animal—a nutria

photosynthetic zone—the ocean's top layer, which receives sunlight. Here plants and phytoplankton use sunlight to make food by *photosynthesis*. **(D50)**

remote sensors—anchored buoys with instruments that take readings of ocean conditions and relay the data to shore. NOMAD is one example of the sensors in use today. **(D29)**

scuba—self-contained *u*nderwater *b*reathing *a*pparatus invented by Jacques Cousteau. Scuba allows a diver to move freely underwater while breathing air from a tank. **(D25)**

snorkel—tube that allows divers to breathe air from the surface. **(D24)**

sonar—*so*und *na*vigation and *r*anging equipment, which can be used to measure depth or to locate objects on the ocean floor. **(D28)**

submersibles—underwater vehicles. **(D26)**

tide pool—ocean water trapped by rocks into small, still bodies of water. Plants and animals that live in tide pools are adapted to the harsh conditions of these habitats. Tide pools are alternately flooded and dried out, and waves often crash onto the rocks. **(D40)**

▼ **Tide pool**

tides—the rises and falls of ocean water that are caused by the pull of gravity of the moon and the sun. *Neap tides* are very small tides that occur when the sun and the moon are at right angles to one another. *Spring tides* are very large tides that occur when the Earth, the sun, and the moon are in a line. **(D58)**

▼ **High tide**

▲ **Low tide**

water cycle—the natural cycle that water goes through, including evaporation, condensation, precipitation, and runoff. **(D48)**

▲ **Water cycle**

BLACKOUT!

I WONDER

Energy—we all need it, we all use it, and we all miss it when it isn't available. Have you ever wondered where energy comes from? What do you wonder about when you look at these photographs of an energy station and of a repair crew fixing downed lines?

Work with a partner to make a list of questions you may have about energy. Be ready to share your list with the class.

Unit E

Blackout!

Energy Uses, Sources, and Alternatives

◀ **Energy station**

▼ **Repairing storm damage**

E3

I PLAN

You may have asked questions such as those below as you wondered about energy and energy production. Scientists also ask questions. Then they plan ways to find answers to their questions. Now you and your classmates can plan how you will investigate energy.

My Science Log

How does an energy station work?

What kinds of energy are used to run an energy station?

How does energy get to the people who use it?

How will energy be produced in the future?

With Your Class

Plan how your class will use the activities and readings from the **I Investigate** part of this unit. Decide what other resources you might use.

On Your Own

There are many ways to learn about energy. Following are some things you can do to investigate energy by yourself or with some classmates. Some explorations may take longer to do than others. Look over the suggestions and choose . . .

- **Projects to Do**
- **Places to Visit**
- **Books to Read**

PROJECTS TO DO

BUILD A MODEL ENERGY STATION

With your class, draw plans for a model energy station. Then build it with cardboard, boxes, plastic from household items, glue, staples, and any other materials you care to use. A large tabletop, perhaps covered with a base of cardboard or plywood, could be used as a display board. Your class might divide into small groups, with each group responsible for one part of the station. Make changes in your model as you study energy stations in this unit.

PUBLISH A BOOK

Collect energy-conservation tips that can be used at home. Compile the tips into a book. Some students might work as editors. Others might use a computer to lay out pages. Still others might draw illustrations for the book or design a cover. Once the book is complete, make copies of it for other people in your school or community. The book can be your contribution to your community's brighter energy future.

SCIENCE FAIR PROJECT

Are there energy topics you want to know more about—for example, how a hydroelectric dam produces energy? A science fair project is one way to explore ideas and answer questions. Think of a question you want answered. Then think of a way to answer that question. Share your ideas with your teacher. With your teacher's permission, plan your project, gather your materials, and begin.

PLACES TO VISIT

ON AN ENERGY TOUR

If there is an energy station near your community, arrange for a class visit so you can get a closeup look at its different parts and how they work. Most energy stations have group tours and provide brochures and other information about the machinery and how it works. You might also get some tips on how to improve your model energy station.

MUSEUM VISIT

Is there a history museum, a museum of natural history, or a science and industry museum nearby? Spend some time at the museum to find out all you can about the use of energy and energy sources. Your visit will help you understand how people used energy in the past and how energy is produced today. You may also find out about alternative energy sources that may help make your community's energy future brighter.

MINE TIME

Arrange to visit a strip mine if one is nearby. Talk to the workers to find out about their work and equipment. Also, find out about their land-reclamation procedures. If you can't visit a mine in person, consider watching a tour on videotape or reading about the history of mining in a reference book.

BOOKS TO READ

Just a Dream

**by Chris Van Allsburg (Houghton Mifflin, 1990),
Outstanding Science Trade Book.**

What's the big deal?
Somebody else will
pick up that piece of
paper. That's what
Ben thought, too. Join
him in this book for
a trip to the future
where he sees a very
different world. It's a
world in which energy
resources are used care-
lessly. Air and water are
polluted as demands for
more energy are met.
Now that Ben knows
what might happen, he
has a second chance to
make the future better.
Will you help him?

JUST A DREAM
STORY AND PICTURES BY CHRIS VAN ALLSBURG

Cartons, Cans, and Orange Peels:
Where Does Your Garbage Go?

by Joanna Foster (Houghton Mifflin, 1991), Outstanding Science Trade Book. We've learned not to throw our garbage away, but to recycle it. We've also learned how to turn garbage into energy, and how to make it into compost to grow plants. If we don't recycle our garbage, what happens to everything we throw out? Read this book to find out.

More Books to Read

Letting Off Steam:
The Story of Geothermal Energy

by Linda Jacobs (Carolrhoda, 1989). Geothermal energy comes from heat deep inside the Earth. This heat from the Earth's molten core is released in many ways. We can't control the energy when it comes out in the form of a volcanic eruption, but we can use it when the energy escapes in other forms. Read to find out about geothermal energy and the way we use this powerful force.

Why Doesn't the Sun Burn Out and Other Not Such Dumb Questions About Energy

by Vicki Cobb (Lodestar Books, 1990). Do you ever wonder about things around you? Why isn't the sky green? How much does energy weigh? Will the sun burn out? Scientists have answered many of these questions for us. In this book, you will find out many things you've always wanted to know.

More Power to You

by Vicki Cobb (Little, Brown, 1986). At your fingertips, you have amazing power! You can turn darkness into light. You can change silence into sound. You can make pictures appear. Are you a magician? No, but you live in a world with electric power available for daily use. Read to learn about different kinds of energy that brings this power to you.

How Did We Find Out About Lasers?

by Isaac Asimov (Walker, 1990), Outstanding Science Trade Book. At stores and libraries, you see people read bar codes with a wand of light. This ray of light, called a *laser*, has been made possible by the discoveries of many scientists. The laser has many uses, from surgery to space exploration. This book tells about the discovery of the laser and how we use it today.

I

INVESTIGATE

To find answers to their questions, scientists read, think, talk to others, and do experiments. Their investigations often lead to new questions.

In this unit, you will have many chances to think and work like a scientist. How will you find answers to questions you posed?

▶ CLASSIFYING/ORDERING When you classify objects, you put them into groups according to how they are alike. Ordering is putting things in an order. For example, you might order things from first to last, smallest to biggest, or lightest to heaviest.

▶ COMPARING When you compare objects or events, you look for what they have in common. You also look for differences between them.

▶ COMMUNICATING When you communicate, you give information. In science, you communicate by showing results from an activity in an organized way—for example, in a chart. Then you and other people can interpret the results.

Are you ready to begin?

SECTIONS

SECTION A
What Energy!

Your alarm clock is buzzing. Could it be morning already? The sun is glaring through the window, hurting your eyes. You turn off the alarm and drag yourself out of bed. It's a cold winter day, and you take a hot shower to warm up. You get dressed and go to the kitchen to get some breakfast. You have already used or been affected by several kinds of energy, and you haven't even left the house yet!

What are these forms of energy? In your Science Log, record answers to these questions. As you work through the investigations that follow, identify ways in which you find, change, and use energy for your daily needs.

1 ENERGY CRISIS

Today is Monday, and it's the first day of school for the week. But this will be no ordinary week at your school. Each day this week, one form of energy will be banned from the school! Let's take a look at how different forms of energy affect our day-to-day lives.

Motionless Monday

As soon as you are seated at your desk, your teacher announces that mechanical energy has been banned from the school for the rest of the day. What will the day be like without the changes caused by this form of energy?

We usually recognize energy by what it does or how it affects things. **Energy** is the ability to cause change, and **mechanical energy** is the energy that moves things.

You realize with excitement that your teachers can't write on the board and they can't hand out any homework! But don't get too happy. The water fountains are dry, your locker won't open, and the doors wouldn't work even if you could walk to get to them! When the day ends, you leave with a sigh of relief. Without mechanical energy, it's no wonder that Monday was so sluggish!

▲ Could you climb the rope on Motionless Monday? Why or why not?

Energetic Clothespins

You will need: rubber bands, 3 clothespins

Wrap a rubber band around two clothespins to secure them tightly. Use "clip," not spring, pins. Wind the pins up tightly. Let them go on a tabletop. What happens? You may want to repeat the experiment, using another rubber band and a third clothespin.

THINK ABOUT IT

How did the clothespins show evidence of mechanical energy?

Tundra Tuesday

After yesterday you think that nothing could be worse than not being able to move around all day. Read to find out what Tundra Tuesday will be like.

Today you come to school and find out that no sunlight will be allowed inside the building. The school's heating system will not produce any heat either, and the water pipes are already frozen! **Thermal energy,** or heat, has been banned today.

It's cold in gym class. How can you warm up? Think about what you might do. You might try exercising to warm up, since thermal energy can be produced as a byproduct of other forms of energy. However, today the mechanical energy you use in gym will not produce any heat! So you can't even rub your hands together to warm them up.

When the last bell rings, you're not sure which was worse—sitting still all day yesterday or walking around in a deep freeze today. Now that Tundra Tuesday has ended, here is an activity that will show you how heat is produced as a byproduct of mechanical energy.

▲ The sun provides Earth with thermal energy.

Working Together

You will need: water, bowl, thermometer, electric mixer

CAUTION: Have an adult help you with the mixer. Put some room temperature water in a bowl, and record its exact temperature. Beat the water with an electric mixer for 3 to 5 minutes. Stop the mixer, and record the temperature again. What happened to the temperature of the water? Why do you think this happened?

THINK ABOUT IT

Think of some other ways in which a lack of thermal energy would affect your school day.

Waveless Wednesday

It's only the third day of the week, and you're already dreading today's announcement. Then you are told that today there will be no radiant energy in the school. How will this affect the school day?

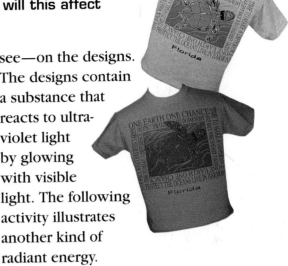

No radio, TV, or light today! These all require radiant energy. **Radiant energy** is energy that is transmitted in the form of waves. The various forms of radiant energy make up the *electromagnetic spectrum.*

Have you ever seen T-shirts with designs that glow when a certain kind of light shines on them? The bulb used to create this effect shines ultraviolet light—a form of radiant energy we can't see—on the designs. The designs contain a substance that reacts to ultraviolet light by glowing with visible light. The following activity illustrates another kind of radiant energy.

▼ **Electromagnetic spectrum**

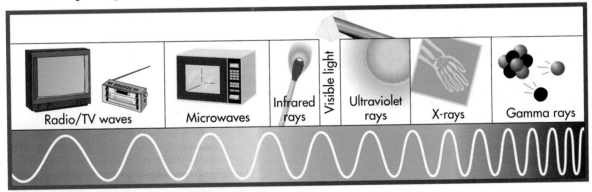

Radio/TV waves | Microwaves | Infrared rays | Visible light | Ultraviolet rays | X-rays | Gamma rays

Zap It

You will need: water, bowl, plastic wrap, microwave

Put water in a microwave-safe bowl.

Cover the bowl tightly with plastic wrap so that the wrap goes all the way under it. Put it in the microwave and set the timer for 3 minutes. What happens?

THINK ABOUT IT

In addition to microwaves and ultraviolet light, what are two other examples of radiant energy in the world around us?

Turmoil Thursday

Everyone shows up for school a little bruised from Wednesday's stumbling in the dark. By now, you are developing a deep respect for energy. You learn that today everyone will go without using chemical energy. Let's find out what happens.

The day seems normal so far, except for your slight case of indigestion. Taking school pictures had been planned for yesterday, but that was postponed until today because of the lack of light. As you stand waiting, the photographer looks confused. "I can't seem to get anything to work," she says. Then someone explains today's rule about chemical energy, and she understands why she can't take pictures. "The batteries in my camera use chemical energy to make electricity, and light produces a chemical change on the film. No wonder they won't work!"

You suddenly understand your indigestion—your digestive system, which changes the chemical makeup of food for your body's use, can't do its job today either. Digestion is a perfect example of using **chemical energy,** the energy in a substance that undergoes a chemical reaction. You can observe another example in the following activity.

Bubbling Over

You will need: goggles, baking soda, flask, vinegar, cork

CAUTION: Wear safety goggles to do this experiment. Put a little baking soda in the bottom of a flask. Add some vinegar to the flask, and seal it firmly, but not too tightly, with a cork. What happens inside the flask?

THINK ABOUT IT

What are some ways in which chemical energy causes change during your day-to-day life?

Finally, Friday

Friday is here at last! Although it's been a crazy week, you're getting an idea about how energy affects your daily life. The minutes drag by, and you begin to wonder if today might actually be a normal day. Suddenly, there's a blackout! Everything that uses electricity blinks out— the clock, the lights, the computers—everything!

The **electric energy**—electricity—to your school has been cut off. All of the electric appliances are useless. Because we are so used to having it around, sometimes we don't even notice electricity!

How would a blackout of all electricity affect what happens at your school? Try the following activities for a firsthand experience with electricity.

The Electric Energy Show

You will need: balloon, paper, comb

- If you're wearing shoes with leather soles, shuffle across a rug. Then touch one of your classmates.

- Blow up and tie a balloon. Rub it on your clothes. Then stick it to the wall.

- Make a paper airplane. Charge your comb by pulling it through your hair. Then share the charge with the plane. Now steer the plane with your comb.

Certain objects get electricity by being rubbed with another object. Since the electricity stays on the objects, this is called *static electricity*—the word *static* means "staying still." Another kind of electricity flows through wires. This kind of electricity is called *current electricity*. Electric appliances use current electricity.

THINK ABOUT IT

What is the difference between static and current electricity?

▲ Lightning during a thunderstorm and the beams in an argon lightning ball are examples of electric energy.

Nuclear Energy

At the end of the day, the electricity comes back on. You are told that the connection to the nuclear energy station has been restored. "What is nuclear energy?" you ask. You're pretty sure that it has something to do with atoms. And you're right.

▼ A fission reaction

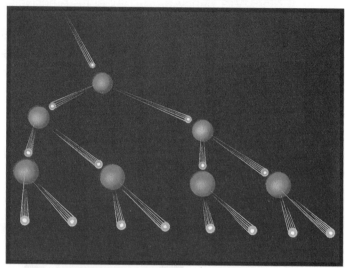

▼ A fission reaction

All matter is made up of tiny particles called *atoms.* According to a simple model, the atom has a core, or *nucleus,* composed of particles called *protons* and *neutrons.* The nucleus is surrounded by orbiting *electrons.*

Scientists have discovered that the nucleus of an atom can be split. This process is called *fission.* You have seen that energy can be released as the result of certain actions; for example, rubbing your hands together produces heat. The energy released when the nucleus of an atom is split is called **nuclear energy.** The diagram shows how nuclear energy is produced in a fission reaction. Nuclear energy stations control the fission reaction and use the heat given off to produce electricity.

Nuclear energy is also produced in other ways. At very high temperatures, two atoms can fuse together. In this process, called *nuclear fusion,* a great amount of energy is released. Our own sun is one huge nuclear fusion reaction. Scientists are trying to find a way to control fusion to produce electricity.

▲ Nuclear fusion occurs on the sun.

If you had been through all these experiences at school, you would have thought you'd had a nightmare. Of course the situations described in this lesson couldn't really happen. But perhaps they helped you think about how we use the many forms of energy every day. How different life would be without energy!

QUICK CHECK

LESSON 1 REVIEW

❶ How do you use various forms of energy during an average day?

❷ How might eliminating one form of energy affect usage of other forms?

2 WHICH ENERGY?

Any of the forms of energy you read about in the previous lesson can change into a different form of energy. For example, some of the mechanical energy of rubbing your hands together changes into heat energy. On this and the following pages, you can explore these changes.

Kinetic and Potential

Look at the photograph of the gymnast. In order to do more difficult flips, he uses a trampoline. Read on to find out what happens to some of the energy as he performs his routine.

The gymnast has *kinetic energy* as he falls toward the trampoline. After his feet hit the trampoline, he slows down as its surface stretches. The gymnast's kinetic energy is being stored in the trampoline as *potential energy* while the surface is forced out of its natural shape. For a split second, he comes to a stop—his kinetic energy is zero. At that moment, the potential energy of the trampoline is greatest. Then the process reverses. The potential energy changes to kinetic energy as the trampoline hurls the gymnast upward. As gravity slows his rise, the gymnast's kinetic energy changes again to potential energy. At the point of his greatest height, the gymnast's potential energy is greatest. As he falls, this energy changes again into kinetic energy.

These changes—from kinetic energy to potential energy and back—illustrate the conservation of energy. This means that energy can't be created or destroyed, but it can change form.

THINK ABOUT IT

Explain how energy changes form during one of your favorite sports or other activities.

The gymnast has potential energy at the peak of the flip.

ACTIVITY

Roller Derby

Not everyone has the time, desire, or talent to be a gymnast, so let's use the following activity to look more closely at the relationship between kinetic energy and potential energy.

DO THIS

1. Make a ramp by stacking two books on the floor and propping one end of the board on them. Mark a starting line with masking tape near the top of the ramp. There should be room behind the starting line for the cart.

2. Hold the cart behind the starting line and then release it. Time how fast it travels down the ramp. Your partner should stop the cart at the bottom of the ramp and return it to you.

3. Add another book to the stack to make the ramp steeper. Then repeat step 2.

4. Finally, add a fourth book to the stack and repeat step 2.

THINK AND WRITE

1. During the first trial, when was the cart's kinetic energy zero? Why? When was its potential energy greatest? Why?

2. Compare the cart's potential and kinetic energy during the second trial with its energy during the first trial. How do they compare?

3. For the three trials, how did the kinetic energy of the moving cart relate to its beginning potential energy?

Changing Energy

Kinetic and potential energy are not the only forms of energy that can be transformed and interchanged. As you do the following activities, think about the other energy forms that you've read about, how they might interact, and what changes take place when they do.

Energy changes are all around us. For example, when you beat the water with the mixer, electric energy changed to mechanical energy, which produced the thermal energy that raised the temperature of the water. The chemical energy in a battery can produce electric energy, and light can produce chemical energy in a plant or on a piece of photographic film.

Hot Stuff!

You will need: leaf, plate, hand lens

CAUTION: Be careful when using a hand lens in this way. Get a leaf from outside and put it on a plate or board. Using a hand lens, focus the sun's light on the leaf. Move the lens up and down until the light is a small, bright dot on the leaf. Hold it there for a short period of time. What happens? What energy changes have taken place?

Light Powered

You will need: radiometer, flashlight

Place a radiometer in semidarkness. Then shine a flashlight beam on the radiometer. What happens? What energy changes have taken place?

Changes All Around

What other changes in energy forms can you think of? Look at the pictures on these pages. Write a brief description of the changes in energy that occur in each of the activities shown.

▲ What energy change takes place in a dry cell?

▶ What energy changes take place from the time the match is struck to the time it is blown out?

▲ What energy change takes place for the plant to make its own food?

▲ What energy changes take place to help make a cyclist visible at night?

▲ What energy changes take place in the toaster?

▲ What energy changes take place in the microwave oven?

▲ What kind of energy do these swimmers have now? Into what kind of energy will it be changed?

THINK ABOUT IT

Which of the activities you performed showed energy changes that were similar to those pictured?

Tool Time

Does a tool or a machine use all of the mechanical energy put into it to do its work? Pound, crank, saw, drill, and bend to find out what really happens to the energy in this activity.

DO THIS

1 **CAUTION: Use the hammer carefully and wear safety goggles.** Pound the nail partway into the block of wood, and then pull it out. Feel the point of the nail. What form of energy do you feel?

2 Sharpen the pencil. Feel the sharpened end of the pencil. What form of energy do you feel?

3 **CAUTION: Handle cutting tools carefully.** Use the saw to cut one piece of wood. Feel the saw blade and the wood near the cut. What form of energy do you feel?

4 Drill a hole in a piece of wood. Feel the wood near the hole and the bit of the drill. What form of energy do you feel?

5 Bend the piece of wire back and forth several times. Feel the wire near the spot where you have been bending it. What form of energy do you feel?

MATERIALS
- safety goggles
- nail
- hammer
- block of wood
- pencil
- pencil sharpener
- 2 pieces of wood
- handsaw
- hand drill
- piece of wire coat hanger
- Science Log data sheet

THINK AND WRITE

1. Do you think that each tool used all of the mechanical energy you put into it to do its work? Explain.

2. Do you think it is possible to make a machine that uses all of its energy for work? Explain.

Heated Discussion

If you have ever touched the hood of a car after it has stopped, you know that the engine produces heat. As you read, think about whether the heat is useful or not.

When a gymnast performs routines, his or her body radiates more heat than when it is at rest. When the sharpener cuts into the pencil, some of the energy changes into heat. During every energy change, some heat that cannot be used to do useful work is produced. The unusable heat is called *waste heat.* This means that even though the total amount of energy is conserved, no machine can use as much energy as is put into it. Name some situations in which waste heat is produced. Jot down your own ideas about why this heat is called waste heat.

▼ Welding produces useful heat.

▲ A lot of a car's energy becomes waste heat.

LESSON 2 REVIEW

What would happen if machines did not waste heat?

DOUBLE CHECK

SECTION A REVIEW

1. Name the forms of energy you use when you play basketball and when you use a hair dryer.

2. How are radiant energy and electric energy alike?

3. List five items that can have potential and kinetic energy. Next to each item, draw one picture of that item storing energy and another picture showing movement. Write a brief description for each pair of drawings.

Producing Electricity

▶ Transformers

Think of a city at night. Warmly lit homes, brightly lit offices and store windows, the colorful glow of neon signs, and patterns of street lights that stretch for miles fill your field of vision. Have you ever wondered where the electricity to light up all of those things comes from? This section discusses many types of energy stations, the fuels they use, and how the energy in the fuel is changed into electricity.

What resources are used to produce electricity? What changes in forms of energy take place in an energy station? Answer these questions in your Science Log as you work through the following investigations.

1 ENERGY STATIONS

When you flip on a light switch to light up your bedroom, you use electricity supplied by an energy station. Energy station technicians operate huge machines that work 24 hours a day to make electricity available to you whenever you need it. In this lesson, you will look at the process of producing electricity and the most common types of energy stations.

What's So Great About Electricity?

We use electricity for so many things and are so used to having it available that usually we don't even think about it. Why is electricity so important? Let's find out.

You will need: Science Log

Look at each picture below, and write a few sentences about how electricity is important to what is shown. Then write a paragraph that explains what's so great about electricity.

Follow the Energy Trail

The most common energy stations are heat engine energy stations. Although these can run on various fuels, they use similar components to convert the energy in those fuels into electric energy. The diagram shows the many energy changes that can take place in the production of electricity.

1 Radiant energy comes from the sun in the form of light.

2 Plants change radiant energy from the sun into chemical energy through photosynthesis.

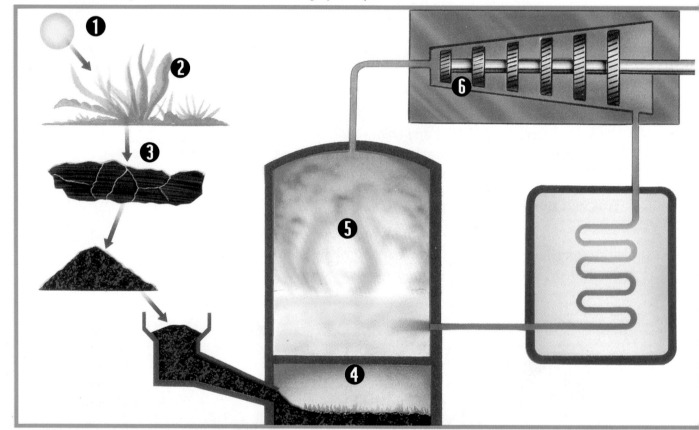

3 Over millions of years, plant matter decays and changes to coal. Chemical energy is stored in coal.

4 In the furnace of a heat engine energy station, coal is burned. This process changes the coal's stored chemical energy to thermal energy.

5 Thermal energy changes water to steam as the water circulates through boiler tubes.

6 Steam pushes against the blades of a turbine, causing it to rotate. The mechanical energy of the rotating **turbine** is used to turn a shaft.

7 The turning shaft sets a generator in motion. The **generator** converts mechanical energy to electric energy.

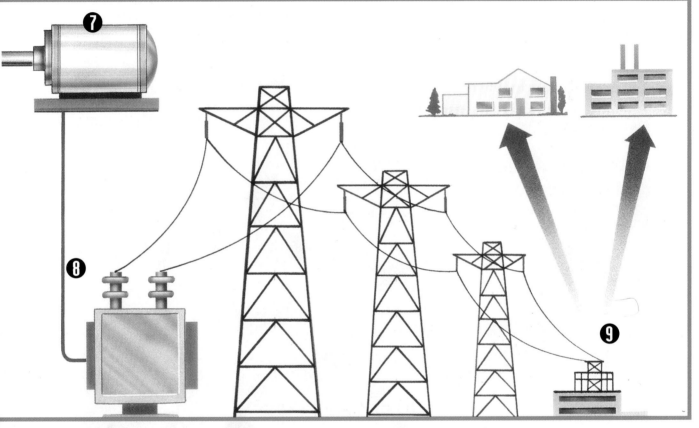

8 Electricity flows through cables to a **transformer**, where the voltage is increased. This allows the electricity to be transmitted over great distances through the wires of an electric grid.

9 Electricity reaches substations, where the energy is reduced to smaller amounts for use in homes and industry.

THINK ABOUT IT

Where do you think energy is wasted in this long series of energy changes?

Heat Engine Energy Stations

The basic components of all heat engine energy stations are the same, but different fuels can be used to change the water to the steam that turns the turbines. Here are two different kinds of heat engine energy stations.

A Coal-Powered Energy Station

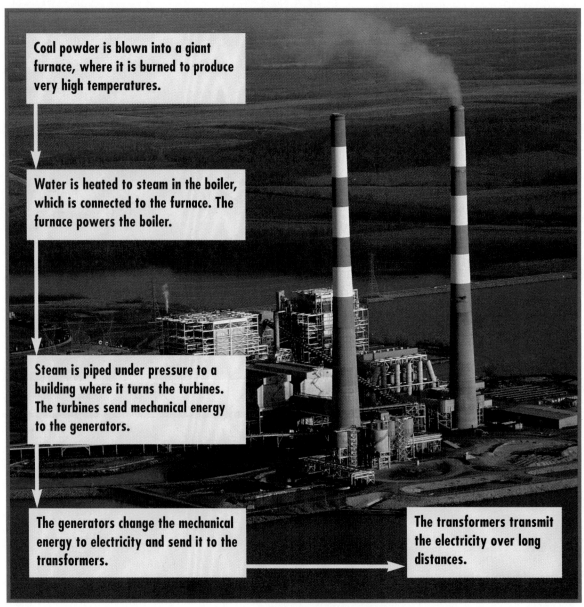

Coal powder is blown into a giant furnace, where it is burned to produce very high temperatures.

Water is heated to steam in the boiler, which is connected to the furnace. The furnace powers the boiler.

Steam is piped under pressure to a building where it turns the turbines. The turbines send mechanical energy to the generators.

The generators change the mechanical energy to electricity and send it to the transformers.

The transformers transmit the electricity over long distances.

A Nuclear-Powered Energy Station

Heat from the fission reaction, which takes place in the reactor core, is used to convert water to steam. The steam turns turbines, which are connected to generators, as in the coal-powered energy station.

Water is returned to its liquid form by the condensers.

Concrete shielding is used in the reactor to protect the environment from dangerous materials.

QUICK CHECK

LESSON 1 REVIEW

How is the production of electricity alike in both of the energy stations described? How does it differ?

2 FUEL SOURCES

In the previous lesson, you looked at two ways in which the energy in fuels can be changed to electricity. We also use the energy in fuels to heat our homes and run our vehicles. Where do fuels come from, and how must they be prepared for our uses? The following activities can give you some ideas.

ACTIVITY

Using Fuels

Wood and wood products are some of the most commonly used fuels in the world today. What makes wood a good fuel? In this activity, you can see why charcoal, a wood product, is used for fuel.

DO THIS

1. Set up the materials as shown.

2. Make a table to record the temperature data. Add 100 mL of water to the can. Measure and record the temperature of the water.

3. **CAUTION: Put on safety goggles.** Your teacher will light the charcoal. After 10 minutes, find the temperature of the water and record it in your table. Find and record the temperature of the water again after 20 minutes and after 30 minutes.

THINK AND WRITE

Do you think all the heat from the burning charcoal went into the water? Explain.

MATERIALS
- ring stand
- 2 rings
- 2 wire screens
- charcoal
- small can
- 50-mL graduate
- water
- thermometer
- goggles
- lighter
- Science Log data sheet

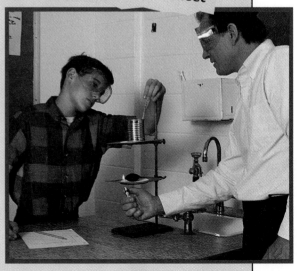

Energy from Fossils

Fuels known as *fossil fuels* are formed from plant material that has been buried for millions of years. To understand how buried plant material becomes fuel, think about a piece of moldy bread.

Bread is made from grain—plant material. If you've ever found a loaf of bread that has been left in a warm, moist place, you've seen the results of a process similar to that of fossil fuel formation. The bread begins to decay because of the action of microorganisms.

In the formation of fossil fuels, microorganisms, heat, and pressure decay buried plant material into **hydrocarbons**— molecules made up of carbon and hydrogen atoms. When hydrocarbons are burned, they release heat, water, and carbon dioxide. Fossil fuels are limited in amount because they take so long to form.

▼ Coal with plant fossil

The most important fossil fuel is coal. People have been burning coal for a long time—in fact, coal was used as fuel in China almost a thousand years ago! It's the most commonly used fuel for the production of electricity. Major deposits of coal are found in the United States, China, Russia, and parts of Europe.

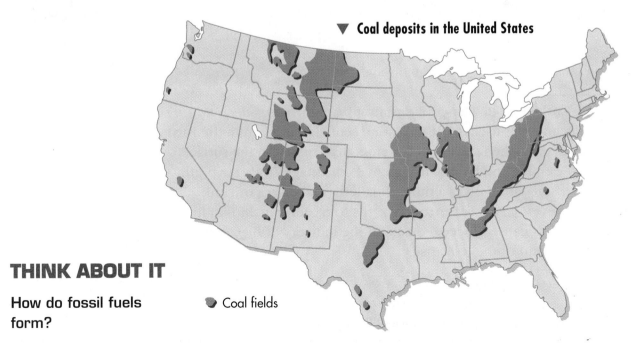

▼ Coal deposits in the United States

THINK ABOUT IT

How do fossil fuels form?

● Coal fields

Mining Coal

The charcoal you used in the last activity is made by heating wood in a container without air. Charcoal is chemically similar to coal. However, coal burns much hotter than charcoal, so less of it is needed to heat homes and produce electricity. It's easy to get wood for making charcoal, but how is coal obtained? You can find out by reading the following.

Coal is *mined,* or taken from the Earth, in two different ways— strip mining and deep mining. In *strip mining,* the top layer of soil is removed to expose the layers of coal underneath. Once the coal is removed, the soil must be restored. The process of restoring strip-mined land is known as *reclamation.*

▼ Strip mining

▲ Underground mining

Coal found in deeper places must be removed by *deep mining.* Machinery is used to dig shafts and tunnels deep within the Earth. The coal is then carried to elevators that bring it to the surface.

Deep mining has environmental advantages over strip mining, since it involves a much smaller surface area of land. However, it presents many hazards to miners, including lung diseases caused by coal dust and the dangers of fire, explosions, and tunnel collapse.

THINK ABOUT IT

Compare and contrast strip mining and deep mining.

Drilling for Oil

Oil is often considered to be a fossil fuel, too. Oil is a hydrocarbon produced from the remains of microscopic sea life. Unlike coal, oil is liquid, and it is often found deep under the sea. How is oil brought to Earth's surface? Read the following story to learn some of the history of oil exploration and drilling in the United States.

GUSHER!!!!

by **Roberta Baxter**
from *Cobblestone*

LITERATURE Captain Anthony F. Lucas was in town when he heard an explosion. The sound rumbled through the streets, shaking windows and startling horses tied to hitching posts.

"What was that?" Lucas wondered. "Could it be my oil well? An accident?"

In a wild scramble, he jumped into his buggy and swung the horse into the muddy street. In the distance, he could see a boiling, black fountain against the sky. As he neared Spindletop, he saw pieces of pipe on the ground, along with rocks and chunks of mud. An avalanche of black slime cascaded down the hill. Several nightmarish figures danced around near the

drilling rig. Lucas tried to grab one slippery apparition. "What is it?" he asked Al Hamill.

"Oil, Captain, it's oil!" Hamill replied. After months of drilling, Lucas and his crew had drilled an oil well that brought a new word into the vocabulary: Gusher!

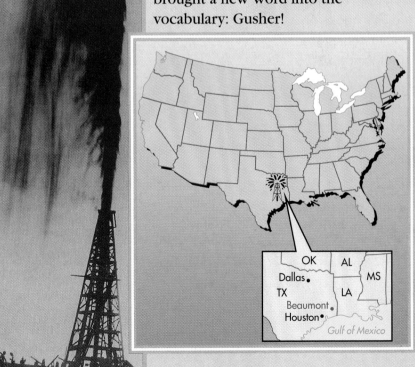

◀ Spindletop gusher

OK
AL
Dallas.
MS
TX
LA
Beaumont.
Houston.
Gulf of Mexico

Ancient people first discovered oil that seeped out of the ground. They used the oil for lamps and the sticky asphalt for holding mosaic floors together. The Chinese drilled for oil as far back as 600 B.C.

The first oil well in the United States was drilled in Pennsylvania. In 1859, Edwin Drake drilled a hole and lined it with stovepipe to keep it from caving in. When the hole was sixty-nine feet deep, oil slowly rose to the surface. The well began producing about ten barrels a day.

Just outside the town of Beaumont, Texas, was a low, round hill called Spindletop. In the 1800s, the boys from town would go out to Spindletop for fun because a hole poked in the soft earth released a gas that would burn after being lit. Sometimes at night, Spindletop would glow with flashing lights.

Paltillo Higgins was the son of a Beaumont gunsmith. He read many books on science, and he believed that

▲ Captain Lucas

◀ First oil well

Spindletop contained oil. After convincing some people to invest in his project, he formed the Gladys City Oil, Gas, and Manufacturing Company in 1892. He began to drill for oil on Spindletop. After three dry holes (wells that did not find oil), Higgins was running out of money, but no one would invest in his enterprise. To attract investors, he placed an ad in a newspaper.

The advertisement caught the eye of Captain Anthony F. Lucas. Lucas migrated to the United States from Austria and was mining salt in Louisiana when he saw the ad. He was convinced that salt, sulfur, and oil often were found together in the earth, so he thought Spindletop might be a salt dome full of oil. He bought the oil company and started drilling.

After six months, only 575 feet had been drilled, mostly through quicksand, and with few traces of oil. By early 1900, Lucas was out of money. An expert from Standard Oil, the largest U.S. oil company at the time, said that southeastern Texas had no resemblance to any known field of oil, so Standard Oil would not invest in Lucas's effort.

Dr. William Battle Phillips, a professor of geology at the University of Texas, believed that oil might be found at Spindletop, so he introduced Lucas to the prospecting firm of Guffey and Gailey. This company decided to invest in Lucas's project, and drilling began on another hole.

Lucas hired J.G., Curt, and Al Hamill, three brothers from Louisiana, to be the drillers. They encountered many problems. Sometimes the drill bit would be drilling through coarse sand that threatened to cave in. Other times the drill hit pockets of gas that would spew up out of the hole. Most of the time, the drilling was rough, through hard rock, so it took a long time to go just a few feet. On December 9, 1900, the drilling suddenly became much easier. At daylight, there was some oil in the pit where the dirt dug out of the hole was put. Al Hamill told Lucas that he might be able to pump fifty barrels of oil a day. But they kept digging deeper.

By the beginning of January, the drill was down to 1,020 feet. On January 10, 1901, the drill was lowered into the hole, and within minutes, the well exploded. A messy shower of oil and mud and four tons of drill pipe shot out of the hole. Then came a roar of gas and a sound like a cannon shot. Finally, a big fountain of oil gushed out of the hole and almost drowned the crew. The noise stampeded cows several miles away. The gusher could be seen for ten miles.

The first well on Spindletop began producing one hundred thousand barrels of oil a day. In six months, Spindletop was covered with oil rigs, with most of the wells producing thousands of barrels a day.

The boom at Spindletop did not last long. Within ten years, the hill was almost a ghost town. But the Lucas Gusher was the beginning of a new era— the age of liquid fuel. The huge quantities found at Spindletop and in other parts of Texas and the Southwest made oil an inexpensive fuel. Compared to wood and coal, it was lightweight and efficient, ideal for powering the recently invented automobile, which soon became America's most popular form of transportation. Oil was put to work heating homes and powering industrial machines. Today thirty million barrels of oil are burned every day, and oil provides more than a third of the world's energy.

▼ **Spindletop oil field**

THINK ABOUT IT

Is oil gushing out of the ground a waste of energy resources? Explain.

Nuclear Fuel

Even though we are quickly using up our fossil fuels, our demand for energy continues to grow. Other sources of energy are always being tested. One of the sources being used is nuclear energy. But where does the fuel to produce nuclear energy come from?

In many countries, nuclear energy is being used to satisfy a growing demand for electricity. The fuel for nuclear energy stations is uranium. Uranium is found in rocks mined from the Earth. Like coal, uranium can be strip-mined from the surface or deep-mined from underground. *Ore,* or rock, containing uranium is crushed so that pure uranium can be taken from it. Very little uranium is needed to run a nuclear energy station.

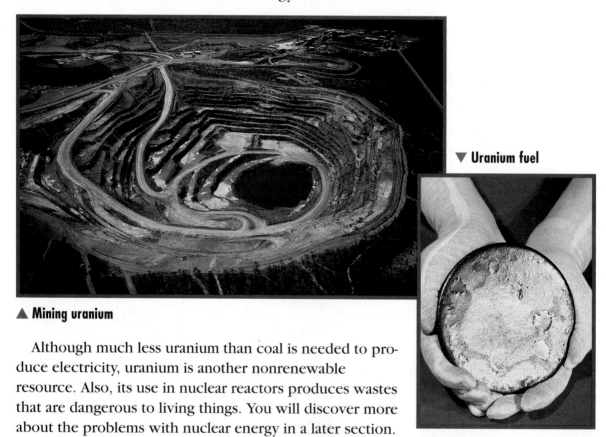

▼ Uranium fuel

▲ Mining uranium

Although much less uranium than coal is needed to produce electricity, uranium is another nonrenewable resource. Also, its use in nuclear reactors produces wastes that are dangerous to living things. You will discover more about the problems with nuclear energy in a later section.

THINK ABOUT IT

Describe the advantages and disadvantages of using uranium to make electricity.

The Earth's Own Fuel

Have you ever seen a picture of a geyser, such as Old Faithful at Yellowstone National Park? Where does the energy come from to produce these explosive sprays?

In some areas of the world, forces within the Earth push large pools of melted rock toward the surface. When water seeps down into these pockets of melted rock, it becomes super hot. Pressure increases as the water turns to steam. Soon hot water and steam shoot up as geysers from cracks in the Earth. This heat from deep inside the Earth is called **geothermal energy.**

Just as heat from the sun can be used to heat homes, heat from inside the Earth can also be used directly. Almost all of the homes in Reykjavik, Iceland, for example, are heated with geothermal energy.

Geothermal energy can also be used to produce electricity. Energy companies drill into the ground where steam is trapped and direct the steam into turbines that convert it to electricity. Many countries now have geothermal energy stations, but geothermal energy is not available in all areas.

THINK ABOUT IT

What are the advantages of using geothermal energy instead of nuclear energy?

▲ Geyser

▲ Buildings in Iceland are heated with geothermal energy.

Talkin' Trash

The search for new sources of fuel can lead us to some pretty strange places—such as our own trash cans! In this activity, you will look at trash as a possible source of fuel.

DO THIS

1. Assemble the paper trash in a pile.

2. Cut large items into small pieces, and soak the trash in a bucket of warm water.

3. Put on the apron and gloves. Empty the bucket, and then squeeze as much water as possible from the trash. Press the pieces of trash into the bottom of the bucket. Keep doing this until you have built up a thick layer of soggy trash.

4. Allow this pressed trash to dry for a few days. When the trash is completely dry, examine your "fuel."

5. **CAUTION: Stay well away from the burning material.** Your teacher will break up the material and burn a little of it in a safe receptacle.

MATERIALS
- paper trash
- scissors
- bucket
- warm water
- apron
- gloves
- Science Log data sheet

THINK AND WRITE

1. Describe the dried-out trash.

2. Do you think trash makes a good fuel? Explain.

Biomass

Burning trash may seem to be a lot more bother than burning wood, coal, or oil. However, it may be worth considering trash as an alternative to our limited supplies of fossil fuels. What other unusual sources of fuel are there? Read to find out.

The fuel you made in the last activity was a form of biomass. Biomass consists of materials from recently living plants and animals. It is a renewable energy resource, since many plants grow quickly.

For thousands of years, people have been using biomass energy to keep warm and to cook. Wood is the most obvious source of biomass. Another example of biomass is *peat*. Peat is coal that has not completely formed. It is softer than coal and contains much more moisture. Because of this, peat doesn't burn as well as coal. However, peat is used as a dependable source of energy in some countries.

Besides releasing energy by burning, biomass can produce a gas called *biogas*. Decomposing garbage in landfills and decomposing waste matter such as manure produce a flammable gas called *methane*. Methane can be collected and burned to produce electricity.

▲ Peat

▲ Landfill

▲ Methane gas vent at a landfill

LESSON 2 REVIEW

Explain how each fuel mentioned in this lesson could be used in a heat engine energy station to produce electricity.

E41

3 FROM STEAM TO ELECTRICITY

Remember, a heat engine produces heat by burning fuel. In a heat engine energy station, the heat is used to produce steam. In this lesson, you will discover how turbines, generators, electric motors, and transformers turn that steam into electricity.

ACTIVITY

Making a Turbine

The turbine in an energy station transfers the mechanical energy of steam to the generator, which produces electricity. The best way to understand how a turbine works is to build one of your own. You can do that in the following activity.

DO THIS

❶ Cut 10 1.25-cm slits around the edge of the cardboard circle. Glue the plastic squares into the slits to make a pinwheel.

❷ Cut a hole in the center of the cardboard circle large enough to slip over the small test tube. Then put the cardboard circle over the test tube.

❸ Place the test tube, with the cardboard circle attached, upside down on top of the ring stand.

❹ Remove the stopper with the glass tube and half-fill the flask with water. Replace the stopper.

MATERIALS
- 20-cm circle cut from heavy cardboard
- scissors
- 10 5-cm squares cut from plastic
- glue
- plastic test tube
- ring stand
- flask with one-hole stopper and bent glass tube
- water
- hot plate
- Science Log data sheet

5 Put the hot plate near the ring stand holding the test tube and cardboard circle. Then put the flask on the hot plate.

6 Direct the glass tube toward the blades on the cardboard circle.

7 **CAUTION: Be careful when using the hot plate.** Turn on the hot plate and observe what happens.

THINK AND WRITE

1. What happened to the plastic blades on your cardboard pinwheel?

2. Do you think that your turbine would be able to produce electricity? Explain.

3. **COMMUNICATING** Being able to communicate effectively is very important to scientists. In this activity, you constructed a model of a turbine. Write a paragraph or draw a diagram that would help someone else build this complex model.

Turbines and generators In an energy station, turbines are enclosed in steel cylinders to direct the flow of steam over the turbine blades. The turning of the test tube in the activity is similar to the turning of the shaft that leads from the turbine to the electric generator. Generators use many of the principles of magnetism, so before we look at generators, let's do some activities with magnets.

▲ **Steam turbine**

Pole to Pole

Remember using magnets as a kid? Maybe you still use them to stick things on the refrigerator at home. In the following activity, you can review some of the properties of magnets.

MATERIALS
- 2 bar magnets
- wooden dowel
- thread
- iron nails
- Science Log data sheet

DO THIS

1 Suspend one of the bar magnets from the dowel with thread so that it swings freely.

2 Holding the other bar magnet, bring the north poles of the magnets together. Then try the same thing with the south poles. Record what happens.

3 Slowly bring together the north pole of one magnet and the south pole of the other magnet. Record what happens.

4 Try picking up some of the nails with the north pole of one magnet and then with the south pole. Record what happens.

5 Pick up a single nail so that only one end of the nail is attached to the magnet. Then try picking up a second nail by touching it with the free end of the first nail. Record what happens.

THINK AND WRITE

1. Based on your observations, write two general rules that describe the way magnets interact with each other.

2. From your observations in step 5, what can you infer about a nail that is touching a magnet?

Force Field

You have observed that magnets exert a force—they can pull or push metallic objects or other magnets. In this activity, you can "see" the field of force of a magnet.

DO THIS

1 Lay the magnet flat on a table. Cover it with the sheet of paper.

2 Sprinkle iron filings across the top of the paper, near the location of the magnet. Shake or tap the paper gently.

3 Use a compass to determine the direction of the lines of force in the magnetic field, as shown by the pattern of the filings. Do this by passing the compass directly above the path of the filings.

MATERIALS
- bar magnet
- sheet of stiff paper
- iron filings
- compass
- Science Log data sheet

THINK AND WRITE

What does the pattern of filings tell you about the magnet's field of force?

Magnets A compass needle, which is a small magnet, aligns itself north and south. The end that points north is called the *north-seeking pole*, and the end that points south is called the *south-seeking pole*. Because the Earth also has a magnetic field, the North Pole of the Earth attracts the north-seeking pole of a compass needle.

Making a Generator

So far, you've done some interesting things with magnets, but what do they have to do with electricity? You can find out by building a model of an electric generator.

DO THIS

1 Keeping 30 cm of wire free at each end, wind the rest of the wire around the outside of the cardboard tube.

2 Attach the bare ends of the wire to the clips of the galvanometer. A galvanometer detects current electricity.

3 Hold one end of a bar magnet, and quickly move it through the cardboard tube in the middle of the coil of wire. Note what happens to the galvanometer needle. Continue to watch the needle as you remove the magnet.

4 Now hold the other end of the magnet and repeat step 3. Again note what happens to the galvanometer needle.

5 Stack two or three magnets together with their poles matching. Then repeat steps 3 and 4. Note what happens to the galvanometer needle.

THINK AND WRITE

1. How did the number of magnets affect the amount of electricity produced?

2. **COMPARING** Look again at steps 3 and 4. What did you do differently in these steps? How was the galvanometer reading different for each step? What determines the direction of the current flowing through the galvanometer?

Generating Electricity

You have made models of two pieces of machinery that an energy station uses—a turbine and a generator. Let's take a look at how these machines work together to produce electricity.

As you discovered, a turbine uses steam under pressure to spin blades attached to a shaft. The shaft runs through a generator. Attached to the shaft, and spinning with it, is a large coil of wire surrounded by a strong magnet. The coil spinning between the poles of the magnet creates a changing magnetic field, which produces current electricity.

In the last activity, you produced current electricity in a similar fashion as you moved the magnet in and out of the coil. As the magnet went into the coil, the current flowed in one direction, and as it was pulled out, the flow direction was reversed. In energy station generators, the rapid movement of the coil within the generator produces a current that constantly changes direction. This is called *alternating current.*

By producing alternating current, energy stations can send more electricity over greater distances than they could with *direct current,* or current that flows only in one direction. Later in this section, you will discover how this is done.

THINK ABOUT IT

A changing magnetic field produces alternating current. Do you think a flow of current could produce a magnetic field? Explain.

▲ **Alternating-current generator**

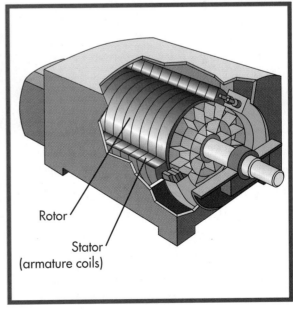

Rotor

Stator (armature coils)

▲ **Inside a generator**

A Current Affair

Alternating current was not always the only type of electricity produced in the United States. In the following article, you can read about two pioneers in electricity who disagreed over which kind of current was better.

The WAR of the Currents

by **Richard L. Mattis**
from *Cobblestone*

Thomas Edison's electric power plant on Pearl Street was a good beginning, but it could serve customers only within about a mile and a half of the plant. The voltage beyond that distance was too low to make Edison's lamps glow brightly.

Edison was using direct current, or DC. Another inventor, George Westinghouse, wanted to use alternating current, or AC, instead. AC sent power over long distances at a higher voltage, then used transformers to reduce the voltage to the right level for service in people's homes.

In 1886, Westinghouse's co-worker William Stanley installed an AC power system in Great Barrington, Massachusetts. About one hundred fifty lamps lighted

▲ George Westinghouse

streets and stores. Soon afterward, orders for Westinghouse power systems began to come in.

The thought of AC making his DC power plants obsolete blinded Edison to the potential benefits of AC power. He stubbornly decided to fight Westinghouse in what has been called "the war of the currents."

Edison began to speak and write about the dangers of AC power. People became frightened, and accidental deaths by electric shock became front-page news. One newspaper article was titled "The Electric Murderer."

Edison supporter Harold Brown applied DC and AC electric shocks to a seventy-six-pound dog in a public demonstration. An AC shock eventually killed the dog. Brown experimented with other dogs, two calves, and a horse. He was convinced that AC was more dangerous than DC. Brown offered to apply DC shocks to himself if Westinghouse would take equal AC shocks. Westinghouse refused, noting that Brown shocked his animals using moistened contacts placed near vital organs. In contrast, an accidental brief contact with household current would be harmless. He pointed to the one hundred thirty Westinghouse systems that were operating successfully in the United States and Canada.

The war continued for several years. In 1896, three Westinghouse generators in a hydroelectric plant at Niagara Falls began delivering power to Buffalo, about twenty miles away. By 1917, only five percent of the electric power in the United States was DC. AC had won the war.

THINK ABOUT IT

Suppose Thomas Edison and DC had won the war of the currents. How might people living in rural areas be affected?

◀ **The lights used at the 1893 Columbian Exposition in Chicago were powered by AC.**

Wind and Water

The energy resources that we most commonly use to produce electricity—fossil fuels and uranium—are cheap and, at the present time, readily available. But other energy resources—wind and water—are alternatives to heat engine energy stations for the production of electricity.

▼ Modern windmills

Windmills have been used for hundreds of years to pump water. *Wind turbines* are modern windmills that use the mechanical energy of the wind for the production of electricity. Wind strikes a wind turbine in much the same way that steam strikes the turbine of a heat engine. When the wind turbine spins, it turns a generator that produces an electric current.

In wind farms around the world, including several in the United States, hundreds of wind turbines are grouped together. In the hills of Tehachapi Pass in California, thousands of wind turbines provide enough electricity for half a million homes! This wind farm produces more wind-generated electricity than any other in the world. You can easily demonstrate the way in which wind produces electricity.

You will need: two window fans, galvanometer, wire.

Place two window fans facing each other, a few centimeters apart. Plug in one fan, and turn it on so that it blows on the blades of the other fan. Connect the prongs of the second fan's plug to a galvanometer and measure the current produced by your wind turbine.

For thousands of years, people have used mills powered by the energy of falling water to grind grain and cut wood. Like wind, falling water can also be used to produce electricity. The mechanical energy of falling water can turn a turbine. As the turbine spins, electricity is produced by an attached generator.

The process of producing electricity from falling water is used in **hydroelectric energy** stations. Dams block the water flow of streams and rivers so that the water level behind the dam is higher than the water level in front of the dam. The force of water falling through the inside of the dam turns the turbines. The turbines turn the generators that produce the electric current. A hydroelectric energy station is like a heat engine energy station without the heat engine.

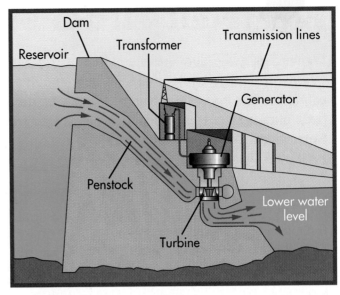

▲ **Hydroelectric energy station**

◀ Hoover Dam, on the Colorado River, created the largest artificial lake in North America. The energy station below Hoover Dam has 17 turbines and generates enough electricity for more than 500,000 homes!

THINK ABOUT IT

The United States gets only about 3 percent of its electricity from wind farms and hydroelectric energy stations. Why do you think this is?

Electricity from Sunlight

Energy from the sun is already being used to produce electricity on a large scale in solar-thermal conversion energy stations. But it is not really necessary to go through a heat engine process to produce electricity from sunlight. Surprised? Continue reading to find out how sunlight can be used to produce electricity directly.

Have you ever used a solar-powered calculator? These instruments are powered by light. Because electric lights are so common, you probably don't use **solar energy,** or the energy of the sun, directly, but you could.

Devices within the calculator, called *photovoltaic cells,* convert light directly into electricity, which then powers the calculator. Photovoltaic cells contain a fairly rare material called *selenium.* When light strikes the selenium in these cells, the selenium gives off electricity.

Photovoltaic cells are used to power everything from calculators to spacecraft. At the present time, photovoltaic cells waste a lot of solar energy—only a small amount of the solar energy that hits the cell is changed into electricity.

▲ Solar-powered calculator with photovoltaic cells

Scientists are continuing to improve photovoltaic cells. Energy stations powered by photovoltaic cells are expected to be commonplace by the middle of the next century. According to the Solar Energy Research Institute, photovoltaic cells could produce more than half of the electricity used in the United States!

Photovoltaic cells could even reduce the need for fuel for transportation. All over the world, races are held to showcase designs for solar-powered cars. In one such race, a car named Sunraycer traveled almost 3,219 kilometers (2,000 miles) across the Australian desert in five and a half days!

Although solar energy is affected by weather and the amount of sunlight that reaches certain parts of the world, it could become an alternative source of energy for the production of electricity.

▲ The Hubble Space Telescope is powered by photovoltaic cells.

QUICK CHECK

LESSON 3 REVIEW

❶ How do a turbine and a generator work together to produce electricity?

❷ What are some disadvantages of using wind, falling water, and photovoltaic cells to produce electricity on a large scale?

▼ **Solar-powered vehicles**

4 THE ELECTRIC GRID

You have looked at several different ways of producing energy. Just as important as producing electricity, however, is distributing it to homes, farms, factories, and offices. In this lesson, you will discover how electricity reaches the people and places that use it.

▲ Transformers

Transformers

Many energy transformations take place in order to produce electricity in an energy station. In fact, so many transformations take place, it's a wonder there is any energy still around at all! Read to find out what happens to electricity after it leaves the energy station.

Energy does not really wear out from the numerous transformations, but a lot of waste heat and other byproducts are produced. So electricity needs a boost in order to reach all of its users.

As electricity passes through power lines, it loses some of its energy. Through the use of *transformers,* energy stations can increase the potential energy, or *voltage,* so electricity can travel long distances with a smaller loss of energy. When the electricity reaches its destination, another transformer reduces the voltage, so it can be used in homes and businesses.

▼ Home circuits

Within a transformer, two separate coils are wound around an iron ring. When an alternating current is passed through one coil, it produces a matching current in the other coil. Changing the size of one of the coils changes the voltage of the electric current.

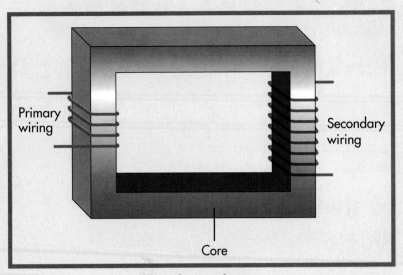

▲ Parts of a transformer

If, for example, the first coil has 10 loops and the second coil has 20 loops, the voltage is doubled. On the other hand, if the first coil has 20 loops and the second coil has 10 loops, the voltage will be reduced by one-half. In this way, 110 volts can be "stepped up" to 220 volts, or 220 volts can be "stepped down" to 110 volts. The amount that the voltage is stepped up or stepped down depends on the number of loops of wire around each part of the ring.

From a transformer station, high-voltage electricity is transmitted through a grid system of overhead lines, or transmission lines, usually made of a good electric *conductor,* such as copper or aluminum. These lines are supported by huge pylons, or steel towers.

At the point where transmission lines enter a city, local transformer substations reduce the voltage for home use—usually to 110 volts.

In your home, or anywhere else that electricity is used, circuits run from the energy source to the electric outlets. Electricity flows through the circuits in your home in much the same way that blood flows through your body. Unlike blood flow, however, the flow of electricity is controlled by a switch that makes or breaks a circuit. In the next activity, you will discover how electric energy is changed back into mechanical energy in an appliance.

THINK ABOUT IT

Why is the voltage of an electric current stepped up before transmission and then stepped down before use?

Making a Simple Motor

Once electricity enters your home, it is changed to mechanical energy in a blender, a drill, a hair dryer, or many other appliances. You can find out how this happens in the following activity.

DO THIS

1 Lay out the wire in a straight line on a table. Place a compass on top of the wire, about midway along its length. Line up the wire with the compass needle.

2 Connect the ends of the wire to a 6-volt battery without disturbing the wire under the compass. Record what happens to the compass needle.

3 Disconnect the wire from the battery. Then switch the ends of the wire and connect them to the opposite posts of the battery. Record what happens to the compass needle.

MATERIALS
- 75-cm wire
- compass
- 6-volt battery
- Science Log data sheet

THINK AND WRITE

Using what you know about magnets and electricity, explain what happened to the compass needle.

Motor Power

An electric motor is a device that transforms electric energy into mechanical energy, or movement. In the activity, you made a simple electric motor. As the current passed through the wire, it produced a magnetic field that moved the compass needle. Continue reading to discover more about electric motors.

Most home appliances have AC motors. In AC motors, the direction of the current, and therefore the magnetic poles, are constantly changing. This switching of magnetic poles causes the coil of wire to spin inside the magnet. Since the coil of wire is part of the shaft, the shaft spins, too. The spinning shaft does the work.

Look at the diagram of an electric motor. It looks a lot like the diagram of a generator. Electric motors and generators have similar designs because they perform similar, but opposite, operations.

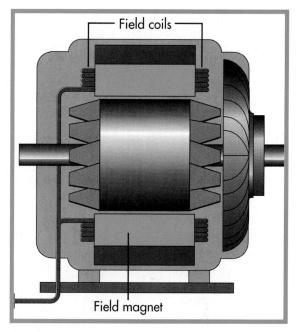

Field coils

Field magnet

▲ AC motor

LESSON 4 REVIEW

Explain how an electric motor is like a generator.

DOUBLE CHECK

SECTION B REVIEW

1. How is using biomass as fuel similar to using fossil fuels? How is it different?

2. What are the advantages and disadvantages of using photovoltaic cells instead of fossil fuels to generate electricity?

3. Explain how a heat engine energy station produces electric energy from a fuel.

SECTION C
Other Uses of Energy

Traffic flowing along a highway, airplanes circling the globe, and homes heated with wood-burning furnaces all consume energy. But most automobiles, airplanes, and fireplaces don't have electric cords coming out of them—they don't rely on electricity for their energy.

In this section, you will discover how we use energy resources in ways other than converting them to electricity. You will also discover alternative energy resources that can be used for these purposes. As you work through the investigations in this section, write new ideas in your Science Log.

① PRODUCING AND USING FUELS

On a cold day, you can turn up the thermostat and enjoy the warmth provided by the furnace in your home. What kind of energy fuels your furnace? It could be electricity, or perhaps your home is heated by coal, oil, natural gas, or another fuel. In the activities that follow, you will discover how processing and refining changes raw energy resources into fuels that can be used directly.

Pipe It In

Many homes use natural gas for heating. This fuel is usually piped into homes. Where does it come from? Think about that question as you read the following.

In the story "Gusher!", you read about a gas that shot up through the well pipe from beneath the ground before the oil appeared. About 2,000 years ago, the Chinese discovered and began using natural gas. They used bamboo poles to pipe the gas from shallow wells and burned it under large pans full of sea water. The sea water evaporated, leaving salt.

People have known for many years that natural gas is very convenient to use—it can usually be piped to wherever it is needed. However, only in some areas have large reserves of natural gas been discovered. For this reason, scientists found ways to convert coal into a less effective, but still useful, manufactured gas through a process called *gasification*.

▼ Natural-gas streetlights in Boston

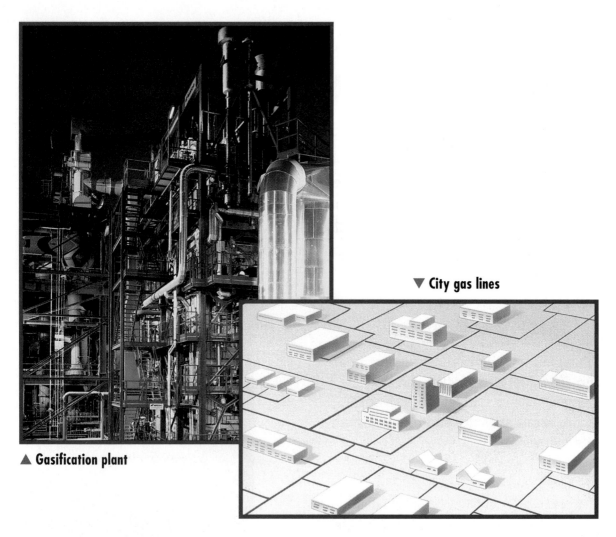

▲ Gasification plant

▼ City gas lines

In gasification, hydrogen and methane gas trapped within the coal are released when coal is heated in an airtight container. The gases are filtered through water and then purified. The coal gas can then be piped to where it is needed. Coal gas is an example of a **synthetic fuel,** that is, a manufactured fuel.

Because of the large reserves of natural gas in the United States, gas made from coal is not as popular here as in some countries where natural gas is not available locally.

Natural gas is pumped through a network of underground pipelines in many of our cities. Natural gas supplies much of the energy used for home heating, water heating, and cooking. However, natural gas is difficult to transport and store in its gaseous form. Just as steam can be condensed to form water, natural gas can be condensed to a liquid fuel. In rural areas where there are no underground pipelines, liquid fuel is delivered by truck and stored in tanks.

THINK ABOUT IT

Why is coal gas not used much in the United States?

ACTIVITY

Coalbusters

Many methods are used to extract gas from coal. You can explore one of these ways in the following activity.

DO THIS

1 Wrap the coal in the rag, and fasten the rag closed with a rubber band. Put the wrapped coal on the plywood, and hammer the coal into a fine powder.

2 Plug the small end of the funnel with a crumpled paper towel. Then carefully pour the coal dust into the top of the funnel.

3 Turn the bucket upside down, and place it over the top of the funnel. Then, holding the funnel tightly against the bottom of the bucket, turn the bucket right side up. Remove the paper towel.

4 Slowly pour water into the bucket while holding the funnel to keep it from floating. Continue pouring until the water is just above the funnel.

5 Fill the jar with water. Then turn it upside down underwater, and place it over the small end of the funnel.

6 Put the bucket aside for a day or two. Then record your observations.

MATERIALS
- bituminous coal
- rag
- rubber band
- plywood
- hammer
- funnel
- paper towel
- plastic bucket
- water
- glass jar
- Science Log data sheet

THINK AND WRITE

1. What happened to the water in the jar?

2. Why do you think it was necessary to crush the coal?

Fill 'er Up

Where does gasoline for cars come from? If you think it comes from service stations, you're only partly correct. Where do service stations get gasoline? Continue reading to find out.

A service station is the end point in a long process that can be traced back to oil wells. But crude oil from wells such as Spindletop can't be poured directly into the gas tank of a car. It first must be changed into lubrication oils and fuels that can be used in cars, trucks, planes, and other vehicles.

▶ Oil refinery

▼ Refining crude oil

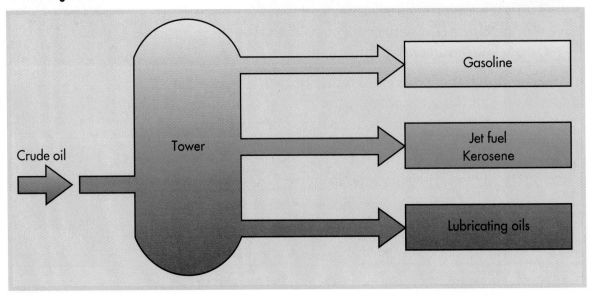

Crude oil → Tower → Gasoline

Jet fuel
Kerosene

Lubricating oils

Coal and natural gas provide us with hydrocarbon fuels in solid and gaseous forms. **Petroleum,** or crude oil, is made up of liquid hydrocarbons. Just as coal has to be processed to extract gas from it, crude oil must also be processed before it can be used as fuel.

Crude oil is shipped to a *refinery*—a plant that separates the oil into products such as gasoline, diesel fuel, jet fuel, heating fuel, motor oil, and other chemicals and lubricants.

In a refinery, crude oil is heated to form a gas, which rises in a tall tower. As the gas rises, it cools. The products in the crude-oil gas return to liquid form at different temperatures and levels in the tower. Each product is removed from the level at which it is liquified in the tower and is pumped into a separate storage tank.

Each product is then shipped to a place where it is stored. Gasoline is stored in large tanks at terminals from which tank trucks transport it to service stations.

▲ Shipping refined-oil products

In addition to producing different fuels for different kinds of vehicles, scientists have found ways to alter oil's chemical make-up in order to produce products such as plastics, cleaners, fabrics, hand lotions, and even chewing gum!

THINK ABOUT IT

What products made from petroleum have you used today?

A Little History

Wood, coal, petroleum, natural gas, uranium—all have been developed as sources of energy for the growth and development of our country. The following article may give you some insight into the history of fuel and energy use in the United States.

FROM **MUSCLE POWER** TO **ATOMIC POWER**

by **Karen E. Hong** from *Cobblestone*

The first American settlers had limited energy resources. They had to rely on muscle power, wood from nearby forests, and candles. Their muscles, assisted by those of their animals, built shelters, cleared and plowed fields, and transported objects. Wood provided fires for warmth and cooking. Candles lit their homes.

As the settlers cut down the eastern forests, however, wood had to be transported over greater distances, making it more expensive. Although coal was mined commercially in Virginia beginning in 1750, it was not widely used until the mid-1800s. The shortage of inexpensive wood created a growing demand for coal to heat homes, cook meals, and fuel the beginnings of American industry. By 1885, more coal than wood was being burned in the United States.

The colonists developed wind and water power more quickly. They harnessed the wind to pump water and grind grain. The first American windmill was erected at Windmill Point near Jamestown, Virginia, in 1620. Settlers moving farther inland along rivers and streams built water mills to grind grain and saw lumber. As early as 1631, water power ran a saw in Maine. In the eighteenth century, people used the

Before the invention of the steam engine and mass-production factories, clothes were made by hand or with foot-pedaled sewing machines.

For hundreds of years, water wheels have turned grindstones to mill flour, saw blades to cut lumber, and, in the past two centuries, the gears of textile looms and industrial machinery in factories. Mill wheels are powered by water flowing either under or over them and are connected by shafts and gears to the machinery they run. This undershot (the water flows under it) paddle wheel at Saugus Iron Works Historic Site in Massachusetts is a reconstruction of a water wheel at America's first successful iron-works, which was built in 1646. The wheel powers bellows that fan the fire of the chafery hearth where cast iron was converted to wrought iron for Colonial iron products.

movement of the ocean to grind spices at a tidal mill in Chelsea, Massachusetts.

But windmills and water mills depended on a steady supply of wind and running water. With the development of an efficient steam engine in 1775, wood and coal were put to new uses. In 1807, Robert Fulton's boat, the *Clermont,* steamed up the Hudson River from New York City to Albany. Soon steam engines were propelling ships and locomotives. Although windmills were still used to pump the great amounts of water required by steam locomotives, steam engines soon took over many manufacturing jobs. Industrial plants were no longer tied to running water and blowing winds.

But as wonderful as steam power was, it could not provide light. In the early nineteenth century, lamps burned whale oil. So many whales were killed for their oil that they almost became extinct. As whale oil became scarcer, it became more expensive. People found a new source of lamplight in a gas manufactured from coal. Although this gas lit streets, homes, and factories in a few large cities, transporting it to rural areas was impractical and expensive.

Kerosene, a satisfactory substitute for whale oil, became available after the country's first oil well was drilled in Titusville, Pennsylvania, in 1859. At first kerosene was the most important petroleum product; gasoline was thought to be a useless and dangerous waste product. However, the development of the internal combustion engine and the automobile made gasoline more important by the end of the 1800s.

The first automobiles were powered by steam or electricity. Steam cars were heavy because they carried wood or coal along as fuel. Electric cars were slow and could travel only a few miles on a charge. Because gasoline was plentiful and inexpensive and it burned efficiently, it soon became the fuel of choice. Petroleum became so valuable that it was sometimes called black gold.

In 1903, Wilbur and Orville Wright put a gasoline engine into a glider and flew for twelve seconds. Before long, this form of petroleum-fueled transportation was common in the United States.

In drilling for petroleum, people often found natural gas. Although natural gas

▲ **The Wright brothers' plane**

provided light for Fredonia, New York, in 1825, most people considered it a nuisance because there was no convenient way to store or transport it. Frequently it was burned off or allowed to escape into the air. By the late 1920s, however, pipes carried gas from the wells to cities, providing light and warmth.

The ability to generate and transport large amounts of electricity revolutionized America. Although electric generators date back to the 1830s, they did not become practical for forty years. Generators turn the power of wood, water, wind, coal, oil, or gas (and, in the twentieth century, nuclear reactions) into electricity. In 1882, the United States' first central power plant burned fossil fuels to create steam and generate electricity for eighty-five customers.

The twentieth century became the century of electricity. Electric streetcars provided transportation. The telegraph, telephone, and, later, television speeded communication. In cities, energy in the form of electricity became available to homes, offices, and factories.

At first, most electricity was used in

cities. People in rural areas relied on older forms of energy. Windmills pumped the water needed for irrigation and household use; kerosene lit the lamps. Some people used generators and batteries to adapt windmills to produce electricity.

In 1935, the Rural Electrification Administration changed that. It provided low-interest loans for building power lines that brought inexpensive electricity to millions of farms. With the widespread availability of electricity generated mainly from fossil fuels, older energy resources fell into disuse.

▲ **Nuclear energy station**

Then a new source of energy was discovered. Uranium atoms were first split in 1938, and the process of fission (the splitting of atoms) produced the atomic bombs dropped on Hiroshima and Nagasaki, Japan, during World War II. After the war, this nuclear energy was put to peacetime uses. In a power plant, a nuclear reactor operates as a sort of furnace, using radioactive metal to provide the heat that powers an electric generator. Because a small amount of radioactive fuel creates an enormous amount of energy, nuclear reactors power submarines as well as electric plants.

At mid-century, the United States' energy potential seemed limitless. As late as 1950, the United States exported its surplus oil. Even remote areas had electricity at the flick of a switch. And there were plans to build numerous nuclear reactors that would produce even more energy.

By the late 1960s, things had begun to change. Half of the United States' petroleum was gone, and it began importing oil. In 1973, the Middle Eastern Arab states refused to ship oil to the United States, and Americans faced an energy shortage. In addition, the burning of petroleum, coal, and natural gas was polluting the air. A 1979 accident at the Three Mile Island nuclear reactors in Pennsylvania released radioactive gases into the outside air, raising the issues of safety and pollution for nuclear power. Americans began to consider the need for conservation and the development of renewable energy sources.

New attention is being paid to wind and water power with the development of increasingly efficient wind turbines and systems using temperature differences in ocean water. Solar collectors are used in some homes and industries, and a few solar farms generate vast amounts of energy. Geothermal energy, the internal heat of the earth, is being developed in the West. In the Midwest, ethyl alcohol, made from surplus grain, is being mixed with gasoline to form a fuel called gasohol. Even trash is a potential source of energy. Some cities add trash to coal, while others use pipes to recover the methane gas being formed under landfills.

Wind power can be captured in many ways. The 2-bladed wind turbine can provide power for 35 average-size homes. The old windmill in front is an example of the type used for power and to pump water on farms before electricity was available. An experimental turbine has blades shaped like the cross section of an airplane wing. These blades operate in wind from any direction.

Great amounts of petroleum are still used, however, and federal energy policy has promoted the use of coal and nuclear energy until alternatives are fully developed. As a result, most federal money has been spent on finding new sources and uses of these conventional fuels to meet immediate needs. Experts say that similar attention must be paid to developing renewable sources of energy and greater energy efficiency in the future.

LESSON 1 REVIEW

Compare the uses of coal, natural gas, gasoline, and uranium as fuels.

2 FUELS FOR THE FUTURE

So far you have explored several methods of producing fuels from natural energy resources. In this lesson, you will find out about alternative fuels and direct energy sources.

Alternative Fuels

As demand for energy increases around the world, a greater effort is being made to develop and use alternative fuels. Continue reading to find out what some of these alternative fuels are.

Today many oil companies add small amounts of ethanol to their gasolines. Ethanol is a colorless liquid made from biomass, usually corn or sugar cane. A mixture of gasoline and ethanol is called *gasohol.*

When engines run on pure ethanol, as some race cars do, they produce almost no carbon monoxide, an air pollutant. Ethanol also has a higher *octane rating* than gasoline, which means that engines using it run more efficiently.

One disadvantage of using ethanol as a fuel is that the crops used to produce it compete with food crops for growing space. Another disadvantage is that it gives fewer kilometers per liter (or miles per gallon) than gasoline.

▲ Gasohol is a gasoline-and-alcohol mixture

Another example of an alternative fuel is methanol, which is made by combining natural gas and coal with renewable resources, such as wood and other biomass. Although its production would not compete with food crops, methanol is very expensive to produce, and using it would require changes in the types of engines we now use. Unlike ethanol, methanol is not as efficient as gasoline.

In the future, there may also be an energy alternative to natural gas. Hydrogen, for example, may be an ideal fuel for many uses. For heating and cooking purposes, hydrogen burns with a hotter flame than natural gas. Compressed hydrogen could also be used in vehicles, since it doesn't produce dangerous air pollutants, as petroleum products do. Hydrogen could also be used to produce electricity in a heat-engine energy station.

▲ **Hydrogen-powered vehicle**

Hydrogen is widely available because it can be extracted from water or any hydrocarbon. However, *electrolysis,* the principal process for extracting hydrogen from water, is very expensive because of the high costs of electricity needed for the process.

When an inexpensive means of obtaining hydrogen is developed, hydrogen may become a more practical fuel alternative. In the next activity, you can discover an energy alternative that can be used directly, and often without added expense.

THINK ABOUT IT

Why is it necessary to begin developing and using alternative fuels as quickly as possible?

ACTIVITY

Collecting Thermal Energy

One of the great things about light is that it produces a form of energy we can use without having to transform it—heat! In this activity, you can examine how light can be used to produce heat.

MATERIALS

- shoe box
- black paper
- scissors
- tape
- 2 thermometers
- clear plastic wrap
- light source
- Science Log data sheet

DO THIS

1 Line the inside of the box with black paper.

2 Tape one thermometer on the inside bottom of the box.

3 Cover the open top of the box with plastic wrap. Tape the edges of the wrap to the box.

4 Place the box and the second thermometer under a bright light for 5 minutes. Then record both thermometer readings.

5 Remove the light source and wait 5 minutes. Again record both thermometer readings.

THINK AND WRITE

1. Why do you think you were asked to line the box with black paper? What role did the plastic wrap play?

2. **COMPARING** When you make comparisons, you look for similarities and differences. How did the temperature readings for the two thermometers compare after the thermometers were exposed to the light source? How did they compare after the source was removed?

Direct Energy Resources

On Tundra Tuesday, your school went without heat for a day. What kind of energy is used to heat your school? It may be heated by electricity or steam, or it may be heated by oil or natural gas. Some energy resources, like oil or gas, can be used directly. Continue reading to find out more about direct energy resources.

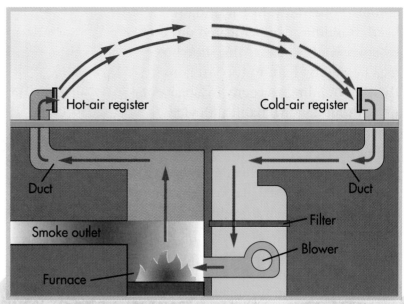

▲ **How a gas furnace works**

Natural gas is one example of an energy resource that can be used directly. Gas can be piped into a home for use in heating and cooking. The diagram shows how gas can be used directly for heating.

Of course, gas isn't the only energy resource that can be used directly. Since the earliest days of civilization, people have used wood for heating and cooking. Many people are returning to this method of using energy directly, thus conserving our dwindling supplies of fossil fuels.

Unfortunately, burning wood pollutes the air, and it requires cutting down a lot of trees. Although wood is a cheap energy resource, our forests are already shrinking because of the number of trees we harvest for lumber and to manufacture paper products.

◄ **Wood may become a scarce energy resource.**

Not all direct energy resources must be burned. Every day, for example, the sun drenches the Earth with huge amounts of energy, just waiting to be used. Buildings can be heated directly by solar energy, just as the shoe box was heated by light in the last activity. Heating buildings directly by solar energy without any mechanical devices being used to distribute the heat is called *passive solar heating.*

In one passive solar-heating system, a layer of double-glazed glass is placed in front of a concrete wall painted black. An air gap separates the glass and the wall. Sunlight shines through the glass and heats the black concrete wall. At the same time, air from the adjoining room enters the gap between the glass and the wall through vents at the base of the wall. The air is heated by the wall and rises, exiting through vents at the top of the wall. The heated air then warms the room. Since the air in the room sinks as it gradually cools, it reenters the lower vents and a circulation is established without the use of fans.

Heating buildings by using mechanical devices to distribute heat produced by

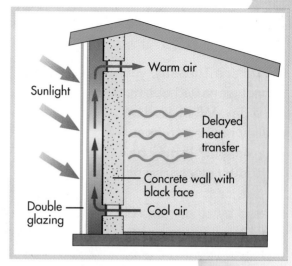

▲ **Passive solar heating**

solar energy is called *active solar heating.*

Many buildings with active solar heating use *solar collectors*, or glass boxes containing tubes filled with liquid or air, to trap heat. Once the heat is trapped, insulators retain the heat for later use. What was the insulator in the heat collector you constructed in the last activity?

In solar collectors that use air, fans force warm air to different areas of the building. In solar collectors that use liquid, pumps send warm liquid, usually water, to a *heat exchanger*. As the outer surfaces of the heat exchanger become hot, heat is transferred to the air around it.

You have already seen how heat from within the Earth can be used to produce electricity. Just as solar energy can be used as a direct energy resource, geothermal energy can also be used directly.

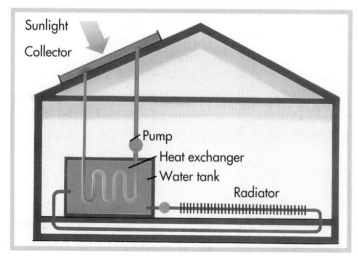

◀ **Active solar heating**

◄ **Geothermal heated pool in Iceland**

Iceland, you may recall, uses geothermal energy to heat most of its homes. The homes are heated with water pumped from hot springs or underground sources. Parts of Russia, Hungary, and France also make direct use of heat from within the Earth. In the United States, geothermal energy is more limited than in other parts of the world, but scientists here are looking for better ways to find and use Earth's own energy.

LESSON 2 REVIEW

1 Why are some people still using wood as fuel for heating?

2 How do active and passive solar-heating systems differ?

DOUBLE CHECK

SECTION C REVIEW

1. Which fuels can be used directly as energy resources?

2. Compare the way natural gas and wood are used for direct heating with the way fuels are used in a heat-engine energy station.

3. What do you think is the most efficient way to heat a home—with electricity, natural gas, or wood? Explain.

SECTION D
Energy Ecology

What comes to your mind when you hear the word *ecology*? Recycling bottles and cans? Landfills? Endangered species? These are all concerns of ecology, but what about energy? What effects do energy production and consumption have on our environment? How can we control these effects? Do we need to find energy alternatives?

In this section, you will see how obtaining and using fuels as sources of energy have harmed Earth's land, air, water, and life. Keep careful notes in your Science Log as you work through the investigations in this section.

1 ENERGY STATIONS' ENVIRONMENTAL IMPACT

If you have ever passed by an energy station that burns fossil fuels, you may have seen plumes of black smoke pouring out. Exactly what is in the smoke, and how does it affect the environment? In this lesson, you will discover answers to these and related questions.

ACTIVITY

Harmful Acid

Some of the pollutants produced by burning fossil fuels can turn rain and snow into an acid. This *acid rain* is harmful to plants, animals, and even buildings. The following activity will show you how acid can be detected.

MATERIALS
- small cup
- tap water
- blue and red litmus paper
- dropper
- vinegar
- Science Log data sheet

DO THIS

1. Fill the glass with tap water.

2. Dip one end of the red litmus paper into the water. Do the same thing with the blue litmus paper. Record your observations.

3. Add a couple of drops of vinegar to the water. Repeat step 2 using the opposite end of each piece of litmus paper. Record your observations.

THINK AND WRITE

1. How were the two tests with litmus paper different?

2. How would you test a sample of rain for the presence of acid?

3. **COMPARING** When you compare, you identify how things are alike and how they are different. What did you compare in this activity? Do you think vinegar water and acid rain would have the same effect on litmus paper? Explain.

Coal Burners

Coal is one of the most common fuels used to produce electricity in the United States. The burning of coal in electric energy stations has some serious environmental effects. The following diagram will help you discover some of them.

▼ In the United States, 200 million tonnes of air pollutants are released annually by electric energy stations.

▼ Sulfur dioxide from the burning of fossil fuels combines with water vapor in the air to form sulfuric acid. This falls to Earth as acid rain.

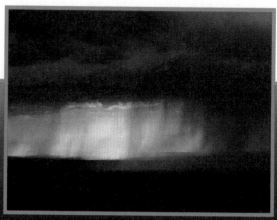

▲ In mountainous areas like the Canadian Shield and the Adirondacks, sulfuric acid builds up in the snowpack. When spring comes, the snow melts, and large amounts of acidic water gush into lakes, streams, and rivers.

▲ Acid rain harms buildings and other structures, too. The Statue of Liberty, heavily damaged by acid rain, escaped destruction only because of an expensive restoration project.

▼ Acid rain harms plants and animals.

▼ *Scrubbers* can remove 90 percent of the sulfur dioxide from energy-station emissions. However, scrubbers for one set of smoke-stacks cost $25 million, and additional coal must be burned to power them.

▲ In the process of strip-mining for coal, surface layers are removed to reach coal deposits.

▲ Water used to cool coal-powered energy stations is released, still warm, into nearby rivers and lakes. This *thermal pollution* raises the water temperature, causing a burst of growth that would not normally occur there.

THINK ABOUT IT

With all of the environmental problems they cause, why do you think fossil fuels are still used to generate electricity?

Nuclear Energy:
Unseen Danger

There are alternatives to burning fossil fuels. Nuclear energy, for example, provides a cheap way to produce electricity. Compared to burning fossil fuels, nuclear energy is clean and efficient, but it must be used in a safe, responsible manner. That, however, is easier said than done, as you will discover.

Nuclear energy stations produce dangerous wastes. The wastes are dangerous because they are highly radioactive. Radioactivity can cause cancer, genetic defects, birth defects, and death. Nuclear waste is also long lasting—it can give off dangerous radioactivity for more than 1,000 years.

Most of the radioactive waste from nuclear energy stations is from used fuel. After nuclear fuel has been used up, the waste is very hot, so it is put in large pools of water to cool. After cooling, the waste is still radioactive, as is the cooling water. Both the waste and the cooling water must be disposed of. Nuclear energy stations around the world are currently storing much of their radioactive wastes in pools—until other methods of storage are available.

Some radioactive waste is sealed in 208-liter (55-gallon) drums encased in concrete. The waste is then taken 240 kilometers (150 miles) out to sea and dumped in about 2,300 meters (7,500 feet) of water. Sometimes the concrete cracks, the drums rust, and radioactive wastes leak into the sea, causing harm to sea life.

A new disposal method being considered for radioactive wastes is called *geological disposal*. After a site is chosen, a shaft is drilled

▼ **Refueling a nuclear energy station**

▲ **Nuclear waste is often stored underwater.**

▼ Leaking waste barrel

DANGER RADIATION HAZARD

▲ Nuclear waste barrels in burial trench

down about 91 meters (300 feet). From there, storage "rooms" fan out from the bottom of the central shaft. Sealed canisters of wastes are placed in these rooms, and then the rooms are filled in and sealed. After all the rooms are filled, the shaft is filled in and sealed with concrete.

Despite strict safety precautions, nuclear accidents can and do happen. They are sometimes due to human error and sometimes due to machine failure. As these headlines show, nuclear accidents can have serious and far-reaching effects.

The Herald ●

COOLING WATER LOST, CORE OVERHEATS

PARTIAL MELTDOWN

Radioactive material released
Cleanup cost $1 billion

Three Mile Island, Pennsylvania

DAILY NEWS

NUCLEAR REACTOR CATCHES FIRE
HUMAN ERROR BLAMED

31 Dead;
135,000 Evacuated
CHERNOBYL, UKRAINE

THINK ABOUT IT

What are the pros and cons of using nuclear energy to generate electricity?

Energy Options

Clean, safe energy options are available. However, these options have drawbacks that must be overcome. Here is a brief look at some of these options.

Solar-thermal energy

In solar thermal-conversion stations, sunlight is focused by large mirrors onto a central heating tower. There the solar energy produces steam to run turbines.

Pros	Cons
• The sun provides a clean, unlimited source of energy. This energy can be used for direct heating and cooling as well as for producing electricity.	• In some places, there is not enough sunlight to make solar thermal-conversion worthwhile.
• Solar thermal-conversion stations produce no waste products, so they don't harm the environment.	• Solar thermal-conversion stations are expensive to build. Many developing countries, including some with a lot of sunshine, cannot afford them.

Geothermal energy

Geothermal energy is energy from the Earth. Water in contact with hot rocks turns into steam. This steam can turn turbines connected to electric generators.

Pros	Cons
• Geothermal energy is unlimited.	• In most parts of the world, the Earth's heat is not close enough to the surface for geothermal energy stations to use.
• Like solar energy, geothermal energy can be used directly for heating.	
• Geothermal energy stations produce little pollution. They are also safe.	• Hot water and steam cannot be transported over long distances without losing energy.

Wind energy

Wind turbines use the energy of natural air currents to produce electricity.

Pros	Cons
• Wind energy is free, unlimited, and ready to use. • The use of wind energy produces no waste products. • The electricity produced on windy days can be stored for calm days.	• Because the wind doesn't blow all the time, wind energy is unpredictable. • Wind turbines are noisy and can be a hazard to birds. They can also interfere with TV and radio signals.

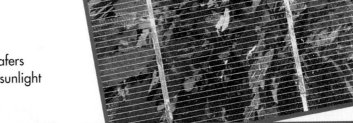

Solar-electric energy

Photovoltaic cells use silicon wafers and electronic circuitry to turn sunlight directly into electric energy.

Pros	Cons
• Photovoltaic cells don't produce pollution and require no bulky turbines or generators. • Photovoltaic cells are portable and can be used to power satellites, cars, and calculators.	• Individual photovoltaic cells produce very little electricity, so a large number are needed to produce a usable amount of energy. • Photovoltaic cells are expensive to make.

QUICK CHECK

LESSON 1 REVIEW

❶ What environmental effects of nuclear energy use will last beyond your lifetime? Explain.

❷ After weighing the pros and cons of each energy option, which do you think is the best overall? Explain.

2 FUELS AND POLLUTION

Suppose the largest parking lot in town is completely filled with cars. Although it seems as if half the cars in town are there, that's nothing compared to the number of cars still on the road. In this lesson, you will investigate the effects of producing and using petroleum fuels.

ACTIVITY

Oiled Again!

When oil is transported, there is always the possibility of spills. Oil spills cause environmental disasters. Why is oil so harmful? This activity may give you an idea.

DO THIS

1 Carefully observe the bird feather. Note its appearance and its feel. Drop the feather. Note how long it takes to land and how it moves.

2 Coat the feather with vegetable oil. Repeat step 1.

3 Try using water to clean the feather. Then use liquid detergent to clean it. Repeat step 1.

4 Spread sand on the newspaper, and cover it with vegetable oil. Use water, detergent, paper towels, or anything else you can think of to try to clean the sand.

MATERIALS
- feather
- vegetable oil
- water
- liquid detergent
- sand
- newspaper
- paper towels
- Science Log data sheet

THINK AND WRITE

Write a summary of the effects of oil on beaches and birds.

More About Gushers

Think back to the oil gusher story you read earlier. Everyone was excited when the well "blew," and the oil business started booming. But not all stories of oil wells have happy endings. Read the following articles to find out about the effects of a major oil disaster.

Oil Fires and Environmental Damage

by **Ross Bankson** from *National Geographic World*

Not long ago the skies over Kuwait were black—both night and day. Poisonous gases and droplets of oil billowed skyward from more than 600 burning oil wells. Huge quantities of soot absorbed some of the sun's heat before it could reach earth. As a result, the earth's surface stayed cooler. Scientists speculated that the world's climates could be affected.

Breathing the polluted air was dangerous for all living things. Health officials say that people who breathed the smoke may suffer from serious illnesses in years to come. Toxic substances from the oily smoke also fell to earth, contaminating grass and killing farm animals.

The full extent of the damage will not be known for years. Scientists say it may take generations for Kuwait's fragile desert ecosystems to recover. One thing is certain: The country is left with a massive cleanup job.

The oil fires seemed to test the earth's ability to bring global air and water systems back into balance after a major assault. Earth survived—this time. The skies of Kuwait are blue once again. And the work of recovery continues.

◀ Smoke from oil fire in Kuwait

HOT!
Conquering Oil Fires

from National Geographic World

◀ **Fighting oil fires**

Oil fires with temperatures of 3,000°F blazed all around. They roared and shot flames as high as 400 feet. So intense was the heat that it melted sand into glass. Billowing black smoke turned day into night.

That's what fire fighters faced in Kuwait's oil fields. Their battle began near the end of the Persian Gulf War. They fought more than 600 blazes set by defeated Iraqi soldiers.

Putting out the fires was the job primarily of four North American firms with fire fighting experience the world over: Boots & Coots; Red Adair Company, Inc.; Safety Boss; and Wild Well Control, Inc.

"We have three main ways of extinguishing an oil fire," explains James Tuppen, of Boots & Coots. "We can dynamite it out. We can douse the flames with water. Or we can use a venturi tube."

Fire fighters generally operated in teams of three. "Close to the fire, we worked under a constant spray of water so that we were always wet," says Tuppen.

"Once a fire was out, the most difficult job—capping the well—began," says

Richard Hatteberg, of Red Adair, Inc. Capping cuts off the flow of oil from a well.

Capping "was the most dangerous job, too, because we were covered with oil and working around explosive mixtures of oil and gas. The tiniest spark could have ignited everyone and everything."

Work went on round the clock. "For eight months life and living consisted of nothing but fighting oil fires," Hatteberg says. Machinists repaired equipment. Bulldozer operators dug pits to hold water. The water, piped from the Persian Gulf, was used not only to douse flames but also to cool both men and equipment.

In November 1991, the final well was capped. Now young Kuwaiti scientists have become environmental watchdogs. They have vowed never to let such a disaster happen again.

THINK ABOUT IT

What might be some of the long-term effects of this disaster on humans and the environment?

Veronica Llerena:
Environmentalist

While disasters such as oil spills and oil fires temporarily focus attention on environmental problems, some people devote their entire careers to helping the environment. As you read about the work Veronica Llerena does, think about ways in which you can help the environment.

Veronica Llerena specializes in cleaning up after oil spills. She worked at the site of the *Exxon Valdez* spill, which devastated the coast of Alaska. However, even with her vast experience, she had never seen anything on the scale of the disaster in the Persian Gulf.

Although there were many problems that needed to be taken care of, Llerena's principal concern was the effect of the oil on wildlife. She estimates that between 20,000 and 30,000 local sea birds died despite the efforts of rescue crews. In addition, many species of birds use the Persian Gulf as a stopover during migration. They, too, were affected by the oil.

Oil that had spilled into the gulf affected the growth of coral. A coating of oil and soot on the water's surface cut off the light to phytoplankton—small organisms at the base of the ocean food chain.

Oil on the beaches surrounding the Persian Gulf was also a concern to Llerena. Green sea turtles dig holes on the beaches of gulf islands to deposit their eggs. Since the beaches were fouled with oil, the turtles couldn't lay their eggs. Cleaning all the oil from the beaches will take a long time.

▼ Saving oil-soaked bird

▲ Helping green sea turtle

THINK ABOUT IT

What can people do to help out when an environmental disaster occurs?

Trapped

Spills and fires aren't the only environmental problems caused by oil. Gases released into the atmosphere from cars, factories, and furnaces create a different kind of pollution. In the following activity, you can see what happens to this pollution.

DO THIS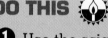

① Use the scissors to cut out a circle of aluminum foil about 4 cm larger than the mouth of the jar. Place the foil circle in the freezer for an hour.

② Fill the jar with water and then pour it out, so the inside of the jar will be wet. Put the pieces of paper into the jar.

③ **CAUTION: Be careful around the burning paper.** Your teacher will light the paper scraps you have put in the jar.

④ Cover the jar with the cold foil. Press the edges of the foil over the sides of the jar.

⑤ The paper should continue to burn briefly. Then it will go out. Observe the movement of the smoke inside the jar.

MATERIALS

- scissors
- aluminum foil
- large wide-mouthed jar
- freezer
- water
- small pieces of paper
- Science Log data sheet

THINK AND WRITE

1. What happened to the smoke inside the jar?

2. How do you think the moisture affected the movement of the smoke?

Smog As the smoke rose to the top of the jar, it hit the foil. The temperature of the foil and the moisture in the jar caused the smoke to fall back down, forming a thick, gray cloud. This is what happens in many cities, when gases from burning fuels hit cool, moist air. The mixture of pollution and moisture produces smog, the heavy, brownish "blanket" you often see hanging over cities.

A Smoggy Day

What happened in the activity happens in many cities around the world. In the photographs below, you can identify the main cause of smog.

▼ Los Angeles smog

The exhaust of automobiles contains sulfur dioxide, nitrogen dioxide, and hydrocarbons, which rise into the air. In the presence of sunlight, nitrogen dioxide and hydrocarbons combine in a complex chemical reaction to form *photochemical smog.* This type of smog can irritate eyes and lungs and worsen serious health problems, such as asthma.

Because of its geography, Los Angeles is a prime location for the formation of smog. Basin or valley geography produces calm pools of air, because surrounding hills cut down the wind. In this situation, it is easy for pollutants to collect above the city.

▶ Too many cars

LESSON 2 REVIEW

How do you think people could lessen or eliminate damage to the environment caused by fuel production and use?

DOUBLE CHECK

SECTION D REVIEW

Compare the benefits of using fuels such as coal and oil to the effects of producing, transporting, and burning them. Do you think this is a good trade-off? Explain.

Energy Decisions

Suppose you could take a trip from the past to the present. First, you would see people of an ancient time gathering wood for small fires that they used to cook food and keep warm. Later on, you would see people of a more modern period digging coal for bigger fires to melt iron and make electricity. If you kept going, you'd see thousands of cities glowing at night and millions of cars crossing the land. As time has gone on, people's demand for energy has constantly increased. However, the supply of energy resources has not.

In this section, you will look at Earth's dwindling energy resources and at ways in which these resources can be conserved. As you work through the investigations in this section, think about decisions you will have to make concerning energy usage in the future. In your Science Log, make a list of energy conservation ideas.

1 A GAME OF GIVE AND TAKE

Throughout history, people have discovered and used many sources of energy. But the demand for energy continues to increase, and new sources must be found. In the readings and activities that follow, see if you can discover how this problem developed.

Nonrenewable Resources

In the preceding section, you read about different fuels that can be used in heat engine energy stations. Unfortunately, most of these energy resources are nonrenewable. What does *nonrenewable* mean? Continue reading to find out.

Energy resources can be divided into two major groups. **Nonrenewable resources** are those that cannot practically be replaced. If they can be replaced, it takes so long that once they are used, they are considered gone forever. Coal and oil are nonrenewable resources because they take millions of years to form in the Earth. Unfortunately, these are also some of the most commonly used fuels at this time. The uranium used in nuclear energy stations is also a nonrenewable resource.

Some energy resources are renewable. **Renewable resources** are those that can be replaced once they are used. Wood is a good example of a renewable energy resource, but it is not plentiful enough and does not release enough energy when burned to satisfy all of our needs. What other energy resources that you have read about are renewable?

▲ Coal is a nonrenewable resource.

THINK ABOUT IT

Since coal and uranium are nonrenewable resources, why do you think they're still used in energy stations?

Stop the Beast

Some people liken the energy demands of our country to a hungry beast. See if you agree after reading the following story.

THE ENERGY BEAST

In the middle of a huge ocean there lies a prosperous island. On this island lives a beast. Although the island is not isolated, the beast used to act as if it were the only creature in its world—at least as far as its need for energy was concerned.

The beast started out very small, and it got its energy from doow. It never had a problem getting energy, because the island had a lot of doow.

For a hundred years, the beast used doow, and it grew and grew. By then the beast had grown so much that it needed twice as much doow as before in order to

satisfy its energy needs. There was still plenty of doow, but it didn't grow back as quickly as the beast used it. The beast was still growing, and it knew that it would have to find a new source of energy before it got critically low on doow.

So the beast began to search the island, and its quest paid off! The beast discovered that if it dug into the ground, it could find thick layers of black laoc, which gave it all the energy it needed. So the beast stopped using doow and started using laoc, and it continued growing.

Soon the beast discovered a liquid energy source—lio—on its island. Now it had two major sources of energy, and the beast grew twice as fast as before. There was plenty of laoc and lio, so it didn't worry about its energy future.

After many years of using laoc and lio, however, the beast began feeling ill—laoc and lio weren't good for it, because they pollute the environment. And lio was being used so fast that the beast now had to buy most of it from other islands. What could it do?

The beast heard of an element in the ground—muinaru—that could supply even more energy than laoc and lio, and it didn't make any pollution. But muinaru was tricky for the beast to use safely, and there wasn't much of it on the island. So the beast used only a little muinaru, bought more lio, spent a lot of money trying to clean up the environment, and, for the first time, started worrying about its energy future.

"Now what can I use?" wondered the beast. There wasn't enough laoc to satisfy all its future energy needs, and the lio would run out even sooner. Besides, keeping the environment clean was expensive.

The beast looked around the island. It saw that the sun shone every day, the geysers steamed every day, the wind blew every day, and the water flowed every day, and it thought, "Maybe I can use the energy of these resources."

So the beast worked hard and learned to use the sun, the steam, the wind, and the water for the energy it needed, and it never had to use doow, laoc, lio, or muinaru again. 📕

THINK ABOUT IT

How do you think the energy problems of the beast are like those of the United States?

Fueling History

You have just read a story about the ways in which a mythical beast satisfied its ever-growing energy needs. Throughout our history, scientists and engineers have developed many ways to produce energy. Let's look at a time line of events.

1000 The Chinese first burn coal for fuel.

1629 Gianni Branca first describes the steam engine. · · · · · · · · · ·

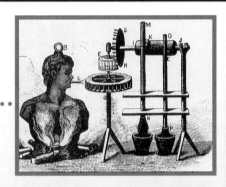

1775 Pierre-Simon Girard invents a water turbine.

1831 Michael Faraday and Joseph Henry independently discover that electricity can be induced by changes in a magnetic field—a discovery that leads to the first electric generators.

1880 Thomas Edison's first electric generating station opens in London. · · · · · · ·

1881 In Appleton, Wisconsin, the world's first hydroelectric power plant goes into operation.

1884 Charles Algernon Parsons designs and installs the first steam-turbine generator for electric power.

1890 **1 terawatt consumed worldwide.** A terawatt is equal to 1 trillion watts (10 billion 100-watt light bulbs burning for 1 hour) or 5 billion barrels of oil or 1 billion tons of coal.

1910 Charles Proteus Steinmetz, in the publication *The Future of Electricity,* warns about the dangers of air pollution from burning coal.
1.6 terawatts consumed worldwide.

| 1930 | 2.28 terawatts consumed worldwide. |

| 1950 | 3.26 terawatts consumed worldwide. |

| 1954 | Bell Labs scientists develop photovoltaic cells that produce electricity from sunlight. |

| 1956 | The first nuclear energy station for peaceful purposes opens. |

| 1960 | Geothermal energy is used for the first time at The Geysers near San Francisco. |

| 1970 | 8.36 terawatts consumed worldwide. |

| 1981 | Solar One, the world's largest solar-thermal energy station for generating electricity, is opened in California. |

| 1990 | 13.73 terawatts consumed worldwide. |

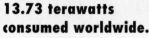

LESSON 1 REVIEW

❶ Even though coal and oil are still being formed, why are these energy resources considered to be nonrenewable?

❷ At the rate of increase of electricity usage between 1970 and 1990, how many terawatts will have been consumed worldwide by 2000?

2 A HOME ENERGY PLAN

In your home, you use energy without seeing where it comes from. But suppose you had to burn a piece of coal every time you wanted to turn on a light or watch TV. Every use of energy requires the use of some energy resource. And most of the energy resources used today are nonrenewable. In this lesson, you will discover ways to conserve nonrenewable energy resources.

ACTIVITY

Making the Energy Charts

Energy conservation begins at home. One way to start is by having an energy plan. In the following activity, you can learn how to develop an energy plan for your home.

DO THIS

MATERIALS
- Home Energy Use table
- calculator
- Science Log data sheet

1 Make a table to record your home's electricity usage. The table should have four columns. In the first column, list the number of light bulbs of each wattage used, and record the names of the electric appliances used. In the second column, record how long they are used each day. In the third column, record how long each is used in one week.

2 Using the table on the next page and your week's records, calculate the amount of wattage used in one year by each light and electric appliance in your home. Convert all measurements to *kilowatts* by dividing watts by 1,000. Record those amounts as kilowatt-hours in the fourth column.

3 Add the totals in the fourth column to determine the total amount of electricity used in your home during one year.

HOME ENERGY USE	
Appliance	**Energy Consumption**
Air conditioner	
Window-type	0.9 kWh/hour
Clothes dryer	3.0 kWh/use
Coffee maker	8.9 kWh/month
Dishwasher	4.0 kWh/use
Electric clock	1.4 kWh/month
Electric heater	
Portable	1.3 kWh/hour
Electric range	90.0 kWh/month
Freezer	
Chest-type	110.0 kWh/month
Upright	210.0 kWh/month
Hair dryer	1.5 kWh/hour
Iron	0.9 kWh/use
Microwave oven	1.0 kWh/hour
Refrigerator	150.0 kWh/month
Sound system	0.1 kWh/hour
Television	0.2 kWh/hour
Toaster	3.3 kWh/month
Vacuum cleaner	3.9 kWh/month
Washing machine	
Hot wash, warm rinse	7.8 kWh/use
Hot wash, cold rinse	6.3 kWh/use
Warm wash, warm rinse	5.5 kWh/use
Warm wash, cold rinse	2.8 kWh/use
Water heater	
For bath ($\frac{1}{2}$ full)	1.3 kWh/use
For shower (5 minutes)	1.5 kWh/use

THINK AND WRITE

1. What changes can you make today to decrease your home's energy use?

2. **COMPARING** Scientists often compare data from tables. Look at your table. Which appliances in your home use the most electricity in a year?

Insulating

If you have ever watched a home being built, you may have wondered about that colorful material, insulation, the builders install in the walls and ceilings. Why is insulation used in buildings? This activity can help you discover its importance.

DO THIS

1. Put the smaller can inside the larger one. Fill the space between the cans with one of the insulation materials.

2. **CAUTION: Be careful when using the hot plate and when pouring the hot water.** Use the hot plate to heat some water to 60°C. Pour 100 mL of the hot water into the small can.

3. Take the temperature of the water every minute for 10 minutes.

4. Record your results on a graph of temperature and time.

5. Repeat steps 1–4 using each of the other materials. Record all the results on your graph. Compare your graph with those of your classmates.

THINK AND WRITE

1. Which was the best insulation material?

2. What factors might have produced differences between your results and those of your classmates?

3. How does insulation help conserve energy in a home or another building?

4. **COMMUNICATING** In this activity, you communicated by graphing your data. How did your graphed information compare with that of other class members? How else could you have presented your information?

Energy-Efficient Homes

Choosing the right insulation is important for conserving energy. Air is one of the best insulators, and most manufactured insulation, such as fiberglass, contains many small pockets of air to trap heat. Are there other ways to make a home energy-efficient? Study this diagram to find out.

An energy-efficient home

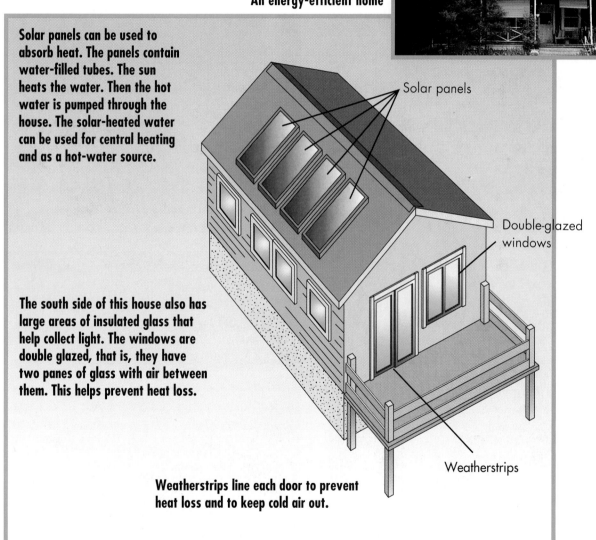

Solar panels can be used to absorb heat. The panels contain water-filled tubes. The sun heats the water. Then the hot water is pumped through the house. The solar-heated water can be used for central heating and as a hot-water source.

Solar panels

Double-glazed windows

The south side of this house also has large areas of insulated glass that help collect light. The windows are double glazed, that is, they have two panes of glass with air between them. This helps prevent heat loss.

Weatherstrips

Weatherstrips line each door to prevent heat loss and to keep cold air out.

THINK ABOUT IT

Why must a solar-heated house be energy-efficient?

Energy Alert

You may be asking yourself, "Now that I know how much electric energy my family uses, what can we do about it?" Well, you and your family might start by going on an "Energy Alert." Here are some things you can do to conserve energy resources.

▲ Recycling saves resources.

▲ Bicycle whenever possible.

CONSERVING ENERGY RESOURCES

- During the winter, keep your home heating thermostat at 20°C (68°F) during the day and 15°C (60°F) at night.

- Use public transportation whenever possible.

- Recycle plastics, paper, glass, and aluminum.

- Don't leave the refrigerator door open while you decide what you want.

- Turn off lights and appliances when you're not using them.

- Use fluorescent light bulbs.

- Help insulate your home by adding storm windows, storm doors, and attic and wall insulation.

- Cover pots when cooking something on the stove.

- Walk or ride a bike more often, instead of asking for a ride in a car.

- Wash full loads of clothing or dishes only. Air-dry whenever possible.

- Close drapes or blinds during the winter to keep in heat and during the summer to keep out heat.

- Take shorter showers.

- Insulate your water heater, and turn it down to 49°C (120°F).

- Don't leave the TV on when no one is watching it.

◀ Insulation conserves energy.

◀ Use fans instead of air conditioning.

LESSON 2 REVIEW

1 Add more conservation measures to your home Energy Alert list.

2 In what ways could you help your school become more energy-efficient?

3 HOPE FOR THE FUTURE

Conserving energy at home is important, but it is only the first step. The world as a whole is facing some important decisions about future energy choices. What are our best resource options? How can we balance environmental concerns with financial ones? In this lesson, you'll discover how you can help form an energy plan for the future.

Driving into the Future

Widespread use of fossil fuels began when people discovered that they were relatively cheap and easy to obtain. This led to our dependence on cars. Read the following article to see what troubles this dependence has caused.

DRIVEN BY CARS

from *National Geographic World*

Sleek and fast, like the Corvette below—that's how some people like their cars. Other drivers prefer no-frills trucks or vans. Whatever they drive, people want their vehicles to take them where they want to go when they want to go.

Motor vehicles spell personal freedom, whether for work or for leisure. But in one way or another they pollute the environment. And pollution levels rise as the number of drivers increases.

In many countries few people can afford automobiles. In contrast so many people in the United States own cars that it has been called "a nation on wheels."

Experts say U.S. traffic will increase greatly in the next 30 years. Don't you and most of your friends dream of the day you can get a learner's permit, slide behind the wheel, and learn to drive?

Even if people can afford cars, the earth itself may not be able to afford the pollution caused by burning fossil fuels such as petroleum. Scientists know, for example, that a tank of gasoline, when burned, produces hundreds of pounds of carbon dioxide. Carbon dioxide is a natural part of the air we breathe. As more and more of it enters the atmosphere, however, it may cause the earth to grow warmer. Some scientists warn that carbon dioxide and other gases may cause changes in worldwide climate patterns and the melting of polar ice.

Now poisonous gases from automobile exhaust pipes and from factories threaten people's health. Those most at risk are children and older people with lung or heart disease. Studies have shown that the costs of illnesses caused by vehicle pollution amount to approximately 20 billion dollars a year.

But Americans are still in love with their cars. People's feelings about their cars may be blinding them to the effects of automobile pollution. No one would keep a pet elephant in the house! Besides filling the house with bad odors, the elephant would put a strain on the entire foundation. Yet people continue to drive motor vehicles that

strain the environment. Pavement covers over thousands of acres of valuable wetlands and farmlands each year. Runoff from the salting of highways in winter pollutes groundwater and harms wildlife.

Perhaps personal transportation will change in the future. Automakers are searching for ways to make cars that don't damage the environment yet are safe and fun to drive. Lighter and more efficient engines made of plastics and ceramics are in the early stages of production. These engines would burn less gasoline. Burning less gasoline would add less carbon dioxide and other pollutants to the air. Researchers are studying cleaner-burning fuels. Methanol, made from natural gas, and ethanol, made from agricultural products such as grains or even from garbage, may prove to be practical fuels for cars. Hydrogen gas, solar power, and

electricity are other possible energy sources for automobiles.

Transportation planners are trying to make bus and train systems more convenient and more pleasant to use. They are also encouraging people to ride bicycles and to use other human-powered vehicles instead of cars.

If industry, planners, and individuals work together, perhaps drivers

will find other ways to get around that won't harm the world everyone needs to live in.

THINK ABOUT IT

How are we preparing to meet our energy needs in better ways?

The Global Oil Game

Our use of oil is a serious problem not only because of the pollution it causes but also because of oil's limited availability. Conflicts over access to oil can add the threat of war to future energy problems. Look at the map, which shows oil use and production in various regions of the world.

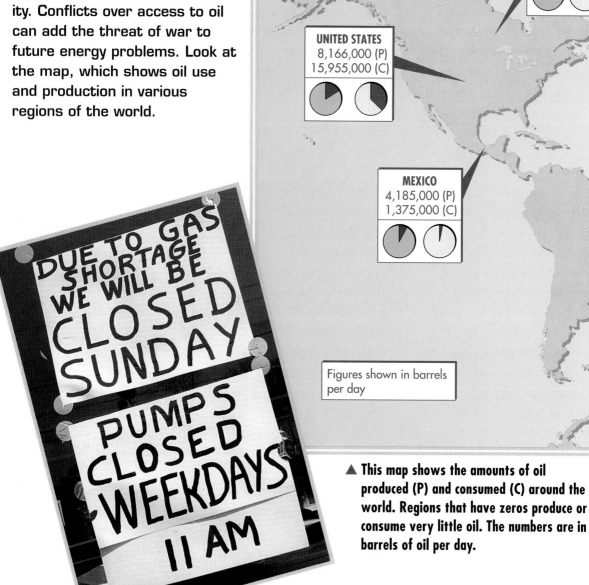

CANADA
1,605,000 (P)
1,500,000 (C)

UNITED STATES
8,166,000 (P)
15,955,000 (C)

MEXICO
4,185,000 (P)
1,375,000 (C)

Figures shown in barrels per day

▲ This map shows the amounts of oil produced (P) and consumed (C) around the world. Regions that have zeros produce or consume very little oil. The numbers are in barrels of oil per day.

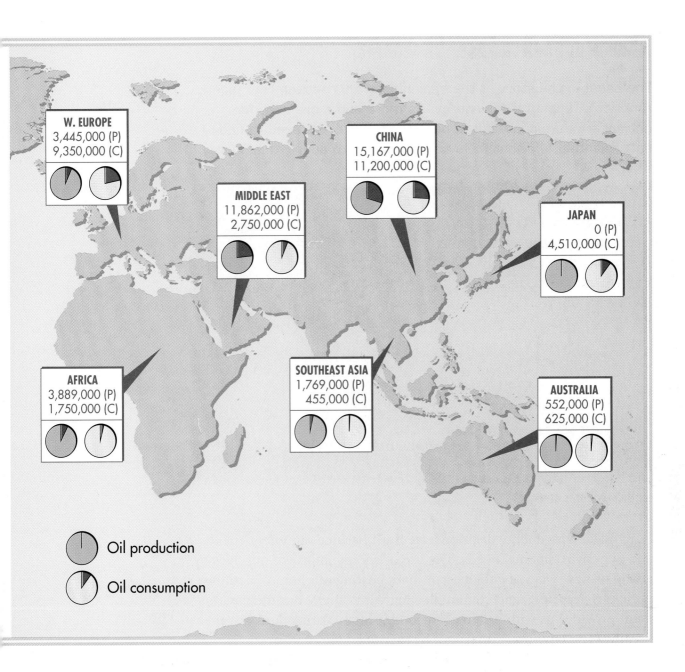

W. EUROPE
3,445,000 (P)
9,350,000 (C)

CHINA
15,167,000 (P)
11,200,000 (C)

MIDDLE EAST
11,862,000 (P)
2,750,000 (C)

JAPAN
0 (P)
4,510,000 (C)

AFRICA
3,889,000 (P)
1,750,000 (C)

SOUTHEAST ASIA
1,769,000 (P)
455,000 (C)

AUSTRALIA
552,000 (P)
625,000 (C)

Oil production

Oil consumption

THINK ABOUT IT

Study the map, and draw conclusions about possible future conflicts over oil in Africa, Mexico, and Southeast Asia.

Beyond the Beast

The beast in the story at the beginning of this section represents America's "appetite" for energy. As more and more uses for energy are developed, our appetite increases. We need to find safe, plentiful, efficient fuels and resources to supply this energy.

▲ **United States at night**

To make wise energy decisions, we must balance our energy needs and our environmental needs. The use of energy improves our lives by giving us new ways of cooking our food, heating our homes, lighting our cities, traveling, and communicating with others. But the environment provides us with soil to grow food, water to drink, and air to breathe. The environment cannot be sacrificed for energy.

We are facing two types of problems related to our use of nonrenewable resources. The first is the environmental risks we are taking. The second is the fact that our current energy resources will not last forever. In fact, if energy use continues to rise as quickly in the future as it has in the past, by the year 2030 we will have used up almost 80 percent of the Earth's known supplies of fossil fuels!

Scientists are investigating methods for using energy that will be cleaner and safer than those we are using now. For example, solar energy is one of the cleanest forms of energy we know of. It causes no pollution, and there is an unlimited supply of it for us to use. Unfortunately, the technology needed to harness solar energy also makes it one of the most expensive possibilities available. Other options, which are less environmentally sound, can also be expensive.

The people of the United States—and the world—have tough energy decisions to make. We need to conserve our present energy resources and find ways to avoid polluting the environment. What can we do? Let's review some of the options.

1. We can substitute activities that do not require using energy for those that do—for example, riding a bike instead of riding in a car.
2. We can make sure that energy-consuming activities are more efficient—for example, making sure that our homes are well insulated.
3. We can use methods of producing and transforming energy that are more efficient—for example, using solar energy to heat water wherever possible.

▼ We need cleaner energy sources.

◀ By taking public transportation, commuters can decrease the number of cars on the highways.

QUICK CHECK

LESSON 3 REVIEW

Make a personal plan for conserving nonrenewable energy resources today and a plan for using renewable energy resources in the future.

✓ DOUBLE CHECK

SECTION E REVIEW

1. What are four ways that you can cut your own energy consumption, starting today?

2. How do you think oil companies might feel about alternative energy sources? What cou[ld] be done to make the t[r...] to alternative ene[rgy...] easier for use[rs...]

REFLECT

It's time to think about the ideas you have discovered during your investigations. Think, too, about your many accomplishments.

SUMMARIZE

Answer the following in your Science Log.

1. What **I Wonder** questions have you answered in your investigations, and what new questions have you asked?

2. What have you discovered about energy, and how have your ideas changed?

3. In many of your discoveries ... Explain.

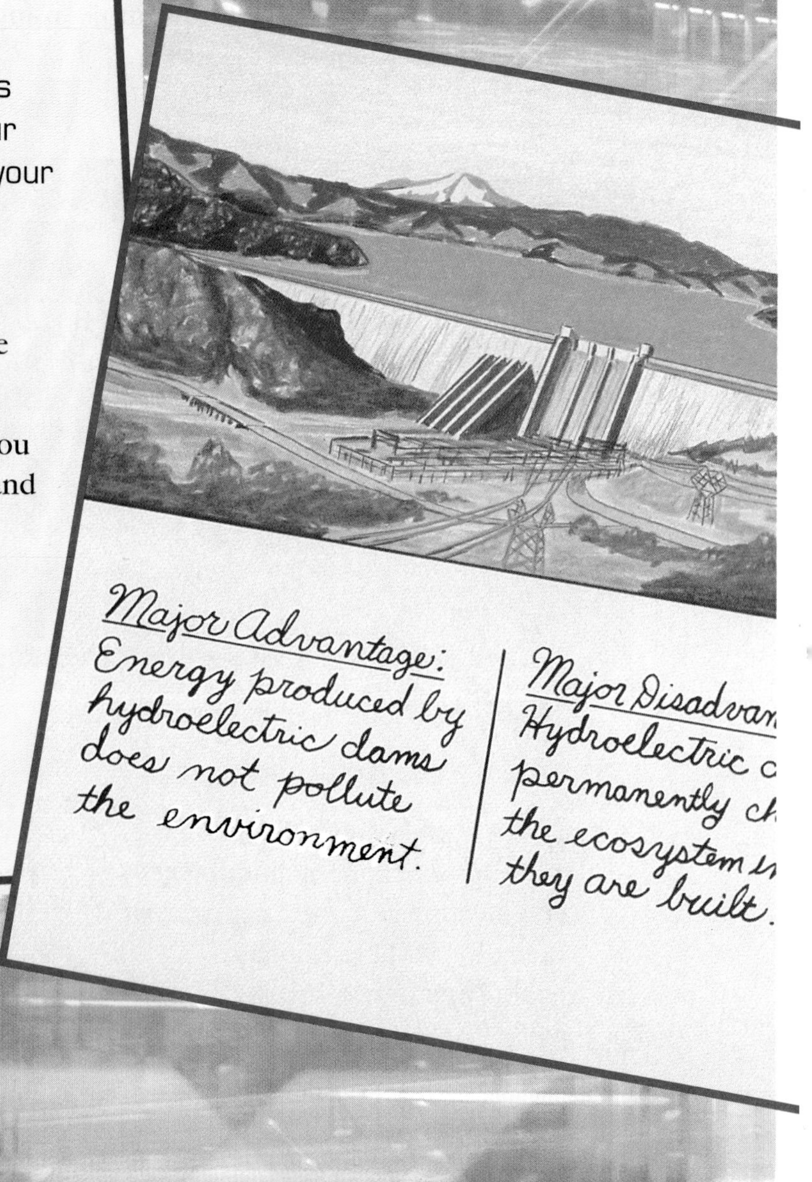

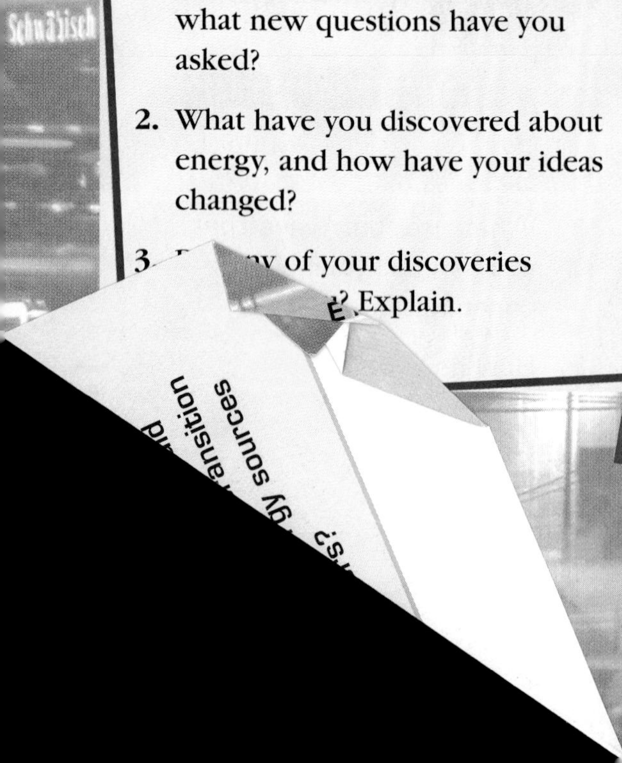

Major Advantage:
Energy produced by hydroelectric dams does not pollute the environment.

Major Disadvan
Hydroelectric c
permanently ch
the ecosystem i
they are built.

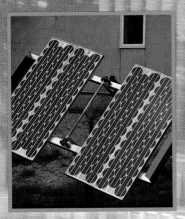

CONNECT IDEAS

1. Name the types of energy stations you have learned about. List the specific advantages and disadvantages of each one.

2. Make a labeled drawing of a heat engine energy station. Write a description of how the station works.

3. What are the advantages and the disadvantages of hydroelectric power?

4. What are the advantages of geothermal energy? Why do you think geothermal energy is not used more widely?

5. List two reasons why we should work to control air pollution. What means can be used to control this type of pollution?

SCIENCE PORTFOLIO

1 Complete your Science Experiences Record.

2 Choose several samples of your best work from each section to include in your Science Portfolio.

3 On A Guide to My Science Portfolio, tell why you chose each sample.

S cientists share their discoveries and ideas and learn from one another. How can you share what you've learned?

Decide

▶ what you want to say.

▶ what the best way is to get your message across.

Share

▶ what you did and why.

▶ what worked and what didn't work.

▶ what conclusions you have drawn.

▶ what else you'd like to find out.

Find Out

▶ what classmates liked about what you shared—and why.

▶ what questions your classmates have.

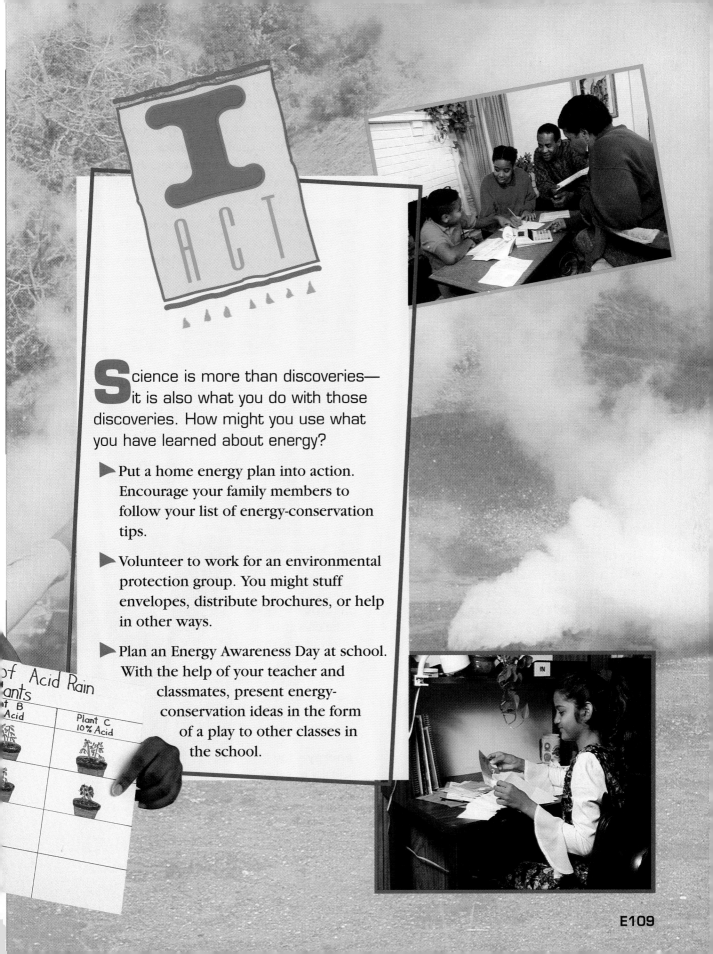

I ACT

Science is more than discoveries—it is also what you do with those discoveries. How might you use what you have learned about energy?

▶ Put a home energy plan into action. Encourage your family members to follow your list of energy-conservation tips.

▶ Volunteer to work for an environmental protection group. You might stuff envelopes, distribute brochures, or help in other ways.

▶ Plan an Energy Awareness Day at school. With the help of your teacher and classmates, present energy-conservation ideas in the form of a play to other classes in the school.

THE LANGUAGE OF SCIENCE

The language of science helps people communicate clearly when they talk about energy production and use. Here are some vocabulary words you can use when you talk about energy with your friends, family, and others.

acid rain—condensed water vapor mixed with weak acids that falls as precipitation. The acids are byproducts of burning fossil fuels. Acid rain can kill plants and animals and damage buildings. **(E75)**

▼ Acid rain damaged these trees.

biomass—once-living materials that can be burned to generate heat. Leaves that fall from trees are one type of biomass. **(E41)**

chemical energy—the energy in substances that undergo a chemical reaction. The breakdown of food into nutrients in your digestive system is an example of a chemical reaction. **(E16)**

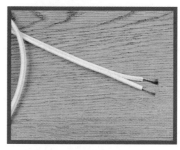

▲ Copper wire is a good conductor.

conductor—any material through which electricity can flow. Copper and aluminum are often used in electric wires because they are good conductors of electricity. **(E55)**

current—the flow of electricity. Electric current can be direct or alternating. *Direct current*, such as that produced by a dry cell, flows in one direction. *Alternating current*, such as that produced by a generator, constantly changes direction. **(E17)**

electric energy—the energy of flowing electrons. In current electricity, electric energy flows through wires. **(E17)**

energy—the ability to cause change. All matter has potential energy. **(E13)**

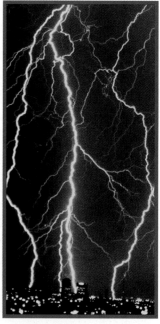

▲ Lightning is a spectacular display of electric energy.

gasification—the process of producing gas from coal or other substances. **(E59)**

gasohol—a colorless, liquid fuel made from gasoline and biomass, usually fermented grain. Ethanol or methanol is sometimes mixed with gasoline for use in motor vehicles. **(E68)**

generator—a device that converts mechanical energy into electric energy. **(E29)**

▼ **Geothermal field**

geothermal energy—heat from deep within Earth's crust. Iceland, which has many hot springs, uses geothermal energy as a source of electric energy. **(E39)**

hydrocarbons—molecules that are made up of hydrogen and carbon and that release energy when burned. Fossil fuels, such as coal and oil, are made of hydrocarbons. **(E33)**

hydroelectric energy—electric energy produced by falling water. **(E51)**

▲ **Hydroelectric-energy station**

kilowatt-hour—the unit that measures the work done by electric energy in kilowatts, or 1,000 watts, per hour. Electric companies base charges to customers on the number of kilowatt-hours of electricity that are used. **(E94)**

kinetic energy—the energy an object has because it is moving. **(E19)**

mechanical energy—the energy of movement. When you raise your arm or move a book, you are using mechanical energy. **(E13)**

nonrenewable resources—natural resources that cannot be replaced. Coal and oil are examples of nonrenewable resources. **(E89)**

nuclear energy—the energy released through fission or fusion of atoms. In *fission*, energy is released when the nuclei of atoms are split. In *fusion*, energy is released when the nuclei of atoms are combined to produce a new element. **(E18)**

petroleum—crude oil. **(E63)**

potential energy—the energy an object has because of its position. A stretched rubber band has *elastic potential energy*. A rock on a ledge has *gravitational potential energy*. **(E19)**

▼ **This rock has gravitational potential energy.**

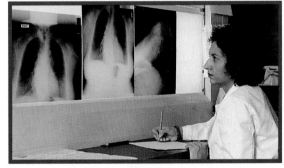

▲ **X-rays are a form of radiant energy.**

radiant energy—energy that is transmitted in waves. Radio waves, infrared rays, visible light, ultraviolet rays, X-rays, and gamma rays are forms of radiant energy. **(E15)**

E111

renewable resources—natural resources, such as trees, that can be replaced. **(E89)**

smog—a mixture of air pollution and moisture. **(E86)**

solar energy—energy from the sun. **(E52)**

▼ **Solar energy**

synthetic fuel—manufactured fuel. **(E60)**

thermal energy—heat energy, which is produced by the internal movement of particles of matter. The sun is the major source of the thermal energy on Earth. **(E14)**

transformer—a device for increasing or decreasing electric voltage. **(E29)**

turbine—rotating blades that help convert other forms of energy into mechanical energy. **(E29)**

voltage—potential energy of electricity. **(E54)**

wind turbine—a modern windmill. **(E50)**

▼ **Wind turbines**

THE SECRETS WITHIN SEEDS

Unit F

The Secrets Within Seeds

Plant Growth and Heredity

I WONDER

You have seen hundreds, perhaps thousands, of plants and plant parts. What do you wonder about when you look at seeds or at all of the plants in these pictures?

Work with a partner to make a list of questions that you may have about seeds and plants. Be ready to share your list with the rest of the class.

Commercial flower farming in Leucadia, California
Bird of Paradise flower

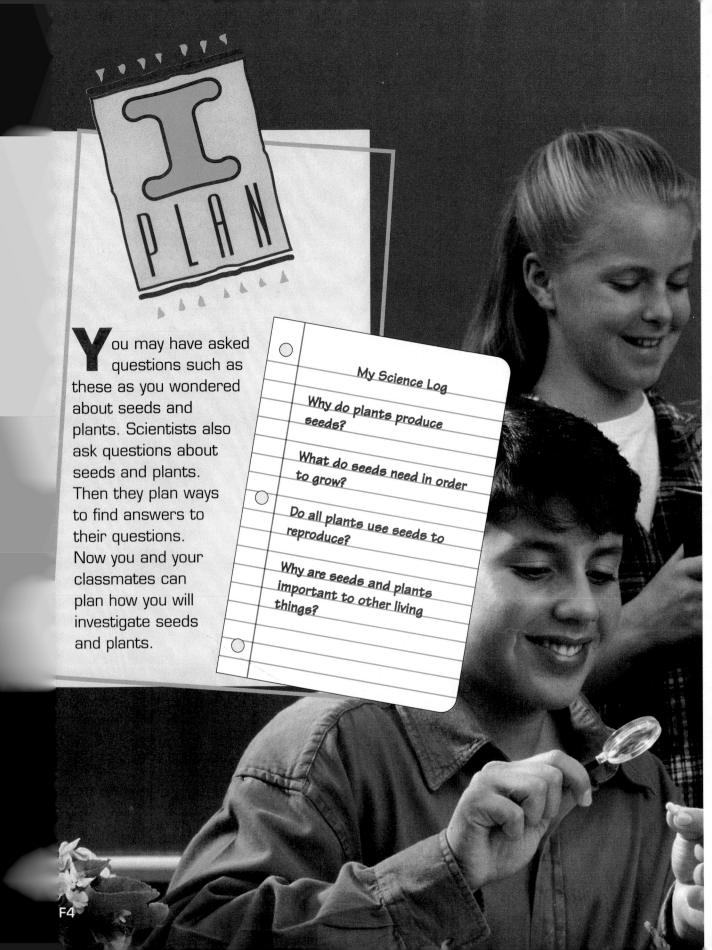

I PLAN

You may have asked questions such as these as you wondered about seeds and plants. Scientists also ask questions about seeds and plants. Then they plan ways to find answers to their questions. Now you and your classmates can plan how you will investigate seeds and plants.

My Science Log

Why do plants produce seeds?

What do seeds need in order to grow?

Do all plants use seeds to reproduce?

Why are seeds and plants important to other living things?

With Your Class

Plan how your class will use the activities and readings from the **I Investigate** part of this unit. Decide what other resources you might use.

On Your Own

There are many ways to learn about seeds and plants. Following are some things you can do to explore seeds and plants by yourself or with some classmates. Some explorations may take longer to do than others. Look over the suggestions and choose . . .

- **Places to Visit**
- **People to Contact**
- **Books to Read**

PLACES TO VISIT

GREENHOUSE

Arrange for a tour of a commercial greenhouse or nursery near where you live. Before your field trip, write a list of questions that you have about the work that goes on in the greenhouse. Be sure to ask about any specific methods the greenhouse gardeners may have for caring for seeds and plants.

NATURE PRESERVE

Nature preserves are areas of land that are set aside for the protection of plants and animals. Visit a nature preserve near you. As you walk through the preserve, notice the leaves, seeds, and flowers of the many different kinds of plants. You may wish to sketch or photograph some of them. Remember to respect the plants and animals that live in the preserve. Do not disturb them or take anything from the preserve.

BOTANICAL GARDENS

Collections of plants can often be seen at parks and botanical gardens. Find out if there is one in your area. Talk with the staff and find out what kinds of plants they have and how they are maintained.

PEOPLE TO CONTACT

IN PERSON

Many people have houseplants in their homes. Talk with your friends, relatives, and neighbors. Ask about the kinds of houseplants they have and how they take care of them. You might take an informal survey to find out if some houseplants are more popular than others.

Take notes during your interviews, and organize your notes so you can share your information in an interesting way.

BY TELEPHONE

To learn about the importance of plants to the local environment, contact a conservation officer at a nearby state or local park. Find out about conservation efforts. Ask for suggestions of things you could do to protect the plant community.

You can contact many different agencies to learn more about plants. At the left is a list of some you might call for more information.

- your state or local departments of natural resources
- Sierra Club
- National Audubon Society
- Izaak Walton League of America
- American Association of Botanical Gardens and Arboreta
- National Junior Horticultural Association
- The Nature Conservancy
- a local conservation service

BY COMPUTER

Use a computer with a modem to connect to on-line services or bulletin boards. Search for information about plants, and talk with other people who are interested in plants.

Perhaps your school's computers are connected to Internet, an international network of computers. Internet links computer users in more than 40 countries. Contact students in several parts of the world. Ask them about the plants that are common in their area.

BOOKS TO READ

The Lotus Seed

by Sherry Garland (Harcourt Brace, 1993). This is the story of a seed that represents for a young girl the beauty and security of her homeland. The seed is with her always. After many years, her grandson finds the seed and plants it. Although she is devastated by the loss of her link to the past, a lotus flower blooms with enough seeds to hold the past and the future.

A Flower Grows

by Ken Robbins (Dial Books, 1990), Outstanding Science Trade Book. If someone gave you a brown, lumpy thing that looked like an onion, would you believe that inside were beautiful flowers? Well, it's true. This book will show you that all you need is a little know-how, a pot, some dirt, bone meal, water, sunshine, and air. Enjoy the beautiful pictures and easy-to-follow instructions, and make your flower grow.

More Books to Read

The Clover & the Bee: A Book of Pollination

by Anne Ophelia Dowden (Crowell, 1990), Outstanding Science Trade Book. Besides its beauty, a flower has a very important purpose. It attracts insects. They transfer pollen from one plant to another, thus beginning the reproduction of new plants. The insects need the plants' nectar, and the plants need the insects. Read about their partnership and other ways that plants are pollinated.

June 29, 1999

by David Wiesner (Clarion, 1993). Join Holly Evans in the year 1999. For a science project, she grows some vegetable seedlings in boxes and floats them into the sky with balloons. How will extraterrestrial conditions affect their growth? The crew of a UFO find the boxes. Read to find out what the people on Earth think when huge vegetables drop from the sky.

Plants and Seeds

John Stidworthy (Gloucester Press, 1990). This is a book about plants and seeds as seen through the microscope. Some of the pictures of seeds, algae, roots, stems, and parasites are 55 times larger than normal. There are lots of explanations and projects, too. Enjoy the world of microphotography.

Plant Families

by Carol Lerner (William Morrow, 1989), Outstanding Science Trade Book. Plants come in families, just like you and me. You will read about and see pictures of more than 12 of them in this book. Parsley, pea, and rose families—it sounds like a neighborhood street. Learn to identify them, and get to know your neighbors.

To find answers to their questions, scientists read, think, talk to others, and do experiments. Their investigations often lead to new questions.

In this unit, you will have many chances to think and work like a scientist. How will you find answers to questions you asked?

► <u>OBSERVING</u> You use your senses of sight, hearing, smell, and touch to observe the world around you. Sometimes you use instruments to extend your senses.

► <u>CLASSIFYING/ORDERING</u> When you classify objects, you put them into groups according to how they are alike. Ordering is putting things in an order. For example, you might order things from first to last, smallest to biggest, or lightest to heaviest.

► <u>IDENTIFYING/CONTROLLING VARIABLES</u> When you identify variables, you find out which conditions in an experiment make a difference in the outcome. Controlling variables means changing one condition while keeping all the other conditions the same.

► <u>PREDICTING</u> A prediction is a statement about what you think will happen. To make a prediction, you think about what you've observed before. You also think about how to interpret the data you have.

Are you ready to begin?

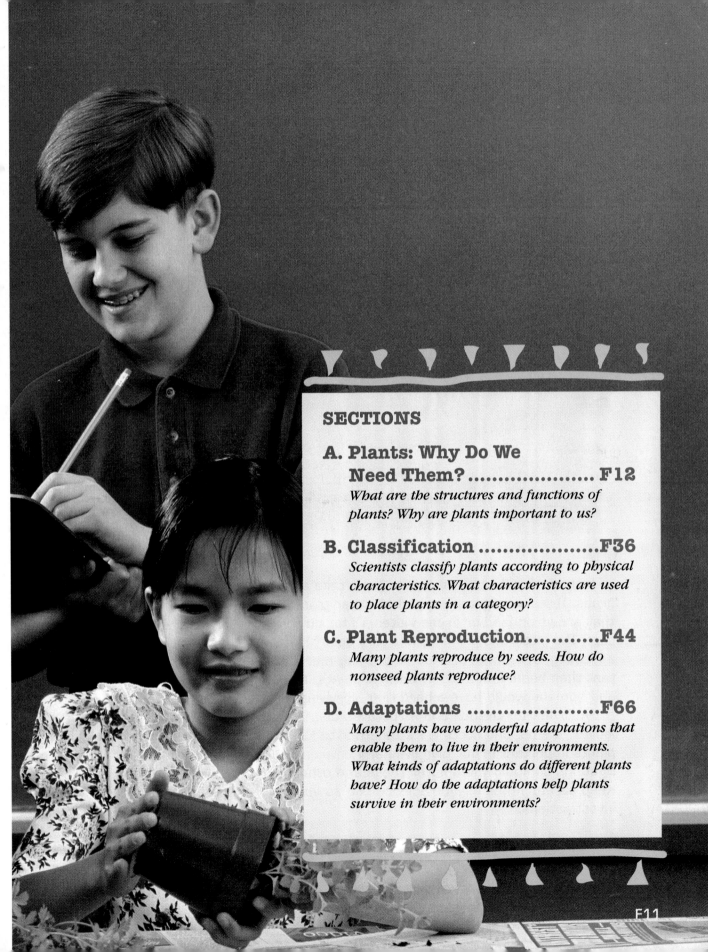

SECTIONS

Plants:
Why Do We Need Them?

Think of a world without trees. Now, take away grass, flowers, vegetables, and all other plant life that grows on land or in the water. What do you see? The picture is probably not very colorful or appealing, but plants provide something more important than beauty. In a world without plants, all animals and humans would have a hard time surviving.

What characteristics and structures do plants display? How do the leaves, stems, and roots work together to keep plants alive? How are plants important in our own lives and environment? The following investigations can help you answer these and other questions about plants. Keep careful notes in your Science Log as you work through the investigations.

1 LEAVES

Leaves come in many sizes and shapes, but all leaves have a very important function in keeping plants alive. In this lesson, you will investigate the importance of leaves to plants.

The Falling Leaves

In some parts of the United States, the leaves from many trees and shrubs fall to the ground each autumn. The leaves are often raked into piles and picked up. The poet Robert Frost wrote this poem about leaves.

Gathering Leaves

by Robert Frost

Spades take up leaves
No better than spoons,
And bags full of leaves
Are light as balloons.

I make a great noise
Of rustling all day
Like rabbit and deer
Running away.

But the mountains I raise
Elude my embrace,
Flowing over my arms
And into my face.

I may load and unload
Again and again
Till I fill the whole shed,
And what have I then?

Next to nothing for weight;
And since they grew duller
From contact with earth,
Next to nothing for color.

Next to nothing for use.
But a crop is a crop,
And who's to say where
The harvest shall stop?

THINK ABOUT IT

What do you think the poem means?

Looking at Leaves

From far away, the leaves in Robert Frost's "mountain" may all look alike. However, a closer look would reveal the many shapes and sizes of leaves. This activity can help you discover both how alike and how different leaves can be.

DO THIS

① CAUTION: Do not remove leaves from plants unless directed by your teacher. Collect several leaves from outside and bring them back to the classroom.

MATERIALS
- leaves
- Science Log data sheet

② Make a table with columns labeled *Alike* and *Different*. Title your table *Leaves*.

③ Examine each of the leaves carefully. Record the ways that the leaves you observe are alike and the ways they are different.

④ Compare your completed table with those of your classmates.

THINK AND WRITE

1. How are the leaves alike? How are they different?

2. **CLASSIFYING/ORDERING** By classifying, you group or organize things into categories based on guidelines. Ordering organizes things in an order. In this activity, you classified and ordered a collection of leaves. Identify three of the characteristics you used to do this.

Turn Over a New Leaf

What methods do scientists use to collect information about leaves? Some plants are in danger of becoming extinct, or vanishing forever. When you don't know which ones these are, it is a good idea to observe all leaves without removing them from the plant. This activity will introduce you to some ways of classifying leaves without removing them from their natural environment.

DO THIS

1 Walk around your school grounds, and look for leaves you can study.

2 Find a leaf that you want to examine. Without removing the leaf from the plant, gently place it on your paper, and use your marker to trace its outline.

3 Using a different sheet of paper for each leaf, repeat the procedure several times.

4 Back in the classroom, use a ruler to measure the length of the leaf at its longest point. Then measure the width of the leaf at its widest point. Record this data next to the outline of each leaf.

MATERIALS
- paper and marker
- ruler
- Science Log data sheet

THINK AND WRITE

1. Scientists have organized the leaves of plants into categories. What might some of these categories be?

2. Why is it better *not* to remove the leaves of a plant?

ACTIVITY

A Closer Look

By observing individual leaves, you have seen how they can be different in some ways and similar in others. Your observations, however, were made simply by using your eyes. How might your observations be different if you looked closer, using a microscope? In this activity, you will examine similarities and differences in leaves from a new perspective.

DO THIS

1 Observe the slide through the microscope. Sketch what you see.

2 Choose a descriptive title for your sketch. Then compare your sketch to those drawn by your classmates. Discuss how the sketches are similar and how they are different.

THINK AND WRITE

1. What did you see with the microscope that you could not see before?

2. Although you may not know the actual names of the things you saw, try to predict their functions or purposes.

MATERIALS
- prepared slide of a leaf section
- microscope
- Science Log data sheet

What's Inside a Leaf?

Have you ever watched an airplane taking off and thought of a bird skimming across the water? Have you ever seen a scuba diver's fins and thought of a frog's webbed feet? What about a submarine and a large, gray whale? You can probably think of many other examples of human tools that resemble things in nature. Why do you think so many things we use are patterned after things in nature?

Applying ideas from nature is not always as easy as imitating a frog's webbed foot. For example, scientists are still trying to perfect an artificial human heart.

You observed with the microscope that leaves are more complex than they appear to the eye. In fact, leaves can do something that we cannot do and have not been able to imitate. They can make their own food! Humans can *prepare* food, but the human body cannot *make* food.

The "Architecture" of a Leaf

An architect who wants to design a building might observe nature to get ideas. Suppose you are an architect. You know that plants make their own food, and you want to design a factory that can imitate this process. However, you know that you need more information about plants in order to design an efficient structure.

Many structures inside a leaf work together to make food. Look at the diagram showing a cross section of a leaf.

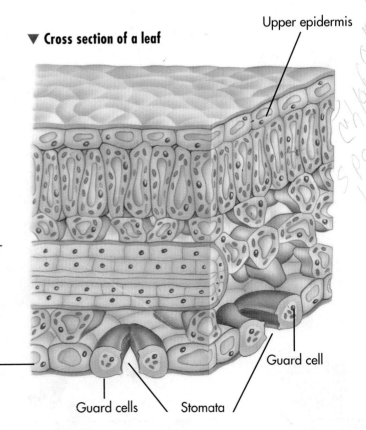

▼ **Cross section of a leaf**

Upper epidermis

Lower epidermis

Guard cell

Guard cells

Stomata

F17

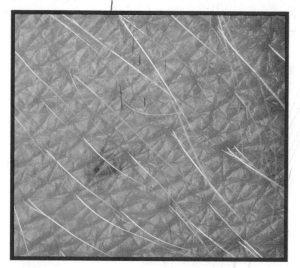

▲ Skin

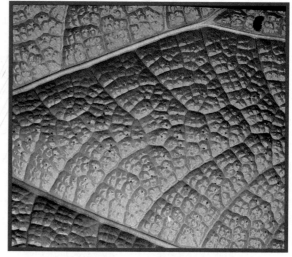

▲ Leaf epidermis

What would happen to your imaginary factory if it had no walls to protect the machinery that makes the food? The leaf, the plant's food factory, has a protective layer of thin, flat cells called the **epidermis.** The epidermis is sometimes covered with a waxlike coating that helps prevent the leaf from losing too much water. The epidermis is similar to the skin on your body, which helps protect you.

The epidermis contains **stomata,** or openings. The stomata are like the pores of your skin: both are openings through which things can enter and exit. The stomata, or stoma, allow water and air to move into and out of the leaf.

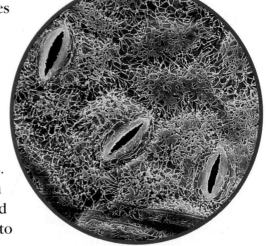

▲ Stomata of a leaf

Sometimes the stomata are open, and at other times they are closed. Structures known as **guard cells** are paired on either side of the stomata. Guard cells control the size of the stomata so that materials can enter and exit the leaf. One way to think about stomata and guard cells is to think of stomata as doors in your imaginary factory and guard cells as security guards. The security guards open and close the doors so that materials can pass through.

THINK ABOUT IT

What can plants do that people cannot?

ACTIVITY

Life Without Leaves

Although some plants are in danger of becoming extinct, in this activity, your teacher will provide you with some that are plentiful enough to study.

MATERIALS
- 3 potted plants
- scissors
- meter stick
- Science Log data sheet

DO THIS

❶ Label the containers of your plants *A*, *B*, and *C*.

❷ **CAUTION: Use care when using sharp tools.** Carefully cut all the leaves from plant *A* and half the leaves from plant *B*. Do not remove any leaves from plant *C*.

❸ Set all three plants in a sunny location, and water them regularly. Predict what will happen to each plant.

❹ Each day, measure the length of the stem of each plant, and record your observations. Also remove any leaves that begin to grow back on plants *A* and *B*.

❺ At the end of two weeks, compare the data you collected each day with the predictions you made.

THINK AND WRITE

1. Explain how your predictions compared with the actual results of the activity.

2. Why are leaves important to a plant?

3. **OBSERVING** In any science investigation, you should make and record observations carefully. How might your observations affect the conclusions you made in this activity?

Photosynthesis

How do we know that plants make their own food? Up until the 1600s, some people thought that plants consumed soil to live! Around that time, J. B. van Helmont, a scientist in Belgium, decided to test this hypothesis.

After drying and recording the weight of some soil, van Helmont placed the soil in a large tub and planted a small willow tree. For five years, van Helmont did nothing more than add water to the soil in the tub.

At the end of the five years, he removed the tree, which by that time had grown much larger. Then he dried and weighed the soil again. He found that it weighed almost the same as it had before! Although van Helmont still didn't understand how plants make their own food, he did prove that plants don't grow by eating soil. Now scientists know how plants make their own food. Let's try to apply this to the factory design that we are working on.

Our imaginary food factory now has walls, doors, and security guards, all inspired by plant structures. We need all of those things, but they can't make the food. The food-making process cannot occur unless there is a supply of

▶ **Plants make food.**

F20

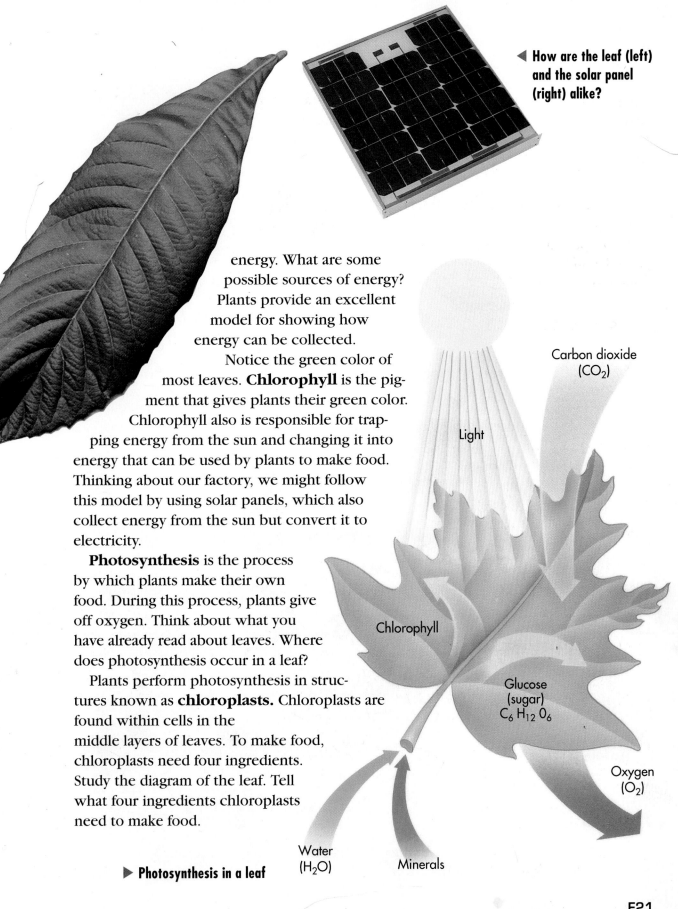

◀ **How are the leaf (left) and the solar panel (right) alike?**

Carbon dioxide (CO_2)

Light

Chlorophyll

Glucose (sugar) $C_6H_{12}O_6$

Oxygen (O_2)

Water (H_2O)

Minerals

energy. What are some possible sources of energy? Plants provide an excellent model for showing how energy can be collected.

Notice the green color of most leaves. **Chlorophyll** is the pigment that gives plants their green color. Chlorophyll also is responsible for trapping energy from the sun and changing it into energy that can be used by plants to make food. Thinking about our factory, we might follow this model by using solar panels, which also collect energy from the sun but convert it to electricity.

Photosynthesis is the process by which plants make their own food. During this process, plants give off oxygen. Think about what you have already read about leaves. Where does photosynthesis occur in a leaf?

Plants perform photosynthesis in structures known as **chloroplasts.** Chloroplasts are found within cells in the middle layers of leaves. To make food, chloroplasts need four ingredients. Study the diagram of the leaf. Tell what four ingredients chloroplasts need to make food.

▶ **Photosynthesis in a leaf**

F21

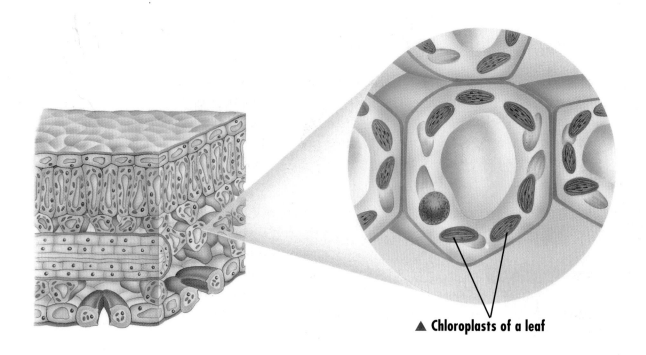

▲ **Chloroplasts of a leaf**

▲ **All energy that passes through a food chain begins with photosynthesis.**

If a plant isn't able to perform photosynthesis, it will die. Think about what would happen if all the plants on Earth failed to perform photosynthesis. How would this affect the other living things on Earth?

The food chain is a model that shows how living things, plants and animals alike, depend on one another for survival.

THINK ABOUT IT

Why is it important for all living things that plants have the ability to make their own food?

Food Factories

There are many different food chains on the Earth. Plants are usually the foundation, or beginning link, of these food chains. This is because, with the exception of a few microorganisms, plants are the only living things that are able to use the energy of sunlight to make food. How does this make other living things dependent upon plants?

We have been modeling our imaginary food factory after a leaf on a plant. The external structures, such as the epidermis and stomata, are easy for us to imitate in the forms of walls and doors. Like the chlorophyll in a leaf, our solar panels can collect energy from the sun. So far, however, scientists have not been able to imitate the actual process of photosynthesis. How we might duplicate the way chloroplasts use light, water, and carbon dioxide to make food is still a mystery to us.

As the problems of extinctions and the struggle to provide food for a rapidly expanding world population increase, the need for alternative food sources becomes more pressing. Perhaps sometime in the future, scientists will actually be able to do what we have only thought about in this unit—duplicate the process of photosynthesis and build food factories that are specifically designed to *make* food.

THINK ABOUT IT

If food factories became possible, how would the quality of people's lives everywhere on Earth change? Would it become better, or would it become worse? Explain.

Why Are Leaves Flat?

One of the characteristics that leaves share is that most are flat. Have you ever wondered why the leaves of plants are flat? If you have, you are not alone. The history of storytelling shows that people have wondered this before.

Legends and myths are stories that are passed down over hundreds of years in a culture. They often try to answer the question *why*. The following Polynesian legend was once used to explain why leaves are flat.

WHY MOST TREES AND PLANTS HAVE FLAT LEAVES

from
Hidden Stories in Plants
by **Anne Pellowski**

 LITERATURE

A long time ago the sky was not very high above the earth. It was the plants that held up the sky, pressing it outward as far as they could. But that was only a short distance from the ground, not even as high as the tree-tops.

The sky was very heavy, and the weight of it caused the leaves of the plants to flatten out more and more. Some, like the leaves of the banana plant, spread into long thick blades as they pressed against the sky. Others, like the taro plants, became as round and broad as elephants' ears as they stretched out to hold the ever-expanding sky.

"We cannot hold out much longer," said the plants. "Soon the sky will fall and crush the earth."

"We must call for help," said the people.

"I will go to Maui," said a woman. "Maui is a trickster, but he is also wise and knows how to do many things."

"Yes, I can raise the sky," said Maui. "But first, you must give me a drink of water from your gourd."

The woman gave him a drink of water and Maui held up his arms. With his broad brown hands he lifted the sky until it came to the treetops. There he let it rest for a time, and the sky flattened the leaves of the trees.

Maui heaved his shoulders, raised his arms, and pushed again.

Soon the sky was resting on the mountaintops.

After he had rested enough, Maui made a mighty effort and hoisted the sky so high it reached the heavens, where it has remained ever since. But the leaves have remained flat, to show that they once held up the sky.

After reading this legend, think about how science has answered some questions and changed some of the ways that we think about nature. Think about science and legends. How are they the same, and how are they different?

By the way, the leaves of plants have adapted over millions of years. The flatness of a leaf allows sunlight to reach more chloroplasts. How does this benefit a plant?

QUICK CHECK

LESSON 1 REVIEW

❶ What raw materials are necessary for a plant to perform photosynthesis?

❷ How does the leaf work as the plant's "food factory"?

❸ How does photosynthesis affect you?

2 STEMS

You have learned that photosynthesis occurs in the leaves of plants. What more do plants need in order to remain alive and healthy? In this lesson, you will examine stems and discover their importance to plants.

ACTIVITY

Stemming from a Plant

Are all stems alike? In this activity, you will have an opportunity to examine stems. What you discover can help you answer the question.

DO THIS

1 Make a table with columns labeled *Alike* and *Different*. Title your table *Stems*.

2 Examine each stem with the hand lens. Record the ways that the stems are alike and the ways they are different.

3 Compare your completed table with those of your classmates.

THINK AND WRITE

How are the stems of plants alike? How are they different? Why?

MATERIALS
- 2 stems from different plants
- hand lens
- Science Log data sheet

Moving Material

Let's suppose that our factory is fully equipped and ready to begin food production. But the factory cannot make food out of nothing. Even though we have a way to collect light energy, we need to find a way to distribute other raw materials within the factory. As the architect, you might again look to plants for ideas. How do plants transport the water and minerals that they obtain? How might the stems of plants play a part in the process of photosynthesis?

DO THIS

MATERIALS
- 2 celery stalks
- knife
- shallow dish
- water
- food coloring
- Science Log data sheet

1 **CAUTION: Handle sharp objects with care. Ask for your teacher's help if you have difficulty removing the tubes in the celery.** Carefully cut off two stalks of celery, each with leaves. Peel off the tubelike structures on the outside edge of one piece.

2 Stand both pieces of celery in the dish, and fill the bottom of the dish with water and food coloring. Set the dish aside overnight.

3 Examine both pieces of celery. How are they alike, and how are they different? How do you account for the differences?

THINK AND WRITE

Describe one function of the stem of a plant.

A Look Inside Stems

In designing the blueprint for your imaginary factory, consider the best way to maximize the energy collected by the solar panels. Suppose your food factory is located in a high-rise building. What are some reasons why you would want to locate the solar panels on the upper floors of the building? Once again, plants provide a solution. How do stems help the leaves of a plant reach sunlight and perform photosynthesis?

Remember, even though most buildings have the same basic framework in their construction, they might not be designed to look the same on the inside. This is also true with plants. There are different types of plant stems. Stems that are green and flexible are described as soft, or **herbaceous**, stems. Stems that contain wood cells and are stiff are called hard, or **woody**, stems.

Think about the ways plants with herbaceous stems are different from those with woody stems. What is the relationship between how long a plant lives, and how big it gets, to the type of stem it has?

▲ Herbaceous and woody stems

▲ Stems provide support.

Stems provide support for leaves, but they also have another important function. Think about our factory for a moment. On its top floors, it collects the energy of the sun. Suppose shipments of raw materials are stored in the basement. How will we get the raw materials to the top floors where the food is made? Think about the experiment in which water moved through one piece of celery but not the other.

Plants contain tubelike tissues called *xylem* (ZY luhm) and *phloem* (FLOH em). Material going from the roots to the leaves moves in **xylem** tissue. Food manufactured in the leaves moves to the rest of the plant in **phloem** tissue. These tissues can be thought of as a plant's system of "plumbing." Both herbaceous and woody stems contain xylem and phloem tissues.

THINK ABOUT IT

The xylem tubes carrying water and minerals up the stem to the leaves are generally larger than the phloem tubes carrying food down to the stem and roots. Why?

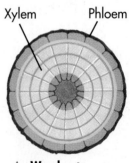

Xylem   Phloem

▲ Woody stem

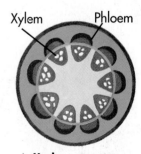

Xylem   Phloem

▲ Herbaceous stem

F29

ACTIVITY

How Old?

A tree trunk is an example of a woody stem. Each year, a tree adds a new layer of growth in its stem. These circular layers of growth, or growth rings, can tell us the age of the tree. In this activity, you will discover one way to tell the age of a tree.

DO THIS

1 Use the hand lens to examine the cross section of the woody stem.

2 Count the number of growth rings that are present. How old is your tree?

3 Note whether some of the growth rings you observe are wide and others are narrow.

THINK AND WRITE

Form a hypothesis about why some growth rings are wide and some are narrow. How could you test your hypothesis?

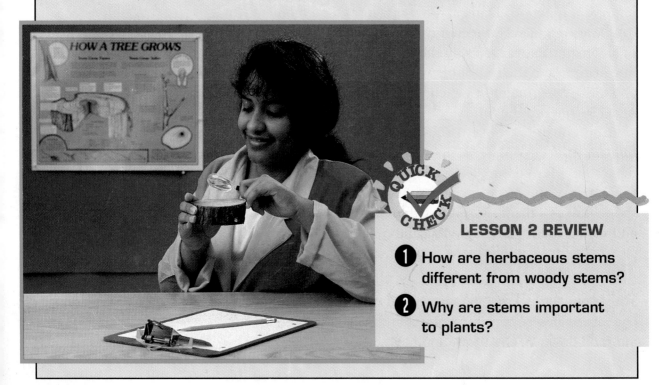

QUICK CHECK

LESSON 2 REVIEW

1 How are herbaceous stems different from woody stems?

2 Why are stems important to plants?

3 Roots

Our imaginary factory is ready to begin production. In this lesson, you will examine how plants gather raw materials.

ACTIVITY

Getting to the Root

A plant uses its roots to absorb the water and minerals it needs from the soil around it. In this activity, you can take a close look at roots.

MATERIALS
- potted plant
- paper towels
- pencil
- hand lens
- Science Log data sheet

DO THIS

1. Carefully remove the plant and soil from the pot by turning the pot upside down and gently tapping the bottom and the sides of the pot.

2. Place the plant over a sink, and gently wash the soil from its roots.

3. Lay the plant on a paper towel. Use a sharp pencil to gently spread its roots apart.

4. Use the hand lens to observe and examine the root system. Draw a picture of the plant and its root system.

5. When you are finished, place the plant back in its pot, and add soil and water. Then place the plant in a warm and sunny location.

THINK AND WRITE

From your observation of the roots, why do you think that they are shaped the way they are?

Growing Roots

Have you ever wondered how things grow? For example, does a hair on your head grow from its tip or from its base? How about the roots of plants? Does a root grow from its tip or from its base? You can explore this question in this activity.

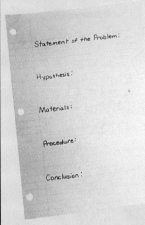

Statement of the Problem:

Hypothesis:

Materials:

Procedure:

Conclusion:

DO THIS

MATERIALS
- materials of your choice
- Science Log data sheet

❶ Make a table with these headings: *Statement of the Problem, Hypothesis, Materials, Procedure,* and *Conclusion.*

❷ Design an experiment that answers the question *Does a root grow from its base or from its tip?* Develop a hypothesis.

❸ List the materials you will use during your experiment.

❹ Develop a detailed procedure that you will follow to answer the question. After your teacher has approved your experiment, gather the materials you will need and perform the experiment.

❺ When your data collection is complete, write a conclusion for your report.

THINK AND WRITE

Does a root grow from its base or from its tip? How do you know?

Root Systems

Your factory is built on a foundation. It helps support the whole building. Read to find out how roots help support the whole plant in much the same way as the foundation.

Suppose your factory is a success and you need a bigger work space. As you expand your factory, the amount of raw materials that you need to keep it working increases. The same thing happens with growing plants. As the stems and leaves of a plant grow, so do its roots.

Roots benefit a plant in the same way that an anchor benefits a ship. Because plants are anchored in place by their roots, they can survive strong winds and heavy rains. Imagine what would happen if plants did not have roots. They would just blow over and tumble away with a gust of wind!

▲ Sometimes even large root systems cannot hold a plant in place.

◄ Roots help a plant to grow.

◄ **Taproot**

▲ **Fibrous roots**

Plants can have either fibrous roots or taproots. The kind of root system a plant has depends on what kind of plant it is. **Fibrous** roots consist of many slender roots in a small area. Lawns, for example, contain grasses that have fibrous roots. **Taproot** roots display a single, thick root.

Dandelions have taproots. If you've ever tried to pull up a dandelion, you know that its taproot will usually break off rather than come out in one piece. When this happens, the piece of taproot left in the soil usually grows again into a dandelion. That's why dandelions can be so hard to get rid of!

What other plants besides grass might have fibrous roots? What other plants besides dandelions might have taproots?

In the experiment you designed and performed, you learned that the roots of plants grow from their tips. The actual growth area of a root tip is known as the **meristem.** If the meristem area of a root is cut off, the root will never grow again! For this reason, it is always a good idea to handle roots with care.

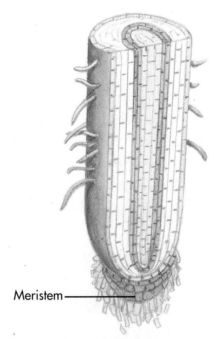

Meristem

▲ **Root growth**

THINK ABOUT IT

Some desert plants have long taproots that may go down several meters. Why?

F34

Food Plants

People adapt their ways of surviving according to their environment. So do plants. Plants that are able to grow in a desert are different from plants that grow in a moist river valley. The many areas of the Earth contain a great variety of plants that people grow and use for food. This activity will help you explore the kinds of plants different people of the Earth use for food.

You will need: reference books, Science Log

Use a world map and reference books to choose the area of the Earth you wish to study. Then use the reference materials to discover the names of plants that people who live in your chosen area use for food. Describe some of the foods.

When your research is completed, prepare a short summary of your findings to present to your classmates. If possible, include pictures of the plants and the foods you discovered.

▲ Loquat and kiwi fruits

Think about the plants and foods you discovered and heard about from your classmates. Which of those would you be willing to try? Explain why you chose these.

 ▶ Foods from plants

QUICK CHECK

LESSON 3 REVIEW

❶ What benefits do root systems provide to plants?

❷ Describe how the functions of a plant are similar to how a factory works.

DOUBLE CHECK

SECTION A REVIEW

1. Why are leaves, stems, and roots important to plants?

2. Why are plants important to other living things?

Classification

Since designing your imaginary food factory in Section A, you have been aware of the efficiency of a plant's xylem and phloem tissues. You go to your local library to learn more. What if your library had no organized way of arranging and filing books? How would you find what you were looking for? Why is it important to organize information?

Fortunately, as in the library, scientists have organized the information about all the different plants in our world. How do scientists do this? Why do they need to do this? The following investigations will help you answer these and other questions about how and why scientists organize plant information. Keep careful notes in your Science Log as you work through the investigations.

1 CLASSIFIED INFORMATION

There are no rules for how information must be organized. People, however, have found efficient ways to organize many things. In this lesson, you will discover how plants are classified.

ACTIVITY

MATERIALS
• shoes
• Science Log data sheet

Classify Them

Classifying plants helps scientists work more efficiently. In this activity, you will practice classifying by using some familiar items.

DO THIS

❶ Take off one shoe and arrange it in a line with your classmates' shoes.

❷ Invent a way to classify the shoes. Begin by separating the shoes into large groups, based on how the shoes are similar and how they are different.

❸ Continue dividing the shoes into smaller and smaller groups, based on more detailed similarities and differences.

❹ Write a description of your group's classification system. Compare it with other groups' systems.

THINK AND WRITE

1. What criteria did you use to develop your categories and subcategories?

2. Why are classification systems useful?

3. **CLASSIFYING/ORDERING** When you classify objects, you examine similarities and differences among them. A major category can be divided into specific subcategories. What were your major categories and subcategories?

Classifying Plants

At first glance, the thousands of books in the library seem to be classified in a complex way. However, you discover that the books are classified into two general categories—fiction and non-fiction. You also find that nonfiction books are further divided into categories according to subject. Once you find the subject that you're looking for, you see that the books are classified into still smaller categories.

▲ **Pine cone**

▼ **Hibiscus flower**

Scientists classify plants in ways that are like a library's classification of books and your own classification of shoes. When scientists classify plants, they group them according to their similarities and differences. You did much the same thing when you grouped the shoes in the last activity.

When scientists classify plants, the first thing they do is separate them into two groups—those that have xylem and phloem tissues and those that do not. Plants that have xylem and phloem tissues are known as **vascular plants.** Plants without xylem and phloem tissues are known as **nonvascular plants.**

Vascular plants are divided into two more groups—seedless plants and seed plants. Seedless vascular plants do not produce seeds. Seed plants produce seeds and some produce fruits. The seed plants are categorized into two more categories—gymnosperms and angiosperms. These groups are determined by how they produce seeds and whether or not the seeds are protected by a covering.

Gymnosperms are seed plants that do not produce flowers or fruit around their seeds. Gymnosperms produce seeds in cones. A pine tree is one example of a gymnosperm.

Angiosperms are seed plants that produce seeds in flowers. The seeds have a protective covering around them called **fruit**. Daisies and roses are examples of angiosperms. You may be surprised to learn that many trees and grasses are angiosperms, too.

Although trees and grasses do not have flowers as distinctive as daisies and roses, they do have flowers.

LESSON 1 REVIEW

Do you think that most of the plants in your area are gymnosperms or angiosperms? Explain your reasoning.

2 PLANTS OF A DIFFERENT STRUCTURE

As you walk along a path in a park, you notice a small plant growing at the base of a tree. It looks like a soft, green carpet. It's different from the vascular plants you have studied. How is it different? You will find out in this lesson.

A C T I V I T Y

What's Missing?

In this activity, you will look for differences between vascular and nonvascular plants.

MATERIALS
- hand lens
- moss
- liverwort
- hornwort
- Science Log data sheet

DO THIS

❶ Use the hand lens to observe and examine the moss.

❷ Repeat the procedure for the liverwort and the hornwort.

❸ Write a description of these nonvascular plants. Include a sketch of each plant, and title your description *Nonvascular Plants.*

THINK AND WRITE

OBSERVING Observing is the most basic science skill. In this activity you observed two nonvascular plants and were then asked to compare them to vascular plants. Describe three ways you observed that nonvascular plants differ from vascular plants.

Nonvascular Plants

How were the nonvascular plants you looked at different from the plants you had studied earlier?

Think about your imaginary food factory. Like the xylem and phloem of a plant, the plumbing of the factory delivers water and minerals from the ground floor to where the food is made, and it distributes food to the rest of the factory.

If your factory had no plumbing, how would you deliver the water and minerals? Your factory wouldn't be very efficient, would it?

Remember that nonvascular plants do not have xylem and phloem tissues. In addition, they do not use seeds to reproduce, and they do not have roots, stems, or leaves, as plants with vascular systems do. In these ways, nonvascular plants are much simpler than seed plants.

A seed plant with its large root system can usually find water easily. Because nonvascular plants do not have true roots, they have more difficulty locating water. As a result, nonvascular plants grow only in moist areas. Swamps are good places to find nonvascular plants. Where else might you expect to find these plants?

THINK ABOUT IT

Most nonvascular plants are not very tall. Why do you think this is the case?

▲ Mosses and ferns like moisture.

Vascular or Nonvascular?

Now that you know about vascular and nonvascular plants, apply your knowledge.

Take a look at the ferns on this page. Based on what you know, would you say they are vascular plants or nonvascular plants? Why?

◀ Spore cases on a fern

If you decided it was a vascular plant, you were right. But the fern isn't like many other vascular plants, because it is seedless. **Seedless vascular plants** are vascular plants that do not reproduce by making seeds. Instead, they produce *spores,* reproductive cells that develop into adult plants. This process differs from the process in seed-producing plants. You'll explore the reproduction of vascular plants in the next section.

Seedless vascular plants have xylem and phloem, just as seed plants do. Like nonvascular plants, seedless vascular plants also need to live near a steady source of moisture.

THINK ABOUT IT

The way that scientists classify plants is shown in the concept map above. Name a plant from each group.

Plants in Your Life

How does the classification system of plants help you look at them in a way that you never have before? Besides giving you tools for learning more about plants, the classification system also gives you a way to think about plants in relation to a large ecosystem. For example, if you see ferns growing near a lake, now you know that the steady moisture is important to them. In the following writing exercise, take your mind on a creative journey as you think about the life of plants.

Poets, artists, and movie directors have all featured plants in their work. Think about how you might describe plant life. Feel free to explore many different aspects of how plant life affects you and other living creatures. Compose a poem, song lyrics, rap, or short story about your thoughts. You can write from your point of view, or you can invent characters. Give your composition a title. Share it with your classmates.

THINK ABOUT IT

If you could use only one sentence to describe the plant life of Earth, what sentence would you use?

▼ **Forest mosses**

▼ **Flower fields in California**

Plants in a greenhouse

A Balanced Diet

You would probably be amazed by all the different plants that people eat. What factors influence the foods people choose to eat?

▼ Tomatoes from the tomato plant

◀ Whole wheat bread from wheat

◀ Lettuce from the lettuce plant

▼ Turkey fed on feed grain

How do you know which foods are part of a balanced diet? A balanced diet includes foods that help your body grow, develop, and be healthy. Plants are a very important part of any balanced diet.

Think of what you know about the different food groups. Keep in mind that humans eat plants directly, such as when they eat carrots, and indirectly, such as when they eat the meat of an animal that ate plants for food. Find out the ingredients of a balanced diet.

Create a menu that describes what you might eat for breakfast, lunch, and dinner for three days. Also include several snacks.

As you design your menu, remember that a balanced diet is important. After your menu is complete, count the number of times in a week you ate plants either directly or indirectly. How are plants important to a balanced diet?

QUICK CHECK

LESSON 2 REVIEW

❶ How can organized scientific information benefit people who are not scientists?

❷ How might the growing conditions suitable for seedless vascular plants be different from those of seeded vascular plants?

DOUBLE CHECK

SECTION B REVIEW

1. How do you think scientists developed their system of classifying plants?

2. How might the differences between vascular and nonvascular plants determine where they grow?

Plant Reproduction

▶ **Hummingbird**

If you flew high above the ground in a plane and looked down, you might see patterns of cities, stretches of golden sand, and large blue basins of water. But you also would see just about every shade of green there is. Green would stretch like a blanket over the Earth—flat stripes of farm crops, tufts of forest trees, and rolling stretches of grasslands.

Where does all this green come from? Plants. Plants have spread over the Earth because they, like other living things, have the ability to reproduce. How do plants reproduce? Why is plant reproduction important? And how are characteristics of plants passed down to their offspring? The following investigations will help you answer these and other questions about plants and some of the different ways they reproduce. Keep careful notes in your Science Log as you work through your investigations.

1 FLOWER POWER

What functions do flowers serve, and why are flowers important to plants? This lesson will help you answer those questions.

ACTIVITY

Take a Close Look

A flower has many different parts. In this activity, you will observe the structure of a typical flower.

MATERIALS
- living flowers
- paper towels
- hand lens
- Science Log data sheet

DO THIS

❶ Select a flower and lay it on a paper towel.

❷ Handle the flower gently while you observe its various structures. Be sure to look inside. What is inside?

❸ Now use the hand lens to examine the structures of the flower. Sketch what you observe.

❹ The inside of the flower contains at least three different structures. Are there at least three different structures in your sketch? If not, look again at the flower and change your sketch.

THINK AND WRITE

1. How would you describe the structures that you found inside your flower?

2. What role do you think these structures might play in the life of a plant?

Reproduction in Seed Plants

You may recall that angiosperms are flowering plants that produce seeds within flowers and that the seeds have a protective covering. The flowers of angiosperms are very important because they contain the plants' reproductive structures. You observed some of these structures when you used a hand lens to examine a flower.

But why is it important that plants have the ability to reproduce? And how do angiosperms reproduce if their flowers can't walk, swim, or fly to other flowers? You can begin to find answers to these questions by studying the flower diagram.

▲ **Wood lily**

The **stamen** is the male part of a flower. This stemlike structure has two parts: the *filament* and the *anther*. The anther contains pollen grains, and pollen grains contain sperm cells. Most flowers have more than one stamen.

The **pistil** is the female part of a flower. This vaselike structure is found in the center of the flower. It has three parts: the *stigma*, the *style*, and the *ovary*. Within the ovary are *ovules*, which contain egg cells.

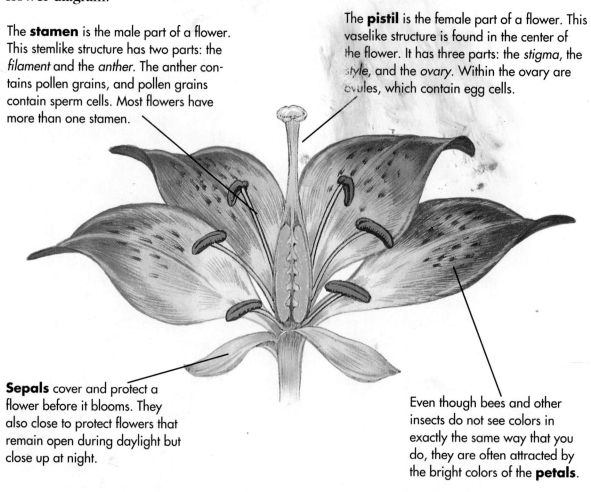

Sepals cover and protect a flower before it blooms. They also close to protect flowers that remain open during daylight but close up at night.

Even though bees and other insects do not see colors in exactly the same way that you do, they are often attracted by the bright colors of the **petals**.

In order for a plant to reproduce, pollen from the male anther must reach the stigma. This is called **pollination.** The pollen grains travel down the style to the ovary. When pollen grains reach the ovules, *fertilization* occurs. Fertilization is the joining of the sperm cell and the egg cell. After fertilization takes place, the plant produces seeds.

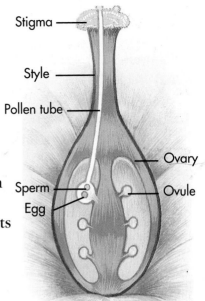

Fertilization is the process necessary to produce seeds, but fertilization can't occur before pollination. Pollination can occur in two different ways. One of these is *self-pollination.* In self-pollination, pollen from a plant finds its way to the stigma of the same plant. The second kind of pollination is *cross-pollination.* Cross-pollination occurs when pollen from a plant finds its way to the stigma of a *different* plant.

Self-pollination

Cross-pollination

THINK ABOUT IT

How do you think pollen gets from one plant to another?

Partners in Pollination

Pollination is needed for the reproduction of flowering plants.
What might happen to a plant if its flowers are not pollinated?
Flowering plants have developed some interesting partnerships.
The yucca plant is an example of this. The following excerpt
describes the yucca's unique method of pollination.

EXTREME CASES & Broken Rules

by Anne Ophelia Dowden
from *The Clover & the Bee: A Book of Pollination*

LITERATURE One of the exclusive partnerships is that of the yucca, or Spanish bayonet, and a small female moth. Yuccas grow wild in the southwestern United States and Mexico, and a few species are found in gardens elsewhere, all bearing tall handsome stalks of drooping white or pinkish flowers. The yucca's little white moth, less than an inch in wingspread, has two very unusual features: parts of her mouth have developed into a pair of spiny tentacles, and the egg-laying tube at the end of her tail—her *ovipositor*—is a horny spike.

The little moths emerge from their cocoons just as the yucca flowers begin to bloom. Soon each female has mated and is ready to lay her eggs, and in the twilight she flies among the tall spires of opening yucca flowers. From each of them she collects pollen and carries it in her tentacles, rolled into a little ball under her chin. When the ball is several times as big as her head, she flies to still another flower and goes directly to the pistil at its center. Here she thrusts her sharp ovipositor through the wall of its ovary and deposits three or four eggs inside. This done, she climbs to

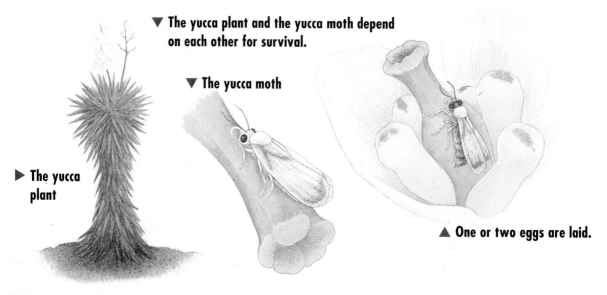

▼ The yucca plant and the yucca moth depend
on each other for survival.

▼ The yucca moth

▶ The yucca plant

▲ One or two eggs are laid.

the tip of the pistil and pushes her ball of pollen into the fork of its stigma, carefully rubbing it in.

This pollen is not food for her larvae nor for herself. (She does not eat at all during her short adult life.) It is purely for the benefit of the flower. Thus fertilized, the flower's ovary will grow into a large pod holding hundreds of seeds. When the moth larvae hatch inside it, they will feed on the seeds, but even when there are several larvae in a pod, the plant can easily afford the loss. Eventually each larva bores a hole through the wall of the pod, drops to the ground, and passes its pupa stage buried there for the winter. Next summer, it will emerge as an adult just when the yucca flowers start to bloom.

This little moth directly arranges the fertilization that is necessary to produce the seeds her offspring need to eat. In the whole field of pollination, it is the only case in which an insect "deliberately" fertilizes a flower for the good of the plant and the future benefit of babies she will never see, and not as an accidental part of her own food gathering. No one knows what started such a habit or how the moth's curious body developed. But the partnership must be very old, since many species of yucca have evolved and, with only one exception, each has a species of *Tegeticula* moth that has evolved with it. Yucca flowers still produce nectar—useless to the moth—and are visited by a number of other insects. But none of those insects play any part in its pollination, and the yucca depends entirely on its little moth.

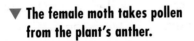

The female moth takes pollen from the plant's anther.

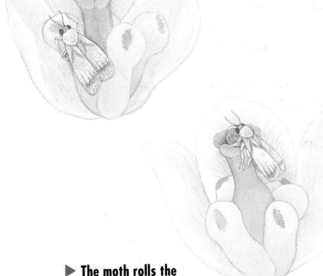

▶ **The moth rolls the pollen into a ball and takes it to the stigma of another plant.**

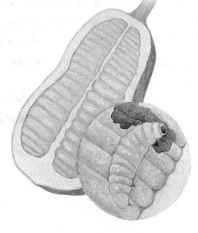

▼ **The larvae feed on the seeds.**

THINK ABOUT IT

How do the yucca plant and the yucca moth help each other survive?

F49

More Help

Like the yucca moth, many other agents help pollinate flowers—
other insects, some birds, and the wind. Here are just a few
examples.

◀ Hummingbirds dart from flower to
flower, using their long bills to suck the
sweet nectar of the flowers. As they do,
pollen sticks to their bills. When they fly
to the next flower and begin drinking, the
pollen rubs off and pollinates that flower.

▶ Bees collect the pollen of
flowers. Pollen is sticky.
When a bee lands on a
flower, pollen grains often
stick to its legs and body.
Attracted by bright petals
and a strong fragrance, the
bee visits another flower.
There, grains of pollen
from the first flower may be
brushed off.

▼ If you have allergies such as hay fever, you know that
pollen can be found in the air. Breezes can loosen pollen
from plants and blow it around. Grasses, wheat, corn,
and many spring-blooming trees are some examples of
wind-pollinated plants.

▲ Ladybugs, mosquitoes, ants, and
many other insects also help pollinate flowers.

THINK ABOUT IT

Invent a new method by which
flowers can be pollinated.

ACTIVITY

Fun with Flowers

If you could design your own flower, what would it look like? The following activity will give you an opportunity to do just that.

DO THIS

1. **CAUTION: Be careful using sharp tools.** Using the materials that you have gathered, make a flower of your own design. In addition to creating the stem and petals, be sure to include sepals, a pistil, and stamens. Use salt to represent pollen.

2. Display your flower in the classroom until your studies of plants are completed.

MATERIALS
- construction paper
- colored pencils
- glue and tape
- flexible straws
- scissors
- paper egg cartons, plastic lids, paper plates, and other similar materials for making a model
- salt
- Science Log data sheet

THINK AND WRITE

Describe how your flower would be pollinated and what outside agents might help in the process.

Flowers in Poetry

Throughout history, flowers have been the subject matter for countless stories, poems, paintings, photographs, and sculptures. The poet William Wordsworth expresses an appreciation of flowers and the plant kingdom in this poem about daffodils.

I Wandered Lonely as a Cloud

by **William Wordsworth**

*I wandered lonely as a cloud
  That floats on high o'er vales and hills,
When all at once I saw a crowd—
  A host of golden daffodils
Beside the lake, beneath the trees,
Fluttering and dancing in the breeze.*

*Continuous as the stars that shine
  And twinkle on the Milky Way,
They stretched in never-ending line
  Along the margin of a bay:
Ten thousand saw I, at a glance,
Tossing their heads in sprightly dance.*

*The waves beside them danced, but they
  Outdid the sparkling waves in glee;
A poet could not be but gay
  In such a jocund company;
I gazed—and gazed—but little thought
  What wealth the show to me had brought.*

*For oft, when on my couch I lie,
  In vacant or in pensive mood,
They flash upon that inward eye
  Which is the bliss of solitude;
And then my heart with pleasure fills,
And dances with the daffodils.*

Write a poem or story telling how you feel about flowers.

QUICK CHECK

LESSON 1 REVIEW

❶ What must happen in order for fertilization to occur?

❷ Explain the role that each structure of a flower plays in pollination.

2 PACKAGES OF LIFE

You have read that plants can produce seeds after pollination and fertilization occur, but what happens next? How do seeds grow? In what ways are seeds important to all living things on Earth? This lesson can help you answer these questions.

ACTIVITY

Seeds

In this activity, you can take a closer look at the structure of some beans, which are actually seeds.

MATERIALS
- lima beans
- paper towel
- hand lens
- Science Log data sheet

DO THIS

1 Place several beans on a paper towel, and observe them with the hand lens. Sketch what you observe. Label your sketch *The Seed Coat of a Bean.*

2 Peel the outside covering, or seed coat, off of each bean. Then carefully open the beans.

3 Observe and sketch the large whitish masses inside each bean. Label your sketch *The Cotyledons of a Bean.*

4 Locate the embryo of each seed. The embryo is a tiny young plant. Sketch what you observe. Label your sketch *The Embryo of a Bean.*

THINK AND WRITE

What might be the functions of the seed coat and the cotyledons?

ACTIVITY

What Do Seeds Need?

MATERIALS

- 8 cups
- marker
- soil
- 24 radish seeds
- water
- refrigerator
- cardboard
- Science Log data sheet

What factors might control whether seeds sprout? In this activity, you can explore some of these factors.

DO THIS

1 Copy the table provided and label the cups A, B, C, D, E, F, G, and H.

2 Put some soil in each cup. Then place three seeds on top of the soil in each cup. Arrange the cups as directed in your table. Water cups A, B, C, and E each day if necessary. Do not water cups D and F.

3 Place cup G in a refrigerator. Cover cup H with a piece of cardboard and keep it at room temperature. Water both cups each day if necessary.

4 Record your observations for five days.

THINK AND WRITE

1. Based on your data, write a statement about the ideal conditions that enable radish seeds to sprout. Explain your reasoning.

2. How can you find out if every kind of seed needs the same growing conditions?

3. **IDENTIFYING/CONTROLLING VARIABLES** Variables are factors that can influence the outcome of an investigation. They can include temperature and light. What variables did you control in this activity?

What Do Seeds Need?

	Water Both		Both In Light		Both In Dark		Water Both & In Dark	
	a	B	C	D	E	F	G	H
Day	Light	Dark	Water	No Water	Water	No Water	Cold	Room Temperature
1								
2								
3								

How Seeds Sprout

As you have discovered, seeds can't just sprout anywhere at any time. What happens to a seed when it sprouts? Read on to find out.

One of the things that you and your classmates and all of the plants of the world have in common is that you all grow at different rates. Unlike people, however, some plants can easily grow several centimeters in one day! If you could grow that fast, just think of how many pairs of shoes you would outgrow in a week!

When you examined the bean seeds, you saw an embryo. The **embryo** of a seed is a tiny young plant. Given the right conditions, an embryo will grow and develop into a complete, mature plant. The **seed coat** of a seed helps protect the embryo. From what do you think an embryo might need to be protected?

The **cotyledons,** the first leaves to emerge, provide food for the growing embryo. Because photosynthesis is carried out in leaves, a growing embryo cannot make its own food until it has leaves. It must develop leaves quickly because the cotyledons contain a limited amount of food.

You performed an activity in which you inferred the func-

tions of the seed coat and the cotyledons of a seed. Look back at your inferences. How accurate were they?

Before a seed sprouts, or **germinates,** it absorbs water. The water makes the seed swell. This makes it easier for the developing embryo to spread the cotyledons apart.

Roots are usually the first structures to develop and emerge from a seed. When the embryo emerges, it is called a **seedling.** Why is life for a young seedling very dangerous?

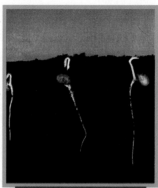
△ Sprouting begins.

△ Cotyledons emerge.

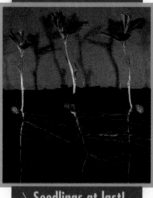
△ Seedlings at last!

▼ Parts of a seed

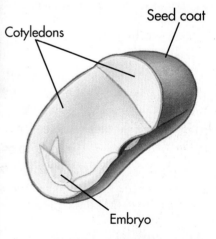

Cotyledons

Seed coat

Embryo

THINK ABOUT IT

Why is the development of leaves important for a seedling?

ACTIVITY

Germinating Seeds

You have found that temperature and moisture are important to seed germination. But even with these needs met, not every seed germinates. In this activity, you will determine the germination rate for a quantity of seeds.

MATERIALS
- packet of seeds
- shallow container
- paper clip
- soil
- flower pots
- water
- Science Log data sheet

DO THIS

1 Carefully open your packet of seeds and pour them into a shallow container.

2 Use the paper clip to help separate the seeds; then count and record the number.

3 Find the germination rate printed on the seed package. The germination rate is the expected percent of seeds that will germinate. Record that number, and predict how many seeds you think will germinate.

4 Plant the seeds according to the directions on the package. Put the pots in a place that has the recommended conditions. Water as directed.

5 Observe the seeds regularly. After two weeks, count the number of seeds that germinated. Record your observations.

THINK AND WRITE

1. How did the number of seeds that germinated compare with the germination rate claimed by the seed company?

2. What might explain any difference you found?

Seed Songs

There are many different ways to learn about science. A fun way to learn and remember facts about seeds and seedlings is to create raps, poems, or songs about them. This exercise will give you the chance to be creative.

With the other members of your group, discuss the different things you have learned about seeds and seedlings. Then create a song, poem, or rap that describes the life of a seed and a seedling. Write it down, and have one member of your group volunteer to read your song, poem, or rap to the class. Or you might decide to perform your creation as a group.

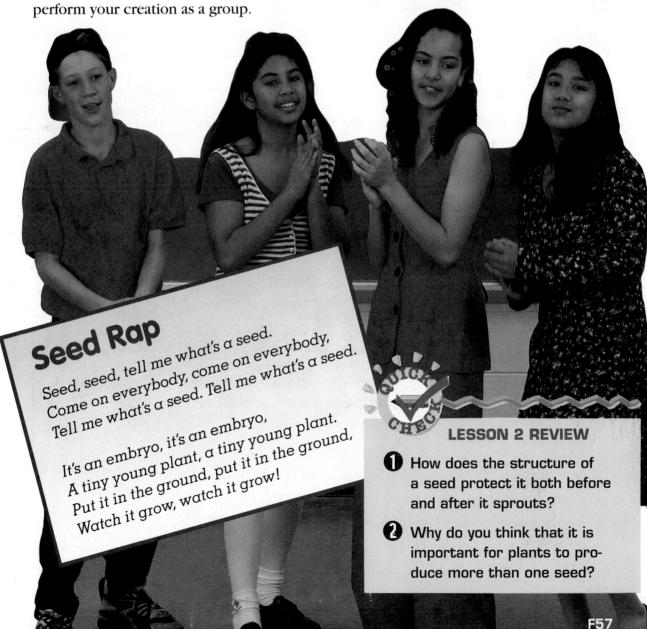

Seed Rap

Seed, seed, tell me what's a seed.
Come on everybody, come on everybody,
Tell me what's a seed. Tell me what's a seed.

It's an embryo, it's an embryo,
A tiny young plant, a tiny young plant.
Put it in the ground, put it in the ground,
Watch it grow, watch it grow!

LESSON 2 REVIEW

❶ How does the structure of a seed protect it both before and after it sprouts?

❷ Why do you think that it is important for plants to produce more than one seed?

3 NEW PLANTS FROM OLD

You know how flowering plants produce seeds. Not all plants reproduce this way. In this lesson, you will examine other ways that plants reproduce.

MATERIALS
- coleus plant
- scissors
- cup of water
- potato with eyes (buds)
- knife
- flower pot
- soil
- water
- Science Log data sheet

ACTIVITY

Plant Cuttings

DO THIS

❶ **CAUTION: Be careful using sharp tools.** Cut a stem about 10 cm long from a coleus plant. Include at least two leaves. Place the cut end in a glass of water.

❷ Carefully remove an eye, or bud, from a potato. Place the eye, pointing downward, in a pot of soil. Cover it with soil.

❸ Place both your coleus stem and your potato eye in a warm, sunny location. Predict what will happen.

❹ Observe your coleus stem and potato eye each day. Add water to each of them when necessary.

❺ After four weeks, gently remove the potato eye from the soil and coleus stem from the glass. Describe your results.

THINK AND WRITE

1. Compare the appearance of the coleus with that of the potato.

2. **PREDICTING** Predicting is anticipating an outcome of future events based on patterns of experience. In this activity, you predicted an outcome. How did your results compare with your predictions?

Asexual Reproduction

Think about the activity you just did. What would life be like if all plants reproduced like the coleus and potato? Just think of the possibilities! A leaf from a tree could grow into an exact copy of the same tree!

What if every weed plant you pulled up grew into another weed plant? What do you think? Maybe it's a good thing that not all plants can reproduce asexually—without both a male and female partner.

How do plants reproduce without both a male and a female partner? You should have an idea from the activity you just did. The stem, leaf, or root of a plant that is removed from the plant is known as a *cutting.* Using a cutting to grow a new plant is called **vegetative reproduction.**

By using a cutting, you can grow a complete, mature plant in much less time than you can with a seed. How might the use of cuttings improve farming?

Some varieties of seedless fruits are grown by vegetative reproduction.

Not all plants can use vegetative reproduction. Let's take a closer look at the ones that can and the methods they use.

▶ **Growing potatoes from buds, or eyes, is a form of vegetative reproduction.**

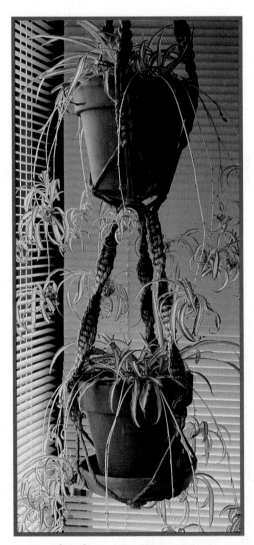

▲ **A spider plant uses runners to reproduce. New plants develop on the ends of the runners.**

Look again at the color patterns of the coleus plant cutting. How do the color patterns from the cutting compare to the plant from which you took the cutting?

Any plant grown by vegetative reproduction is identical to its parent plant. It doesn't matter whether you use cuttings, buds, bulbs, eyes, or runners. Vegetative reproduction *always* produces a plant that is identical in every way to its parent plant.

Why do you think seed reproduction does not produce a plant that is identical to either parent? Hint: Think about pollination and fertilization.

▶ Strawberries grow by sending out runners. Why do you think that these stems are called *runners*?

◀ In another form of vegetative reproduction, flowers such as tulips, lilies, and daffodils can be grown from bulbs. Bulbs are short underground stems.

QUICK CHECK

LESSON 3 REVIEW

❶ Describe four ways that plants can be grown by vegetative reproduction.

❷ What advantages do plants grown by vegetative reproduction have when compared to plants grown from seeds?

4 INHERITED CHARACTERISTICS

Think of ways that you are like your mother or your father. In what ways are you different from one or both of them? You are probably able to see some similarities and some differences between you and your parents just by looking. You may be able to do the same with seeds that develop from cross-pollination. In this lesson, you will examine how characteristics are passed from parents to offspring.

Mendel's Discovery

Many scientists have studied plants and their characteristics. Read to find out about the work of one scientist.

When scientists study how living things are similar to their parents, they are studying inherited characteristics. *Inherited* means "received from parents." The first person to study how plants inherited characteristics from their parents was an Austrian named Gregor Mendel.

Throughout his life, Mendel had an interest in plants and gardening. He began in the 1850s to study the characteristics of the common garden pea plant. The garden pea has an interesting flower. The petals cover the pistil and stamens, so pollination takes place within one flower.

Mendel noticed that the plants with purple flowers always produced offspring that had purple flowers. Likewise, the plants with white flowers always produced offspring with white flowers.

What would you expect if you cross-pollinated a plant with purple flowers and a plant with white flowers? Would you expect some purple flowers and some white flowers? Would the flowers

Parent plants

Purple   White

First generation

Purple   Purple   Purple   Purple

Second generation

Purple   Purple   Purple   White

have purple-and-white stripes? Would they be white with purple dots? Mendel did not know what to expect, but he was surprised! Look at the diagram below and follow Mendel's experiments. What was Mendel's surprise?

Mendel made hundreds of crosses, resulting in thousands of seeds. He also studied a variety of *traits*, or characteristics, such as stem length, seed color, seed shape, and pod color.

When Mendel cross-pollinated a pea plant that had green pods with a pea plant that had yellow pods, he found that all of the offspring had green pods. The yellow-pod trait seemed to disappear. But in the next generation of self-pollinated plants, the yellow pods reappeared. The trait that seemed to disappear in the second generation appeared in about one-fourth of the plants in the third generation.

While performing his experiments, Mendel hypothesized that each parent pea plant had two factors for each characteristic and contributed one of the factors to each offspring. The offspring's two factors then included one from each parent.

▲ Gregor Mendel

Mendel described these factors as either *dominant* or *recessive*. A **dominant** factor produces a characteristic that is visible in the offspring. A **recessive** factor is sometimes hidden. Mendel's pea plants—and other living things, such as yourself—include both dominant factors and recessive factors. We now call these factors *genes*. Genes are units that are inherited from parents and that determine the characteristics of an offspring.

In pea plants, the dominant characteristic for stem length is tall stems, and the recessive characteristic is short stems. The dominant characteristic for pod color is green pods, and the recessive characteristic is yellow pods. In humans, the dominant characteristic for eye color is brown eyes, and the recessive characteristic is blue eyes.

THINK ABOUT IT

Using your current knowledge of heredity, explain why plants produced by vegetative propagation are always identical to the parent plant. How is this different from the other type of plant reproduction you have explored?

Parent plants

Green   Yellow

First generation

Green   Green   Green   Green

Second generation

Green   Green   Green   Yellow

Squaring Things Away

You've read how Mendel discovered inherited traits. Now here is a way you can look at the inheritance of characteristics.

Let G stand for a dominant factor, corresponding to green pea pods. Let g stand for the recessive factor, corresponding to yellow pea pods. Remember, each organism has two factors for each characteristic—one factor from each parent. If a pea plant has two identical factors for a characteristic, it is called *homozygous* (HOH moh ZY guhs). If it has two different factors, such as one for green pods and one for yellow pods, then it is called *heterozygous* (HET uhr oh ZY guhs).

Homozygous plants can be GG (dominant, green) or gg (recessive, yellow). Heterozygous plants—Gg—have green pods, because the recessive factor is hidden.

The possibilities can be illustrated with a *Punnett square.* A Punnett square is a tool used to predict how a genetic cross might turn out. Let's see what happens if we cross a plant that is homozygous for green pods with a plant that is homozygous for yellow pods. Look at the first Punnett square below. The offspring are all heterozygous and have green pods.

Now let's see what happens if we cross two heterozygous plants. Look at the second Punnett square below. Three-fourths of the offspring have green pods, and one-fourth have yellow pods. What would happen if you crossed a heterozygous plant (with green pods) and a homozygous plant with yellow pods? Try creating a Punnett square yourself.

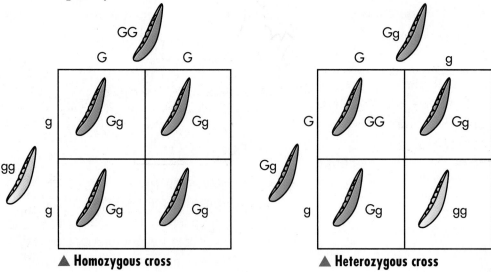

▲ **Homozygous cross**   ▲ **Heterozygous cross**

Mendel's work was radical in his day. At the time, scientists did not know about cells and how they reproduce. The scientists of today know a great deal more about cells. They know about genes and DNA—the material of which genes are made. Mendel was a pioneer, but the scientists who came after him helped explain the process he had discovered. Mendel's work with pea plants helps scientists today explain heredity in plants and animals, including humans.

The study of human inheritance has helped scientists understand hereditary diseases. They hope one day to be able to cure or even prevent such problems. Scientists learn more and more amazing things every year about genetics, although much of it still remains a mystery to humankind.

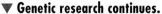
▼ **Genetic research continues.**

LESSON 4 REVIEW

❶ How could two brown-eyed parents have a blue-eyed offspring? Draw a Punnett square to illustrate your findings.

❷ Why was the garden pea such a useful organism in the discovery of hereditary characteristics?

 DOUBLE CHECK

SECTION C REVIEW

1. Why do you think greenhouse workers would use vegetative reproduction for their plants whenever possible?

2. Why does a plant have flowers?

3. Explain how genetics determines which characteristics we inherit from our parents.

Adaptations

Suppose that it is a hot, humid summer afternoon. You are walking to a picnic in the park. As you walk, you wipe the sweat off your forehead and fan yourself with your cap. How is your behavior affected by the weather? In what ways does your body react to the environment around you? How does your environment influence the choices that you make in day-to-day living?

While you are walking, you stop to observe the plant life. The plants seem to tolerate the weather silently. After all, they are rooted in one location and can't walk around. How do plants respond to their environment? What do they do to survive unfavorable conditions? As you find answers to these and other questions about how plants respond, adapt, and survive, keep careful notes in your Science Log.

1 IN RESPONSE

What would the Earth be like if plants could move from one location to another all by themselves? That would be strange, but there are ways that plants can move. In this lesson, you will discover ways that plants respond to their environment.

ACTIVITY

In Search of Light

You know plants need light to make their own food. How do they "move" to make sure they get the light they need? You can find the answer to this question by doing this activity.

MATERIALS
- marker
- 2 removable labels
- 2 potted seedlings
- light source
- water
- Science Log data sheet

DO THIS

1. Write *A* on one label and *B* on the other. Put a label on each plant pot.

2. Place both plants on a windowsill of your classroom. If you are using artificial light, place the light next to your plants. The light should not be directly overhead.

3. Rotate plant *A* one-half turn each day. Do not rotate plant *B*.

4. Observe the plants each day, and record your observations. Water the plants as needed.

5. After ten days, summarize your observations. Use illustrations in your summary.

THINK AND WRITE

Explain how the plants responded to light.

ACTIVITY

The Light of My Life

MATERIALS
- marker
- 4 identical young plants
- ruler
- water
- red, blue, and yellow cellophane
- string
- Science Log data sheet

What is your favorite color of sunlight? Sunlight is a mix of the colors red, orange, yellow, green, blue, and violet. In this activity, find out which color of sunlight plants seem to like best.

DO THIS

1 Make a table like the one shown, and use the marker to label the plants A, B, C, and D.

2 Measure the length and width of the top leaf of each plant. Record this data in your table. Water the plants.

3 Loosely wrap plant A with red cellophane, plant B with blue cellophane, and plant C with yellow cellophane. Use loops of string to hold the cellophane in place. Do not cover plant D. Then place the plants in a warm, bright location.

4 Every two days, remove the cellophane and measure the length and width of the top leaf of each

plant. Record your data in the table. Water the plants if necessary. Then cover each plant again, and move it back to its warm, bright location.

5 After ten days, compare the data that appears in your table.

THINK AND WRITE

1. What color light do the plants seem to respond to most and least? Explain.

2. **IDENTIFYING/CONTROLLING VARIABLES** Identifying and controlling the variables in an experiment can affect the outcome. In this activity you tested the effect of colors. Explain what other variables might affect plant growth.

Effect of Light on Plants		Plant A	Plant B	Plant C	Plant D
Day 1	Width				
	Length				
Day 3	Width				
	Length				
Day 5	Width				
	Length				
Day 7	Width				
	Length				

The Root of the Problem

Do you remember when most of your baby teeth fell out and were replaced by adult teeth? Somehow, your adult teeth managed to fill the space left by your baby teeth instead of moving into your chin and sinuses! It seems as if your teeth had a sense of direction about where to go. What about plants? In what direction do their roots grow? What makes them grow that way? You can explore these questions in this activity.

DO THIS

1 Line the cup with several layers of paper towels.

2 Place the beans between the paper towels and the side of the cup. Position the beans as shown.

3 Moisten the paper towels with water, and place the cup in a cabinet or room that is dark all the time.

4 Observe the beans every day until the roots have grown to about 5 cm. Keep the paper towels moist.

THINK AND WRITE

1. In which direction did the roots of each bean grow?

2. What might have caused the roots to respond in this way?

▶ Soybeans

Plant Responses

Plants respond to and are influenced by the environment in which they live. But why is it important that plants respond to their environment?

▲ Seedlings need sunlight.

▲ Sunlight stimulates growth.

Think about a seedling growing among towering trees in a forest. Filtered through spaces between leaves of the trees, sunlight falls in small patches on the ground. The survival of the seedling depends on many things, including its ability to photosynthesize. But how will the seedling, growing in a somewhat shady place, reach the sunlight?

In the first activity, you discovered that plants bend toward a source of light. You also saw that roots emerging from a seed grow down. Plants adjust their patterns of growth and development in response to environmental factors. What causes plants to respond in this way?

Every response of a plant to its environment requires a stimulus. A **stimulus** is anything in the environment that causes a response in a plant or other living thing.

An example of a stimulus for humans is sunlight causing blinking. If you've been indoors and you walk outside into the bright sunlight, what are you stimulated to do?

Light is an example of a plant stimulus. Light will stimulate a seedling in a forest to adjust its growth so that it bends toward the closest source of light. Without light, the seedling will not respond in the same way.

A plant's response to a stimulus in its environment is known as a **tropism** (TROH piz uhm). A tropism can be caused by light, gravity, water, or touch.

THINK ABOUT IT

What do you think will happen to a sapling that can't get enough light for photosynthesis?

Response Ability

In your last activity, you observed how bean seeds responded to gravity. Although the bean seeds were placed on their sides, you noticed that the roots still grew downward. This response by a plant to gravity is known as *geotropism*. Plants have many different tropisms. Here are some other examples.

▶ A plant's response to light is known as *phototropism*. The plant leans toward a source of light and its leaves turn in the direction of the light.

▼ A plant's response to a water stimulus is known as *hydrotropism*. The resurrection fern is an example. It looks brown and dead when it's dry, but it rebounds and becomes green once it rains.

◀ These vines also exhibit thigmotropism. They grow upward until they touch something. This stimulates them to coil around things, which gives them the appearance of climbing.

▲ A plant's response to touch is known as *thigmotropism*. When this mimosa plant is touched, its leaves fold and its branches droop.

THINK ABOUT IT

Plants have a tropism called *chemotropism*. What kind of tropism do you think it is? Use a dictionary to check your answer.

In Control

What causes plants to react to a stimulus? Let's take a look at the control mechanisms that operate within plants.

Tropisms are controlled by substances called *auxins*. **Auxins** are hormones, or controlling chemicals, that regulate the growth of plants. Plants of the Earth contain many auxins, but each auxin in a plant has a specific job to do.

Light may cause auxins to move from the lighted side of a stem to the side that is not in the light. This unequal distribution of auxins causes cells on the darker side of the stem to grow longer than cells on the side in the light. This uneven growth of cells causes the stem to bend. Whenever you see a plant that is bent toward a source of light, you see the work of auxins.

▼ Ox-eye daisy

Auxins also control flowering within a plant. At some times of the year, days have more daylight hours than at other times of the year. Auxins in flowering plants respond to the number of daylight hours in a day.

▼ Auxins respond to light.

▲ Chrysanthemums are short-day plants that bloom in the fall. *Short-day plants* flower only when the number of daylight hours is small.

◀ Petunias are long-day plants. *Long-day plants* flower only when the number of daylight hours is great.

▶ Marigolds are an example of day-neutral plants. *Day-neutral plants* do not respond to the length of daylight hours in the day. They can flower anytime.

Scientists have developed artificial auxins. These auxins are used to stimulate plant growth. Some artificial auxins cause such rapid growth, that they kill plants. These auxins are widely used to kill weeds.

THINK ABOUT IT

How might an understanding of controlling plant growth benefit you?

ACTIVITY

Blowing in the Wind

You have learned that plants respond to different factors in their environment. This activity will allow you to investigate how plants might respond to wind.

MATERIALS
- small potted tomato plants
- materials of your choice
- Science Log data sheet

DO THIS

1 With a small group of your classmates, design an experiment that determines how wind might affect the way tomato plants grow.

2 Record your design. Be sure to include a statement of the problem, the hypothesis and prediction of each group member, a list of materials that will be used, and the procedure that will be followed. Also, leave space to record your conclusion.

3 Begin the experiment after it has been approved by your teacher. At the end of the experiment, use the data you collected to make a graph that displays the growth rate of each plant you observed.

THINK AND WRITE

1. What variables did you have to control in your activity? Why?

2. What conclusions can you draw from your results?

3. **PREDICTING** A prediction is based on prior observations. You use your knowledge to help you interpret the information you've gained and then to project the outcome for a given situation. Explain how the data from your experiment agreed or disagreed with your predictions.

QUICK CHECK

LESSON 1 REVIEW

1 What might happen to plants during a short summer drought?

2 A potted geranium plant kept indoors will bloom all year long. What kind of flowering plant is it?

2 SURVIVAL

In order to survive, plants have adapted. This lesson examines some of those adaptations.

ACTIVITY

Field of Seeds

You may recall that plants cannot move from place to place. So how do they spread their seeds? In this activity, you will discover some ways that plants scatter their seeds.

DO THIS

1 **CAUTION: Do this activity only under adult supervision and never alone.** Wear the socks outside other clothing you are wearing, and walk through an overgrown field.

2 After walking for several minutes, return to the place where you first entered the field. Remove your socks and place them in the plastic bag.

3 Use a hand lens to examine the seeds that were collected by your socks.

MATERIALS
- old knee-high socks
- plastic bag
- hand lens
- Science Log data sheet

THINK AND WRITE

How might the structures of seeds help the plants that produce them?

Seeds on the Move

In the activity that you performed wearing knee-high socks, you had an opportunity to observe one way that seeds **disperse,** or scatter. They dispersed by clinging to your socks. Some seeds also disperse by clinging to the fur of animals. By doing this, they get a free ride to another location, where they can fall off or be bumped or brushed off and grow into new plants. You can see here some additional ways that plants spread their seeds.

▲ A coconut from a coconut tree growing near the ocean can fall into the ocean and float for thousands of kilometers to another place, where it might grow into a new tree.

▶ The seeds of many fruits have a thick, tough covering that is not damaged by the intestines of animals that eat them. The seeds pass through undigested and are deposited along with the animals' wastes.

▲ Maple seeds have structures that look and act like wings. When the seeds are released from a tree, they resemble miniature helicopters as they "fly" through the air.

▲ Dandelion seeds are feathery light. A slight breeze can disperse them. The lawn full of dandelions shows that dandelion seeds have been easily dispersed.

◀ Cocklebur

THINK ABOUT IT

Look around at the plants where you live. Describe some examples of seed dispersal that you find.

ACTIVITY

Leaving Home

Once seeds are dispersed, conditions must be right for them to germinate. But sometimes certain conditions are necessary for seed dispersal. In the following activity, observe how some gymnosperms disperse their seeds.

MATERIALS
- pine cone
- zip-type plastic bag
- measuring spoon
- water
- Science Log data sheet

DO THIS

1 Place an opened pine cone in the plastic bag. Add about a teaspoon of water, and zip the bag shut.

2 After a few hours, take the pine cone out of the bag, and observe what has happened to it. Record your observations.

3 Leave the pine cone out of the bag. After a few hours, observe the pine cone again. Record your observations.

THINK AND WRITE

1. What do the results of your experiment tell you about the weather conditions that favor pine seed dispersal?

2. How do you think the pine cone's means of seed dispersal contributes to the survival of the pine tree?

Surviving Harsh Climates

In what ways do people adapt their ways of living to their surrounding environment? Think of a desert, for example. If you have always lived in a place where water is plentiful, desert dwelling might seem difficult to you. But people who live in very dry areas have adapted their lifestyle to conform to the environmental demands of the region.

▼ Cholla cactus

Plants are no different. In the pine cone activity, you discovered that a pine tree favors certain weather conditions. Pines have effectively adapted ways to release their seeds when conditions are favorable for their dispersal and germination.

There's a problem if plants are unable to adapt in some way to environmental changes and unfavorable conditions. If they fail to reproduce themselves, they might become extinct. So plants have adapted in many ways to survive.

Many fruits are covered by a thick, waxy covering. This covering is waterproof and helps prevent the seeds inside from drying out.

▶ The leaves and stems of some plants are covered by a waxy coating. This coating helps prevent water inside the plant from evaporating.

THINK ABOUT IT

What kinds of fruit have thick, waxy coverings?

A Real Survivor

Plants have ways of coping with a lack of water. This is especially important during dry conditions, a time when plants have to conserve what little water they can find. You can learn more about desert plant adaptations by reading the following selection.

DESERT PLANTS: Secrets of Survival

by **Eileen Ross** from *Children's Playmate*

 Did you ever put a leafy green plant in a sunny window, then forget to water it? Too much heat and too little water will cause most plants to die. But what about desert plants? How do they survive in the scorching heat with so little water? Let's see if we can discover some of their special survival secrets.

All plants contain water. Most plants lose some of this water through tiny openings in their leaves. Many types of cactus have sharp prickly needles instead of leaves. The needles don't let much water escape into the hot, dry desert air.

One interesting type of desert cactus is the spiny ***cholla*** (pronounced CHOL-yah). This plant has clusters of prickly joints that seem to jump out at you and stick to your shoes and clothing. These sharp needles hurt, but they are there for a reason. They protect the spiny cholla from hot desert winds. If the winds can't reach the surface of the plant, then water doesn't evaporate into the air.

▼ **Life in the desert**

▼ **Saguaro**

▲ **Palo verde tree**

▶ **Palo verde tree in bloom**

Not every desert plant has sharp needles. Some desert plants do have leaves. A waxy coating on the leaves helps prevent water loss. Plants with leaves have another secret.

To survive in the desert, they shed their leaves during the long dry season.

Without leaves, most plants could not survive, because leaves contain *chlorophyll*, the green substance plants use to make food. But desert plants such as the palo verde tree and the *ocotillo* (pronounced oh-koh-TEE-oh) bush don't need leaves to make food. They store chlorophyll in their greenish colored bark. Many cactus plants are green for this same reason.

Color provides another important clue to plant survival in the desert. Light color reflects sunlight and dark colors absorb it. So most desert plants are light in color. Plants that blend in with the light-colored desert stay cool by reflecting sunlight.

To survive long dry spells, desert plants absorb and store moisture. Many of them store water in long roots that travel deep into the ground in search of moisture.

But the *saguaro* (pronounced sa-WHAR-o) cactus has the special ability to store water in its thick trunk. After a heavy rainstorm, the trunk of the saguaro swells as it stores tons of water. As the water is gradually used up, the saguaro's trunk begins to shrink. By noticing whether the trunk is swollen or shrunken, you might be able to guess how long it's been since the saguaro cactus had a drink of water!

◀ **Plants along an arroyo**

▲ **Ephemerals in bloom**

▼ **Shrunken saguaros**

▲ **Canyon environment**

Other desert plants with an unusual secret for survival are called *ephemerals.* Ephemeral means "living for a brief time," and that's exactly what these plants do! For most of the year, ephemerals live as tiny seeds. When heavy rains finally come, these little seeds sprout quickly, grow, and blossom. At this time of year, the desert is a glorious garden of wildflowers.

After only a few weeks, the flowers die and the seeds again lie hidden in the desert soil, waiting for another heavy rain. They will sprout a year or more later, and the cycle is repeated.

Sometimes, the location in which desert plants grow provides a clue to their survival. Many desert plants grow along the edges of dry stream beds called *arroyos* (pronounced a-ROY-os). That way they will be close to water when flash floods occur. Some desert plants grow in rock canyons where steep canyon walls provide shade. But one thing is certain. All desert plants have found ways of adapting to hot, dry surroundings. Plants that live and thrive in the desert have learned a special secret . . . the secret of survival!

THINK ABOUT IT

Do you think an apple tree could survive in the desert? Explain.

The Big Chill

The tundra is a cold, dry environment almost all year long. Trees cannot grow there, but other plants do. Most of the plants grow low to the ground so that they are protected from the wind.

The cold winters of some environments present another challenge to plants. As winter approaches, they prepare for the cold and survive until spring.

Plants all over the Earth are able to survive harsh temperatures and many other unfavorable conditions surprisingly well. But it's difficult for them to survive without water. Very few things threaten plants as much as a shortage of water.

THINK ABOUT IT

How do some plants protect themselves against cold and loss of water?

▶ Trees and bushes become dormant and develop thick bud scales on their stems where the leaves grow. This protects the meristem in even the coldest weather. When spring arrives, the scales peel off and new leaves and flowers grow.

▲ In the tundra, the growing season is very short. Because of this, plants there grow to maturity and produce seeds very quickly. Everything happens in a hurry because there is little time.

ACTIVITY

Too Much of a Good Thing

You have learned that one of the biggest needs of plants is water. Without enough water, plants can't survive. But can plants get too much water? How much is too much? You can get an idea by doing this activity.

MATERIALS
- marker
- 2 small potted plants
- 2 drainage pans
- plastic container
- water
- newspaper
- pencil
- hand lens
- Science Log data sheet

DO THIS

1. Use the marker to label one pot A and the other B. Place both plants inside the drainage pans, and put them in a well-lighted area.

2. Every day for ten days, pour a full container of water into the pot holding plant B. Water plant A as needed.

3. At the end of ten days, cover a table with newspaper and remove the plants from their pots. Carefully spread the roots using a pencil point.

4. Use a hand lens to examine the roots. Record your observations.

THINK AND WRITE

1. What happened to the roots of the overwatered plant? Why do you think this happened?

2. Based on your observations, what effect do you think a flood might have on plants?

Life in the Water

Desert plants have adapted to live in an environment where water is scarce. Other plants have had to adapt to environments that have abundant water. Read and discover how some plants do this.

◄ The roots and stems of water lilies grow in water or mud that has little or no air. To survive, the plant's stems have large, open spaces that fill with air. The oxygen the roots need moves from these spaces to the roots. The stomata of a water lily are mostly in the top of the leaves at the water's surface. There the plant gets the carbon dioxide it needs.

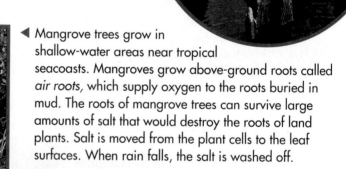

▶ Bald cypress trees grow in freshwater swamps in the southern United States. The trees get oxygen to their roots through structures called *knees*. The knees grow above water, and from them oxygen is transported to the roots.

◄ Mangrove trees grow in shallow-water areas near tropical seacoasts. Mangroves grow above-ground roots called *air roots*, which supply oxygen to the roots buried in mud. The roots of mangrove trees can survive large amounts of salt that would destroy the roots of land plants. Salt is moved from the plant cells to the leaf surfaces. When rain falls, the salt is washed off.

▶ The water milfoil has below-water leaves that absorb carbon dioxide from the water. Its above-water leaves are like those of land plants.

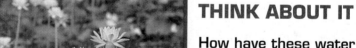

THINK ABOUT IT

How have these water plants adapted to life in the water?

Meat-Eating Plants

Besides adapting to climate, a few plants have developed unusual ways to satisfy their needs. Some plants live in areas in which the soil does not supply all of the minerals the plants need. How do these plants get the nutrients they need? You can find the answer to this question in this activity.

With several of your classmates, select one of the carnivorous, or meat-eating, plants shown here. Use reference materials to research the characteristics of both the plant and its natural habitat.

Write a short, imaginative story about the plant. In your story, try to include facts about the plant that you learned in your research. Then share your story with your classmates.

▼ Pitcher plant

◀ Venus' flytrap

▼ Sundew

▶ Bladderwort

Tasteless Herbage

Just as animals have different ways of protecting themselves from predators, plants have ways of protecting themselves. Some plants produce and use chemicals to protect themselves against attacks by animals and other plants.

Grazing animals, such as cows, are a serious threat to plants. The animals may eat so much of a plant that it dies. To prevent this, some plants, such as milkweed, produce chemicals that taste terrible. Because of milkweeds' bad taste, grazing animals soon learn that there are better things to eat for lunch than milkweed plants.

Other plants produce and use chemicals in a different way. If you're allergic to poison ivy, you've already encountered this plant adaptation. Plants such as poison ivy, poison oak, and poison sumac contain chemicals that can irritate the skin of people and animals. It doesn't take long for animals or people to learn that it's better to stay away from these plants!

One of the most common ways that plants protect themselves from animals is by growing sharp thorns. The stems of roses

▼ **Butterfly milkweed**

▲ **Poison ivy**

▲ **Poison oak**

▲ **Poison sumac**

▼ **Roses with thorns**

◀ **Stinging nettle**

▶ **Pincushion cactus**

and cactuses, for example, have thorns. Although plants with thorns may look appealing, animals quickly learn that poking around thorny plants can be painful.

Some plants make sure that at least some seeds survive by varying the number of seeds they produce. The oak tree is a good example. In some years, the oak tree produces large numbers of acorns. There are so many acorns that squirrels and other animals can't eat them all. In other years, it produces very few acorns. There are not enough acorns for animals to rely on them as their main source of food. The animals have to find other sources of food. As the animals begin to rely on other food sources, the oak again produces large numbers of seeds. In this way, it makes sure that at least some acorns survive to become oak trees.

Some kinds of plants need to protect themselves from other plants. For example, black walnut trees have a hard time growing with other plants near them. So, as a means of survival, black walnut trees release a chemical from their roots that prevents other plants from growing in the area.

THINK ABOUT IT

Many unripe fruits taste bitter. How do you think this bitter taste helps protect the growing seed inside the fruit? How might the bitter taste affect seed dispersal?

◀ **Common oak**

F87

Shirley Mah Kooyman:
Plant Scientist at Work

Much of what we know about plants is because of the work of plant scientists. How important is the work of plant scientists? What are some facts they have discovered about plants that can benefit you? Come meet a real-life plant scientist. Learn how some discoveries about plants can benefit you.

If you visit the Minnesota Landscape Arboretum at the University of Minnesota in Chanhassen, Minnesota, you might meet Dr. Shirley Mah Kooyman. An *arboretum* is a place where plants and trees are grown for study. Kooyman is a *botanist.* A botanist is a scientist who studies plants.

Kooyman also studies trees and plants at the arboretum. Kooyman feels that understanding plants is important. "We take plants for granted," says Kooyman. "Because we don't see movement as with animals and humans, we don't think of plants as living, breathing things. They grow just like all living organisms, getting their energy from light, water, and hormones."

Understanding how these processes enable plants to grow can be beneficial to people. For example, when weather and climate conditions change, plants either adapt or die. Knowing how plants grow and respond to these kinds of changes can help us grow healthier plants. Since we rely on plants for food, healthier plants would help us ensure the survivability of our own food supply.

One of the ways botanists can make plants healthier is by using hormones. Hormones are chemical messengers that tell a plant to produce chemicals that stimulate plant growth. Botanists such as Kooyman have discovered that artificial hormones can encourage a plant to grow. Using hormones on plants is necessary, says Kooyman, "because we're into production and we need to feed more people." In addition to creating bigger and

▲ Picking beans in the arboretum.

better plants, artificial hormones can prevent fruit from prematurely dropping off the tree and can enhance the growth of root crops, such as potatoes and carrots. How might this benefit farmers and you?

"I like working with plants," adds Kooyman. "I like seeing them grow, and I like their pretty colors. I even like trees whose flowers are not quite as pretty. The fact that here you have tiny little things that can grow and produce more seeds and the seeds can produce more plants—that's kind of a fun thing—seeing things grow."

Kooyman's career as a botanist required a college education. After getting a bachelor's degree in botany, most botanists can find jobs in private industry, working for plant nurseries or seed companies. There are also job opportunities in federal, state, and local governments. Some botanists teach in schools, colleges, and universities.

▲ Dr. Kooyman

LESSON 2 REVIEW

❶ Although water covers much of the Earth, the amount of drinkable water is becoming a scarce resource in some areas. How might this affect future generations of plants?

❷ How do plants protect the seeds they disperse?

DOUBLE CHECK

SECTION D REVIEW

1. Describe kinds of tropisms that plants exhibit. What factors control these tropisms?

2. How do a plant's responses to its environment contribute to its survival and to the survival of future generations of plants?

3. How can the study of plant adaptations benefit life for human beings and animals?

REFLECT

It's time to think about the ideas you have discovered during your investigations. Think, too, about your many accomplishments.

SUMMARIZE

Answer the following in your Science Log.

1. What **I Wonder** questions have you answered in your investigations, and what new questions have you asked?

2. What have you discovered about seeds and plants, and how have your ideas changed?

3. Did any of your discoveries surprise you? Explain.

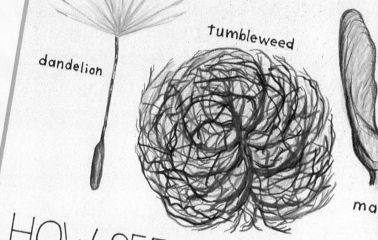

dandelion

tumbleweed

ma

HOW SEEDS ARE SPRE

1. Seeds blow in the wind.
2. Burrs stick to animals' fur a people's clothing.
3. Berry seeds may be spread when animals eat the berrie
4. Squirrels and other small animals may pick up acorns and bury them.

aple

EAD

and

d

es.

CONNECT IDEAS

1. Describe how leaves, stems, and roots benefit plants.

2. Explain how the survival of plants is important to the survival of animals.

3. Identify the plants around your neighborhood as gymnosperms or angiosperms.

4. Describe how plants around your home are responding to the environment.

5. Look around your school. Find examples of plants surviving under unfavorable conditions.

SCIENCE PORTFOLIO

1. Complete your Science Experiences Record.

2. Choose several samples of your best work from each section to include in your Science Portfolio.

3. On A Guide to My Science Portfolio, tell why you chose each sample.

I SHARE

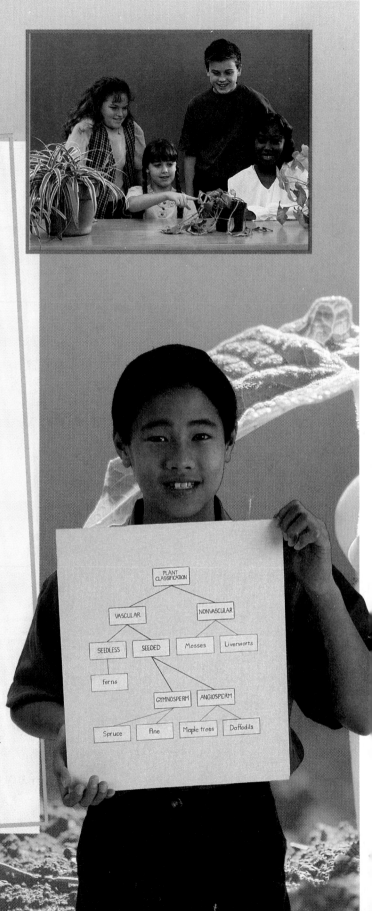

Scientists share their discoveries and ideas and learn from one another. How can you share what you've learned?

Decide

▶ what you want to say.

▶ what the best way is to get your message across.

Share

▶ what you did and why.

▶ what worked and what didn't work.

▶ what conclusions you have drawn.

▶ what else you'd like to find out.

Find Out

▶ what classmates liked about what you shared—and why.

▶ what questions your classmates have.

I ACT

Science is more than discoveries—it is also what you do with those discoveries. How might you use what you have learned about seeds and plants?

▶ Draw up a plan for planting a flower box or an area around your home; or with your classmates, make a plan for planting flowers in your schoolyard.

▶ Grow plants from cuttings of a plant in your home. Give the new plants to friends or relatives.

▶ In the spring, get involved with volunteers from your community by helping to plant trees on Earth Day.

THE LANGUAGE OF SCIENCE

The language of science helps people communicate clearly when they talk about nature. Here are some vocabulary words you can use when you talk about plants and seeds with your friends, family, and others.

angiosperms—vascular plants that produce flowers and have a protective covering around their seeds. Apple trees, pear trees, and maple trees are examples of angiosperms. **(F38)**

chlorophyll—a pigment that traps energy from the sun and changes it into energy that can be used by plants to make food. Chlorophyll gives plants their green color. **(F21)**

chloroplast—a structure in which chlorophyll is found and in which photosynthesis takes place. **(F21)**

cotyledons—the first leaves of an emerging seedling. **(F55)**

embryo—a tiny young plant within a seed. **(F55)**

epidermis—the protective layer of a leaf. It helps prevent water loss. **(F18)**

fertilization—the process by which pollen reaches ovules inside a flower's ovary. **(F47)**

germinate—to sprout. **(F55)**

gymnosperms—vascular plants that do not produce flowers and lack a protective covering around their seeds. Conifers, such as pine, spruce, and cypress, are examples of gymnosperms. **(F38)**

Pine cone

heterozygous—having two different factors for a characteristic. **(F64)**

homozygous—having two identical factors for a characteristic. **(F64)**

meristem—new plant cells that grow at the root tips and buds of plants. **(F34)**

nonvascular plants—plants without xylem and phloem tissues. Mosses are nonvascular plants. **(F38)**

petals—leaflike structures of a flower that display interesting shapes and beautiful colors. **(F46)**

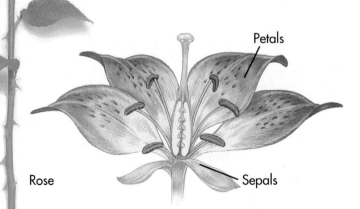

Rose

Petals

Sepals

phloem—tubelike structures through which materials manufactured in the leaves of a plant move throughout the plant. **(F29)**

photosynthesis—the process by which plants, using chlorophyll, capture energy from sunlight and combine it with water, minerals, and carbon dioxide to make their own food. **(F21)**

CO_2
Carbon dioxide

Light

Chlorophyll

Glucose (sugar)
$C_6H_{12}O_6$

H_2O
Water

Minerals

O_2
Oxygen

pollination—the spreading of pollen to female reproductive organs in a flower. Insects such as bees help pollinate plants. **(F47)**

root—a plant part that grows in the ground, where it anchors the plant and takes up water and nutrients from the soil. There are two kinds of roots: a *fibrous root* is slender and grows with others in a small area; a *taproot* is a single, thick root. **(F34)**

Fibrous roots (left), taproot (right)

Corn kernel

seed coat—the covering that protects the embryo in a seed. **(F55)**

seedless vascular plants—vascular plants that do not reproduce by making seeds, but instead produce spores. **(F41)**

sepals—leaflike structures that cover and protect a flower before it blooms. **(F46)**

stem—a plant's main body or stalk that rises from the ground. *Herbaceous* stems are green, flexible stems. *Woody* stems are stiffer stems that contain wood cells. Dandelions have herbaceous stems, and trees have woody stems. **(F28)**

stimulus—anything in the environment that causes a response in a plant or other living thing. **(F70)**

stomata—openings in the epidermis of a leaf, through which materials enter and exit. **(F18)**

traits—characteristics inherited from parents. Traits can be *dominant,* visible in an offspring, or *recessive,* hidden. **(F63)**

tropism—a plant's response to a stimulus in its environment. Some examples are *phototropism,* a plant's response to a source of light; *geotropism,* a plant's response to gravity; *hydrotropism,* a plant's response to water; and *thigmotropism,* a plant's response to touch. **(F70)**

Tropisms

Maple tree

vascular plants—plants with xylem and phloem tissues. Marigolds, oak trees, maple trees, and other flowering plants are examples of vascular plants. **(F38)**

vegetative reproduction—a way of producing offspring that are identical to a parent plant. Removing a cutting from a plant is one example of vegetative reproduction. **(F59)**

xylem—tubelike structures through which materials move from the roots of a plant to the leaves. **(F29)**

REFERENCE HANDBOOK

Safety in the Classroom

Doing activities in science can be fun, but you need to be sure you do them safely. It is up to you, your teacher, and your classmates to make your classroom a safe place for science activities.

Think about what causes most accidents in everyday life—being careless, not paying attention, and showing off. The same kinds of behavior cause accidents in the science classroom.

Here are some ways to make your classroom a safe place.

WATCH YOUR EYES.

Wear safety goggles anytime you are directed to do so. If you should ever get any substance in your eyes, tell your teacher right away.

THINK AHEAD.

Study the steps of the activity so you know what to expect. If you have any questions about the steps, ask your teacher to explain. Be sure you understand any safety symbols that are shown in the activity.

BE NEAT.

Keep your work area clean. If you have long hair, pull it back so it doesn't get in the way. If you have long sleeves, roll them or push them up to keep them away from your experiment.

YUCK!

Never eat or drink anything during a science activity unless you are told to do so by your teacher.

OOPS!

If you should have an accident that causes a spill or breaks something, or if you get cut, tell your teacher right away.

DON'T GET SHOCKED.

Sometimes you need to use electric appliances, such as lamps, in an activity. You always need to be careful around electricity. Be sure that electric cords are in a safe place where you can't trip over them. Don't ever pull a plug out of an outlet by pulling on the cord.

KEEP IT CLEAN.

Always clean up when you have finished your activity. Put everything away and wipe your work area. Last of all, wash your hands.

Safety Symbols

In some activities, you will see a symbol that stands for what
you need to do to stay safe. Do what the symbol stands for.

 This is a general symbol that tells you to be careful.
Reading the steps of the activity will tell you exactly what
you need to do to be safe.

 You will need to protect your eyes if you see this symbol.
Put on safety goggles and leave them on for the entire
activity.

This symbol tells you that you will be using something
sharp in the activity. Be careful not to cut or poke yourself
or others.

 This symbol tells you something hot will be used in the
activity. Be careful not to get burned or to cause someone
else to get burned.

 This symbol tells you to put on an apron to protect
your clothing.

 Don't touch! This symbol tells you that you will need to
touch something that is hot. Use a thermal mitt to protect
your hand.

 This symbol tells you that you will be using electric
equipment. Use proper safety procedures.

Using a Hand Lens

A hand lens magnifies objects, or makes them look larger than they are.

▲ **This object is not in focus.**

Sometimes objects are too small for you to see easily without some help. You might want to see details that you cannot see with your eyes alone. When this happens, you can use a hand lens.

To use a hand lens, first place the object you want to look at on a flat surface, such as a table. Next, hold the hand lens over the object. At first, the object may appear blurry, like the object in **A**. Move the hand lens toward or away from the object until the object comes into sharp focus, as shown in **B**.

▲ **This object is focused clearly.**

Making a Water-Drop Lens

There may be times when you want to use a hand lens but there isn't one around. If that happens, you can make a water-drop lens to help you in the same way a hand lens does. A water-drop lens is best used to make flat objects, such as pieces of paper and leaves, seem larger.

MATERIALS
- sheet of acetate
- 2 rectangular rubber erasers
- water
- dropper

DO THIS

1 Place the object to be magnified on a table between two identical erasers.

2 Place a sheet of acetate on top of the erasers so that the sheet of acetate is about 1 cm above the object.

3 Use the dropper to place one drop of water on the surface of the sheet over the object. Don't make the drop too large or it will make things look bent.

▶ **A water-drop lens can magnify objects.**

Caring For and Using a Microscope

A microscope, like a hand lens, magnifies objects. However, a microscope can increase the detail you see by increasing the number of times an object is magnified.

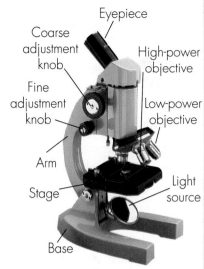

▲ **Light microscope**

CARING FOR A MICROSCOPE

* Always use two hands when you carry a microscope.
* Never touch any of the lenses of the microscope with your fingers.

USING A MICROSCOPE

1 Raise the eyepiece as far as you can using the coarse-adjustment knob. Place the slide you wish to view on the stage.

2 Always start by using the lowest power. The lowest-power lens is usually the shortest. Start with the lens in the lowest position it can go without touching the slide.

3 Look through the eyepiece and begin adjusting the eyepiece upward with the coarse-adjustment knob. When the slide is close to being in focus, use the fine-adjustment knob.

4 When you want to use the higher-power lens, first focus the slide under low power. Then, watching carefully to make sure that the lens will not hit the slide, turn the higher-power lens into place. Use only the fine-adjustment knob when looking through the higher-power lens.

Some of you may use a Brock microscope. This is a sturdy microscope that has only one lens.

1 Place the object to be viewed on the stage. Move the long tube, containing the lens, close to the stage.

2 Put your eye on the eyepiece, and begin raising the tube until the object comes into focus.

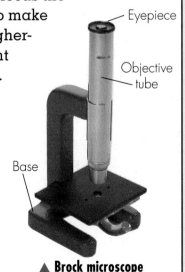

▲ **Brock microscope**

Using a Dropper

Use a dropper when you need to add small amounts of a liquid to another material.

A dropper has two main parts. One is a large empty part called a *bulb*. You hold the bulb and squeeze it to use the dropper. The other part of a dropper is long and narrow and is called a *tube*.

Droppers measure liquids one drop at a time. You might need to figure out how much liquid is in one drop. To do that, you can count the number of drops in 1 mL and divide. For example, if there are about 10 drops in 1 mL, you know that each drop is equal to about 0.1 mL. Follow the directions below to measure a liquid by using a dropper.

DO THIS

1 Use a clean dropper for each liquid you measure.

2 With the dropper out of the liquid, squeeze the bulb and keep it squeezed. Then dip the end of the tube into the liquid.

3 Release the pressure on the bulb. As you do so, you will see the liquid enter the tube.

▲ **Using a dropper correctly**

4 Take the dropper from the liquid, and move it to the place you want to put the liquid. If you are putting the liquid into another liquid, do not let the dropper touch the surface of the second liquid.

5 Gently squeeze the bulb until one drop comes out of the tube. Repeat slowly until you have measured out the right number of drops.

▲ **Using a dropper incorrectly**

Measuring Liquids

Use a beaker, a measuring cup, or a graduated cylinder to measure liquids accurately.

Containers for measuring liquids are made of clear or translucent materials so that you can see the liquid inside them. On the outside of each of these measuring tools, you will see lines and numbers that make up a scale. On most of the containers used by scientists, the scale is in milliliters (mL).

DO THIS

1 Pour the liquid you want to measure into one of the measuring containers. Make sure your measuring container is on a flat, stable surface, with the measuring scale facing you.

2 Look at the liquid through the container. Move so that your eyes are even with the surface of the liquid in the container.

3 To read the volume of the liquid, find the scale line that is even with the top of the liquid. In narrow containers, the surface of the liquid may look curved. Take your reading at the lowest point of the curve.

4 Sometimes the surface of the liquid may not be exactly even with a line. In that case, you will need to estimate the volume of the liquid. Decide which line the liquid is closer to, and use that number.

▲ There are 32 mL of liquid in this graduated cylinder.

▲ There are 27 mL of liquid in this beaker.

Using a Thermometer

Determine temperature readings of the air and most liquids by using a thermometer with a standard scale.

Most thermometers are thin tubes of glass that are filled with a red or silver liquid. As the temperature goes up, the liquid in the tube rises. As the temperature goes down, the liquid sinks. The tube is marked with lines and numbers that provide a temperature scale in degrees. Scientists use the Celsius scale to measure temperature. A temperature reading of 27 degrees Celsius is written 27°C.

DO THIS

❶ Place the thermometer in the liquid whose temperature you want to record, but don't rest the bulb of the thermometer on the bottom or side of the container. If you are measuring the temperature of the air, make sure that the thermometer is not in direct sunlight or in line with a direct light source.

❷ Move so that your eyes are even with the liquid in the thermometer.

❸ If you are measuring a material that is not being heated or cooled, wait about two minutes for the reading to become stable. Find the scale line that meets the top of the liquid in the thermometer, and read the temperature.

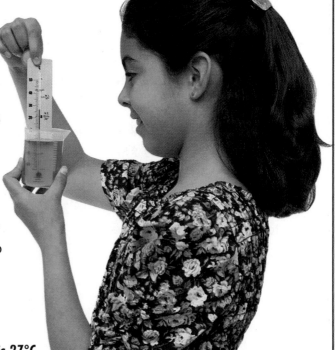

❹ If the material you are measuring is being heated or cooled, you will not be able to wait before taking your measurements. Measure as quickly as you can.

▶ **The temperature of this liquid is 27°C.**

Making a Thermometer

If you don't have a thermometer, you can make a simple one easily. The simple thermometer won't give you an exact temperature reading, but you can use it to tell if the temperature is going up or going down.

DO THIS

❶ Add colored water to the jar until it is nearly full.

❷ Place the straw in the jar. Finish filling the jar with water, but leave about 1 cm of space at the top.

❸ Lift the straw until 10 cm of it stick up out of the jar. Use the clay to seal the mouth of the jar.

❹ Use the dropper to add colored water to the straw until the straw is at least half full.

❺ On the straw, mark the level of the water. "S" stands for *start*.

❻ To get an idea of how your thermometer works, place the jar in a bowl of ice. Wait several minutes, and then mark the new water level on the straw. This new water level should be marked C for *cold*.

❼ Take the jar out of the bowl of ice, and let it return to room temperature. Next, place the jar in a bowl of warm water. Wait several minutes, and then mark the new water level on the straw. This level can be labeled W for *warm*.

—W

—S

—C

▶ You can use a thermometer like this to decide if the temperature of a liquid or the air is going up or down.

Using a Balance

Use a balance to measure an object's mass. Mass is the amount of matter an object has.

Most balances look like the one shown. They have two pans. In one pan, you place the object you want to measure. In the other pan, you place standard masses. Standard masses are objects that have a known mass. Grams are the units used to measure mass for most scientific activities.

DO THIS

1 First, make certain the empty pans are balanced. They are in balance if the pointer is at the middle mark on the base. If the pointer is not at this mark, move the slider to the right or left. Your teacher will help if you cannot balance the pans.

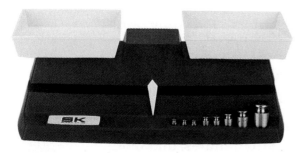

◀ **These pans are balanced and ready to be used to find the mass of an object.**

2 Place the object you wish to measure in one pan. The pointer will move toward the pan without the object in it.

3 Add the standard masses to the other pan. As you add masses, you should see the pointer begin to move. When the pointer is at the middle mark again, the pans are balanced.

4 Add the numbers on the masses you used. The total is the mass of the object you measured.

▶ **These pans are unbalanced.**

Making a Balance

If you do not have a balance, you can make one. A balance requires only a few simple materials. You can use nonstandard masses such as paper clips or nickels. This type of balance is best for measuring small masses.

DO THIS

1. If the ruler has holes in it, tie the string through the center hole. If it does not have holes, tie the string around the middle of the ruler.

2. Tape the other end of the string to a table. Allow the ruler to hang down from the side of the table. Adjust the ruler so that it is level.

3. Unbend the end of each paper clip slightly. Push these ends through the paper cups as shown. Attach each cup to the ruler by using the paper clips.

4. Adjust the cups until the ruler is level again.

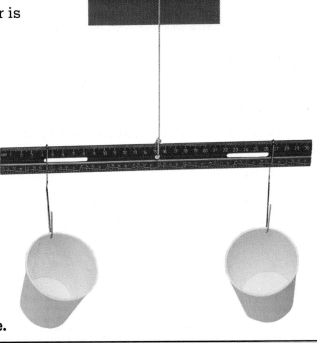

▶ This balance is ready for use.

Using a Spring Scale

A spring scale is a tool you use to measure the force of gravity on objects. You find the weight of the objects and use newtons as the unit of measurement for the force of gravity. You also use the spring scale and newtons to measure other forces.

A spring scale has two main parts. One part is a spring with a hook on the end. The hook is used to connect an object to the spring scale. The other part is a scale with numbers that tell you how many newtons of force are acting on the object.

DO THIS

With an Object at Rest

1 With the object resting on the table, hook the spring scale to it. Do not stretch the spring at this point.

2 Lift the scale and object with a smooth motion. Do not jerk them upward.

3 Wait until any motion in the spring comes to a stop. Then read the number of newtons from the scale.

With an Object in Motion

1 With the object resting on the table, hook the spring scale to it. Do not stretch the spring.

2 Pull the object smoothly across the table. Do not jerk the object. If you pull with a jerky motion, the spring scale will wiggle too much for you to get a good reading.

3 As you are pulling, read the number of newtons you are using to pull the object.

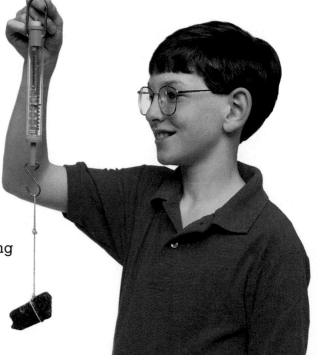

Making a Spring Scale

If you do not have a spring scale, you can make one by following the directions below.

DO THIS

1 Staple one end of the rubber band (the part with the sharp curve) to the middle of one end of the cardboard so that the rubber band hangs down the length of the cardboard. Color the loose end of the rubber band with a marker to make it easy to see.

2 Bend the paper clip so that it is slightly open and forms a hook. Hang the paper clip by its unopened end from the rubber band.

3 Put the narrow paper strip across the rubber band, and staple the strip to the cardboard. The rubber band and hook must be able to move easily.

4 While holding the cardboard upright, hang one 100-g mass from the hook. Allow the mass to come to rest, and mark the position of the bottom of the rubber band on the cardboard. Label this position on the cardboard 1 N. Add another 100-g mass for a total of 200 g.

5 Continue to add masses and mark the cardboard. Each 100-g mass adds a force of about 1 N.

MATERIALS
- heavy cardboard (10cm x 30cm)
- large rubber band
- stapler
- marker
- large paper clip
- paper strip (about 1 cm x 3 cm)
- 100-g masses (about 1 N each)

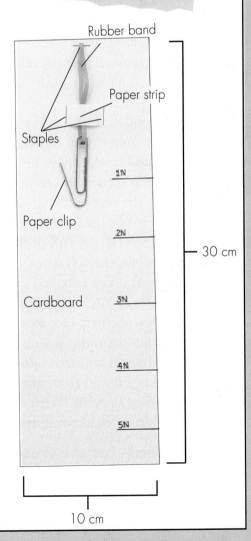

R13

Working Like a Scientist
How Does Your Garden Grow?

The first step in any scientific investigation is *asking a question.* You may think that asking a question is easy. Most of the time it is. But sometimes you have to ask a lot of questions before you get to the one that you really want to have answered. The process of asking a question starts when you use what you already know to evaluate a situation. After you have thought about what you already know, you can begin to ask about what you do not know.

Alexia had some questions about her garden. She was weeding the garden one day when she noticed that one corner of the garden seemed empty. Alexia had tried planting all sorts of things in that corner, but nothing seemed to grow. Still, she wanted to make that corner of her garden as beautiful as the rest.

Alexia wondered, "Why don't things grow there?" She examined the soil. It seemed harder than the soil in the rest of the garden. It was a little higher than the rest of the garden. Water didn't soak into the ground—it simply ran off into the rest of the garden. As a result, the soil received very little water. And it was baked by the sun all the time. The soil in this part of the garden seemed a lot more closely packed than the soil elsewhere. Perhaps it was that tightness that prevented things from growing.

Alexia asked herself, "What can I do to make the soil in this part of the garden more like the rest of the soil?"

Alexia used what she already knew about the garden and the soil to ask a question. She asked several questions before she got to one that stumped her. Now she had to figure out an answer.

DO THIS

Ask a question.
Form a hypothesis.
Design a test. Do the test.
Record what happened.
Draw a conclusion.

Alexia had asked a question. Now she had to think of some possible answers. When you have thought of a possible answer, you may be able to test it. An answer that can be tested is called a *hypothesis.* A hypothesis is more than a guess, because it is based on all your previous knowledge and understanding of a situation. One test will not prove a hypothesis. But one test may be enough to show that your hypothesis is incorrect.

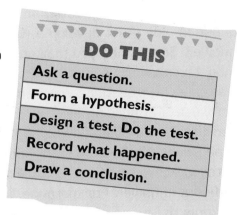

DO THIS

Ask a question.
Form a hypothesis.
Design a test. Do the test.
Record what happened.
Draw a conclusion.

The other important thing about a hypothesis is that an incorrect one is as useful as a correct one, and sometimes more useful. An incorrect hypothesis does not mean that you have failed, but that you have eliminated one possibility. You can begin to look in a new direction for other answers.

Sometimes you may do several tests before you discover that your hypothesis is incorrect. This can be frustrating, but you are still moving forward. Remember, a hypothesis that has been disproved can help show the direction to the right answer.

Alexia just stood in her garden for a while, thinking about her problem and observing. The soil where nothing grew seemed a little paler and dustier but otherwise the same as all the other soil. She turned the soil over. It was dark brown and very heavy, much heavier than the soil in the rest of the garden.

As she thought about it, she had the idea that maybe there was more clay in this part of the garden than in other parts. If that were the case, what might be a solution to the problem? Alexia thought that if she added something to the soil to make it lighter, then plants would be able to grow. This was Alexia's hypothesis.

After you have suggested an answer to your question, you must develop a way to test that answer. Sometimes you may choose to build a model to answer your question. Building models was one way questions were answered in the early years of building aircraft. Sometimes you can't make a model and you can't really do an experiment. Then you might choose to record detailed observations of natural occurrences to find an answer. For instance, if you wanted to know the types of fossils in different layers of rocks, you would collect the rocks and make detailed observations. But the approach to solving problems in science that most people are aware of is experimenting. An *experiment* is a planned test under controlled conditions. An experiment should test the solution you have proposed. The experiment should be repeatable by other people who study similar things.

An experiment must be carefully planned. You change only one variable at a time. Suppose Alexia wanted to test the effect of watering the soil more. She might add different amounts of water to different samples of soil. But the samples should otherwise be as nearly the same as possible—for example, in the materials they contain.

DO THIS

| Ask a question. |
| Form a hypothesis. |
| Design a test. Do the test. |
| Record what happened. |
| Draw a conclusion. |

In addition, an experiment often includes a control. A *control* is a sample that you do not treat in any unusual way. The control serves as a standard for comparison. For example, if Alexia chose to test the effects of different amounts of water, her control would be a soil sample receiving the amount of water that is usual for her garden. Then, if Alexia discovered that plants grew just as well in the control as in the other samples, she would know that watering was not an important factor.

Adding something to loosen the soil is the answer that Alexia chose for her hypothesis. She wanted to develop a way to test it.

She went into the garage and looked at her gardening supplies. She had potting soil, some sand, some fertilizer, and some vermiculite, a material that has highly water-absorbent particles in it. At one time or another, she had added all of these things to the soil of her garden. Maybe some of these things would make the soil looser. How could she find out?

Alexia knew that water flowed through looser soil more swiftly. She could test her soils by seeing how long it took for water to flow through them.

After she had gotten her parents' permission, she designed her experiment. She needed to dry out five equal-sized samples of the soil from the part of the garden where nothing grew. She would do nothing to one of the samples. To each of the other samples, she would add one of the things she had found in the garage.

When she had done that, she found some wide plastic tubes. She placed each of her soils into a different plastic tube. She made sure that all of the tubes had the same amount of soil. She added the same amount of water to each tube and recorded the amount of time it took for the water to seep through the soil.

Data is another word for information. The data from an experiment includes observations and measurements. It is important that everything about an experiment is carefully recorded—not only the data but also the problem you are investigating, the methods you use, and the solution you propose. Other people who work on the same problem should be able to do your experiment again and see if they come up with the same or similar results.

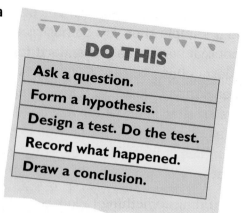

DO THIS

Ask a question.
Form a hypothesis.
Design a test. Do the test.
Record what happened.
Draw a conclusion.

Scientists use many different ways to record data. Two of the most common ways are making tables and making graphs. These are very useful because they help to organize the information that is collected. They serve as a summary of the results of an experiment. Think about it—if you had to write out each of your measurements and observations in a separate sentence, the report on the experiment would be very long. However, you can shorten all of that by recording the data in a table. Sometimes, depending on the data, you can make a graph to serve as a visual summary. Looking at the data in more than one way can make some of the results clearer.

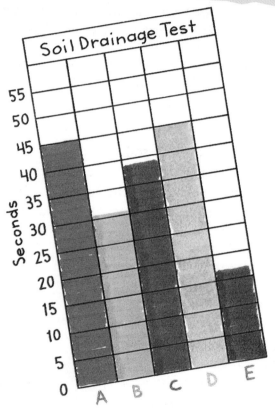

Soil Drainage Test Results

	Material	Time
A	Plain Soil	45 Seconds
B	Soil/Sand	31 Seconds
C	Soil/Potting Soil	38 Seconds
D	Soil/Fertilizer	45 Seconds
E	Soil/Vermiculite	17 Seconds

Alexia made a table to record the time it took the water to reach the bottom of each tube. The table summarized her information, but Alexia thought that she should look at the data in another way. The table and graph summarize what Alexia discovered. Through which soil did water run most rapidly?

DO THIS

| Ask a question. |
| Form a hypothesis. |
| Design a test. Do the test. |
| Record what happened. |
| Draw a conclusion. |

There is no point at all to doing an experiment if you do not reach some sort of conclusion. You might conclude that your hypothesis was incorrect. You might conclude that the experiment did not give enough information and that another test must be performed.

You *draw a conclusion* when you analyze the data and decide whether your hypothesis is supported or not. You use what you already know about the situation to decide what your data is telling you.

Alexia saw that the soil with the vermiculite allowed water to run through it the fastest. She concluded that if she used vermiculite in the corner of her garden, the soil might be loose enough for water to soak through more easily and, therefore, plants might grow there.

You can see that Alexia reached a conclusion. Part of her hypothesis was support- ed. However, another part of her hypothesis was not tested. Remember, she thought that making the soil looser would enable plants to grow. Alexia did not test plant growth. So she had support for one part of her hypothesis, but she must design another experiment to test the other part.

INDEX

Note: Page numbers in italics indicate illustrations.

TV script writer, C13
"TV special bulletin" activity, B75
TV studio, visit to, C6
"TV Pioneer" (Olson), C85–C87

U

Underground mining, E34
Underwater currents, D63, D94
Underwater labs, *D27*
Underwater mountain ranges, *A26*, A31, *A37*
University of Minnesota,
    Chanhassen, MN
    Minnesota Landscape Arboretum
    at, F88
Uranium, *E38*
    as nonrenewable resource, E89
U. S. Geological Survey, A7, A63

V

Valleys, formation of, A45
Valparaiso, Chile, B59
Van Allsburg, Chris, E8
Van Dover, Cindy, D70–D71
Vance, Robert H., C35
Vascular plants
    activity, F39
    defined, F38, *F95*
    seedless, *F41*
Vegetative reproduction, F59, *F60*, *F61*
    defined, F59, F95
Venus's flower basket, *D55*
Venus' flytrap, *F85*
Vibrations, *C56*
Video effects, C15
Videographer, *C14*, *C15*
Viewfinder (camera), *C36*
Vines, rain forest, B44
Violet, *B30*
Violin, *C64*
Virola (plant), B54
Visible spectrum, C40
Volcano(es), *A3*, A64–A73
    activity, A68
    defined, A31
Volcano bake, A6
Volcanoes and Earthquakes (Elting), A9
Voltage, defined, E54, E112
Voltmeter, C80
Volume, defined, C64, C95
Vorticellids, *D41*
Voyage of the Beagle, The (Hyndley), B9,
    B57–B59
Vulcan, *A66*

W

Wales, folded rock in, *A41*
Walker, Lou Ann, C60–C61

"Walk in the Deep, A" (Earle), D88–D89
Walls
    activity, A43
    defined, A42, A79
Walrus, B24–*B25*
Wamsley, John, B26–*B29*
"War of the Currents, The" (Mattis),
    E48–E49
Warm–water vents, *D69*
Waste heat, *E25*
Water
    activity, D49, *F83*
    in coal–powered energy station, E30
    in energy trail, E28
    in estuary, D44–D45
    life in, F84
    need in germination, F55, *F81*
    in nuclear–powered energy station,
    E31
    and sound, C55, *C57*
Water circuit, *C73*
Water cycle, D48, D95
Water lily, *F84*
Water milfoil, *F84*
Water power, E64, *E65*, E67
Water pressure
    buoyancy and, D22–D23
    and personal diving equipment,
    D25
Water wheels, *E65*
Wavelength, *C56*
Waves, earthquake, *A54*, *A79*
    activity, A55
    defined, A54, A79
Waves, water
    satellite photo of, *D30*
    video of, *D60–D61*
Wayang, described, *C17–C18*
Wayang kulit, *C17–C18*
"We Finally Got Your Drift" (Bacena),
    A26–A27
Weatherstrips, *E97*
Wedgewood, Thomas, C34
Wegener, Alfred, A21–A22, A27
Weight belt, *D23*
Wern, Judy, D37
Westinghouse, George, C79, *E48–E49*
Whale oil, E65
Wheat, *F43*
Whisper, sound of, *C65*
White light, activity, C39
White Star Line, D74
Whooping crane, *B79*
*Why Doesn't the Sun Burn Out and
    Other Not Such Dumb Questions
    About Energy* (Cobb), E9
"Why the Kangaroo Hops on Two Legs"
    (Australian aborigine legend),
    B64–B65
"Why Most Trees and Plants Have Flat
    Leaves" (Pellowski), F24–F25
Wiesner, David, F9
Wild Well Control, Inc., E84
Wildlife, effect of oil spills on, *E85*
Wildlife refuge, visit to, B6
Wind(s)
    and ocean currents, D64–D65
    plants response to activity, F74
    and pollination, F50
Windmill Point, Jamestown, VA,
    E64

*Window on the Deep: The Adventures of
    Underwater Explorer Sylvia
    Earle* (Conley), D9
Windpower, E64, E65, E66, *E67*
Wind turbines, *E50*, E112
    as energy option, *E81*
Wood
    as direct energy resource, *E71*
    and sound, *C57*
Wood lily, *F46*
Woods Hole Oceanographic Institution,
    D68
    Deep Submergence Laboratory of,
    D79
    summer program at, D85
Woody stems, *F28*, *F29*, F95
    activity, F30
Wordsworth, William, F52
Working like a scientist, *R14–R19*
World Resources Institute, B7, D7
World Wildlife Fund, B7, B87
Wright, Orville, E65, *E66*
Wright, Wilbur, E65, *E66*

X

X-rays, *E111*
Xylem, F29, F95

Y

Yellow sea fan, *D55*
Young, care of
    duck–billed dinosaurs, B71
    platypus, *B29*
Yucca, pollination of, *F48–F49*
Yucca moth, *F48–F49*

Z

Zaire, Africa, *B48–B49*
Zoo, visit to, B6
Zooplankton, D50
Zubrowski, Bernie, C9
Zworykin, Vladimir K., C7

ACKNOWLEDGMENTS

For permission to reprint copyrighted material, grateful acknowledgment is made to the following sources:

Harry N. Abrams, Inc.: Cover illustration from *The Sign of the Seahorse* by Graeme Base. Copyright © 1992 by Doublebase Pty. Ltd.

Boys' Life Magazine: From "'The Titanic Has Gone Down!'" and from "They've Found the Titanic" (Retitled: "Finding the Titanic" and "They Found the Titanic") by Jon C. Halter in *Boys' Life* Magazine. Text © 1989 by the Boy Scouts of America. Reprinted from the October and November 1989 issues. Published by Boy Scouts of America.

Children's Better Health Institute, Indianapolis, IN: "Desert Plants: Secrets of Survival" by Eileen Ross from *Children's Playmate* Magazine, January/February 1993. Text copyright © 1992 by Children's Better Health Institute, Benjamin Franklin Literary & Medical Society, Inc.

Clarion Books, a Houghton Mifflin Company imprint: Cover illustration from *Cartons, Cans, and Orange Peels: Where Does Your Garbage Go?* by Joanna Foster. Copyright © 1991 by Joanna Foster.

Cobblestone Publishing, Inc., 7 School Street, Peterborough, NH 03458: "Gusher!" by Roberta Baxter, "From Muscle Power to Atomic Power" by Karen E. Hong, and "The War of the Currents" by Richard L. Mattis from *Cobblestone: Energy, Powering Our Nation,* October 1990. Text © 1990 by Cobblestone Publishing, Inc. From "Philo Farnsworth: Forgotten Inventor" by Jeanne Field Olson in *Cobblestone: Tuning In to Television,* October 1989. Text © 1989 by Cobblestone Publishing, Inc. "The Daguerreotype in America" by June L. Sargent from *Cobblestone: The Art of Photography,* April 1985. Text © 1985 by Cobblestone Publishing, Inc.

Dial Books for Young Readers, a division of Penguin Books USA Inc.: Cover illustration from *A Flower Grows* by Ken Robbins. Copyright © 1990 by Ken Robbins.

Disney Magazine Publishing, Inc.: "Deep Trouble" from *Disney Adventures: The Magazine for Kids,* September 1993. © by Disney.

Harcourt Brace & Company: Cover photograph by Michael Wallace from *On the Brink of Extinction: The California Condor* by Caroline Arnold. Photograph copyright © 1993 by Greater Los Angeles Zoo Association Condor Fund. Cover illustration by Tatsuro Kiuchi from *The Lotus Seed* by Sherry Garland. Illustration copyright © 1993 by Tatsuro Kiuchi. Cover illustration by David Kahl from *Earthquake at Dawn* by Kristiana Gregory. Copyright © 1992 by Kristiana Gregory.

HarperCollins Publishers: From *The Clover & the Bee: A Book of Pollination* by Anne Ophelia Dowden. Text copyright © 1990 by Anne Ophelia Dowden. Cover illustration by Dan Brown from *The Missing 'Gator of Gumbo Limbo: An Ecological Mystery* by Jean Craighead George. Illustration © 1992 by Dan Brown.

Henry Holt and Company, Inc.: "Gathering Leaves" by Robert Frost from *The Poetry of Robert Frost,* edited by Edward Connery Lathem. Text copyright 1951 by Robert Frost; text copyright 1923, © 1969 by Henry Holt and Company, Inc.

Holt, Rinehart and Winston, Inc.: "Karen McNally, Seismologist" from *Holt Earth Science* by Robert Fronk and Linda Knight. Text copyright © 1994 by Holt, Rinehart and Winston, Inc.

Houghton Mifflin Company: Cover illustration from *Just a Dream* by Chris Van Allsburg. Copyright © 1990 by Chris Van Allsburg.

Houston Chronicle: From "Field Days in the Marsh" by Kevin Moran in *Houston Chronicle,* July 18, 1993. Text © by Houston Chronicle.

Hyperion Books for Children, an imprint of Disney Book Publishing Group, Inc.: Cover photograph by Sigurgeir Jónasson from *Surtsey: The Newest Place on Earth* by Kathryn Lasky, photographs by Christopher G. Knight. Cover photograph copyright © 1992 by Sigurgeir Jónasson.

Marjorie Jackson: "Shadow Puppets of Indonesia" by Marjorie Jackson from *Cricket* Magazine, January 1992. Text © 1992 by Marjorie Jackson.

Alfred A. Knopf, Inc.: Cover illustration by David J. Catrow from *Backstage with Clawdio* by Harriet Berg Schwartz. Illustration copyright © 1993 by David J. Catrow.

Lodestar Books, an affiliate of Dutton Children's Books, a division of Penguin Books USA Inc.: From *Amy: The Story of a Deaf Child* by Lou Ann Walker, photographs by Michael Abramson. Text copyright © 1985 by Lou Ann Walker; photographs copyright © 1985 by Michael Abramson.

Macmillan Publishing Company, a Division of Macmillan, Inc.: "How Gray the Rain" from *Five Bushel Farm* by Elizabeth Coatsworth. Text copyright 1939 by Macmillan Publishing Company, renewed 1967 by Elizabeth Coatsworth Beston. "Why Most Trees and Plants Have Flat Leaves" from *Hidden Stories in Plants* by Anne Pellowski. Text copyright © 1990 by Anne Pellowski.

Morrow Junior Books, a division of William Morrow & Company, Inc.: Cover photograph by Richard Hewett from *Look Alive: Behind the Scenes of an Animated Film* by Elaine Scott. Photograph © 1992 by Richard Hewett. From pp. 54–55 in *RAMONA: Behind the Scenes of a Television Show* by Elaine Scott, photograph by Margaret Miller. Text copyright © 1988 by Elaine Scott; photograph copyright © 1988 by Margaret Miller.

National Geographic Books for World Explorers: From pp. 43–44 in *Dolphins: Our Friends in the Sea* by Judith E. Rinard. Text copyright 1986 by National Geographic Society.

National Geographic Society: From "A Walk in the Deep" by Sylvia A. Earle in *National Geographic* Magazine, May 1980. Text copyright © 1980 by National Geographic Society.

National Geographic WORLD: "Driven by Cars" from *National Geographic WORLD* Magazine, May 1991. Text copyright 1991 by National Geographic Society. "Meet...Bob Ballard, Undersea Explorer" from *National Geographic WORLD* Magazine, December 1993. Text copyright 1993 by National Geographic Society. Illustration by Dale Glasgow. "Hot! Conquering Oil Fires" by Ross Bankson from *National Geographic WORLD* Magazine, May 1992. Text copyright 1992 by National Geographic Society.

National Wildlife Federation: "RAP Team to the Rescue" by Deborah Churchman from *Ranger Rick* Magazine, April 1993. Text copyright 1993 by the National Wildlife Federation. "The Puzzling Platypus" by Kathy Walsh from *Ranger Rick* Magazine, May 1992. Text copyright 1992 by the National Wildlife Federation. "Away on the Bay" from *Ranger Rick's NatureScope®, Pollution: Problems and Solutions.* Copyright 1990 by the National Wildlife Federation. From "A Jungle Journey" in *Ranger Rick's NatureScope®, Rain Forests: Tropical Treasures.* Copyright 1989 by the National Wildlife Federation.

OMNI Publications International, Ltd.: Adapted from "Rediscovering Tesla" by Bill Lawren in *OMNI* Magazine, March 1988. Text © 1988 by OMNI Publications International, Ltd.

Jane R. Ray: "Shadow Puppets" cover illustration by Jane R. Ray from *Cricket* Magazine, January 1992.

Kay Saetre: From "Living by a Volcano" by Kay Saetre in *Cricket* Magazine, June 1985. Text © 1985 by Kay Saetre.

Thames and Hudson Inc.: Cover photograph by Len Rubenstein from *Real Kids Real Science, Marine Biology* by Ellen Doris. Copyright © 1993 by Thames and Hudson.

Viking Penguin, a division of Penguin Books USA Inc.: "How the People Sang the Mountains Up" from *How the People Sang the Mountains Up* by Maria Leach. Text copyright © 1967 by Maria Leach.

Franklin Watts Inc., New York: From *The Voyage of the Beagle* by Kate Hyndley. Text copyright © 1989 by Wayland (Publishers) Limited.

PHOTOGRAPHY CREDITS:

Key: (t)top, (b)bottom, (l)left, (r)right, (c)center, (bg)background

Front Cover, Harcourt Brace & Company Photographs: (bl), (br), Greg Leary.
Front Cover, All Other Photographs: (t) Fujiphotos/The Image Works; (cl), Tom Walker AllStock; (c), Paul Chesley /Tony Stone Images.
Back Cover, Harcourt Brace & Company Photographs: (t), (bl), Greg Leary.
Front Cover, All Other Photographs: (br) Porterfield Chickering/Photo Researchers.
To The Student, Harcourt Brace & Company Photographs: iv(bc), Greg Leary; v(bl), Weronica Ankarorn; vi(tl), Photo Studio; viii(bc), David Phillips; xi(t), Delinda Karnehm; xiv(r), Terry McManamy.
To The Student, All Other Photographs: iv(t), The Granger Collection; iv(bl), Photri/ The Stock Market; iv(br), Pictor/Uniphoto; v(t), Stephen Dalton/Photo Researchers; v(br), Brian Parker/Tom Stack & Assoc.; vi(tr), Richard Adams; vi(c), Grag Vaughn/ Tom Stack & Assoc.; vi(bl), SuperStock; vi(br), H.R. Bramaz/Peter Arnold, Inc.; vii(tl), Mike Bacon/Tom Stack & Assoc.; vii(b-inset), Kjell Sandved/Uniphoto; viii(tl), Damm/ Zefa/H. Armstrong Roberts, Inc.; viii(tr), Keith Kent/Peter Arnold, Inc.; viii(br), The Bettmann Archive; ix(tl), H. Armstrong Roberts, Inc.; ix(tr) SuperStock; ix(tc), Uniphoto; ix(bc), Scott Camazine/Photo Researchers; ix(b), SuperStock; x, David Young-Wolff/PhotoEdit; xi(b) Michael S. Thompson/Comstock; xii, Gabe Palmer/The Stock Market; xiii, Bruce M. Wellman/Stock, Boston; xiv(l) Comstock; xv(t), Mary Kate Denny/PhotoEdit; xv(b), Superstock; xvi(l), David Young-Wolff/PhotoEdit; xvi(r), Amy C. Etra/PhotoEdit.
Unit A, Harcourt Brace & Company Photographs: A4-A5, A6(t), A6(c), A6(b), A7, Greg Leary; A8, A9, Photo Studio; A10-A11, A12, A12(inset), A13, A16, A17, A18, A20, A23, A24, A25, A32, A33, A35, A40, A43, A46, A47, A52, A53, A55, A58, A68, A74-A75, A75(tc), A76(t), A76(b), A77(t), A77(b), Greg Leary.
Unit A, All Other Photographs: A01, Ric Ergenbright; Unit Divider Page, Salmioraghi/The Stock Market; A2-A3, Ric Ergenbright Photography; A3(inset), B.Barbey/Magnum Photos; A19, Reuters/Bettmann; A22, The Granger Collection, New York; A28, G.R. Roberts/ Documentary Photographs; A28, Richard Hutchings/Photo Researchers; A28(inset), Simon Fraser/Science Photo Library/Photo Researchers; A29(tr), Bob Abraham/The Stock Market; A29(br), A.Taylor/PhotoReporters; A29(l), Photri Inc./The Stock Market; A32-A33(bg), Paul Berger/Tony Stone Images; A34, Tony Waltham/Robert Harding Picture Library; A41, G.R.Roberts/Documentary Photographs; A42, Tony Stone Images; A44-A45(t), David R.Frazier; A44(b), Rick Browne/PhotoReporters; A45, A48-49(b), Ric Ergenbright Photography; A49, Bob Clemenz Photography; A50(bg), Robert Yager/Tony Stone Images; A50, Piotr Kapa/The Stock Market; A50(inset), Herman Kokojan/Black Star; A51, Lance Schriner-Holt, Rinehart & Winston; A56-57(t), Barbara Laing/Black Star; A56-57(b), Dennis Cipnic/Black Star; A57(inset), The Granger Collection, New York; A58-59(bg), E.Sander/Liaison International; A59(l), Tom Myers; A59(r), William S. Helsel/Tony Stone Images; A60(l), A60(r), E.Sander/Liaison International; A61(l), Noel Quidu/ Liaison International; A61(c), David Ryan/Uniphoto; A61(r), Pictor/Uniphoto; A62, A63, Don Fukuda/USC Photo Library; A64, Giraudon/Art Resource; A65(t), Scala/Art Resource; A65(bl), Mike Mazzaschi/Stock, Boston; A65(br), Figaro Magazine/Liaison International; A67, Ken Sakamoto/Black Star; A69(t), Franco Salmoiraghi/The Stock Market; A69(b), Rene Burri/Magnum; A74-A75(bg), Tony Stone Images; A75(tl), Photri Inc./The Stock Market; A75(tr), David Weintraub/Photo Researchers; A76-A77(bg), James Balog/Black Star; A79(l), G.R. Roberts/Documentary Photographs; A79(r), Tom Myers.
Unit B, Harcourt Brace & Company Photographs: B4-B5, Greg Leary; B8, B9, Photo Studio; B10-B11, B16, B22, B31(bl), B31(bc), B31(br), Greg Leary; B36-B37, B36(tl), Michael Smith/Black Star; B40, Rob Downey; B45, Greg Leary; B51, Weronica Ankarorn; B61, B70, B75, B80, B81, B82, B89, Greg Leary; B90-B91, Weronica Ankarorn; B91(tr), B92(t), Greg Leary; B92(b), Weronica Ankarorn; B93(t), Greg Leary.
Unit B, All Other Photographs: B01, Superstock; Unit Divider Page, Pat Crowe/Animals, Animals; B2-B3, SuperStock; B3, Alan D. Carey/Photo Researchers; B4-B5(bg), Julie Habel/ WestLight; B6(tr), SuperStock; B6(l), Tom & Pat Leeson/Photo Researchers; B6(br), Brian Parker/Tom Stack & Assoc.; B7, Roger Aitkenhead/Animals, Animals; B10-B11(bg), W. Cody/WestLight; B12(border), Aaron Haupt/David R. Frazier Photolibrary; B12(c),

Grant Heilman Photography; B12(inset), SuperStock; B13, Ralph A. Reinhold/Animals Animals; B14(tr), Grant Heilman/ Grant Heilman Photography; B14(cl), Leonard Lee Rue III/Photo Researchers; B14(c), Harry Rogers/Photo Researchers; B14(bl), Marcia W. Griffen/Animals, Animals; B14(bc), Bonnie Rauch/Photo Researchers; B15(tr), Pat & Tom Leeson/Photo Researchers; B15(l), Pat Crowe/Animals, Animals; B15(br), Joe McDonald/Animals, Animals; B18(t), Marcia W. Griffen/Animals, Animals; B18(c), Leonard Lee Rue III/Animals, Animals; B18(l), National Library of Medicine/Mark Marten/Photo Researchers; B18(r), B.G. Murray, Jr./Animals, Animals; B19, Henry Ausloos/Animals, Animals; B20(l), Earth Scenes; B20(r), Gregory K. Scott/ Photo Researchers; B21(l), Ed Elberfeld/Uniphoto; B21(r), Charles Gupton/Uniphoto; B22-23(bg), Barry L. Runk/Grant Heilman Photography; B24(top to bottom), E. Hanumantha Rao/Photo Researchers; B24(top to bottom), SuperStock; B24(top to bottom), Perry D. Slocum/Earth Scenes; B24(top to bottom), Abbey Photo/Photo Researchers; B24(top to bottom), Lee D. Simon/Photo Researchers; B25(tl), Photo Researchers; B25(tr), Ralph A. Reinhold/Animals, Animals; B25(b), SuperStock; B26, Ford Kristo/Animal Image Photography; B27(l), Photo Researchers; B27(r), Tom McHugh/Photo Researchers; B28, SuperStock; B29(t), Hans & Judy Beste/Animals, Animals; B29(b), Photo Researchers; B30(tl), J.L. Lepore/Photo Researchers; B30(tc), B30(tr), SuperStock; B30(bl), Fritz Prenzel/ Animals, Animals; B30(bc), David Falconer/David R. Frazier Photolibrary; B30(br), Richard R. Hansen/Photo Researchers; B31(tl), M. Anoterman/Animals, Animals; B31(tc), SuperStock; B31(tr), Leonard Lee Rue III/Animals, Animals; B31(cl), John Kaprielian/ Photo Researchers; B31(c), Breck P. Kent/Earth Scenes; B31(cr), Grant Heilman Photography; B32(border), Rod Planck/Tony Stone Images; B32(c) Tom McHugh/Photo Researchers; B32(inset), Michael Fogden/Animals, Animals; B33(all), Gregory G. Dimijian/Photo Researchers; B34, Richard K. LaVal/Animals, Animals; B35(t), Zig Leszczynski/Animals, Animals; B35(bl), Francois Gohier/Photo Researchers; B35(br), Richard K. La Val/Animals, Animals; B38(l), Michael Fogden/Animals, Animals; B38(r), J.H. Robinson/Earth Scenes; B39(l), SuperStock; B39(r), J.A.L. Cooke/Animals, Animals; B41, Breck P. Kent/Earth Scenes; B42(t), Tim Holt/Photo Researchers; B42(b), Breck P. Kent/Earth Scenes; B43(t to b), G.I. Bernard/Animals, Animals; Zig Leszczynski/Animals, Animals; Francois Gohier/Photo Researchers; Merlin D. Tuttle/Photo Researchers; B44(tl), G.I. Bernard/Earth Scenes; B44(tr), Michael Fogden/Earth Scenes; B44(bl), Patti Murray/Earth Scenes; B44(br), Stephen E. Cornelius/Photo Researchers; B45(bg), Arthur Gloor/Earth Scenes; B46(t), Michael Dick/Animals, Animals; B46(c), Richard K. La Val/Earth Scenes; B46(b), L. West/Photo Researchers; B46-B47(tl), Gilbert Grant/ Photo Researchers; B47(r), Jeremy Burgess/Photo Researchers; B47(b), Adrienne T. Gibson/Earth Scenes; B48(c), Dr. Nigel Smith/Earth Scenes; B48-B49(bg), Victor Englebert/Photo Researchers; B49(t), Patti Murray/Earth Scenes; B49(b), George Holton/Photo Researchers; B50(all), Holt Studios, Ltd./Earth Scenes; B52, B53(all), B54(tl), B54(tr), B54(bl), Randall Hyman; B54(br), James H. Carmichael, Jr./Nature Photographics; B55(all), Randall Hyman; B56(border), M. Thonig/H. Armstrong Roberts, Inc.; B56(inset), Jerry Cooke/Animals, Animals; B60-B61(bg), H. Armstrong Roberts, Inc.; B63(all), Breck P. Kent/Animals, Animals; B64, Gerard Lacz/Animals, Animals; B67, James L. Amos/Photo Researchers; B68(t), Stephen J. Krasemann/Photo Researchers; B71, Lee Balterman/ MGA/Photri, Inc.; B72(t), Phil Schofield Photography; B72(b), Bruce Selyem/Museum of the Rockies; B74(border), W. Metzen/H. Armstrong Roberts, Inc.; B74(c), Alan L. Detrick/Photo Researchers; (inset), David R. Frazier Photolibrary; B76(t), Tom McHugh/Photo Researchers; B76(b), Animals, Animals; B76-B77, Stephen Dalton/Photo Researchers; B77(t), Zig Leszczynski/Animals, Animals; B77(c), SuperStock; B77(b), Fritz Prenzel/ Animals, Animals; B78(l), SuperStock; B78(r), Joe McDonald/ Animals, Animals; B79(t), Stanley Schoenberger/Grant Heilman Photography; B79(bl), Ken Cole/Animals, Animals; B79(br), Stan Osolinski/Animals, Animals; B80(bg), Dean Lee/Wildlife Collection; B83(l), SuperStock; B83(r), Bruce Davidson/Animals, Animals; B84, Shane Moore/Animals, Animals; B85(t), G.I. Bernard/Animals, Animals; B85(bl), Michael & Elvan Habicht/Earth Scenes; B85(br), Dr. Nigel Smith/Earth Scenes; B86(t) & B86(l), Monkey Jungle Miami, Fl Tom McHugh/Photo Researchers B86(b), Kenneth W. Fink/Photo Researchers; B87(t), Tim Laman/Wildlife Collection; B87(b), Randall Hyman; B88(tl), Miami Herald Publishing Co.; B88(tr), Miami Herald Publishing Co.; B88(b), Florida Keys National Wildlife Refuges; B90-B91(bg), Martyn Colbeck/Animals, Animals; B91(l), Karl Weidmann/Photo Researchers; B91(c), G.I. Bernard/Animals, Animals; B92-B93(bg), SuperStock; B93(b), Kent & Donna Dannen/Photo Researchers; B94, Ralph A. Reinhold/Animals, Animals; B95(t), E.R. Degginger/Earth Scenes; B95(bl), USDA/Science/Photo Researchers; B95(br), E.R. Degginger/Earth Scenes

Unit C, Harcourt Brace & Company Photographs: C4-C5, Greg Leary; C6(c), Rich Franco; C8, C9, Photo Studio; C10-C11, Greg Leary; C19, C22, C23, David Phillips; C24, Weronica Ankarorn; C25, David Phillips; C27, C27(bg), Greg Leary; C31, C39, David Phillips; C41, C42, Rich Franco; C43, Greg Leary; C44(l), C44(tv-inset), Photo Studio; C45, C44-C45(bg), Rich Franco; C45(tv-inset), Photo Studio; C46(all), Weronica Ankarorn; C47, Photo Studio; C48(bg), C49, Maria Paraskavas; C51(t), Rich Franco; C52, C53, C55, David Phillips; C57(c), Rich Franco; C58(t), Greg Leary; C62-C63(bg), Maria Paraskavas; C63(t), Photo Studio; C63(b); Greg Leary; C65(b), Photo Studio; C66, Rich Franco; C67, Greg Leary; C69(bl), Rich Franco; C72, Weronica Ankarorn; C74, C75, Photo Studio; C77, Rich Franco; C81(all), Maria Paraskavas; C83, David Phillips; C88, Rich Franco; C89, Greg Leary; C90-C91(b), Weronica Ankarorn; C91(l), Rich Franco; C91(r),C92(t), Greg Leary; C92(b), Photo Studio; C93(t), C93(b), Rich Franco.

Unit C, All Other Photographs: C01, Teri Bloom Photography; Unit Divider Page, SuperStock; C2-C3(bg), Teri Bloom Photography, Inc.; C3, Junebug Clark/Photo Researchers; C6(tr), David R. Frazier Photolibrary; C6(br), Lou Jacobs, Jr./Grant Heilman Photography; C7(t), Rafael Macia/Photo Researchers; C7(tr), Rafael Macia/Photo Researchers; C7(l), FPG International; C7(br), Dr. Winifred Latimer Norman; C12(border), LLNL/Science Source/Photo Researchers; C12(c), Gerard Fritz/Uniphoto; C12(inset), Oscar Burriel/ Latin Stock/Science Photo Library/Photo Researchers; C13(bg), Carl Purcell/ Uniphoto; C13(t), Gary A. Conner/PhotoEdit; C13(b), Teri Bloom Photography, Inc.; C14(t), SuperStock; C14(c), Peggy/Yoram Kahana/Peter Arnold, Inc.; C14(b), D.A. Emmrich/ Uniphoto; C14-C15(bg), Carl Purcell/Uniphoto; C15(t), Helen Marcus/Photo Researchers; C15(b), Art Stein/Photo Researchers; C16(bg), Carl Purcell/Uniphoto; C16(t), Jan Halaska/Photo Researchers; C16(b), Jeff Isaac Greenberg/Photo Researchers; C17, Walter H. Hodge/Peter Arnold, Inc.; C21, Margaret Miller; C22-C23(bg), SuperStock; C26(bg), Jim Corwin/Photo Researchers; C28(t), Leonard Lessin/Peter Arnold, Inc.; C28(b), Thomas Kitchin/Tom Stack & Assoc.; C29(tl), Leonard Lessin/Peter Arnold, Inc.; C29(tc), Will & Deni McIntyre/Photo Researchers; C29(tr), Leonard Lessin/Peter Arnold, Inc.; C29(bl), SuperStock; C29(bc), Greg Vaughn/Tom Stack & Assoc.; C29(br), David Young-Wolff/PhotoEdit; C31(bg), Pete Turner/The Image Bank; C34-C35(bg), C35(t), The Bettmann Archive; C35(b), National Portrait Gallery, Smithsonian Institution/Art Resource; C37, Richard Adams; C38(border), Vaughan Fleming/Science Photo Library/Photo Researchers; C38(c), Terry Donnelly/Tom Stack & Assoc.; C38(inset), Joe McDonald/Tom Stack & Assoc.; C40(bg), Phil Jude/Science Photo Library/Photo Researchers; C41(t), C41(inset), Leonard Lessin/Peter Arnold, Inc.; C42-43(bg), SuperStock; C44(c), H. Armstrong Roberts, Inc.; C44(r), W. Geiersperger/H. Armstrong Roberts, Inc.; C44-C45, H.R. Bramaz/Peter Arnold, Inc.; C48(t), Photo Researchers; C50(c), Mark Burnett/PhotoEdit; C50(inset), Runk/Schoenberger/Grant Heilman Photography; C51(c), Barry L. Runk/Grant Heilman Photography; C51(b), John W. Warden/SuperStock; C54(bg), H. Armstrong Roberts, Inc.; C54(r), David Doubilet/Doubilet Photography, Inc.; C56-C57(bg), SuperStock; C57(tl), Kelvin Aitken/Peter Arnold, Inc.; C57(bl), Ann Duncan/Tom Stack & Assoc.; C58(bl), Stephen J. Krasemann/Photo Researchers; C58(bc), Gerard Lacz/Peter Arnold, Inc.; C58(br), Merlin D. Tuttle/Bat Conservation International/Photo Researchers; C60(all), C61, Michael Abramson; C64(tl), Lawrence Migdale/Photo Researchers; C64(tc), Gerry Souter/Photo Researchers; C64(tr), Nancy Pierce/Photo Researchers; C64(bl), Blair Seitz/Photo Researchers; C64(br), Tim Davis/Photo Researchers; C64-C65, David Hill/Photo Researchers; C65(tr), Blair Seitz/Photo Researchers; C69(tl), PhotoEdit; C69(tr), Billy E. Barnes/PhotoEdit; C69(cl), C69(c), SuperStock; C69(cr), Kim Heacox/Peter Arnold, Inc.; C69(br), George Chan/Photo Researchers; C70(border), Alfred Pasieka/Peter Arnold, Inc.; C70(c), J. Raffo/Photo Researchers; C70(inset), Bill Longcore/Photo Researchers; C71, SuperStock; C78(bg), Culver Pictures, Inc.; C78(b), The Bettmann Archive; C79(bg), C79(l), Culver Pictures, Inc.; C79(r), The Bettmann Archive; C81(bl), Leonard Lessin/Peter Arnold, Inc.; C84(t), Felicia Martinez/PhotoEdit; C84(c), Comstock; C84(b), Teri Bloom Photography, Inc.; C85(l), Lionel F. Stevenson/Photo Researchers; C86(t), Courtesy of AT&T Archives; C86(b), C90-C91(bg), Lawrence Migdale/Photo Researchers; C92-C93(bg), Rafael Macia/Photo Researchers; C94, J&L Weber/Peter Arnold, Inc.; C95, Phil Jude/Science Photo Library/Photo Researchers

Unit D, Harcourt Brace & Company Photographs: D4-D5, Greg Leary; D6(t), Rich Franco; D6(c), D6(b), Greg Leary; D8, D9, Photo Studio; D10-D11, Greg Leary; D13, Weronica Ankarorn; D16, D18(t), Greg Leary; D18(b), Weronica Ankarorn; D32, D33, Greg Leary; D34, Maria Paraskavas; D38, D49, D56, D57, D59, D62, D63, D73, D77, D78, Greg Leary; D90, Maria Paraskavas; D91(tr), D92(t), D92(b), D93(b), Greg Leary.

Unit D, All Other Photographs: D01(bg), Doug Sokell/Tom Stack & Associates; Unit Divider Page, Marc Chamberlain/Tony Stone Images; D2-D3(bg), Doug Sokell/Tom Stack & Assoc.; D3, Brian Parker/Tom Stack & Assoc.; D7(l), Jim Nilsen/Tom Stack & Assoc.; D7(r), Francis Lepine/Earth Scenes; D12(border), Marc Chamberlain/Tony Stone Images; D12(c), Giraudon/Art Resource; D12(inset), John Novak/Earth Scenes; D14-D15, David Doubilet/Doubilet Photography, Inc.; D16-D17(bg), Superstock; D16-D17(c), Tammy Palusol/Tom Stack & Assoc.; D19(tr), Mark Lewis/Tony Stone Images; D19(c), D19(br), Japan National Tourist Organization; D24(l), UPI/Bettmann; D24(c), Mike Severns/Tom Stack & Assoc.; D24-D25, Earth Scenes; D25(c), UPI/Bettmann Newsphotos; D25(r), Al Giddings/Images Unlimited; D25(b), Oceaneering; D26(l), Archive Photos; D26(r), John Tee-Van/National Geographic Society; D27, Naval Undersea Museum/Department of the Navy; D28(c), Courtesy Mr. D.J. Blackwell/American Clock & Watch Museum; D28(r), Culver Pictures, Inc.; D29, National Data Buoy Center; D30, Greg Vaughn/Tom Stack & Assoc.; D30(inset), NASA; D32-D33(bg), Culver Pictures, Inc.; D34(border), Willard Clay/Tony Stone Images; D34(inset), W. Gregory Brown/Animals, Animals; D35(t), Mike Bacon/Tom Stack & Assoc.; D35(b), S.J. Krasemann/Peter Arnold, Inc.; D36-D37, D37, Betty Tichich/Houston Chronicle Library; D38-D39(bg), Manfred Gottschalk/Tom Stack & Assoc.; D40, Scott Blackman/Tom Stack & Assoc.; D41(tl), Jeffrey L. Rotman/ Peter Arnold, Inc.; D41(tc), Animals, Animals; D41(tr), Zig Leszczynski/Animals, Animals; D41(cl), Patti Murray/ Animals, Animals ; D41(cr), Breck P. Kent/Animals, Animals; D41(bl), Fred Bruemmer/ Peter Arnold, Inc.; D41(bc), D. Holden Bailey/Tom Stack & Assoc.; D41(br), Brian Parker/ Tom Stack & Assoc.; D42, Kevin Schafer/Tom Stack & Assoc.; D43(tl), F.E. Unverhau/ Animals, Animals; D43(tc), Kevin Schafer/Peter Arnold, Inc.; D43(tr), John Shaw/Tom Stack & Assoc.; D43(b), Leslie Jackman/NHPA; D44(c), C.C. Lockwood/Earth Scenes; D44(inset top to bottom), Jeffrey L. Rotman/Peter Arnold, Inc.; D44(inset top to bottom), Zig Leszczynski/Animals, Animals; D44(inset top to bottom), John Shaw/Tom Stack & Assoc.; D44(inset top to bottom), Zig Leszczynski/Animals, Animals; D44(inset top to bottom), Colin Milkins/Animals, Animals; D45, Brian Parker/Tom Stack & Assoc.; D46(t), Kerry T. Givens/Tom Stack & Assoc.; D46-D47(bg), Gene Ahrens/Natural Selection; D47(b), Cameron Davidson/ Comstock, Inc.; D50, Sea Studios, Inc./Peter Arnold, Inc.; D52(t), Uniphoto; D52(b), Kjell Sandved/Uniphoto; D53(t), Norbert Wu/Peter Arnold, Inc.; D53(c), Norbert Wu/Tony Stone Images; D53(b), Richard Herrmann/The Wildlife Collection; D54(tl), Animals, Animals; D54(tr), Fred Bavendam/Peter Arnold, Inc.; D54(cl), Norbert Wu/Peter Arnold, Inc.; D54(cr), D54(br), Norbert Wu Wildlife Photographer; D55(t), Patti Murray/ Animals, Animals; D55(tl), Sea Studios, Inc./Peter Arnold, Inc.; D55(tr), Kelvin Aitken/ Peter Arnold, Inc.; D55(cl), Norbert Wu/Peter Arnold, Inc.; D55(cr), Fred Bavendam/ Peter Arnold, Inc.; D55(br), Mike Bacon/Tom Stack & Assoc.; D59(bg), Ulrike Welsch/PhotoEdit; D60(t), J.A.L. Cooke/Earth Scenes; D60(c), Ralph A. Reinhold/Earth Scenes; D60(b), Anne Wertheim/ Earth Scenes; D61(t), Brian Parker/Tom Stack & Assoc.; D61(c), D61(b), Greg Vaughn/ Tom Stack & Assoc.; D66(border), Joseph H. Bailey/National Geographic Society; D66(c), Emory Kristof/National Geographic Society; D66(inset), Rod Catanach/Woods Hole Oceanographic Institute; D68, Emory Kristof & Alvin Chandler/National Geographic Society; D69, J. Frederick Grassle/ Woods Hole Oceanographic Institute; D70, Rod Catanach/Woods Hole Oceanographic Institute; D71, Emory Kristof/National Geographic Society; D72-D73(bg), M.A. Chappell/ Earth

074-D75, Drawing by Richard Schlecht/ National Geographic Society; D75(t), ...ale/National Geographic Society; D75(b), Culver Pictures, Inc.; D76, ...Archive Photos; D79, D80, Emory Kristof/National Geographic Society; D82(l), ...nett W. Francois; D82(r), Emory Kristof/National Geographic Society; D83, Dudley ...ster/ Woods Hole Oceanographic Institute; D84(tl), Culver Pictures, Inc.; D84(c), Woods Hole Oceanographic Institute; D84(b), APA/Archive Photos; D85, SuperStock; D86(t), Artwork by Dale Glasgow/National Geographic Society; D86(b), Maria Stenzel/National Geographic Society; D87(t), Joseph H. Bailey/National Geographic Society; D87(c), © Quest Group, Ltd./The JASON Foundation/Woods Hole Oceanographic Institute; D87(b), Artwork by E. Paul Oberlander/Woods Hole Oceanographic Institution; D88, Charles Nicklin/Images Unlimited; D89(t), D89(b), Al Giddings/Images Unlimited; D90-D91(bg), Greg Vaughn/Tom Stack & Assoc.; D91(l), Christopher Swann/Peter Arnold, Inc.; D92-D93(bg), Emory Kristof/National Geographic Society; D93(t), Craig Newbauer/Peter Arnold, Inc.; D94, C.C. Lockwood/Animals, Animals; D95(tc), D95(tr), Stephen J. Krasemann/Peter Arnold, Inc.; D95(b), Larry Lefever/Grant Heilman Photography

Unit E, Harcourt Brace & Company Photographs: E4-E5, Greg Leary; E6(t), David Phillips; E6(b), Rich Franco; E8, E9, Photo Studio; E10-E11, Greg Leary; E13(t), E13(b), E14(b), Richard Nowitz; E15(t), E15(c), Weronica Ankarorn; E16(b), Richard Nowitz; E17(inset), E20, E21, Greg Leary; E21(inset), Maria Paraskavas; E22(t), E22(b-inset), E22-E23(t), E23(tr), E23(bl), David Phillips; E24, E32, E40, Richard Nowitz; E42, Maria Paraskavas; E44, Richard Nowitz; E45, David Phillips; E46, Weronica Ankarorn; E50(b), Maria Paraskavas; E56, E56(bg), Greg Leary; E61, E70, Maria Paraskavas; E75, E82, Richard Nowitz; E86, Weronica Ankarorn; E95, Rich Franco; E96, Richard Nowitz; E98(tr), E99(inset), Greg Leary; E106-E107, Photo Studio; E107(tc), E108(t), Rich Franco; E108-E109(b), Photo Studio; E109(t), E109(b), David Phillips; E110(t), Photo Studio.

Unit E, All Other Photographs: Unit Divider Page, IFA/Peter Arnold; E2-3(bg), Peter Arnold, Inc.; E3, E7(t), Comstock; E7(c), Kevin O. Mooney/photo taken at The Power House, Commonwealth Edison; E7(b), W. Perry Conway/Tom Stack & Assoc.; E12(c), Ray Pfortner/Peter Arnold, Inc.; E12(inset), L. Fritz/H. Armstrong Roberts, Inc.; E14(t), Malcolm Kirk/Peter Arnold, Inc.; E16(t), J. Patton/H. Armstrong Roberts, Inc.; E17(bg), Keith Kent/Peter Arnold Inc.; E18, Douglas Faulkner/Photo Researchers; E19, Bruce Curtis/Peter Arnold, Inc.; E22(br), Alfred Pasieka/Peter Arnold, Inc.; E23(br), Tim Davis/Photo Researchers; E25(t), Spencer Grant/ Photo Researchers; E25(b), J. Gerard Smith/Photo Researchers; E26(border), W. Cody/ West-Light; E26(c), Jim Corwin/Photo Researchers; E26(inset), Matt Meadows/Peter Arnold, Inc.; E27(tl), Rafael Macia/Photo Researchers; E27(tc), H. Armstrong Roberts, Inc.; E27(c), Sam Pierson/Photo Researchers; E27(bl), Alain Evrard/Photo Researchers; E27(bc), Lawrence Migdale/Photo Researchers; E27(br), Jack Elness/Comstock; E30, Jeri Gleiter/Peter Arnold, Inc.; E31, Earl Roberge/Photo Researchers; E33, Kage/Peter Arnold, Inc.; E34(l), Lowell Georgia Arctic Resources/Photo Researchers; E34(r), Harvey Lloyd/Peter Arnold, Inc.; E35(bg), E35, E36(t), Spindletop/Gladys City Boomtown Museum; E36(b), Drake Well Museum; E37, Spindletop/ Gladys City Boomtown Museum; E38(l), Australian Picture Library/WestLight; E38(r), U.S. Department of Energy; E39(t), W. Perry Conway/Tom Stack & Assoc.; E39(b), Randall Hyman; E41(t), Horst Schafer/Peter Arnold, Inc.; E41(c), Larry Lefever/Grant Heilman Photography; E41(b), Phil Degginger/Color-Pic, Inc.; E43, E.R. Degginger/Color-Pic, Inc.; E44-E45(bg), Tony Freeman/PhotoEdit; E47, E.R. Degginger/Color-Pic, Inc.; E48, E48-E49, Westinghouse Electric Corporation; E50(t), H.R. Bramaz/Peter Arnold, Inc.; E51, Brian Parker/Tom Stack & Assoc.; E52(tr), Martin Bond/Photo Researchers; E52(cl), Steven E. Sutton/Duomo Photography; E52(bl), Steven E. Sutton/Duomo Photography; E52(bc), Steven E. Sutton/Duomo Photography; E52-E53, Greg Vaughn/Tom Stack & Assoc.; E53(t), NASA; E53(b), Dingo/ Photo Researchers; E54(t), IFA/Peter Arnold, Inc.; E54(b), David R. Frazier Photo-library; E54-E55(bg), Thomas Kitchin/Tom Stack & Assoc.; E58(border), B. Kliewe/H. Armstrong Roberts, Inc.; E58(c), Bjorn Bolstad/Peter Arnold, Inc.; E58(inset), Damm/ Zefa/H. Armstrong Roberts, Inc.; E59(t), R. Michael Stuckey/ Comstock; E59(b), Jim Strawser/Grant Heilman Photography; E60, Tommaso Guicciardini/Photo Researchers; E61(bg), Donna Bise/Photo Researchers; E62, David Halpern/Photo Researchers; E63, Alan Pitcairn/Grant Heilman Photography; E64, Culver Pictures, Inc.; E65, U.S. Department of the Interior/ National Park Service, Saugus Iron Works National Historic Site; E66(t), Culver Pictures, Inc.; E66(b), U.S. Department of Energy; E67, U.S. Department of Energy; E68, Grant Heilman Photography; E69, UPI/Bettmann; E71, Runk/Schoenberger/Grant Heilman Photography; E71(bg), Leonard Lee Rue III/Earth Scenes; E72-E73(bg), Farrell Grehan/Photo Researchers; E73, Randall Hyman; E74(border), H. Armstrong Roberts, Inc.; E74(c), Ray Pfortner/Peter Arnold, Inc.; E74(inset), Grant Heilman/Grant Heilman Photography; E76(tl), Ray Pfortner/Peter Arnold, Inc.; E76(tr), Richard Weiss/Peter Arnold, Inc.; E76(bl), Clyde H. Smith/Peter Arnold, Inc.; E76(br), Walker/Peter Arnold, Inc.; E77(tl), Robert Winslow/Tom Stack & Assoc.; E77(tr), David Frazier/Sipa Press; E77(bl), Air Products and Chemicals, Inc.; E77(bc), Matt Meadows/Peter Arnold, Inc.; E77(br), Doug Sokell/Tom Stack & Assoc.; E78(t), E78(b), Yann Arthus-Bertrand/Peter Arnold, Inc.; E79(l), Matthew Neal McVay/Tony Stone Images; E79(r), Barry L. Runk/ Grant Heilman Photography; E80(t), Francois Gohier/Photo Researchers; E80(b), Gerald A. Corsi/Tom Stack & Assoc.; E81(t), U.S. Department of Energy; E81(b), Hank Morgan/ Photo Researchers; E83, Bruno Barbey/Magnum Photos; E84, Steve McCurry/Magnum Photos; E85(t), Randy Brandon/Tony Stone Images; E85(b), Ann Duncan/Tom Stack & Assoc.; E87(t), Margaret McCarthy/Peter Arnold, Inc.; E87(b), Thomas Kitchin/Tom Stack & Assoc.; E88(border), National Snow and Ice Data Center/Photo Researchers; E88(c), E.R. Degginger/Color-Pic, Inc.; E88(inset), Mark Burnett/PhotoEdit; E89, William Felger/ Grant Heilman Photography; E92(t), E92(b), The Bettmann Archive; E93(t), Tom Pix/Peter Arnold, Inc.; E93(c), E93(b), Gerald A. Corsi/Tom Stack & Assoc.; E97, Erika Stone/Peter Arnold, Inc.; E98(l), Lawrence Migdale/Tony Stone Images; E98-E99, David M. Doody/Tom Stack & Assoc.; E100, David R. Frazier Photolibrary; E100-E101(bg), Pete Saloutos/Tony Stone Images; E101, Bill DeKay/ National Geographic Society; E102, Larry Voigt/Photo Researchers; E105(l), Dan Porges/Peter Arnold, Inc.; E105(r), Malcolm S. Kirk/Peter Arnold, Inc.; E106-E107(bg), Werner H. Muller/Peter Arnold, Inc.; E107(l), John Cancalosi/Tom Stack & Assoc.; E107(r), John Shaw/Tom Stack & Assoc.; E108-

E109(bg), Gerald A. Corsi/Tom Stack & Assoc.; E110(bl), David M. Dennis/Tom Stack & Assoc.; E110(br), Keith Kent/Peter Arnold, Inc.; E111(tl), Kevin Schafer/Tom Stack & Assoc.; E111(tr), Gary Milburn/Tom Stack & Assoc.; E111(bl), Brian Parker/Tom Stack & Assoc.; E111(br), Matt Meadows/Peter Arnold, Inc.; E112(l), IFA/Peter Arnold, Inc.; E112(r), Kevin Schafer/Peter Arnold, Inc.

Unit F, Harcourt Brace & Company Photographs: F4-F5, F7(t), F7(c), F7(b), Greg Leary; F8, F9, Photo Studio; F10-F11, F14, F15, F16, F19, F21(tl), Greg Leary; F21(tr), Photo Studio; F26(t), Greg Leary; F27, Maria Paraskavas; F30, F31, F32(t), F32(b), F37, F39, F42(l-inset); F43(bl), F45, F51, F53, F54, F56, F57, F58, F67, F68, F75, F77(l), F83, Greg Leary; F90, Weronica Ankarorn; F91(r), F92(t), Greg Leary; F92(b), Weronica Ankarorn; F93(t), F93(b), Greg Leary.

Unit F, All Other Photographs: Unit Divider Page, Comstock; F02-03(bg), Shirley Richards/Photo Researchers; F03, Joan Iaconetti/Bruce Coleman, Inc.; F06(t), Eunice Harris/Photo Researchers; F06(c), Alexander Lowry/Photo Researchers; F06(b), Rick Buettner/Bruce Coleman, Inc.; F12(border), Robert Frerck/Tony Stone Images; F12(c), F12(inset), SuperStock; F13(bg), H. Armstrong Roberts, Inc.; F14-15(bg), F18(tl), SIU/Photo Researchers; F18(tr), Norman Owen Tomalin/Bruce Coleman, Inc.; F18(br), Dr. Jeremy Burgess/Photo Researchers; F19(bg), Pasieka/Zefa/H. Armstrong Roberts, Inc.; F20, Ray Simons/Photo Researchers; F23, SuperStock; F26(bl), Jane Burton/Bruce Coleman, Inc.; F26(br), Richard Parker/Photo Researchers; F28, Judy McDuffy/Photo Researchers; F29, F33(t), Holt Confer/Grant Heilman Photography; F33(b), Joy Spurr/Bruce Coleman, Inc.; F35(t), SuperStock; F35(c), G. Büttner/Naturbild/OKAPIA/Photo Researchers; F35(b), Van Bucher/Photo Researchers; F36(border), Richard J. Green/Photo Researchers; F36(c), SuperStock; F36(inset), Michael P. Gadomski/Photo Researchers; F37(t), Steve Solum/ Bruce Coleman, Inc.; F38(t), Gilbert S. Grant/Photo Researchers; F38(b), Wardene Weisser/Bruce Coleman, Inc.; F40, SuperStock; F41(t), E.R. Degginger/Bruce Coleman, Inc.; F41(b), Dan Suzio/Photo Researchers; F42(tr), Bud Lehnhausen/Photo Researchers; F42(b), Lawrence Migdale/Photo Researchers; F43(tl), Lee Foster/Bruce Coleman, Inc.; F43(tr), SuperStock; F43(cr), G. Büttner/Naturbild/OKAPIA/Photo Researchers; F43(br), Erwin and Peggy Bauer/Bruce Coleman, Inc.; F44(border), Comstock; F44(c), E.R. Degginger/Photo Researchers; F44(inset), Bob & Clara Calhoun/Bruce Coleman, Inc.; F46, Rod Planck/Photo Researchers; F50(t), Anthony Mercieca/Photo Researchers; F50(cl), J.H. Robinson/Photo Researchers; F50(cr), Hans Reinhard/Photo Researchers; F50(bl), SuperStock; F51(bg), D. Long/Visuals Unlimited; F52(bg), Alan L. Detrick/Photo Researchers; F55(t), F55(c), F55(b), Stephen J. Krasemann/Photo Researchers; F59(l), Wardene Weisser/Bruce Coleman, Inc.; F59(r), P. Munchenberg/SuperStock; F60(tr), Jane Burton/Bruce Coleman, Inc.; F60(l), Tom McHugh/Photo Researchers; F60-61, SuperStock; F61(tr), Uniphoto; F61(cl), John Kaprielian/Photo Researchers; F61(cr), Kenneth W. Fink/Photo Researchers; F63, Bettmann; F65, Pat Lanza/Bruce Coleman, Inc.; F66(border), Patricio Robles Gil/Bruce Coleman, Inc.; F66(c), SuperStock; F66(inset), Rod Planck/Photo Researchers; F69(b), Garry D. McMichael/Photo Researchers; F70(l), Waina Cheng/Bruce Coleman, Inc.; F70(r), John Shaw/Bruce Coleman, Inc.; F71(bg), Stephen P. Parker/Photo Researchers; F71(tl), F71(tc), John Kaprielian/ Photo Researchers; F71(tr), C.C. Lockwood/Bruce Coleman, Inc.; F71(c), Stephen J. Krasemann/Photo Researchers; F71(cr), C.C. Lockwood/Bruce Coleman, Inc.; F71(bl), John Kaprielian/Photo Researchers; F72(l), D. Long/ Visuals Unlimited; F72(r), Jane Grushow/Grant Heilman Photography; F73(tl), Joy Spurr/Bruce Coleman, Inc.; F73(tr), Runk/Schoenberger/Grant Heilman Photography; F73(bl), D. Lada/H. Armstrong Roberts, Inc.; F73(br), Guy Gillette/ Photo Researchers; F74, SuperStock; F76(tr), John Kaprielian/Photo Researchers; F76(l), Nuridsanv et Pérennou/Photo Researchers; F76(c), H. Armstrong Roberts, Inc.; F76(cr), Alan L. Detrick/Photo Researchers; F76(br), Scott Camazine/Photo Researchers; F77(r), S. Nielsen/Bruce Coleman, Inc.; F78(t), Matt Bradley/Bruce Coleman, Inc.; F78(b), SuperStock; F79, Jen & Des Bartlett/Bruce Coleman, Inc.; F80(l), Wardene Weisser/Bruce Coleman, Inc.; F80(c), Jen & Des Bartlett/Bruce Coleman, Inc.; F80(r), John H. Hoffman/Bruce Coleman, Inc.; F81(t), Keith Gunnar/Bruce Coleman, Inc.; F81(l), Renee Lynn/Photo Researchers; F81(r), Rod Planck/Photo Researchers; F81(b), Gary R. Zahm/Bruce Coleman, Inc.; F82(tr), SuperStock; F82(l), John Shaw/Bruce Coleman, Inc.; F82(br), Michael P. Gadomski/Bruce Coleman, Inc.; F84(tl), SuperStock; F84(r), Douglas Faulkner/Photo Researchers; F84(bl), Mark N. Boulton/Photo Researchers; F84(bc), Len Rue Jr./Bruce Coleman, Inc.; F85(tl), J.H. Robinson/Photo Researchers; F85(tr), Dr. Paul A. Zahl/Photo Researchers; F85(bl), Stephen P. Parker/Photo Researchers; F85(br), Norm Thomas/Photo Researchers; F86(tl), SuperStock; F86(tr), Robert P. Carr/Bruce Coleman, Inc.; F86(cl), Renee Lynn/Photo Researchers; F86(bl), John M. Burnley/Photo Researchers; F86(bc), Joy Spurr/Bruce Coleman, Inc.; F86(inset), Terry Ross/Visuals Unlimited; F86-87, Hans Reinhard/Bruce Coleman, Inc.; F87(t), Kim Taylor/Bruce Coleman, Inc.; F87(c), SuperStock; F88, Minnesota Landscape Arboretum; F89, Dennis Carlyle Darling-Holt, Rinehart & Winston; F90-91(bg), S. Nielsen/Bruce Coleman, Inc.; F91(tl), Tim Davis/Photo Researchers; F91(tc), Robert E. Pelham/Bruce Coleman, Inc.; F92-93(bg), H. Abernathy/H. Armstrong Roberts, Inc.; F94(t), Michael P. Gadomski/Bruce Coleman, Inc.; F94(b), SuperStock; F95(l), John E. Sass/Photo Researchers; F95(cl), Gilbert S. Grant/Photo Researchers; F95(cr), Michael S. Renner/Bruce Coleman, Inc.; F95(r), Runk/Schoenberger/Grant Heilman Photography

Reference Handbook, Harcourt Brace & Company Photographs: R4(all), Ralph J. Brunke; R5(b), Weronica Ankarorn; R9, Earl Kogler; R7(all), R8, R10(all), R11, R12, R13, R14, R15, R16, R17, R19, Ralph J. Brunke.

Reference Handbook, All Other Photographs: R5(t), Science Kit & Boreal Laboratories.